W9-BDM-173

Biennial Review of Counseling Psychology

Biennial Review of Counseling Psychology

Volume 1, 2008

Edited by W. BRUCE WALSH

Ψ17 Society of **Counseling Psychology** Division **17**

ISSN 1941-4250

Psychology Press
Taylor & Francis Group
270 Madison Avenue
New York, NY 10016

Psychology Press
Taylor & Francis Group
27 Church Road
Hove, East Sussex BN3 2FA

Printed in the United States of America on acid-free paper
10 9 8 7 6 5 4 3 2 1

International Standard Book Number 13: 978-0-8058-6279-9 (0)

Visit the Taylor & Francis Web site at
http://www.taylorandfrancis.com

and the Psychology Press Web site at
http://www.psypress.com

Contents

Preface

The idea behind the *Biennial Review of Counseling Psychology* was generated to keep pace with the field's change, addressing key developments in theory, research, and practice. The *BR* will serve as a means of coping with the information explosion by reviewing, writing chapters, criticizing, and synthesizing research, theory, and application of psychological principals in the field of counseling psychology. The content will represent and be relevant for science, education and training, public interest and diversity, and professional practice. Thus, the primary goal of the *BR* is to present current knowledge in the field. However, the *BR* will be different from review journals by planfully requesting content, rather than by spontaneous submissions. Instead of waiting for submitted contributions, the *BR* will pursue manuscripts from different perspectives and will present topics that may not be spontaneously submitted. The *BR* will consist of about 12 to 14 chapters per volume and over time will cover the field of counseling psychology. Choices of chapters are guided by a master plan of topics in counseling psychology and will be revised as the field changes and develops. Topics will come up in rotation, and the editorial committee will issue invitations. For Volume 1, 95% of the invited authors accepted, and 100% of those then delivered a manuscript.

As mentioned earlier, chapter authors for each *BR* volume will be nominated by the members of the editorial committee. Invitations will indicate the general topic to be covered, but authors will have considerable freedom in shaping their chapters. Some authors may provide a conceptual framework that not only pulls the available evidence together, but points in new directions. Other authors may provide a synthesis or an overview of the current literature. Still other authors may present different approaches or interpretations of the data.

Overall, we believe that this process will permit the recognition of new areas of work and areas that have evolved in the field of counseling psychology. The *BR* will serve as a means of coping with the information explosion by reviewing and synthesizing research, theory, and the practice of psychological principals in the field of counseling psychology. It makes some sense that scientists, teachers, and practicing professionals as well as those on their way to these careers will read the *BR* precisely as a form of continuing education.

W. Bruce Walsh, Editor

Editorial Committee:
Ruth Fassinger
Nadya Fouad
Bruce Wampold

Contributors

David B. Baker, PhD, is the Margaret Clark Morgan Director of the Archives of the History of American Psychology and professor of psychology at the University of Akron. He received his PhD in 1988 from Texas A&M University. He is a Fellow of the American Psychological Association and the Association for Psychological Science. As a historian of psychology, he teaches the history of psychology at the undergraduate and graduate level, and does research and writing on the rise of professional psychology in America during the 20th century.

Kathleen J. Bieschke, PhD, is currently a professor at Pennsylvania State University in the Department of Counselor Education, Counseling Psychology, and Rehabilitation Services. She received her degree in counseling psychology from Michigan State University in 1991. Dr. Bieschke's research efforts focus primarily on how attitudes influence the delivery of affirmative counseling and psychotherapy to gay, lesbian, and bisexual clients. In 2006, she was awarded Fellow status by the American Psychological Association, and she currently serves as the Associate Editor of Training and Education in Professional Psychology.

Jean Carter, PhD, is a counseling psychologist in independent practice in Washington, DC, specializing in serious trauma. She is on the editorial board of *Psychotherapy: Theory, Research, Practice and Training* and an associate editor of *Professional Psychology: Research and Practice.* She is an APA Fellow, and she has served as president of three APA divisions (17, Society of Counseling Psychology; 42, Psychologists in Independent Practice; 29, Division of Psychotherapy), and in other leadership positions in psychology.

Madonna G. Constantine, PhD, is a professor of psychology and education in the Department of Counseling and Clinical Psychology at Teachers College, Columbia University. The scope of her work includes exploring the psychological, educational, and vocational issues of African Americans; developing models of multicultural competence in counseling, training, and supervision; and examining the intersections of variables such as race and ethnicity in relation to mental health and educational processes and outcomes.

Stewart Cooper, PhD, ABPP, is Director of Counseling Services and professor of psychology at Valparaiso University. He is a Fellow of both Divisions 17 (Counseling) and 13 (Consulting Psychology) of the American Psychological Association and is board certified (ABPP) in both counseling and consulting psychology. He has published four books on college mental health as well as articles, book chapters, and monographs on prevention, psychometric analysis, substance abuse, dual-career issues, organizational consultation, and sex therapy.

James M. Croteau, PhD, is a professor at Western Michigan University. His specific areas of scholarship include lesbian, gay, bisexual, and transgender (LGBT) issues and issues of race and racism in White Americans. His newest area of scholarship focuses on the intersection between race and sexual orientation, particularly among White LGBT people. In 2003, he received the Outstanding Achievement Award from APA's Committee on Lesbian, Gay, and Bisexual Concerns.

Timothy R. Elliott, PhD, ABPP, is a professor in the Department of Educational Psychology at Texas A&M University. He is a Fellow of the American Psychological Association (in the divisions of Health, Rehabilitation and Counseling Psychology). His research has been supported by the Centers for Disease Control, the National Institute of Child and Human Development, and the National Institute on Disability and Rehabilitation Research. In 2004, he received the Dorothy Booz Black Award from the Society of Counseling Psychology.

Ruth E. Fassinger, PhD, is professor and interim chair of the Department of Counseling and Personnel Services and a distinguished scholar-teacher at the University of Maryland, College Park. She specializes in gender, sexuality, work, and social justice issues. She is an APA Fellow in several divisions, serves on the editorial boards of the *Journal of Lesbian Studies* and *The Counseling Psychologist,* and has received numerous awards for her scholarship, teaching, and professional contributions.

Nadya A. Fouad, PhD, is professor and training director of the Counseling Psychology program at the University of Wisconsin–Milwaukee. She was the recipient in 2003 of the John Holland Award for Outstanding Achievement in Career and Personality Research. She is the editor of *The Counseling Psychologist*. She has published articles and chapters on cross-cultural vocational assessment, career development of women and racial/ethnic minorities, interest measurement, cross-cultural counseling, and race and ethnicity.

Lawrence H. Gerstein, PhD, is a professor of psychology; director, Counseling Psychology Doctoral Program; and director, Center for Peace and Conflict Studies at Ball State University, Muncie, Indiana. He is coeditor of the *Handbook for Social Justice in Counseling Psychology: Leadership, Vision, and Action* and *International Handbook of Cross-Cultural Counseling: Cultural Assumptions and Practices Worldwide*. He is a Fellow of the American Psychological Association, co-chair of the American Psychological Association Division 17 International Section, and president, International Tibet Independence Movement.

Carol D. Goodheart, EdD, is in independent practice in Princeton, New Jersey, and a clinical supervisor at the Graduate School of Applied and Professional Psychology, Rutgers University. She is a Fellow of the American Psychological Association and has chaired the APA Presidential Task Force on Evidence-Based Practice, which developed the policy recommendation adopted by APA. She publishes extensively on health, women, and the practice of psychology.

Michele R. Guzmán is assistant vice president for Diversity Education Initiatives in the Division of Diversity and Community Engagement at the University of Texas at Austin and a clinical associate professor in the Counseling Psychology Program in the Department of Educational Psychology. Dr. Guzmán is a native of Austin, Texas. She completed her undergraduate studies at Vassar College and her PhD at the University at Albany, State University of New York.

Jennifer Hardy is currently a second-year counseling psychology doctoral student at the Pennsylvania State University in the Department of Counselor Education, Counseling Psychology, and Rehabilitation Services. She completed her master's degree in community counseling at Ball State University in 2004. She is interested in investigating the interpersonal process of psychotherapy, particularly how attachment impacts the therapeutic relationship.

P. Paul Heppner, PhD, is currently a professor at the University of Missouri–Columbia, co-founder and co-director of the Center for Multicultural Research, Training, and Consultation, and the inaugural co-chair of the International Section of the Society of Counseling Psychology. He has over 130 scholarly publications and five books, he has made hundreds of presentations at national conferences, and he has delivered over 40 invited presentations in 14 countries. He has served on several national/international editorial boards, was past editor of *The Counseling Psychologist*, and was president of Division 17. He has been honored to receive a named professorship, awarded Fellow status in the American Psychological Association (Deivsions 17 and 52) as well as the American Psychological Society, and the recipient of several awards for his leadership, research, teaching, mentoring, international work (three Fulbrights), and promoting diversity and social justice issues.

Morgan Hurst is currently a doctoral candidate in the Department of Educational Psychology at Texas A&M University. She received her master's degree in psychology from Northwestern University. Her current research and clinical interests are looking at the effects of stress and trauma on physical and mental health in minority women.

Frederick T. L. Leong, PhD, is professor of psychology and director of the Center for Multicultural Psychology Research at Michigan State University. Dr. Leong is a Fellow of the American Psychological Association (Divisions 1, 2, 17, 45, and 52) and the American Psychological Society. He was also the recipient of the 1998 Distinguished Contributions Award from the Asian American Psychological Association and the 1999 John Holland Award from the APA Division of Counseling Psychology. In 2007, he received the APA Award for Distinguished Contributions for the International Advancement of Psychology. He is the past president of the Asian American Psychological Association, the Division of Counseling Psychology of the International Association of Applied Psychology, and the Society for Psychological Study of Ethnic Minority Issues (APA Division 45).

Shane J. Lopez, PhD, received his doctorate in counseling psychology from the University of Kansas, where he is an associate professor of psychology and research in education and a Gallup Senior Scientist. Lopez is coeditor of *Positive Psychological Assessment* (APA) and the *Handbook of Positive Psychology* (Oxford), and co-author of *Positive Psychology* (Sage). His research foci include examining the effectiveness of strengths-enhancing programs and refining a model of and measure of psychological courage.

Jeana L. Magyar-Moe, PhD, is an assistant professor at the University of Wisconsin–Stevens Point, where she is a Teaching Fellow and the recipient of Excellence in Teaching, University Scholar, and Leadership Mentor awards. Her research interests include positive psychology, therapy process and outcome, and the scholarship of teaching and learning. She is on the Board of Trustees for the National Wellness Institute and is a member of

Divisions 2 and 17 of the APA. Within Division 17, Jeana serves as the treasurer and chair-elect of the Positive Psychology Section.

Takuya Minami, PhD, is an assistant professor in the Counseling Psychology Program, Department of Educational Psychology, at the University of Utah. His research areas are psychotherapy process and outcome, therapist effects, and psychotherapy modeling, particularly within the context of natural clinical settings.

Terry M. Pace, PhD, is professor and director of the Counseling Psychology Clinic in the Department of Educational Psychology at the University of Oklahoma. Dr. Pace completed his undergraduate studies at Texas Tech University in 1980, then earned a master's degree in counseling (1985) and a PhD in counseling psychology (1989) from the University of Nebraska–Lincoln. Dr. Pace has been a full-time faculty member at the University of Oklahoma since 1989 and is a licensed psychologist.

Jaquelyn Liss Resnick, PhD, is professor and director of the Counseling Center at the University of Florida. She is a Fellow of APA (Division 17) and chair-elect of the APA Board of Professional Affairs. She is the past president of both the International Association of Counseling Services, Inc., and the Association for University and College Counseling Center Directors (AUCCCD). Resnick is a 2007 recipient of the AUCCCD Lifetime Achievement Award.

Emil Rodolfa, PhD, is the director of the University of California, Davis Counseling and Psychological Services, where he has worked since 1988. Dr. Rodolfa completed his internship at the University of Iowa and received his PhD from Texas A&M University in 1981. He is a Fellow of the American Psychological Association, a former chair of the Association of Psychology Postdoctoral and Internship Centers (APPIC), a former president of the State of California Board of Psychology, a former chair of the Council of Chairs of Training Councils (CCTC), and a former president of the Association of Counseling Center Training Agencies (ACCTA). Dr. Rodolfa is the founding editor of *Training and Education in Professional Psychology,* a member of the governing board of the Association of University and College Counseling Center Directors (AUCCCD), and a member of the Board of Directors of the Association of State and Provincial Psychology Boards (ASPPB). He's received numerous awards, including the Distinguished Contributions of Applications of Psychology to Education and Training Award from the American Psychological Association and the John D. Black Award for Outstanding Achievement in the Practice of Counseling Psychology from the APA Society of Counseling Psychology.

Azara L. Santiago-Rivera, PhD, is a professor in the Department of Educational Psychology, Counseling Psychology program with a joint appointment in the Department of Health Sciences at the University of Wisconsin–Milwaukee. Her areas of research and publications include the development of culturally and linguistically appropriate treatment approaches for Latinos and the impact of environmental contamination on the biopsychosocial well-being of Native Americans. She has held numerous leadership positions in professional organizations, such as president of the National Latino/a Psychological Association, an affiliate of the American Psychological Association, and president of Counselors for Social Justice (CSJ), a division of the American Counseling Association.

Cal D. Stoltenberg, PhD, received his doctorate from the University of Iowa in counseling psychology in 1981 and is currently a David Ross Boyd Professor and director of the counseling psychology and community counseling programs at the University of Oklahoma. He is a Fellow of Divisions 17 (Counseling Psychology) and 43 (Family Psychology) of the American Psychological Association and the recipient of the APA 2005 Distinguished Contributions of Applications of Psychology to Education and Training Award. He is a licensed psychologist and health services provider in Oklahoma.

Linda M. Subich, PhD, is a professor of psychology at the University of Akron and co-training director of its collaborative program in counseling psychology. Her professional interests include vocational psychology theory and research, with special emphasis on issues relevant to women and members of various minority groups. In 2000, she received the Holland Award for outstanding achievement in career or personality research from the Society for Counseling Psychology and is a Fellow of American Psychological Association Divisions 17 and 45.

Bruce E. Wampold, PhD, ABPP, is professor of counseling psychology at the University of Wisconsin–Madison. He is a Fellow of APA (Divisions 12, 17, 29, 45), a Diplomat of the American Board of Professional Psychology, and a recipient of the APA Distinguished Professional Contributions to Applied Research Award. Currently his work involves understanding psychotherapy from empirical, historical, and anthropological perspectives.

Chapter One

Counseling Psychology

Historical Perspectives

David B. Baker
Linda M. Subich

Counseling psychology is an area of professional psychology accredited by the American Psychological Association (APA). According to Division 17 (Society of Counseling Psychology) of the APA, the definition of this specialty is as follows:

> Counseling psychology is a general practice and health service provider specialty in professional psychology. It focuses upon personal and interpersonal functioning across the life span and on emotional, social, vocational, educational, health-related, developmental and organizational concerns. Counseling psychology centers on typical or normal developmental issues as well as atypical or disordered development as it applies to human experience from individual, family, group, systems, and organizational perspectives. Counseling psychologists help people with physical, emotional and mental disorders improve well-being, alleviate distress and maladjustment, and resolve crises. In addition, practitioners in the professional specialty provide assessment, diagnosis and treatment of psychopathology. (APA, 1999, p. 589)

The statement reflects an ambitious specialty, one that offers a wide range of services to a variety of populations in many different settings. The uniqueness of counseling psychology is often attributed to its current breadth and depth, but a deeper understanding of counseling psychology can be revealed with a look back at its inception and development.

Beginnings, for the most part, tend to be arbitrary. Whether chosen for historical precision, maintenance of myth, convenience, or necessity, beginnings tell us something of how we want our story to be told. For counseling psychology, how that history is told and what it tells has been the subject of considerable interest for over two decades. Documentation of our collective memory began with the work of John Whiteley in 1980 (Whiteley, 1980). He was able to assemble a mix of primary sources and reflections that helped to focus on the ever vexing questions of identity with which counseling psychology continues to struggle. P. Paul Heppner's "Pioneers in Counseling and Development: Personal and Professional Perspectives" (1990) contributed to the genre of biographical and autobiographical narrative that is essential to the historical record. Formalization of the historical imperative led to the creation of the Legacies and Traditions forum in the Division 17 journal *The Counseling Psychologist*. The end of the 20th century tempted a number of counseling psychologists to tackle the bigger picture and offer institutional histories of counseling psychology (Blocher, 2000; Hansen & Fouad, 2001; Meara & Myers, 1998).

Modern historiography demands that we avoid a number of pitfalls in telling the story of our past. Presentism is the tendency to view the past in terms of current values and beliefs. Internalist history focuses solely on developments within a field and fails to acknowledge the larger social, political, and economic contexts in which events and individual actions unfold. Great Man theories credit single, unique individuals (most often White males) as makers of history without regard for the impact that the spirit of the times (often referred to as the zeitgeist) has on the achievements of individuals. To avoid these errors calls for a different approach that Stocking (1965) has labeled "historicism": an understanding of the past in its own context and for its own sake. Such an approach requires that historians immerse themselves in the context of the times they are studying.

Given these considerations, a retrospective look at counseling psychology should help to tell us where we are from and illuminate the impact that social forces have had on what we do, where we do it, and who is permitted to do it. This chapter examines the context in which counseling psychology emerged at the beginning of the 20th century and the ways in which it has been unfolded over the course of a century. In many ways, the history of counseling psychology is a story of the 20th century in America.

SOCIAL CHANGE

America in 1900 was a place of rapid change. There was no longer a frontier, rather a growing industrial base that drove the economy to new heights while transporting millions from a rural to an urban life. Faster travel, the making of fuel from oil, and the building of structures from steel transformed the continent and the culture. The national industrial machine cleared a path east and west, north and south, transforming native lands, and displacing and frequently exterminating wildlife and native peoples.

The culture of change was everywhere in the new urban centers of the industrial northeast and midwest. City life was mesmerizing with a dizzying array of new technologies, including telephones, radios, movies, electricity, and automobiles. The captivating quality of the new held the promise that modernity would improve individual lives and advance the collective good. Information, goods and services, and people could move more rapidly, and processes could be mechanized. Machines could replace human toil and turmoil, and could do so with great strength and precision. It was believed that machines could remove error, increase production, and improve efficiency.

Achieving precision meant avoiding waste, a concept that could be applied to products as well as people. In industry, efficiency was embodied in the work of Frederick Taylor, whose scientific study of jobs was designed to streamline human performance and increase production. Taylor believed his system would benefit management and the worker. The better-trained worker was likely to be more productive, thus increasing the possibility of promotion and improved wages. Gains in productivity would translate into greater profit for management, and, at the end of the cycle, the consumer would benefit from a better and more cost-efficient product (Taylor, 1911). The enthusiasm for precision and efficiency became codified in the progressive political movement of the early 1900s (Mann, 1975; Watts, 1994).

PROGRESSIVE CHANGE

Those identified as progressives sought a better social order through the application of scientific principles and Christian charity. A central tenet of the Progressive Party was that the government had an obligation to see to it that the institutions of society responded to the needs of all its members. On the national scene, political progressives would lobby on behalf of such issues as women's suffrage, government regulation of industry, child labor laws, and educational reform (Mann, 1975).

The progressive movement expressed faith in science and technology, tempered by an equal measure of public concern for the well-being of the individual. At the start of the 20th century, there were signs of worry. Those who migrated to America's urban centers were often poor and uneducated. The new immigrants did not know the language or the culture. Exploitation was always a concern, but immediate needs such as food and shelter were often all with which the newly arrived could concern themselves. The most vulnerable of this already vulnerable group were children. America, a young nation itself, took a significant interest in its youngest citizens. The result was the child-saving movement, a national commitment to protect children from the ravages of poverty, exploitation, and neglect. It was a time when children's aid societies flourished and child labor laws were instituted (Davidson & Benjamin, 1987; Levine & Levine, 1992). The impulse toward child saving was propelled by a belief that perfectibility began with the young, and the focus on the saving of the young marked the beginnings of the vocational guidance movement, a major precursor to the development of counseling psychology (Baker, 2002).

Child savers and many others were eager to see children receive an adequate education, one that would last beyond the primary grades. Children leaving school to drift aimlessly was seen as a tremendous waste of human potential and an inefficient use of human resources. The concern over school leaving was embedded within the larger context of the place of public education in American society, a debate that gave rise to a variety of visions for the future of the nation and its youth. There were many who saw the school system as failing the students it was charged with serving. They called for public education to complement the world outside of the classroom and provide tools for success in the new American urban industrial center. For immigrant children, the system struggled to provide thoughtful alternatives; for Native American and African American children, the system was and would remain limited, segregated, and largely indifferent.

A variety of alternatives were offered. Booker T. Washington called for national programs of industrial education for African American children; the psychologist Helen Thompson Woolley conducted scientific studies of school leaving; and philanthropic reformers including Jane Addams established settlement homes (Baker, 2002).

In the cities of Boston, Chicago, New York, and Philadelphia, settlement homes were a common feature of the progressive landscape (Carson, 1990). Seeking to respond to the plight of inner-city poor, socially minded students, professors, clergy, and artists would take up residence in working-class neighborhoods, becoming part of the community's social, educational, political, artistic, and economic life. The settlement home provided a place for neighborhood residents to complete high school, learn about the arts, and organize efforts to lobby local government for needed services. Of particular importance in the history of counseling psychology was Boston's Civic Service House. Opened in 1901, it is recognized by many as the birthplace of modern guidance (Brewer, 1932).

THE EARLY ORIGINS OF COUNSELING PSYCHOLOGY

The Civic Service House was envisioned in large part as an educational facility, a community center where immigrants could learn English and participate in a wide range of educational activities. A frequent visitor to the House was Boston attorney Frank Parsons (1854–1908). Well educated and socially minded, he was an advocate for the rights and needs of those who he believed were exploited by industrial monopolies (Davis, 1969).

As a progressive, Parsons advocated for efficiencies, believing a proper balance of federal control, scientific reasoning, and thoughtful planning could improve the quality of life of individuals and of society (Stevens, 1970). Parsons described human efficiency as inextricably linked to the choice of a life's work:

> The wise selection of the business, profession, trade, or occupation to which one's life is to be devoted and the development of full efficiency in the chosen field are matters of the deepest moment to young men and to the public. These vital problems should be solved in a careful, scientific way, with due regard to each person's aptitudes, abilities, ambitions, resources, and limitations, and the relations of these elements to the conditions of success than if he drifts into an industry for which he is not fitted. An occupation out of harmony with the worker's aptitudes and capacities means inefficiency, unenthusiastic and perhaps distasteful labor, and low pay; while an occupation in harmony with the nature of the man means enthusiasm, love of work, and high economic values, superior product, efficient service, and good pay. (Parsons, 1909, p. 3)

Parsons was fond of speaking on occupational choice to students at the Civic Service House. The talks were well received and brought numerous requests for personal meetings. Parsons soon found himself at the center of a need that was going unmet, the provision of guidance in helping students plan their vocational futures. Apparently the need was great enough that a new office was opened at the Civic Service House. In January 1908, the Vocational Bureau was created under the motto "Light, Information, Inspiration, and Cooperation" (Watts, 1994).

Parsons's beliefs were actualized in a program of individual guidance that he developed based on the triadic formulation of: (a) knowledge of oneself, (b) knowledge of occupations, and (c) knowledge of the relationship between the two. Parsons had to develop many of the methods he used or borrow from questionable practices such as physiognomy and phrenology. The matching of self and job traits retained popular appeal, and Parsons earned a place of historical distinction in the history of guidance and counseling. His legacy, threatened by his premature death in 1908, lived on in the posthumous publication in 1909 of his treatise on vocational guidance, *Choosing a Vocation* (Parsons, 1909).

Soon after Frank Parsons began his efforts at the Civic Service House, vocational guidance was on its way to a place of national visibility and support. While Parsons was busy with individual guidance, others such as educator Jesse Davis (1871–1955) were exploring methods of group guidance. Davis, a high school principal in Grand Rapids, Michigan, developed a guidance curriculum that extended into all subject areas. In his autobiography, Davis (1956) recalled:

> The teachers of Latin had their pupils preparing lists of words derived from Latin that were of special interest to the lawyer, the doctor, the scientist, or writer. History teachers had their pupils looking up the origins or historical backgrounds of the vocations in which they were interested. The applications of science, mathematics, and the practical arts to engineering, manufacturing, and to business made most interesting reports. Periodically we held exhibits of charts, diagrams, and written materials that aroused much competition and inspired the use of the career motive throughout the school. (pp. 179–180)

Davis believed that vocational guidance was not simply a process of job choice. It involved a serious obligation to develop the moral fabric of students. According to Davis (1914), the purpose of guidance was:

> The pupil's better understanding of his own character: it means an awakening of the normal consciousness that will lead him to emulate the character of the good and the great who have gone on before; it means a conception of himself as a social being in some future occupation, and from this viewpoint the appreciation of his duty and obligation toward his business associates, toward his neighbors, and toward the law. (p. 17)

The fusion of moral guidance with vocational guidance suggested by Davis was common throughout the period, reflecting the progressive emphasis on rational humanism. Thus, the beginnings of the guidance movement showed interest not only in vocational guidance, but guidance in living a good life. This humanism remained a constant throughout the evolution of guidance and counseling, becoming a central feature of counseling psychology.

The times were ready and, in many ways, called for the work of people such as Parsons and Davis. Their work was quickly absorbed into school-based vocational guidance programs and vocational bureaus across

America. The timing was right, for there was an ample supply of jobs and plenty of people to fill them. There was an ethos of efficiency that valued the individual as much as the swift completion of tasks. Interest in vocational guidance was significant and widespread. Against this backdrop, David Snedden, Massachusetts Commissioner of Education, convened the first national meeting on vocational guidance in Boston in 1910. The meeting, in a sense, was a national summit on vocational guidance. It was well attended, and the Vocational Bureau that Parsons had established at the Civic Service House was a source of much pride. By 1910, many of the Bureau's board members were on the faculty of nearby Harvard University. Working off the success of this initial meeting, the group met each year and in 1913 were officially organized as the National Vocational Guidance Association (NVGA) (Norris, 1954).

Harvard University had a substantial interest in the Vocational Bureau, and in 1917 the Bureau was transferred from the Civic Service House to Harvard University's Division of Education. It was here that educators and psychologists framed some of the earliest debates about the nature of guidance and counseling, debates that have echoed throughout the history of counseling psychology.

AT HOME IN EDUCATION AND PSYCHOLOGY

There were those who saw vocational guidance as an educational function and those who saw it as a province of the new applied psychology. This was embodied in Harvard faculty members such as John Brewer (1877–1950) of education and Hugo Münsterberg (1863–1916) of psychology. Brewer argued that guidance was a part of the educational experience, a process by which the student is an active agent in seeking out experiences that help determine the appropriate choice of an occupation (Brewer, 1932). Psychologists such as Münsterberg viewed guidance as an activity well suited to the new applied psychology. Münsterberg, director of the psychological laboratory at Harvard and a pioneer in applied psychology, was familiar with and supportive of Parsons's work but offered a warning (1910):

> We now realize that questions as to the mental capacities and functions and powers of an individual can no longer be trusted to impressionistic replies. If we are to have reliable answers, we must make use of the available resources of the psychological laboratory. These resources emancipate us from the illusions and emotions of the self-observer. The well-arranged experiment measures the mental states with the same exactness with which the chemical or physical examination of the physician studies the organism of the individual. (p. 401)

Brewer eschewed the experimental approach offered by psychology in favor of an experiential approach. Of testing, he noted (1918):

> Vocational guidance has still another score to settle with a pseudo-psychology, and this is the belief in the "spread" or transfer of mental qualities. Can the attention of a boy be tested, so that the conclusion can be drawn that he is attentive or inattentive? Can a simple examination be devised to test the powers of observation? Can honesty in examinations qualify a girl for the label, "honest girl?" In short, are such activities as attending, observing, concentrating, persisting, using energy, being fair, being honest, remembering, analyzing, etc., if applied to one situation, likely to be applicable to all? We are of course, touching on the whole question of general training or formal discipline. It is the belief in the general nature and transferability of mental and moral qualities that is at the bottom of the beliefs that we have just been examining: the beliefs in types and in the efficacy of psychological types. (pp. 161–162)

Brewer believed that experiential approaches would introduce students to a variety of ideas and experiences. Over time, interests and abilities would emerge, leading eventually to occupational choice. It was a process that took time and required familiarity between counselors and those counseled.

Brewer further believed that schools provided the perfect setting for vocational exploration. As Davis had demonstrated, vocational activities could be incorporated into the curriculum with teachers and administrators providing the needed guidance and counsel. Brewer had established himself as a key figure in the vocational guidance movement, bringing him many key national appointments. Of particular importance was his appointment to the Commission on the Reorganization of Secondary Education, a group that developed a national plan of vocational guidance. Vocational education already had a strong record of service and funding—now vocational guidance was poised to get its share of federal dollars and support. The report of the committee, released in 1918 (Department of the Interior Bureau of Education, 1918), placed education at the center of guidance and counseling:

> It will be some time before actual proof of the validity of psychological tests for vocational guidance can be established, meanwhile, young people must be guided. It is also to be noted that the psychologist "tests" and that there are many other factors in the problem of vocational guidance all of which the counselor must consider, for his problem is one demanding immediate solution. At the present time few tests have been given in such a way as to determine the ability of youth to improve with instruction and training. The province of the

> vocational counselor, however, is to see that education and training become prominent elements in guidance. Therefore the ideal vocational counselor will be something of a psychologist, but he will also be a sociologist, an economist, and most of all an educator in the best modern sense of the word. The committee believes that we should welcome continued experimentation in the field of vocational psychology, but that we should put the present emphasis upon education, training, and supervision. We are of the opinion that when false expectations are abandoned and unreasonable demands are withdrawn, psychology will be able to render worthy service in vocational guidance, and the psychologist may have a large share in making adjustments between individuals and society. (p. xvi)

The report accomplished what it had intended; after 1918, vocational guidance received substantial funding from the federal government and established a presence throughout America's public schools. Colleges of education could now offer training and guidance alongside teacher training. The role of psychology was limited, and Münsterberg (1913) himself commented:

> All taken together, we may, therefore, say that in the movement for vocational guidance practically nothing has been done to make modern experimental psychology serviceable to the new task. But on the other side, it has become evident that in the vocation bureaus appropriate social agencies are existing which are ready to take up the results of such work, and to apply them for the good of the American youth and of commerce and industry, as soon as the experimental psychologist has developed the significant methods. (p. 26)

As vocational guidance flourished in the public schools, psychology increasingly focused on the assessment of individual differences as a part of the scientific management of vocational guidance, which was termed *vocational psychology* (Savickas & Baker, 2005). Münsterberg was joined in his efforts by psychologists such as Harry Hollingworth (1880–1956) and Leta Hollingworth (1886–1939). All three were wary of pseudo scientific means of assessing individual traits. In 1916, Harry Hollingworth published the book *Vocational Psychology* (Hollingworth, 1916). Designed to debunk such character reading techniques as physiognomy, it promoted the benefits the new science of psychology could lend to the assessment of individual abilities. Leta Hollingworth, an early advocate for the psychological study of women and women's issues, added a chapter on the vocational aptitudes of women. The purpose of the chapter she wrote is:

> . . . to inquire whether there are any innate and essential sex differences in tastes and abilities, which would afford a scientific basis for

> the apparently arbitrary and traditional assumption that the vocational future of all girls must naturally fall in the domestic sphere, and consequently presents no problem, while the future of boys is entirely problematical and may lie in any of a score of different callings, according to personal fitness. (p. 223)

Reflective of much of her work on gender differences and mental abilities, she concluded that, "so far as is at present known, women are as competent in mental capacity as men are, to undertake any and all human vocations" (p. 244).

The uneasy alliance between psychologists and educators was held together by the fact that each had a stake in the other's work. Even if some educators were resistant to the use of psychological tests and measures in the educational guidance process, such instruments were becoming increasingly necessary. Rising enrollments (due to immigration, migration, and compulsory attendance laws) made the selection and classification of students a necessity. In the gulf between the psychology lab and the lab school, educational psychology grew and flourished. Its champion, Edward L. Thorndike (1874–1949), made significant contributions to education and learning. He sought to improve classroom instruction and worked to develop objective measures of learning. A highly productive and prolific researcher, he played a major role in the rise of educational testing in 20th-century America (Joncich, 1968). The application of the new science of psychology to the problems of vocational psychology through the provision of tests of individual differences would soon transform psychology and the nation and usher in a new era in the development of counseling.

PSYCHOLOGY GOES TO WAR

As America entered World War I, psychologists sought to win public approval by demonstrating their value to society during a wartime emergency. Soon after America entered the war, American Psychological Association (APA) President Robert Yerkes organized psychologists to assist with the war effort. Yerkes quickly organized a number of committees—among them was a committee on the classification of personnel. By developing and implementing group tests of achievement and ability, the committee bolstered the place of applied psychology in America (Napoli, 1981). For all the possibilities there were also limitations. Group testing, still in its infancy, had problems, none more apparent than the questions of the reliability and validity of intelligence tests that failed to recognize cultural bias. The questionable use of questionable tests led to numerous claims of racial differences in intelligence and education that contributed to continued perpetuation of racial stereotyping and bias (Fancher, 1985; Guthrie, 1998; Yerkes, 1921).

Returning from the war, psychologists found that their success in measurement was needed on many different fronts. Clinical psychology benefited from developments in tests of intelligence and personality, industrial psychology found utility in tests measuring aptitudes and abilities, and counseling and guidance discovered that almost all of these developments could be applied to the scientific management of the student. The decades after the war were a time of incredible development in the psychometrics of selection. Tests of interest, aptitude, and ability were developed and studied by such well-known figures as E. K. Strong (1884–1963), L. L. Thurstone (1887–1955), and E. L. Thorndike (1874–1949). The vocational guidance of the early century was transforming and branching out into areas such as student personnel work and industrial psychology (Paterson, 1938; Super, 1955). The greatest need for selection and placement came with the Great Depression of the 1930s. With high rates of unemployment and the success of the classification, federal assistance for large-scale studies of selection in industry and education was widely available. The government was eager to get people to work, and placement activities grew and agencies seemed to appear overnight. The *Dictionary of Occupational Titles* began at this time, as did the United States Employment Service.

An important player in all this was the University of Minnesota. Members of the Minnesota psychology department were well positioned. Many had served on the classification committee during World War I and had a good reputation with officials in Washington. Money flowed into Minnesota for innovative programs such as the Minnesota Employment Stabilization Research Institute. A Depression-era project, it was an early model of the integration of science and practice. It was designed to scientifically study occupations and employment, while simultaneously finding jobs for its unemployed subjects. The director of the program, Donald G. Paterson, would soon merge all the branches of vocational guidance, applied and scientific, into a program of counseling and guidance that would serve as a model for the later formalization of counseling psychology (Baker, 2006; Blocher, 2000).

The 1930s also saw a rise in the number of psychologists interested in applying testing and counseling to those with more severe forms of maladjustment. Most often these psychologists were found in hospitals and clinical settings where they worked under the direction of a psychiatrist. Many were linked to clinical work with children in clinics and schools like those associated with Lightner Witmer and his psychological clinic at the

University of Pennsylvania (Baker, 1988). This was a time, however, when psychologists used few labels to self-identify, and there were not organized and systematic training programs for mental health professionals. It would take another world war to change everything.

THE MODERN EMERGENCE OF COUNSELING PSYCHOLOGY

Much like World War I, America's entrance into World War II greatly expanded the services that American psychologists offered the nation. Classification and other assessment activities remained an integral part of the work, but a new issue emerged, that of mental health.

The incidence of psychiatric illness among new recruits was surprisingly high, averaging around 17% (Deutsch, 1949). The majority of discharges from service were for psychiatric reasons, and psychiatric casualties occupied over half of all beds in Veterans Administration (VA) hospitals. The available supply of trained personnel was a fraction of the need. In a response that was fast and sweeping, the federal government passed the National Mental Health Act of 1946, legislation that has been a major determinant in the growth of the mental health profession in America (Baker & Benjamin, 2004). The act provided a massive program of federal assistance to address research, training, and service in the identification, treatment, and prevention of mental illness. It created the National Institute of Mental Health (NIMH), and provided broad support to psychiatry, psychiatric social work, psychiatric nursing, and psychology for the training of mental health professionals. For psychology, it was a time of tremendous change.

Through the joint efforts of the United States Public Health Service (USPHS) and the VA, funds were made available to psychology departments willing to train professional psychologists. Together, the APA, the VA, and the USPHS convened the Boulder Conference on Graduate Education in Clinical Psychology in 1949 to find a way to create a competent and trained cadre of mental health professionals.

Although the federal government wanted trained mental health professionals, psychologists wanted to be sure that the growing family of psychology did not split apart. Applied psychology had been on the rise for years. Still, applied psychologists did not feel part of the mainstream of psychology, especially as it was represented by the academic membership of the APA. The American Association for Applied Psychology (AAAP) was the organization that best represented the interests of applied psychologists before World War II. When the nation went to war, there was pressure from within and without for psychology to unify. The result was the merging of the AAAP with the APA in 1945. A new APA emerged, one that included a divisional structure that included Division 17, the Division of Personnel and Guidance Psychologists (quickly changed to the Division of Counseling and Guidance). Division 17 came into existence due in large part to faculty members at the University of Minnesota, including Donald Paterson, E. G. Williamson (1900–1979), and John Darley (1910–1990).

At the Boulder conference, the newly formed Division 17 held a place at the table. The conference was ambitious. For 15 days, 73 representatives of academic and applied psychology, medicine, nursing, and education debated and discussed the establishment of the professional psychologist. The result was the scientist-practitioner model of training that has stayed with us to this day (Baker & Benjamin, 2000).

The Boulder conference also highlighted the emerging differences between those affiliated with either clinical or counseling psychology. It was a conflict that was present at Boulder and that caused participants to make a call for unity (Raimy, 1950):

> The majority of the conference was clearly in favor of encouraging the broad development of clinical psychology along the lines that extend the field of practice from the frankly psychotic or mentally ill to the relatively normal clientele who need information, vocational counseling, and remedial work. Specialization in any of these less clearly defined branches has now become an open issue that must be faced sooner or later. (pp. 112–113)

The conferees went so far as to offer a vote of support for the recommendation that, "The APA and its appropriate division should study the common and diverse problems and concepts of clinical psychology and counseling and guidance with a view to immediate interfield enrichment of knowledge and methods. Consideration should also be given to the possibility of eventual amalgamation of these two fields" (p. 148).

Such an amalgamation never occurred, and, in fact, the gulf only grew wider.

Division 17 included members of varying backgrounds and interests. They could be found in any number of applied and educational settings. In many cases, however, the growing mental health movement brought them closer to clinical psychology (Pepinsky, Hill-Frederick, & Epperson, 1978).

The interest in and support for mental health issues caused many counseling psychologists to question who best represented their interests. The National Vocational Guidance Association (NVGA) was no longer the best fit, nor did Division 12 (Clinical Psychology) seem appropriate. The answer for Division 17 members was to establish their own standards of training.

With the support of the USPHS, a meeting on the training of counselors was held at the University of Michigan on July 27 and 28, 1949, and again on January 6 and 7, 1950. The deliberations at the Ann Arbor conference illustrated the divergence in counseling and clinical approaches to training and teaching of professional psychology. Psychological counselors and counseling were differentiated from clinical psychologists and psychotherapy. The attendees attempted to highlight commonalities but could not disguise some true differences. The psychological counselor was likely to be found in an educational setting, working with essentially normal individuals. This was in contrast to the clinical psychologist, who was most likely to be in a hospital setting working with mentally ill populations whose treatment was aimed at personality reorganization.

The roads began to diverge more fully when subdoctoral training was discussed. Boulder affirmed the primacy of the doctoral degree as the entry-level degree in professional psychology, but the Ann Arbor group was willing to consider a program of training for the master's-level psychological counselor (Bordin, 1950).

The deliberations at Ann Arbor were brought before the larger group of Division 17 representatives meeting on the campus of Northwestern University just prior to the annual meeting of the APA in Chicago in 1951. Known as the Northwestern Conference, its purpose was to produce a formal statement on the training of counseling psychologists. At the meeting a statement on the doctoral training of counseling psychologists was approved (APA, 1952). Among other things, it upheld the Boulder standard of the scientist-practitioner model of training, and defined the goal of counseling psychology as:

> . . . fostering the psychological development of the individual. This included all people on the adjustment continuum from those who function at tolerable levels of adequacy to those suffering from more severe psychological disturbances. Counseling psychologists will spend the bulk of their time with individuals within the normal range, but their training should qualify them to work in some degree with individuals at any level of psychological adjustment. Counseling stresses the positive and the preventative. It focuses upon the stimulation of personal development in order to maximize personal and social effectiveness and to forestall psychologically crippling disabilities. (pp. 175–181)

In a further attempt to declare an independent identity, the conferees voted to change the name of the division from Counseling and Guidance to Counseling Psychology.

The adoption of recommended training standards at the doctoral level brought with it many new opportunities and brought counseling psychology closer to its current identity as a health service profession. Shortly after the Northwestern Conference, the APA began accrediting doctoral training programs in counseling psychology, and the VA sought to incorporate counseling psychologists into its list of approved mental health service providers. Alongside the new mental health services, counseling psychologists still provided the more traditional services of the division. Those working in the Vocational Rehabilitation and Education (VR&E) Service helped returning veterans find suitable employment, obtain needed rehabilitation (for both physical and emotional problems), and gain placement in training and educational programs. These VR&E services were provided through VA regional offices with satellite clinics located on many university campuses.

The demand for these services after the war prompted the VA to establish a new counseling service that would serve its expansive hospital system. In 1952, counseling psychologist Robert Waldrop (b. 1912) became the first chief of the newly founded Vocational Counseling Service of the Department of Medicine and Surgery of the VA. It was the persistence of Waldrop that persuaded the VA to have counseling psychologists classified at the same rank as clinical psychologists. His insistence that counseling psychologists in the VA's medical service have doctoral-level training caused consternation among many in the VR& E service who perceived his efforts as a threat to their employment (Benjamin & Baker, 2004).

IDENTITY

In the 1950s, counseling psychology continued to stray further from its historical roots in vocational guidance. Many in Division 17 held joint membership in the APA and the NVGA, which as a result of its own internal differences joined together with others interested in guidance and student personnel work to form the American Personnel and Guidance Association (APGA) in 1951 (now known as the American Counseling Association).

A number of factors influenced the direction that counseling psychology took in the 1950s. Returning veterans required counseling of all types. The transition from war to civilian life could be difficult. Soldiers had to get reacquainted with friends and family who knew little of the experience of war. Many returned home to find themselves and their surroundings changed. Returning to work was an adjustment, as was the decision to return to school. The GI Bill of Rights afforded a college education to many who otherwise might not have been able to afford one. Counseling needed to be able to account for the adjustment of the whole person, and counseling methods and theories began to reflect this emphasis, especially the nondirective approach of Carl Rogers (1902–1987).

Rogers's first major statement on his approach to counseling appeared in his 1942 publication, *Counseling and Psychotherapy* (Rogers, 1942). Rogers advocated that counselors be nondirective, allowing clients to take the lead in the counseling session. Through active listening and reflection of feeling, the counselor helped the client explore concerns and seek possible solutions. There were no tests and no advice. Rogers believed that each person had the capacity for emotional growth and adjustment. It was the counselor's role to provide a safe and supportive environment that allowed the client to safely explore thoughts and feelings. To some, this was heresy. Since the time of Frank Parsons, counselors learned about clients through responses to interviews and tests, and after the data had been gathered, the counselor instructed clients what to do. Known as the trait and factor approach, its adherents were aghast at Rogers's seeming inaction and lack of direction. This was particularly true at the University of Minnesota, where the counseling faculty was considered among the most influential in the field. Addressing a group there in 1940, Rogers (1961) recalled, "I was totally unprepared for the furor the talk aroused. I was criticized, I was praised, I was attacked, I was looked on with puzzlement" (p. 13). Somewhere in between the directive and nondirective approaches were a host of theories and practices advanced by other significant figures in the history of counseling psychology, including Leona Tyler (1906–1993) and C. Gilbert Wrenn (1902–2001).

Vocational behavior and career development remained popular topics among counseling psychologists, with advances in theory and research led by such people as Donald Super (1910–1994), David Tiedeman (b. 1919), and Anne Roe (1904–1991). Multivariate statistics and computer-assisted data analysis contributed to more elaborate and original uses of measurement tools such as the Strong Interest Inventory and the Kuder Preference Record Test (Holland, 1964).

Toward the end of the 1950s, yet another world event would have implications for counseling psychology. The launch of the Russian satellite *Sputnik*, on October 4, 1957, instilled considerable panic in the American public. To many, *Sputnik* represented Russian superiority in science and technology. There was widespread concern that American public schools were not producing enough students interested in math and science, and the finger of blame was pointed directly at progressive education for being too lax and child-centered. There was a rallying cry for an increased emphasis on ability and intellect, an area in which educational psychologists in the tradition of E. L. Thorndike had much to offer. President Eisenhower, under considerable pressure, pushed for new legislation. The National Defense Education Act (NDEA) was drafted.

At the heart of the NDEA was the identification and guidance of students who showed promise in math and science at all levels of schooling. In higher education, there were provisions for aid to students at both the undergraduate and graduate level. To better identify able students in elementary and secondary schools, significantly more school counselors were needed.

In 1957 it was estimated that there were 11,000 full-time counselors in the public schools, with a need for 26,000. The NDEA set aside a large portion of funds for a national program of testing (including aptitude, vocational, and scholastic) and guidance. Just as World War II had pointed out the dire need for mental health professionals, the Sputnik scare pointed out the dire need for school counselors.

The NDEA was signed into law on September 2, 1958. The range and scope of the act was sweeping. Of particular interest to counseling psychologists was Title V of the NDEA: Guidance, Counseling and Testing, Identification and Encouragement of Able Students. This section of the act made funding available to colleges and universities to conduct counseling and guidance institutes. Approximately 80 institutes were conducted a year. These could be summer institutes of 6–8 weeks or year-long sequences. Participants were typically drawn from the ranks of high school guidance counselors, many of whom were attracted to the opportunities and the stipends the institutes offered.

Institute staffs were frequently counseling psychologists. Topics of study included tests and measurement, statistics, and individual and group counseling methods. The use of group experiences was common, as was supervised practicum experience. The institutes increased demand for professors of counselor education and also made training requirements for graduate degrees in counseling and guidance more concrete. In the 8 years of the program some 44,000 counselors were trained (Tyler, 1960).

IDENTITY DISPUTES

As the 1950s came to a close, the status of counseling psychology appeared good. There were doctoral training programs, strong job opportunities, an established division of APA, and a professional journal, the *Journal of Counseling Psychology* (established in 1954). Yet, there was a chorus of detractors, and in 1959 they persuaded the Education and Training (E & T) Board of the APA to appoint a committee to investigate the status of counseling psychology. The committee members were three counseling psychologists: Irwin Berg (1913–2001), Harold Pepinsky, (1917–1998), and Joseph Shobin (1918–1996), and the report they produced was scathing (Berg, Pepinsky, & Shobin, 1980). The tone of the opening paragraph provided some indication of what was to follow:

> The reasons for the Board's action was a general feeling that all was not well with counseling psychology. Although counseling as an activity in fields other than psychology appeared to be flourishing, as witness the provisions of the National Defense Education Act, *counseling psychology* appeared, in the opinion of some members of the Board, to have lagged behind other specialty areas of psychology. Two or three decades ago, counseling psychology was immensely prestigious as a specialty, but now it appears to be in some ways on the wane. (p. 105)

The report went on to provide a laundry list of complaints and problems with counseling psychology, including a lack of a research emphasis, a continuing decline in the number and quality of students, few candidates holding or seeking certification by the American Board of Examiners in Professional Psychology (ABEPP), and a poor status ranking among psychologists. In conclusion, it was recommended that consideration be given to dissolving Division 17, and moving it under the auspices of Division 12, Clinical Psychology.

Needless to say, the report touched off a firestorm of controversy and was never released. The Executive Committee of Division 17 protested, claiming they were never asked to participate in the preparation of the report, and demanding that they appoint their own committee to prepare a status report of their own. The APA agreed, and Leona Tyler, C. Gilbert Wrenn, and David Tiedeman prepared the new report (Tyler, Tiedeman, & Wrenn, 1980). In preparing the report, they noted:

> Counseling psychology, particularly in its important components of vocational psychology and vocational counseling, is in need of careful reexamination and clarification at this time. The scientific and professional interests of the members of Division 17 are multiple and complex. Some pulling together of some of the main threads in the more recent development of the Division is desirable. The relatively new label, *Counseling Psychology,* has caused this well-established field of work to be frequently compared with *Clinical Psychology* and other areas of specialization. Evaluation of the overlapping and differentiating features of these various areas of specialization is desirable. If Counseling Psychology, or any other field of psychology, appears to be contributing to human welfare, this distinctive contribution should be

> defined from time to time and suggestions for strengthening it should be proposed. (p. 115)

Data describing counseling psychology and psychologists were presented. Drawing from a variety of published sources, the report concluded that counseling psychology was indeed alive and well. It was noted that division membership was growing, as was the number of graduates, and that the similarities and differences between counseling psychology and other areas of professional psychology made for a more rounded and balanced offering of mental health services to the public. According to the report, counseling psychology was unique in that it focused on helping people make plans to play productive roles in the social environment. This required special skills and training, as they noted:

> It does not seem to matter whether the curriculum is placed in an arts and science psychology department or under a psychology staff in a school of education. It matters a great deal whether the curriculum is psychologically sound and whether psychologists teach the courses. The practice in some institutions of adding courses in group measurement and occupational information to a clinical psychology program or of adding courses in personality dynamics and clinical psychology to an educational psychology program or a pupil personnel program does not provide a counseling psychology program. Nor does it develop respect for the program. (p. 122)

The report closed with a series of recommendations aimed at educating others about the unique features of counseling psychology, and improving existing programs of study.

Counseling psychology ended the decade of the 1950s just as it had begun, focused on the question of identity. An emerging theme was that of social action. Counseling psychology was a specialty area that helped people find a place in the world, regardless of their condition, physical, emotional, or otherwise. It had special tools and techniques to guide people into thoughtful consideration of a plan of life; it was in essence an extension of the work of early pioneers like Parsons who sought to maximize human potential through the thoughtful choice of a life's work.

CONSOLIDATING IDENTITY

In the 1960s, counseling psychologists did what they had been doing for two decades, meeting to consider their identity. For a 3-day period in January 1964, 60 participants, representing a broad spectrum of the counseling psychology community, gathered at the Greyston Mansion (then a part of Teachers College, Columbia University) to consider their specialty. The conference deliberations were organized under four themes: (a) the roles of counseling psychologists, (b) the content of professional preparation, (c) organizational aspects of training, and (d) unity and diversity (Thompson & Super, 1964).

At the meeting, support was offered for the evolving role of counseling psychology in larger social issues such as poverty, equal rights, and education. There was extensive discussion of the place of subdoctoral training. The longtime association of counseling psychology and education meant that many were familiar and comfortable with the training of subdoctoral personnel. No doubt, federal programs such as the NDEA, which offered opportunities for counseling psychologists to train and supervise master's-level counselors, encouraged Division 17 to look more kindly upon the issue of subdoctoral training. However, to call oneself a counseling psychologist still required the doctoral degree. Greyston affirmed the scientist-practitioner model of training with the addition of coursework that reflected the core values and unique nature of counseling psychology. Thus, it was recommended that attention be given to coursework in sociology, the world of work, and education. Many at Greyston believed that counseling psychology needed to be much more proactive, explaining and educating others about the specialty area. This included more and better information to students and faculty, public service agencies and training centers, and the APA (Thompson & Super, 1964).

If nothing else, Greyston helped to unite counseling psychologists in a spirit of shared mission. After Greyston, there was less talk about disbanding and more talk of unity and identity.

RECENT DEVELOPMENTS

The history of counseling psychology over the last 30 years points to continued growth and expansion of the specialty as a health service profession. The interest in personal growth, declining federal support of training and research, and retrenchment in academia all contributed to the growth of independent practice in the 1970s and 1980s. Licensure and third-party (insurance) reimbursement for psychological services has continued the development of counseling psychology as a health-service specialty.

Counseling psychology has retained a record of advances in theory, research, and practice, especially in the area of vocational psychology. It is the one area in which counseling psychology has a clear link to its past. The template of vocational psychology can be applied to many of the topical areas of interest to counseling psychologists such as gender, ethnicity, sexual orientation, and life-span development.

Organizationally, counseling psychology has grown in size and strength. Division 17 (the Society for Counseling Psychology) has over 3,000 members (APA Division Services, personal communication, August 2, 2007) and remains the largest representative body of counseling psychologists. There are 67 active APA-accredited doctoral programs (APA, 2006) and two major journals, *The Journal of Counseling Psychology* and *The Counseling Psychologist*. The organizational structure of Division 17 reflects the major themes that persistently characterize the field: diversity/public interest, practice, science, and education/training.

Within Division 17, paralleling APA's division structure, there are areas of special interest and activity. This is accomplished through the mechanisms of sections and special interest groups (SIGs). Currently there are 12 sections and 8 SIGs associated with Division 17. Sections exist as formal subgroups of the division to connect counseling psychologists with shared interests in diversity (e.g., Section on Ethnic and Racial Diversity, Lesbian, Gay and Bisexual Awareness), individual differences (e.g., Section for the Advancement of Women), psychological science (e.g., Section for the Promotion of Psychotherapy Science), training (e.g., Supervision and Training Section), and particular research and practice domains (e.g., Counseling Health Psychology, Independent Practice, Prevention, Positive Psychology, University and College Counseling Centers, Vocational Psychology). The relatively new International Section promotes global connections among counseling psychologists, a recent emphasis of Division 17 as well as APA. The SIGs are smaller, less formal, more fluid, and often interdisciplinary groups that focus on topics such as adoption, couples and families, older adults, organizations, and religious and spiritual issues. The persistent themes and emphases of the field of counseling psychology, especially its foci on diversity and social issues, science, work, and health, are well represented in these subgroups, which offer a mechanism for Division 17 to accommodate and serve the varied interests of its members.

The division also works closely with other groups whose work impacts directly upon counseling psychologists. In the 1970s, directors of training programs in counseling psychology sought to increase their presence in professional psychology through the establishment of the Council of Counseling Psychology Training Programs (CCPTP). The group, which now has representation on APA's Committee on Accreditation (CoA), provides a common meeting ground for training directors across the country to discuss training issues and trends. Likewise, the Association of Counseling Center Training Agencies (ACCTA) exists to represent the needs and interests of those working in one of counseling psychology's primary settings (Heppner, Casas, Carter, & Stone, 2000).

Issues of training and accreditation remain constant. What changes is the content and context in which these issues unfold. In 1988, counseling psychologists convened in Atlanta for what was termed the Third National Conference for Counseling Psychology: Planning the Future (Blocher, 2000). It was agreed at the conference that counseling psychology needed to pay attention to issues of diversity and inclusivity, and this focus was woven into all other major foci of the conference, including research, practice, training, organizational, and public image issues. Many of the recommendations forwarded from this conference sought to broaden the composition, perspective, and knowledge base of the field of counseling psychology to better reflect American society and those persons whom counseling psychologists serve. The recommendations from this conference are collected in a series of papers published in 1988 in *The Counseling Psychologist* (Volume 16, Number 3).

Especially since the Atlanta conference, counseling psychology has taken considerable initiative in forwarding an inclusive agenda. Counseling psychology and psychologists played a major role in the National Multicultural Summit of 1999 and subsequent biennial summits. Women and ethnic minorities have leadership roles in Division 17, and consideration of individual and group differences such as age, gender, ethnicity, sexual orientation, disability, and socioeconomic status are now commonplace in counseling psychology theory, research, and practice.

Indeed, the 2001 Houston Counseling Psychology Conference had as its theme "Counseling Psychologists, Making a Difference." The conference's ambitious agenda included keynotes, symposia, posters, and continuing education programs that addressed themes of health, inclusion, and social action. Past president Rosie Bingham's keynote address on the "power of inclusion" offered a poignant acknowledgment of the exclusive origin of the field of counseling psychology and the growth and benefits that have accrued as counseling psychology has "drawn the circle bigger." Illustrative of her call to continue on this course, a unique and perhaps defining component to the conference was its creation of working social action groups (SAGs). The SAGs addressed specific aspects of oppression such as community and domestic/family violence, homelessness and class issues, and racism. Each of these groups met extensively during the conference to develop an action agenda for counseling psychologists to pursue in order to address their specific focus. An intended legacy of the Houston conference was to incorporate social justice as a fundamental part of the identity and practice of counseling psychology.

This goal has perhaps been realized to some extent in that social justice is a central component of the March 2008 International Counseling Psychology Conference that will convene in Chicago. This conference builds on prior conferences that have addressed health, science and practice, training, diversity, and social justice. It moves beyond prior conferences in its explicit focus on international and global perspectives and the impact of technology. This focus represents another step on the road to "drawing the circle bigger" and enriching the field and those whom it serves as a result.

Issues of social justice, inclusion, and the pursuit of a healthier society have become a part of our larger national dialogues and are certainly not unique to professional psychology. However, a case can be made that counseling psychology has a long history of social action and justice. We have traced the roots of counseling psychology to the beginning of the 20th century and the social progressives and reformers who shared a concern for the well-being of those who were disenfranchised and at the mercy of the new industrial order. Over the span of 100 years, that mission has expanded to include many more who are excluded from the ideals of a democratic society. Long in coming, and with much still to be done, counseling psychology has made social action a central feature of its current mission.

BIBLIOGRAPHY

American Psychological Association, Division of Counseling and Guidance, Committee on Counselor Training. (1952). Recommended standards for training counselors at the doctoral level. *American Psychologist, 7,* 175–181.

American Psychological Association (Division 17). (1999). Archival description of counseling psychology. *The Counseling Psychologist, 27,* 589–592.

American Psychological Association. (2006). Accredited doctoral programs in professional psychology: 2006. *American Psychologist, 61,* 991–1005.

Baker, D. B. (1988). The psychology of Lightner Witmer. *Professional School Psychology, 3,* 109–121.

Baker, D. B. (2002). Child saving and the emergence of vocational counseling. *Journal of Vocational Behavior, 60,* 374–381.

Baker, D. B. (2006). An individual difference: The career of Donald G. Paterson. In L. T. Benjamin, & D. Dewsbury (Eds.), *Portraits of pioneers in psychology* (Vol. 6, pp. 115–135). Washington, DC: American Psychological Association.

Baker, D. B., & Benjamin, L. T., Jr. (2000). The affirmation of the scientist-practitioner: A look back at Boulder. *American Psychologist, 55,* 241–247.

Baker, D. B., & Benjamin, L. T., Jr. (2004). Creating a profession: NIMH and the training of psychologists, 1946–1954. In W. Pickren (Ed.), *Psychology and the National Institute of Mental Health* (pp. 181–207). Washington, DC: American Psychological Association.

Benjamin, L. T., & Baker, D. B. (2004). *From séance to science: A history of the profession of psychology in America.* Belmont, CA: Wadsworth.

Berg, I., Pepinsky, H. B., & Shobin, E. J., Jr. (1980). The status of counseling psychology: 1960. In J. M. Whitely (Ed.), *The history of counseling psychology* (pp. 105–113). Monterey, CA: Brooks/Cole.

Blocher, D. H. (2000). *The evolution of counseling psychology.* New York: Springer Publishing Company.

Bordin, Edward. (1950). *Training of psychological counselors: Report of a conference held at Ann Arbor, Michigan, July 27 and 28, 1949, and January 6 and 7, 1950.* Ann Arbor: University of Michigan Press.

Brewer, J. M. (1918). *The vocational guidance movement: Its problems and possibilities.* New York: Macmillan.

Brewer, J. M. (1932). *Education as guidance; an examination of the possibilities of a curriculum in terms of life activities, in elementary and secondary school and college.* New York: Macmillan.

Brewer, J. M. (1942). *History of vocational guidance.* New York: Harper and Brothers.

Carson, M. J. (1990). *Settlement folk: Social thought and the American settlement movement,* 1885–1930. Chicago: University of Chicago Press.

Davidson, E., & Benjamin, L. T., Jr. (1987). A history of the child study movement in America. In J. A. Glover & R. R. Ronning (Eds.), *Historical foundations of educational psychology* (pp. 187–208). New York: Plenum Press.

Davis, H. V. (1969). *Frank Parsons: Prophet, innovator, and counselor.* Carbondale, IL: Southern Illinois University.

Davis, J. B. (1914). *Vocational and moral guidance.* New York: Ginn and Company.

Davis, J. B. (1956). *The saga of a schoolmaster: An important, personal account of American secondary education 1886–1950.* Boston: Boston University Press.

Department of the Interior Bureau of Education (1918). *Vocational guidance in secondary education.* Bulletin no. 19, Washington, DC: Government Printing Office.

Deutsch, A. (1949). *The mentally ill in America: A history of their care and treatment from colonial times* (2nd ed.). New York: Columbia University Press.

Fagan, T. K., & Warden, P. G. (Eds.) (1996). *Historical encyclopedia of school psychology.* Westport, CT: Greenwood Press.

Fancher, R. E. (1985). *The intelligence men.* New York: W. W. Norton.

Guthrie, R. V. (1998). *Even the rat was white: A historical view of psychology.* Boston: Allyn and Bacon.

Hansen, N. D., & Fouad, N. A. (2001). Service, scholarship, serendipity, and students: Their roles in the lives of three prominent counseling psychologists. *The Counseling Psychologist, 29,* 331–335.

Heppner, P. P. (Ed.) (1990). *Pioneers in counseling and development: Personal and professional perspectives.* Alexandria, VA: American Association for Counseling and Development.

Heppner, P. P., Casas, J., Carter, J., & Stone, G. L. (2000). The maturation of counseling psychology: Multifaceted perspectives, 1978–1998. In Steven D. Brown & Robert W. Lent (Eds.), *Handbook of counseling psychology* (3rd ed., pp. 3–49). New York: Wiley.

Hilgard, E. R. (1987). *Psychology in America: A historical survey.* San Diego, CA: Harcourt Brace Jovanovich.

Holland, J. L. (1964). Major programs of research on vocational behavior. In Henry Borow (Ed.), *Man in a world of work* (pp. 259–284). Boston: Houghton Mifflin.

Hollingworth, H. (1916). *Vocational psychology: Its problems and methods*. With a chapter on the vocational aptitudes of women by Leta Stetter Hollingworth. New York: D. Appleton and Company.

Joncich, G. M. (1968). *The sane positivist: A biography of Edward L. Thorndike*. Middletown, CT: Wesleyan University Press.

Levine, M., & Levine, A. (1992). *Helping children: A social history*. New York: Oxford University Press.

Mann, A. (Ed.) (1975). *The progressive era* (2nd ed.). Hinsdale, IL: Dryden Press.

Meara, N. M., & Myers, R. A. (1998). A history of division 17 (counseling psychology): Establishing stability amidst change. In D. A. Dewsbury (Ed.), *Unification through division: Histories of the divisions of the American Psychological Association* (Vol. 3, pp. 9–41). Washington, DC: American Psychological Association.

Münsterberg, H. (1910). Finding a life work. *McClures, 34*, 398–403.

Münsterberg, H. (1913). *Psychology and industrial efficiency*. New York: Macmillan.

Napoli, D. S. (1981). *Architects of adjustment: The history of the psychological profession in the United States*. Port Washington, NY: Kennikat Press.

Norris, W. (1954). *The history and development of the National Vocational Guidance Association*. Unpublished doctoral dissertation, George Washington University.

Parsons, F. (1909). *Choosing a vocation*. New York: Houghton Mifflin.

Paterson, D. G. (1938). The genesis of modern guidance. *The Educational Record, XIX*, 36–46.

Pepinsky, H. B., Hill-Frederick, K., & Epperson, D. L. (1978). The *Journal of Counseling Psychology as a matter of policies*. *Journal of Counseling Psychology, 25*, 483–498.

Raimy, V. C. (Ed.). (1950). *Training in clinical psychology*. Englewood Cliffs, NJ: Prentice Hall.

Rogers, C. R. (1942). *Counseling and psychotherapy: Newer concepts in practice*. Boston: Houghton Mifflin.

Rogers, C. R. (1961). *On becoming a person*. Boston: Houghton Mifflin.

Routh, D. K. (1994). *Clinical psychology since 1917: Science, practice, and organization*. New York: Plenum Press.

Savickas, M. L., & Baker, D. B. (2005). The history of vocational psychology: Antecedents, origin, and early development. In B. Walsh, & M. Savickas (Eds.), *The handbook of vocational psychology* (3rd ed., pp. 15–50). Thousand Oaks, CA: Sage Publications.

Stevens, W. R. (1970). *Social reform and the origins of vocational guidance*. Washington, DC: Monograph of the National Vocational Guidance Association.

Stocking, G. W., Jr. (1965). On the limits of "presentism" and "historicism" in the historiography of the behavioral sciences. *Journal of the History of the Behavioral Sciences, 1*, 211–218.

Super, D. E. (1955). Transition: From vocational guidance to counseling psychology. *Journal of Counseling Psychology, 2*, 3–9.

Taylor, F. W. (1911, May). The gospel of efficiency: III. The principles of scientific management. *American Magazine*, 101–113.

Thompson, A. S., & Super, D. E. (Eds.). (1964). *The professional preparation of counseling psychologists: Report of the 1964 Greyston Conference*. New York: Teachers College, Columbia University.

Tyler, L. E. (1960). *The national defense counseling and guidance training institutes program; a report of the first 50 institutes sponsored during the summer of 1959 by 50 colleges and universities under contract with the U. S. Office of Education authorized by the National defense Education Act of 1958*. Washington, DC: Office of Education.

Tyler, L., Tiedeman, D., & Wrenn, C. G. (1980). The current status of counseling psychology: 1961. In J. M. Whitely (Ed.), *The history of counseling psychology* (pp. 114–124). Monterey, CA: Brooks/Cole.

Washington, B. T. (1909). Relation of industrial education to national progress. *Annals of the American Academy of Political and Social Science, 33*, 1–12.

Watts, G. A. (1994). Frank Parsons: Promoter of a progressive era. *Journal of Career Development, 20*, 265–286.

Whiteley, J. M. (Ed.). (1980). *The history of counseling psychology*. Monterey, CA: Brooks Cole.

Yerkes, R. M. (Ed.). (1921). *Psychological examining in the United States Army*. Memoirs of the National Academy of Sciences, Volume 15. Washington, DC: U.S. Government Printing Office.

Chapter Two

Adult Psychotherapy in the Real World

Takuya Minami
Bruce E. Wampold

A perusal of the published literature on psychotherapy reveals that what we know about psychotherapy is limited by the context in which the research is conducted and the priorities of the researchers with regards to questions, hypotheses, variables, and methods. In the past few decades, the emphasis in psychotherapy research has been investigating the efficacy of treatments using randomized controlled trials (Goldfried & Wolfe, 1998; Wampold, 2001). As well, increasingly counseling and psychotherapy process research has been conducted in the context of clinical trials; when such research is conducted in naturalistic settings, the sample sizes are relatively small and the variables studied are meant to explore theoretical aspects of therapy. As a result, we actually know relatively little about how psychotherapy is practiced in the real world. The purpose of this chapter is to review what we do know about the practice of psychotherapy.

A DESCRIPTION OF THE PRACTICE OF PSYCHOTHERAPY

Wampold (2001) defined psychotherapy as follows:

> Psychotherapy is a primarily interpersonal treatment, based on psychological principles, and involves a trained therapist and a client who has a mental disorder, problem, or complaint, is intended by the therapist to be remedial for the client disorder, problem, or complaint, and is adapted or individualized for the particular client and his or her disorder, problem, or complaint. (p. 3)

Psychotherapy is a generic term in the sense that the practitioners of psychotherapy belong to a variety of professions including counseling, social work, medicine, and psychology, among others; in psychology, there are specialties in school, counseling, and clinical, each of which are involved in the training of psychotherapists. Moreover, psychotherapists practice in a variety of settings, including private practice, community agencies, hospitals and clinics, and counseling centers, among others (VandenBos, Cummings, & DeLeon, 1992). Furthermore, the sources of payment for the services are varied, including self (i.e., the client), managed care, institutions (e.g., universities, as in college counseling centers), various governmental agencies, and nonprofit agencies. Because of the variability in professions, settings, and financial systems involved, it is difficult to portray the modal practice of psychotherapy. Nevertheless, over the years, a number of surveys have been conducted by governmental agencies, professional organizations, and researchers that provide some elucidation of psychotherapy practice.

Psychotherapy as a Treatment for Mental Disorders

One important issue inherent in psychotherapy practice is with regard to the degree to which psychotherapists treat mental disorders. Information about this issue for adults emanates from the National Comorbidity Survey (NCS) conducted in 1990–1992 ($N = 5{,}388$) and the NCS Replication in 2001–2003 ($N = 4{,}319$) (Kessler et al., 2005; Wang et al., 2005, 2006). Based on the latter replication, Wang et al. (2005) reported that about 25% of the respondents would qualify as having a *DSM* diagnosis in the past 12 months. The most prevalent disorders were anxiety disorders (71% of those with disorders had some type of anxiety disorder, 18% of all respondents), mood disorders (62% of those with disorders, 16% of all respondents), impulse disorders (17% of those with disorders, 5% of all respondents), and substance abuse disorders (15% of those with disorders, 4% of all respondents).

It is interesting to know the rate at which those with mental disorders received mental health services and who were the service providers. About 18% of respondents indicated that they had used services for emotional or substance abuse issues. However, only about 40% of those who could be classified as having a *DSM* diagnosis in the past 12 months received mental health services. Interestingly, of those with disorders, only 16% were seen by a mental health professional, which was defined as a psychologist or other nonpsychiatrist mental health professional in any setting, a social worker or counselor in a mental health specialty setting, or use of a mental health hotline. By contrast, those with disorders were treated by psychiatrists (12%), general medical practitioners (23%), and non–health care providers (13%). Kessler et al. (2005) noted that from the original NCS to the replication, there was an increase in the proportion of those with mental disorders who received some form of treatment, but the treatment rate remained low. As Wang et al. (2005) noted, "Most people with mental disorders in the United States remain either untreated or poorly treated" (p. 629).

Wang et al. (2006) examined trends from the 1990–1992 NCS to the 2001–2003 replication. Six profiles among service providers and services were defined: (a) psychiatrist only, (b) general medical practitioners combined with mental health specialists, (c) general medical only profile, (d) other mental health specialty only profile, (e) human services only (religious or spiritual advisor or a social worker or counselor not in a mental health setting), or (f) complementary/alternative treatment. A clear trend was that the use of medical services, presumably involving psychotropic medication, increased over time, with psychiatrists only, general medical combined with mental health specialists, and general medicine only increased by 29%, 72%, and 153%, respectively. The use of mental health specialty, which is the profile that includes for the most psychotherapy, decreased by 72%; human services only and complementary and alternative treatments also decreased. Olfson, Marcus, Druss, & Pincus (2002), using household sections of the 1987 National Medical Expenditure Survey and the 1997 Medical Expenditure Panel Survey, found similar trends. Although the overall rate of psychotherapy use did not change significantly over this time period (3.2 to 3.6 per 100 persons in 1987 and 1997, respectively), the rate of psychotropic medication for psychotherapy clients increased (antidepressant medications increased from 14.4% to 48.6% of psychotherapy clients, mood stabilizers from 5.3% to 14.5%, and stimulants from 1.9% to 6.4%). Clearly, while the proportion of the population receiving psychotherapy from a nonphysician mental health specialist has remained constant, there has been a dramatic increase in the use of medications, with the largest increase coming from general practice medicine. This trend has occurred while the prevalence of mental disorders has remained fairly constant (Kessler et al., 2005; Wang et al., 2005, 2006). Given that recent research has shown that psychotherapy typically is as effective as pharmacological treatments of mental disorders, and more enduring (e.g., Barlow, Gorman, Shear, & Woods, 2000; Hollon, Stewart, & Strunk, 2006; Robinson, Berman, & Neimeyer, 1990), the increase in the use of medications for mental disorders is a cause of concern for many psychotherapists. The influence of the pharmaceutical companies, through direct advertising to the general population and marketing with physicians, has changed the manner in which people conceptualize mental health problems and the behavior of mental health professionals, particularly general practice physicians (Wampold, 2001).

One perspicuous trend is that, although the proportion of the population receiving psychotherapy has remained constant, the duration of treatment has decreased. The proportion of psychotherapy clients who received more than 20 visits dropped from over 15% in 1987 to approximately 10% in 1997. Whether this trend is a result of more effective services or pressure from payers (e.g., managed care, government agencies) is not clear from these data.

An important question with regard to psychotherapy is the degree to which various underserved populations are receiving psychotherapy. As we discussed earlier, an alarmingly small proportion of people who qualify for a mental health diagnosis receive mental health services. The delivery of psychotherapy services is dependent on ethnic group, with a greater proportion of European Americans receiving psychotherapy in 1997 (4.26 per 100 persons) than other groups (African Americans, Hispanic, and Other at 1.97, 1.94, and 0.93 per 100, respectively; Olfson et al., 2002). However, between 1987 and 1997, the proportion of poor and unemployed who received psychotherapy increased significantly, and the poor or nearly poor receive as much or more psychotherapy than more well-off individuals (Olfson et al., 2002). As is well known, over one and a half as many women receive psychotherapy as men (4.16 to 2.96 per 100). When examining all mental health services vis-à-vis prevalence rates, Wang et al. (2005) noted, "Unmet need for treatment is greatest in traditionally underserved groups, including elderly persons, racial-ethnic minorities, those with low incomes, those without insurance, and residents of rural areas" (p. 629).

Because psychotherapy is not provided by a single professional, it is useful to know what professions are providing this service. Again, the data come from surveys, most importantly from the 1987 National Medical Expenditure Survey and the 1997 Medical Expenditure Panel Survey (Olfson et al., 2002). According to these surveys, most respondents reported that they receive their psychotherapy from physicians and that this increased over time, from 48% of all psychotherapy provided by physicians in 1987 to 65% in 1997. However, because the definition of psychotherapy is ambiguous to respondents, it might well include medicine checks and clinical management for psychotropic medication. The proportion of people who receive psychotherapy from a psychologist has remained fairly steady at around 33%. The proportion of people receiving psychotherapy from social workers nearly doubled, from 7% to 13%, whereas the proportion from other providers (e.g., marriage and family therapists, counselors, and other nonphysician, nonpsychologist, and non–social workers) declined (from 23% in 1987 to 15% in 1997).

Payment for Psychotherapy

Who pays for psychotherapy? This is a complicated question, given that payments vary as a function of a number of factors, including location, employment status, and socioeconomic status; as well, the landscape is always changing as parity laws are passed in some states and are being considered nationally. Nevertheless, some attempts have been made to address this issue, again primarily from national surveys. It is estimated that nearly 10 million Americans receive psychotherapy annually, at a cost of between $5.7 and $9.6 billion; as a comparison, the annual sales of antidepressants alone is approximately $13.5 billion (Olfson et al., 2002; Langreth, 2007). Recently, Zuvekas and Meyerhoefer (2006) reported the results of the 1996 and 2003 Medical Expenditure Panel Survey (MEPS). They found that, although the out-of-pocket expenses as a proportion of total costs of outpatient mental health services declined slightly from 1996 to 2003, it remains significantly higher than it is for physical health services. Importantly, the out-of-pocket expenses for mental health services from mental health specialists were substantially greater than they were for nonpsychiatrist physicians, the latter services being covered under the general provisions of health insurance whereas the former are covered under the behavioral health components. Incidentally, this might explain why the general practitioners are treating a great proportion of mental health clients.

For psychologists, there was a troubling trend in these data with regard to income (Zuvekas & Meyerhoefer, 2006). In 1996, the mean expense per visit to a psychologist was $112, of which $65 was paid by a payer other than the client (i.e., a third-party payer), leaving an out-of-pocket expense of $47; in 2003, the mean expense per visit was $88 of which $55 was paid by a third-party payer, leaving an out-of-pocket expense of $33. So, although the proportion of out-of-pocket expense vis-à-vis the cost of a visit has decreased slightly (a good thing for clients), and the absolute amount of out-of-pocket expense has also decreased (a good thing for clients), the income of psychologists appears to have dropped precipitously (for practicing psychologists, not a good thing). There are also troubling aspects of out-of-pocket expenses from the patient perspective, as such expenses appear to increase as the intensity of treatment increases, so the more severe the disorder and the more treatment that is needed, the greater the relative out-of-pocket expenses. Out-of-pocket expenses were relatively less if the client (a) was a member of an HMO, (b) was African American, and (c) was poor, although one has to be careful to interpret these results, as various populations use very different services and the payers and subsidies differ.

Type of Psychotherapy Delivered

It is also interesting to know what types of psychotherapy are being delivered. Every 10 years, Norcross and colleagues survey members of the Division 29 (Psychotherapy) of the American Psychological Association relative to a number of practices, including type of treatment provided. In the 2001 survey (Norcross, Hedges, & Castle, 2002), over one-third of the psychologists indicated that their theoretical orientation was eclectic or integrative. Next in order were psychodynamic or psychoanalytic (29%), behavioral or cognitive (19%, which is about double what it was in 1981), and, in a distant third, some form of humanistic (client-centered, Rogerian, existential, Gestalt, or other humanistic; 6%, down from 14% in 1981). Of course, psychotherapy is not only practiced by psychologists, but it appears nevertheless that not only have humanistic approaches been abandoned by (or perhaps have abandoned) mainstream theoretical psychology, as Rice and Greenberg (1992) suggest, but psychotherapists (at least psychologists) have abandoned these approaches as well.

The foregoing discussion of the role of psychotherapy in the treatment of mental disorders begs an important question—is psychotherapy, as practiced in the real world, effective? We now turn to that important question.

QUALITY OF CURRENT PRACTICE IN GENERAL CLINICAL SETTINGS

From the clients' standpoint, obviously the most important question is whether or not psychotherapy delivered in practice is effective. Interestingly, little is known about this—in the past 30 years since Smith and Glass's (1977) seminal meta-analysis that established the efficacy of psychotherapy (i.e., is it beneficial in clinical trials?), few studies have attempted to investigate the degree of effectiveness (i.e., is it beneficial in actual practice?) despite consistent calls for its importance (e.g., Barlow, 1981; Cohen, 1965; Goldfried & Wolfe, 1998; Luborsky, 1972; Seligman, 1995; Smith, Glass, & Miller, 1980; Strupp, 1989; Weisz, Donenberg, Han, & Weiss, 1995a). The lack of research on the effects of psychotherapy as it is regularly practiced in the field (i.e., effectiveness) is perhaps a result of the field's position that the randomized controlled trials are the "gold standard" of research, as evidenced by the propagation of clinical trials during the past five decades (Goldfried & Wolfe, 1998). Indeed, the majority of the criticism against Seligman's (1995) *Consumer Reports Study*, which reported consumers' opinions about the effectiveness of psychotherapy, were directed toward its methodology, notably threats to internal validity, as this well-known survey lacked control groups. Although few disagree that effectiveness studies are necessary, there is little consensus about what constitutes a valid effectiveness study. For example, the title of Mintz, Drake, and Crits-Christoph's (1996) comment on Seligman (1995) was "Efficacy and Effectiveness of Psychotherapy: Two Paradigms, One Science"; they argued for stringent research designs that involved randomization, control group(s), diagnostic homogeneity of clients, and use of treatment manuals, components that frankly are unrealistic in naturalistic settings and would alter the treatments being delivered, thus obviating an estimation of the effects of psychotherapy as "actually practiced." Reflecting this lack of consensus, there are now many variations of "effectiveness" studies investigating adult psychotherapy in the real world. In general, these studies could be classified into three categories based on research design and analysis: (a) clinical representativeness studies, (b) treatment studies that compare psychotherapy that is generally practiced within the setting (i.e., treatment-as-usual; TAU) and empirically supported treatments (EST; e.g., Chambless & Ollendick, 2001), and (c) benchmarking studies.

Clinical Representativeness Studies

Clinical representativeness studies do not actually collect data from the field. Rather, these studies analyze previously published studies to see whether or not factors that would distinguish between the real world and the laboratory (e.g., setting, client recruitment method, random client assignment to treatment, use of treatment manual) are present and moderate outcomes. Typically, these studies are meta-analyses that code the degree to which treatments resemble those offered in clinical settings and then investigate whether those treatments that more closely resemble those provided in practice settings produce poorer (or greater) outcomes than those administered in laboratory settings.

Interestingly, the first clinical representativeness study was conducted by Smith and colleagues (Smith & Glass, 1977; Smith et al., 1980). In their book (i.e., Smith et al.), they included two factors that contrast clinical trials and clinical settings, notably, treatment setting and client recruitment method. With regard to treatment setting, they found that the estimated effect size was the largest for psychotherapy conducted in college facilities (d = 1.04, SE = 0.06) defined as "psychology laboratory, therapy training center, or student mental health clinic" (p. 117) and the smallest in mental health centers (d = 0.47, SE = 0.13). However, the analysis was plagued by the fact that less than two percent of the studies were conducted in mental health centers. With regard to client recruitment method, they found that the largest effect size estimates were from studies in which participants responded to special advertisements for the study (d = 1.00, SE = 0.06) and when experimenters solicited participants (d = 0.92, SE = 0.06), whereas the effect size estimates from studies where participants were self-referred were smaller (d = 0.71, SE = 0.03). Smith et al. concluded that the "reliable differences in effects associated with the true-to-life methods and the laboratory methods of obtaining clients is evidence against the generalizability of results of laboratory-based therapies and argues for field-based evaluation to back up research conducted under artificial arrangements" (p. 122).

Since Smith et al. (1980), there have been several studies that also investigated clinical representativeness (e.g., Shapiro & Shapiro, 1982). However, it was difficult to interpret the results from these studies because each potential moderator was tested alone rather than in conjunction. In other words, although the potential impact of each factor was assessed, the impact that these factors as a group have on psychotherapy outcome has not been investigated. Shadish and colleagues remedied this gap by examining the potentially compounding effect of numerous factors including treatment setting, therapist characteristics, referral sources, use of manuals, adherence monitoring, additional training, client heterogeneity, and flexibility in length of treatment (Shadish et al., 1997; Shadish, Matt, Navarro, & Phillips, 2000). Based on their statistical analysis of a large number of studies, Shadish et al. (2000) concluded that an ideal, clinically representative psychotherapy should yield effect size estimates that are similar to or slightly less than what is observed in clinical trials. However, these studies cannot ultimately provide evidence for effectiveness of psychotherapy in the real world because they do not directly assess outcomes in the field. Moreover, very few of the treatments in the studies in these meta-analyses closely resembled real-world psychotherapy; indeed, of the more than 1,000 studies reviewed, only 56 contained treatments that met criteria for being "somewhat similar" to clinic therapy, and only 1 met all criteria for clinic therapy (Wampold, 2001).

ESTs versus TAUs

In the second type of effectiveness study, an EST is transported into a clinical setting and its outcomes are compared against TAUs. Although there is little consistency as to how these studies are conducted (as will be detailed), a representative procedure is demonstrated by Addis et al. (2004). The design of this study was similar to a clinical trial, where therapists are provided training in the particular EST, are supervised throughout the study, and their sessions are recorded and checked for adherence to the treatment protocol specified by a manual. Specifically, Addis et al. randomly assigned volunteer therapists to either deliver panic control therapy (PCT; Craske, Meadows, & Barlow, 1994) or to deliver their usual therapy. The therapists who delivered PCT participated in a 2-day workshop on panic and PCT, and, after conducting two trial cases using PCT, they were further provided 30-minute phone consultations with the expert who provided the workshop as well as biweekly 1-hour group consultations with the principal investigator and the research team to "discuss cases and refine therapists' knowledge of PCT and its underlying cognitive-behavioral principles" (p. 627). The sessions were audiotaped and were randomly checked for adherence based on a rating manual developed for PCT.

Several difficulties are encountered when reviewing studies that compare ESTs against TAUs, of which the first and foremost is what constitutes TAU. Although the acronym TAU has become quite popular in the psychotherapy literature (e.g., Weisz, Jensen-Doss, & Hawley, 2006), many "TAUs" are in fact not psychotherapy. The TAUs included medication management by general practitioners or psychiatrists (e.g., Guthrie et al., 1999; Proudfoot et al., 2004), case management (e.g., Dare, Eisler, Russell, Treasure, & Dodge, 2001), self-help (e.g., Baker et al., 2006), mixture of different interventions (e.g., Bowen et al., 2006; De Leon, Sacks, Staines, & McKendrick, 2000), whatever the clients wished (e.g., Granholm, et al., 2005; Lang, Norman, & Casmar, 2006; Linton & Ryberg, 2000; Williams, Teasdale, Segal, & Soulsby, 2001), or even nothing (e.g., Spector et al., 2003). Therefore, although an outcome evaluation of an EST against a "TAU" may provide an impression that the TAUs are bona fide psychotherapy provided in clinical settings, this is rarely the case. Even in the event that the TAU does appear to be psychotherapy, very little information is provided in the studies regarding the treatment itself, the context in which the treatment was delivered, the therapists who delivered the treatment, and the duration, frequency, and intensity of the treatment. One notable exception is by Rawson et al. (2004), which devoted a separate publication to provide the descriptions of the different TAUs that were used (Galloway et al., 2000).

Another issue with studies comparing TAU and EST in clinical studies is that unlike clinical trials comparing two ESTs head-to-head, the ESTs and TAUs are rarely matched with regard to the dose of treatment. In fact, rather than allocating clients to TAU or EST, many studies assign clients to TAU or TAU plus EST (e.g., Bach & Hayes, 2004; Bockting et al., 2005; Ma & Teasdale, 2004; Morgenstern, Blanchard, Morgan, Labouvie, & Hayaki, 2001; Zlotnick, Johnson, Miller, Pearlstein, & Howard, 2001). Even in the case in which clients are allocated to either the TAU or EST, many studies explicitly acknowledge that clients in the EST condition received a significantly higher number of sessions vis-à-vis the TAU condition (e.g., Bohus et al, 2004; Linehan et al. 1999; Rawson et al., 2004; Verheul et al. 2005). This is a significant problem with these studies because most claim that the ESTs were superior to the TAUs despite such differences in dosage.

Another significant issue with these studies is that the amount of training, supervision, and/or consultation significantly differs between conditions. The TAU therapists typically do not receive additional training, supervision, and/or consultation during the study, which could create differences in expectancy and motivation. For example, Addis et al. (2004) reported that they were very explicit with regard to the training and expectancy in that they were "encouraging therapists to attend meetings by repeatedly expressing our confidence in the treatment and the value of consultation" (p. 628), but dismissed its possible effect by reporting that "[i]f expectancy effects were the preliminary mechanisms of change, the results would have been more likely to be restricted to panic-specific problems measured by self-report" (p. 634). Nevertheless, providing additional training, supervision, and/or consultation to therapists providing the EST not only is an advantage but alters the nature of how treatments are delivered in practice settings where therapists do not have the luxury of intensive training and supervision by the developers of a particular treatment.

The problems of comparing treatments whose efficacy is established in clinical trials to TAU is illustrated by a meta-analysis conducted by Weisz et al. (2006), who compared "evidence-based" treatments (EBT) and usual care (UC). They concluded, "Our findings support the view that EBTs have generally outperformed UC in direct, randomized comparisons" (p. 684). However, they also noted that there were possible confounds related to patients, therapists, settings, and dose—indeed, no study adequately controlled these variables! Importantly, when any one of the confounds are controlled, the superiority of the EBT disappears, as illustrated in Figure 2.1, which is based on the summary statistics provided by Weisz et al. The small superiority of ESTs noted in several studies of adult TAU (e.g., Addis et al., 2004) are likely a result of the same confounds that plague the childhood comparisons.

Benchmarking

The third category of effectiveness research is benchmarking. This is a fairly new method in which the delivery of TAUs in clinical settings does not need any modification except for implementing outcome measures (if they do not do so already). Rather than statistically estimating the effectiveness or implementing a different treatment, benchmarking assesses effectiveness of

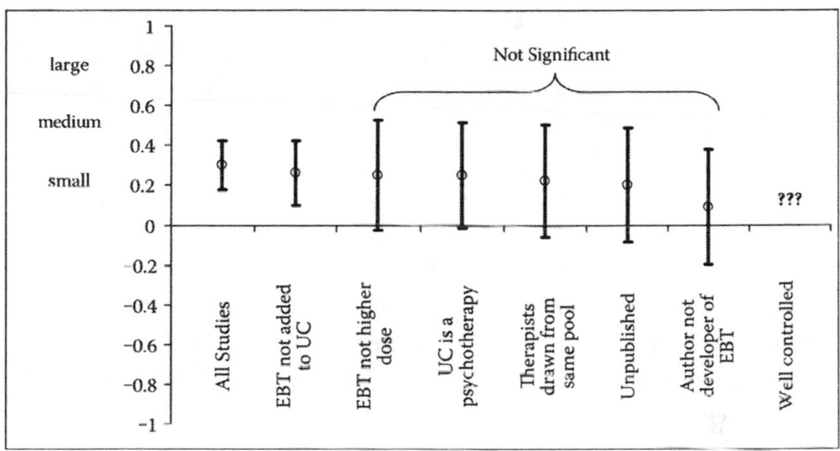

Figure 2.1 Effect size and 95% confidence intervals for all studies and studies that control for one confound in Weisz et al. (2006) comparisons of evidence-based treatments and usual care for youth.

TAUs by comparing its observed pre-post effect size estimates against an effect size criterion (i.e., benchmark) derived by aggregating outcomes in clinical trials.

Ironically, the first psychotherapy benchmarking study assessed the "effectiveness" of CBT transported to a community mental health center (i.e., a disseminated EST) rather than TAU. Wade et al. (1998) compared the clinical outcomes of CBT administered to 110 clients seeking treatment for panic disorder, benchmarked their results against two clinical trials, and found that treatment outcomes of their participants and those of the clinical trials were "similar" (p. 237). In addition to their study being a transported EST, the degree of dissimilarity between this treatment and TAU was magnified by fixed treatment length, therapist training, use of a treatment manual, and monitoring adherence to treatment protocol, which are all procedures rarely seen in clinical settings. In sum, it would be hard to argue that the clinical outcomes obtained in this study are representative of TAU in this setting.

The study was replicated at the same treatment center using clients seeking treatment for depression (Merrill, Tolbert, & Wade, 2003). Similar to Wade et al. (1998), they provided CBT training to their therapists using a treatment manual; however, in this study, the length of treatment was not fixed and adherence was not monitored. Although Merrill et al. claimed that their results compared "favorably to the two RCT studies" (p. 406), their results were plagued with a very high attrition rate (68%). Like Wade et al., their results are also far from representative of TAU.

Weersing and Weisz (2002) conducted the first study that benchmarked TAU against clinical trials. Their methodology significantly improved on that of Wade et al. (1998), in that rather than using two clinical trials as benchmarks, they conducted a benchmark by meta-analyzing published clinical trials of youth depression treatment so as to assess the outcomes of 67 children who received treatment at six community mental health centers in the Los Angeles area. Using hierarchical linear modeling, they found that the mean level of depression measured at 3 months into treatment was nearly identical to the control benchmark (aggregated using wait-list, no treatment, or placebo control groups) and was significantly higher than that of the clinical trials treatment benchmark. Consistent with a previous review of effectiveness studies (Weisz, Donenberg, Han, & Kauneckis, 1995b), their results provided little support for TAUs for children and adolescents.

As of this date, only one study has benchmarked TAU for adults. Using benchmarks that aggregated effect size estimates observed in clinical trials of adult depression treatment, Minami et al. (2008) conducted a benchmarking study assessing the effectiveness of TAU for adult clients with major depression delivered in a managed care environment. In their benchmarking study, they improved on Weersing and Weisz's (2002) methodology in two ways. First, as Minami, Wampold, Serlin, Kircher, and Brown (2007) found that effect size estimates in clinical trials significantly differed based on reactivity (i.e., whether the outcome was measured by a blind clinician or client self-report) and specificity (i.e., whether or not the outcome measure was tailored to a specific diagnosis), the benchmark that they used for comparison was matched with regard to reactivity and specificity with the outcome measure used in the clinical settings. These effects based on the nature of outcome measures are consistent with previous meta-analyses (e.g., Lambert, Hatch, Kingston, & Edwards, 1986; Smith et al., 1980). Second, as analyses using a traditional point-null hypothesis attain statistical significance in large sample sizes even when differences are clinically trivial, Minami et al. (2007) utilized a range-null hypothesis testing to avoid rejection of the null hypothesis when effects are clinically equivalent based on the "good-enough principle" (Minami et al. 2007; Serlin & Lapsley, 1985, 1993). Specifically, when comparing against the treatment efficacy benchmarks, they considered that effect size estimates that are within 10% below the benchmarks are clinically equivalent. When comparing against the natural history benchmark (i.e., no-treatment control), clinical settings data needed to exceed it by $d = 0.2$. These criteria were selected to conduct conservative comparisons.

In this study, three clinical settings samples were benchmarked. The samples differed in degree of equivalence between the clinical settings data and the clinical trials based on client clinical characteristics. In particular, the first sample (i.e., Clinical) was most representative of clients who seek treatment for depression in a managed care setting. In stark contrast to typical exclusion criteria of RCTs, clients were not excluded based on comorbidity. The second sample (i.e., Noncomorbid) excluded clients with comorbidity from the first sample; thus, the clinical characteristics of these participants were much similar to RCTs. The third sample (i.e., Completer) further excluded clients from the second sample based on the number of sessions and duration of treatment in attempt to replicate the conditions observed in RCTs among clients who "complete" treatment.

Three benchmarks from Minami et al. (2007) were used, notably, intent-to-treat treatment efficacy, completer treatment efficacy, and natural history (i.e., no-treatment control). The Clinical and Noncomorbid samples were compared against the intent-to-treat treatment efficacy, and the Completer sample was compared against the treatment efficacy. Results indicated that TAUs delivered in a managed care environment attain clinically equivalent outcomes as compared to RCTs. In all three comparisons, the samples met statistical criteria for clinical equivalence—that is, the outcomes attained by providers in a managed care environment were comparable to the outcomes attained in clinical trials. Minami et al. (2008) also assessed the effect of concurrent antidepressants and found that, on average, they increased the effect size estimates by approximately $d = 0.15$. In addition, while not included in the manuscript, they also found that practitioners in group practice had significantly better outcomes than those who were in solo practices (differences of $d = 0.24 \sim 0.30$).

CONCLUSIONS

Characterizing adult psychotherapy in the real world is difficult, as direct evidence for the type of service provided, the payment for such services, and the effectiveness of services are sparse. Nevertheless, we have been able to present some evidence that clarifies the situation, and some tentative conclusions can be made. Psychotherapy is a modality frequently used to treat mental disorders and is widely practiced in the United States. However, the treatment of mental disorders with psychotropic medication, either as the primary treatment or in conjunction with psychotherapy, is increasing dramatically; the medications are often prescribed by general practice physicians. Nevertheless, a large proportion of persons with mental disorders are untreated, and there is particular concern about services provided to minorities and low socioeconomic status

(SES) persons. Payment for psychotherapy services comes from a number of sources, and although out-of-pocket expenses for patients have been relatively stable, psychologists' fees have apparently been decreasing. For the most part, psychologists practice eclectic or integrative psychotherapy, followed in order with psychodynamic and cognitive-behavioral psychotherapy. Although it is difficult to estimate the effectiveness of psychotherapy, it appears that, when rigorously evaluated, the quality of services provided in practice rival that of the treatments provided in clinical trials.

BIBLIOGRAPHY

Addis, M. E., Hatgis, C., Krasnow, A. D., Jacob, K., Bourne, L, & Mansfield, A. (2004). Effectiveness of cognitive-behavioral treatment for panic disorder versus treatment as usual in a managed care setting. *Journal of Consulting and Clinical Psychology, 72*, 625–635.

Bach, P., & Hayes, S. C. (2004). The use of acceptance and commitment therapy to prevent the rehospitalization of psychotic patients: A randomized controlled trial. *Journal of Consulting and Clinical Psychology, 70*, 1129–1139.

Baker, A., Bucci, S. A., Lewin, T. J., Kay-Lambkin, F., Constable, P. M., & Carr, V. J. (2006). Cognitive-behavioural therapy for substance use disorders in people with psychotic disorders. *British Journal of Psychiatry, 188*, 439–448.

Barlow, D. H. (1981). On the relation of clinical research on clinical practice: Current issues. *Journal of Consulting and Clinical Psychology, 49*, 147–155.

Barlow, D. H., Gorman, J. M., Shear, M. K., & Woods, S. W. (2000). Cognitive-behavioral therapy, imipramine, or their combination for panic disorder: A randomized controlled trial. *Journal of the American Medical Assocation, 283*, 2529–2536.

Bockting, C. L. H., Schene, A. H., Spinhoven, P., Koeter, M. W. J., Wouters, L. F., Huyser, J., et al. (2005). Preventing relapse/recurrence in recurrent depression with cognitive therapy: A randomized controlled trial. *Journal of Consulting and Clinical Psychology, 73*, 647–657.

Bohus, M., Haaf, B., Simms, T., Limberger, M. F., Schmahl, C., Unckel, C., et al. (2004). Effectiveness of inpatient dialectical behavioral therapy for borderline personality disorder: A controlled trial. *Behaviour Research and Therapy, 42*, 487–499.

Bowen, S., Witkiewitz, K., Dillworth, T. M., Chawla, N., Simpson, T. L., Ostafin, B. D., et al. (2006). Mindfulness meditation and substance use in an incarcerated population. *Psychology of Addictive Behaviors, 20*, 343–347.

Chambless, D. L., & Ollendick, T. H. (2001). Empirically supported psychological interventions: Controversies and evidence. *Annual Review of Psychology, 52*, 685–716.

Cohen, J. (1965). Some statistical issues in psychological research. In B. Wolman (Ed.), *Handbook of clinical psychology* (pp. 95–121). New York: McGraw-Hill.

Craske, M. G., Meadows, E., & Barlow, D. H. (1994). *Therapist's guide for the mastery of your anxiety and panic II & agoraphobia supplement (Map II) program.* Albany, NY: Graywind.

Dare, C., Eisler, I., Russell, G., Treasure, J., & Dodge, L. (2001). Psychological therapies for adults with anorexia nervosa. *British Journal of Psychiatry, 178,* 216–221.

De Leon, G., Sacks, S., Staines, G., & McKendrick, K. (2000). Modified therapeutic community for homeless mentally ill chemical abusers: Treatment outcomes. *American Journal of Drug and Alcohol Abuse, 26,* 461–480.

Franklin, M. E., Abramowitz, J. S., Kozak, M. J., Levitt, J. T., & Foa, E. B. (2000). Effectiveness of exposure and ritual prevention for obsessive-compulsive disorder: Randomized compared with nonrandomized samples. *Journal of Consulting and Clinical Psychology, 68,* 594–602.

Galloway, G. P., Marinelli-Casey, P., Stalcup, J., Lord, R., Christian, D., Cohen, J., et al. (2000). Treatment-as-usual in the Methamphetamine Treatment Project. *Journal of Psychoactive Drugs, 32,* 165–175.

García-Palacios, A., Botella, C., Robert, C., Baños, R., Perpiña, C., Quero, S., et al. (2002). Clinical utility of cognitive-behavioural treatment for panic disorder. Results obtained in different settings: A research centre and a public mental health unit. *Clinical Psychology and Psychotherapy, 9,* 373–383.

Gillespie, K., Duffy, M., Hackmann, A., & Clark, D. M. (2002). Community-based cognitive therapy in the treatment of post-traumatic stress disorder following the Omagh bomb. *Behaviour Research and Therapy, 40,* 345–357.

Goldfried, M. R., & Wolfe, B. E. (1998). Toward a more clinically valid approach to therapy research. *Journal of Consulting and Clinical Psychology, 66,* 143–150.

Granholm, E., McQuaid, J. R., McClure, F. S., Auslander, L. A., Perivoliotis, D., Pedrelli, P., et al. (2005). A randomized, controlled trial of cognitive behavioral social skills training for middle aged and older outpatients with chronic schizophrenia. *American Journal of Psychiatry, 162,* 520–529.

Guthrie, E., Moorey, J., Margison, F., Barker, H., Palmer, S., McGrath, G., et al. (1999). Cost-effectiveness of brief psychodynamic-interpersonal therapy in high utilizers of psychiatric services. *Archives of General Psychiatry, 56,* 519–526.

Hahlweg, K., Fiegenbaum, W., Frank, M., Schroeder, B., & von Witzleben, I. (2001). Short- and long-term effectiveness of an empirically supported treatment for agoraphobia. *Journal of Consulting and Clinical Psychology, 69,* 375–382.

Henggeler, S. W., Melton, G. B., Brondino, M. J., Scherer, D. G., & Hanley, J. H. (1997). Multisystemic therapy with violent and chronic juvenile offenders and their families: The role of treatment fidelity in successful dissemination. *Journal of Consulting and Clinical Psychology, 65,* 821–833.

Hollanders, H., & McLeod, J. (1999). Theoretical orientation and reported practice: A survey of eclecticism among counsellors in Britain. *British Journal of Guidance and Counselling, 27,* 405–414.

Hollon, S. D., Stewart, M. O., & Strunk, D. (2006). Enduring effects for cognitive behavior therapy in the treatment of depression and anxiety. *Annual Review of Psychology, 57,* 285–315.

Kessler, R. C., Demler, O., Frank, R. G., Olfson, M., Pincus, H. A., Walters, E. E., et al. (2005). Prevalence and treatment of mental disorders, 1990 to 2003. *New England Journal of Medicine, 352,* 2515–2523.

Lambert, M. J., Hatch, D. R., Kingston, M. D., & Edwards, B. C. (1986). Zung, Beck, and Hamilton Rating Scales as measures of treatment outcome: A meta-analytic comparison. *Journal of Consulting and Clinical Psychology, 54,* 54–59.

Lang, A. J., Norman, G. J., & Casmar, P. V. (2006). A randomized trial of a brief mental health intervention for primary care patients. *Journal of Consulting and Clinical Psychology, 74,* 1173–1179.

Langreth, R. (2007, April 9). Patient, fix thyself. *Forbes,* 80–86.

Lincoln, T. M., Rief, W., Hahlweg, K., Frank, M., von Witzleben, I., Schroeder, B., et al. (2003). Effectiveness of an empirically supported treatment for social phobia in the field. *Behaviour Research and Therapy, 41,* 1251–1269.

Linehan, M. M., Schmidt, H., Dimeff, L. A., Craft, J. C., Kanter, J., & Comtois, K. A. (1999). Dialectical behavior therapy for patients with borderline personality disorder and drug-dependence. *American Journal on Addictions, 8,* 279–292.

Linton, S. J., & Ryberg, M. (2000). A cognitive-behavioral group intervention as prevention for persistent neck and back pain in a non-patient population: A randomized controlled trial. *Pain,* 90, 83–90.

Luborsky, L. (1972). Research cannot yet influence clinical practice. In A. Bergin & H. Strupp (Eds.), *Changing frontiers in the science of psychotherapy* (pp. 120–127). Chicago: Aldine.

Luborsky, L., McLellan, T., Woody, G. E., O'Brien, C. P., & Auerbach, A. (1985). Therapist success and its determinants. *Archives of General Psychiatry, 42,* 602–611.

Ma, S. H., & Teasdale, J. D. (2004). Mindfulness-based cognitive therapy for depression: Replication and exploration of differential relapse prevention effects. *Journal of Consulting and Clinical Psychology, 72,* 31–40.

Merrill, K. A., Tolbert, V. E., & Wade, W. A. (2003). Effectiveness of cognitive therapy for depression in a community mental health center: A benchmarking study. *Journal of Consulting and Clinical Psychology, 71,* 404–409.

Minami, T., Serlin, R. C., Wampold, B. E., Kircher, J. C., & Brown, G. S. (In press). Using clinical trials to benchmark effects produced in clinical practice. *Quality and Quantity.*

Minami, T., Wampold, B. E., Serlin, R. C., Hamilton, E. G., Brown, G. S., & Kircher, J. C. (2008). Benchmarking the effectiveness of psychotherapy treatment for adult depression in a managed care environment: A preliminary study. *Journal of Consulting and Clinical Psychology,* 76, 116–124.

Minami, T., Wampold, B. E., Serlin, R. C., Kircher, J. C., & Brown, G. S. (2007). Benchmarks for psychotherapy efficacy in adult major depression. *Journal of Consulting and Clinical Psychology, 75,* 232–243.

Mintz, J., Drake, R., & Crits-Christoph, P. (1996). Efficacy and effectiveness of psychotherapy: Two paradigms, one science. *American Psychologist, 51,* 1084–1085.

Morgenstern, J., Blanchard, K. A., Morgan, T. J., Labouvie, E., & Hayaki, J. (2001). Testing the effectiveness of cognitive-behavioral treatment for substance abuse in a community setting: Within treatment and posttreatment findings. *Journal of Consulting and Clinical Psychology, 69,* 1007–1017.

Morrison, A. P., Renton, J. C., Williams, S., Knight, D. H., Kreutz, M., Nothard, S., et al. (2004). Delivering cognitive therapy to people with psychosis in a community mental health setting: An effectiveness study. *Acta Psychiatrica Scandinavica, 220,* 36–44.

Norcross, J. C., Hedges, M., & Castle, P. H. (2002). Psychologists conducting psychotherapy in 2001: A study of the Division 29 membership. *Psychotherapy: Theory, Research, Practice, Training, 39,* 97–102.

Norcross, J. C., Karpiak, C. P., & Santoro, S. O. (2005). Clinical psychologists across the years: The division of clinical psychology from 1960 to 2003. *Journal of Clinical Psychology, 61,* 1467–1483.

Olfson, M., Marcus, S. C., Druss, B., & Pincus, H. A. (2002). National trends in the use of outpatient psychotherapy. *American Journal of Psychiatry, 159,* 1914–1920.

Persons, J. B., Bostrom, A., & Bertagnolli, A. (1999). Results of randomized controlled trials of cognitive therapy for depression generalize to private practice. *Cognitive Therapy and Research, 23,* 535–548.

Proudfoot, J., Ryden, C., Everitt, B., Shapiro, D. A., Goldberg, D., Mann, A., et al (2004). Clinical efficacy of computerised cognitive-behavioural therapy for anxiety and depression in primary care: Randomised controlled trial. *British Journal of Psychiatry, 185,* 46–54.

Rawson, R. A., Marinelli-Casey, P., Anglin, M. D., Dickow, A., Frazier, Y., Gallagher, C., et al. (2004). A multi-site comparison of psychosocial approaches for the treatment of methamphetamine dependence. *Addiction, 99,* 708–717.

Rice, L. N., & Greenberg, L. S. (1992). Humanistic approaches to psychotherapy. In D. K. Freedheim (Ed.), *History of psychotherapy: A century of change* (pp. 197–224). Washington, DC: American Psychological Association.

Robinson, L. A., Berman, J. S., & Neimeyer, R. A. (1990). Psychotherapy for the treatment of depression: A comprehensive review of controlled outcome research. *Psychological Bulletin, 108,* 30–49.

Seligman, M. E. P. (1995). The effectiveness of psychotherapy: The Consumer Reports Study. *American Psychologist, 50,* 965–974.

Serlin, R. C., & Lapsley, D. K. (1985). Rationality in psychological research: The good-enough principle. *American Psychologist, 40,* 73–83.

Serlin, R. C., & Lapsley, D. K. (1993). Rational appraisal of psychological research and the good-enough principle. In G. Keren & C. Lewis (Eds.), *A handbook for data analysis in the behavioral sciences: Methodological issues* (pp. 199–228). Hillsdale, NJ: Erlbaum.

Shadish, W. R., Matt, G. E., Navarro, A. M., & Phillips, G. (2000). The effects of psychological therapies under clinically representative conditions: A meta-analysis. *Psychological Bulletin, 126,* 512–529.

Shadish, W. R., Matt, G. E., Navarro, A. M., Siegle, G., Crits-Christoph, P., Hazeligg, M. D., et al. (1997). Evidence that therapy works in clinically representative conditions. *Journal of Consulting and Clinical Psychology, 65,* 355–365.

Shapiro, D. A., & Shapiro, D. (1982). Meta-analysis of comparative therapy outcome studies: A replication and refinement. *Psychological Bulletin, 92,* 581–604.

Smith, M. L., & Glass, G. V. (1977). Meta-analysis of psychotherapy outcome studies. *American Psychologist, 32,* 752–760.

Smith, M. L., Glass, G. V., & Miller, T. I. (1980). *The benefits of psychotherapy.* Baltimore: Johns Hopkins University Press.

Spector, A., Thorgrimsen, L., Woods, B., Royan, L., Davies, S., Butterworth, M., et al. (2003). Efficacy of an evidence-based cognitive stimulation therapy programme for people with dementia. *British Journal of Psychiatry, 283,* 248–254.

Strupp, H. H. (1989). Psychotherapy: Can the practitioner learn from the researcher? *American Psychologist, 44,* 717–724.

Tuschen-Caffier, B., Pook, M., & Frank, M. (2001). Evaluation of manual-based cognitive-behavioral therapy for bulimia nervosa in a service setting. *Behaviour Research and Therapy, 39,* 299–308.

VandenBos, G. R., Cummings, N. A., & DeLeon, P. H. (1992). A century of psychotherapy: Economic and environmental influences. In D. K. Freedheim (Ed.), *A history of psychotherapy: A century of change.* Washington, DC: American Psychological Association.

Verheul, R., van den Bosch, L. M. C., Koeter, W. J., de Ridder, M. A., Stijnen, T., & van den Brink, W. (2003). Dialectical behavior therapy with women with borderline personality disorder: 12-month, randomised clinical trial in the Netherlands. *British Journal of Psychiatry, 182,* 135–140.

Wade, W. A., Treat, T. A., & Stuart, G. L. (1998). Transporting an empirically supported treatment for panic disorder to a service clinic setting: A benchmarking strategy. *Journal of Consulting and Clinical Psychology, 66,* 231–239.

Wampold, B. E. (2001). *The great psychotherapy debate: Model, methods, and findings.* Mahwah, NJ: Lawrence Erlbaum Associates.

Wang, P. S., Demler, O., Olfson, M., Pincus, H. A., Wells, K. B., & Kessler, R. C. (2006). Changing profiles of service sectors used for mental health care in the United States. *American Journal of Psychiatry, 163,* 1187–1198.

Wang, P. S., Lane, M., Olfson, M., Pincus, H. A., Wells, K. B., & Kessler, R. C. (2005). Twelve-month use of mental health services in the United States: Results from the National Comorbidity Survey Replication. *Archives of General Psychiatry, 62,* 629–640.

Warren, R., & Thomas, J. C. (2001). Cognitive-behavior therapy of obsessive-compulsive disorder in private practice: An effectiveness study. *Journal of Anxiety Disorders, 15,* 277–285.

Weersing, V. R., & Weisz, J. R. (2002). Community clinic treatment of depressed youth: Benchmarking usual care against CBT clinical trials. *Journal of Consulting and Clinical Psychology, 70,* 299–310.

Weisz, J. R., Donenberg, G. R., Han, S. S., & Weiss, B. (1995a). Bridging the gap between laboratory and clinical in child and adolescent psychotherapy. *Journal of Consulting and Clinical Psychology, 63,* 688–701.

Weisz, J. R., Donenberg, G. R., Han, S. S., & Kauneckis, D. (1995b). Child and adolescent psychotherapy outcomes in experiments versus clinics: Why the disparity? *Journal of Abnormal Child Psychology, 23,* 83–106.

Weisz, J. R., Jensen-Doss, A., & Hawley, K. M. (2006). Evidence-based youth psychotherapies versus usual clinical care: A meta-analysis of direct comparisons. *American Psychologist, 61,* 671–689.

Williams, J. M. G., Teasdale, J. D., Segal, Z. V., & Soulsby, J. (2001). Mindfulness-based cognitive therapy reduces overgeneral autobiographical memory in formerly depressed patients. *Journal of Abnormal Psychology, 109,* 150–155.

Wilson, G. T. (1996). Manual-based treatments: The clinical application of research findings. *Behaviour Research and Therapy, 34,* 295–314.
Zlotnick, C., Johnson, S. L., Miller, I. W., Pearlstein, T., & Howard, M. (2001). Postpartum depression in women receiving public assistance: Pilot study of an interpersonal-therapy-oriented group intervention. *American Journal of Psychiatry, 158,* 638–640.
Zuvekas, S. H., & Meyerhoefer, C. D. (2006). Coverage for mental health treatment: Do the gaps still persist? *Journal of Mental Health Policy and Economics, 9,* 155–163.

Chapter Three

The Proper Focus of Evidence-Based Practice in Psychology

Integration of Possibility and Probability[1]

Carol D. Goodheart
Jean A. Carter

Evidence-based practice in psychology (EBPP) is an integrative approach in which practitioners actively and deliberately use scientific findings to provide effective treatment to clients. It is embedded in health care marketplace concerns as well as the scientist-practitioner model that is foundational for counseling psychology (Chwalisz, 2003). The Society of Counseling Psychology (Division 17 of the American Psychological Association [APA]), other divisions, and the APA have developed approaches to EBPP that offer valuable guidance to researchers, educators, and practitioners about its implementation and implications. It is important for counseling psychologists to understand the meaning of EBPP, the ways in which it may be put to good use, how it relates to the values and principles of counseling psychology, and the different epistemologies on which it is based.

THE CURRENT CONTEXT FOR EVIDENCE-BASED PRACTICE

Despite psychology's long history as an academic discipline resting on a core foundation of scientific evidence for its application to human welfare, the history of an integrated scientist-practitioner model is not so long. Debates about how best to implement such a model have persisted throughout the life of the applied specialties within psychology. Counseling psychology is no different from the other specialties as it engages in discussion, deliberation, and debate about the scientist-practitioner model (Chwalisz, 2003). Although these discussions are important, interesting, engaging, and lead to various models of training, in recent years they have become part of a different context.

The current context arises primarily out of evolutions in the health care system that require accountability and attempt to enhance quality by containing costs and reining in inefficient or ineffective treatment efforts. There are calls to reduce waste and error in the health care system through quality improvement; to establish the effectiveness of treatments, demonstrate outcomes, and hold those providing the treatments accountable for results; and to reduce health care costs through demonstrating the value added for mental health services and the cost effectiveness of treatment (Reed & Eisman, 2006). In addition, stigma, doubt, and uncertainty about mental health services and their value persist. A wider view of evidence suggests that an increase, not a decrease, in the provision of mental health services is warranted: The onset of many psychological disorders occurs early in life, the conditions are frequently chronic and affect functioning and development, the delay in seeking treatment from the onset of a disorder ranges from 5 to 23 years, and many people never receive any treatment at all despite severe psychological problems (Reed & Eisman, 2006). Nevertheless, in an environment with skyrocketing costs, it is not surprising that services without demonstrated effectiveness are viewed with skepticism and doubt.

The positive aspects of the impetus for evidence-based practice within psychology are also unsurprising, given psychology's origins and continuing identification as a social science, its empirical foundation, its methodologies, and its results as justification for the applications of psychological principles. However, defining and implementing evidence-based practice initiatives has not been a simple matter, and organized psychology's initiatives to define the proper focus for the integration of evidence and practice have taken various forms.

THE DEVELOPMENT OF EVIDENCE-BASED PRACTICE MODELS

In an effort to define the ways in which practitioners might use empirical evidence arising out of psychology's scientific foundation, the Society of Clinical Psychology (Division 12) approached the issue through the *delineation of specific techniques, treatments, or interventions with demonstrated efficacy and/or effectiveness.* Hallmarks of this approach include a requirement for high levels of internal validity and, drawing on a biopsychosocial science akin to the natural sciences, a narrow, positivistic empiricism (Hoshmand, 2003). Division 12 created a task force to identify empirically validated treatments (a term that has evolved into the descriptor "empirically supported treatments" in subsequent years) and to publicize them (Chambless et al., 1996, 1998; Task Force, 1995). The division's purpose was to demonstrate that psychological treatments are as effective, and in some cases more effective, than medical drug treatments. Although intended as a strong response to a medicalized treatment approach that relies primarily on pharmacotherapy, the rigorous methodologies that emphasized internal validity over external validity resulted in lists of "empirically validated treatments" that raised enthusiasm in some quarters, but started a firestorm in others. Large segments of both the practitioner community and the research community found the approach unrepresentative of the realities of practice and of a large body of psychotherapy research.

The American Psychiatric Association and other medical groups have adopted a related approach, which is the *delineation of treatment guidelines for particular target populations or diagnostic groups.* The APA has not adopted this approach for reasons similar to those that led to resistance to the Division 12 efforts described earlier (American Psychological Association Task Force on Psychological Intervention Guidelines, 1995).

An alternative approach emphasizes *delineation of procedures or principles for the integration of research evidence into practice applications.* This is the approach taken by the APA Divisions of Humanistic Psychology (Division 32, through principles for the provision of humanistic psychosocial services), Psychotherapy (Division 29, through principles of empirically supported relationships), (Ackerman et al., 2001; Norcross, 2002), and the Society of Counseling Psychology (Division 17, through principles of empirically supported interventions (Wampold, Lichtenberg, & Waehler, 2002). This approach to EBPP relies on significant sources that enlarge the framework for appropriate and necessary research evidence and methodological approaches. It relies on the long history of research on common factors and the psychotherapy relationship, as well as on basic psychological science and an assumption that psychologist practitioners can be good consumers of the psychological literature. This is an integrative approach that prizes multiple strands of research evidence and clinical expertise to enhance outcomes and quality. It requires an understanding of fundamental principles of change, and the utility of a variety of techniques that can be integrated within a fluid practice context and tailored to individual patient characteristics.

Counseling Psychology's Model of EBPP

The Society of Counseling Psychology (Division 17) undertook an initiative to delineate an evidence-based practice model appropriate for counseling psychology. Its goals were: "(a) making counseling psychologists and students more aware of the current empirical status of interventions in counseling psychology, (b) increasing predoctoral and postdoctoral training in psychological interventions that have been supported by empirical research, and (c) fostering public understanding and appreciation of empirically supported interventions offered by counseling psychologists" (Wampold et al. 2002). The outcome was a set of principles for understanding and assessing evidence as a basis for practice. The seven Principles of Empirically Supported Interventions are:

Principle 1: Level of Specificity Should Be Considered When Evaluating Outcomes.
Principle 2: Level of Specificity Should Not Be Restricted to Diagnosis.
Principle 3: Scientific Evidence Needs to Be Examined in Its Entirety and Aggregated Appropriately.
Principle 4: Evidence for Absolute and Relative Efficacy Needs to Be Presented.
Principle 5: Causal Attributions for Specific Ingredients Should Be Made Only if the Evidence Is Persuasive.
Principle 6: Outcomes Should Be Assessed Appropriately and Broadly.
Principle 7: Outcomes Should Be Assessed Locally and Freedom of Choice Should Be Recognized.

These principles offer guidance to researchers, educators, and practitioners on the development of treatment approaches and the research foundation on which they are based. This model accommodates the competing tensions of internal and external validity in which experimental rigor and real-world clinical application are both valued.

The APA's Policy on Evidence-Based Practice in Psychology

The APA, with its responsibility to represent the breadth of the discipline, recognizes the importance of EBPP issues for health care policy development and the health care marketplace. In order to establish a policy that could advance the organization's ability to advocate with one voice for psychology in government and private health systems, APA President Ronald F. Levant appointed the 2005 Presidential Initiative Task Force on Evidence-Based Practice (TF). Members of the task force were chosen to represent expertise in the research, delivery, and evaluation of psychological services, from a variety of perspectives. Counseling psychologists Ronald Levant (ex officio), Carol Goodheart (chair), Jean Carter, and Bruce Wampold participated on the TF. The goal of the TF was to develop policy language and a report containing the rationale and references for the policy. These documents are designed to show how evidence should be used to design and offer services of benefit to patients, as well as demonstrate to the public and health care systems that psychologists are providing evidence-based services.

The TF began with the Institute of Medicine's (IOM) definition of evidence-based medicine, because it is widely accepted in science and health care practice. Given the dominant role of the IOM in defining medical treatments and the models on which the health care market would rely, it is essential that psychology's model be aligned with the IOM definition, albeit modified as appropriate for psychological practice.

Evidence-based medicine is a three-legged stool, as described by the IOM (2001):

> Evidence based [medicine] is the integration of best research evidence with clinical expertise and patient values. Best research evidence refers to clinically relevant research, often from the basic health and medical sciences, but especially from patient centered clinical research. . . . Clinical expertise means the ability to use clinical skills and past experience to rapidly identify each patient's unique health state and diagnosis, individual risks and benefits of potential interventions, and personal values and expectations. Patient values refers to the unique preferences, concerns and expectations that each patient brings to a clinical encounter and that must be integrated into clinical decisions if they are to serve the patient. (p. 147)

The APA TF engaged in considerable dialogue about the nature and streams of evidence emphasized in psychology, about appropriate research designs to incorporate both internal and external validity, the role of clinical expertise, and the incorporation of patient characteristics in addition to values, as well as many other philosophy of science and feasibility of practice issues. Ultimately, the TF crafted the definition and explication for psychology to reflect sound evidence on therapeutic effectiveness and the vital role played by the therapist and the patient working in a collaborative endeavor undertaken for optimal results.

The definition and recommendations of the TF were adopted by the APA Council of Representatives as policy for the Association (APA, 2005):

> Evidence-Based Practice in Psychology (EBPP) is the integration of the best available research with clinical expertise in the context of patient characteristics, culture and preferences. (p. 1)

This definition of EBPP closely parallels the one adopted by the Institute of Medicine. The purpose of EBPP is to promote effective psychological practice and enhance public health by applying empirically supported principles of psychological assessment, case formulation, therapeutic relationship, and intervention (APA, 2005).

An essential component of EBPP, which has significant implications for the policy and its implementation, focuses on psychological practice as an *integrative approach* to practice, rather than on specific practices, interventions, or treatments using defined strategies for particular populations or disorders. In other words, EBPP as articulated by the TF is a superordinate concept, which recognizes that clinical trials provide optimal evidence on treatment efficacy because they rule out threats to internal validity, but does not prescribe particular data collection methods nor privilege certain types of evidence.

Within this context, it is essential to reconcile disparate bodies of knowledge based on research evidence and clinical expertise that differentially emphasize the role of common factors and the therapeutic relationship in mental health treatment and the role of specific techniques or interventions. A significant area of debate concerns how to balance an intervention approach in which the emphasis is on particular treatments and techniques, with a relational perspective that emphasizes the therapeutic relationship (and in particular the working alliance) as the vehicle for change. There is a long history of research supporting the essential roles of both the relationship and the intervention.

Clinical expertise is the prism through which the integration of research evidence, clinical data gathered over the course of treatment, and patient characteristics occurs. The treating psychologist is responsible for understanding and incorporating research findings as they may be appropriate for the individual patient. This is not always easy or straightforward, because research evidence is probabilistic and not always predictive of efficacy under localized circumstances. Thus, it cannot be applied directly with assurance to any particular individual, and clinical decisions must be made in collaboration with patients to fit the individual situation.

In the APA definition of EBPP, "patient values" is expanded to include patient characteristics, including such variables as level of function and readiness for change, race, ethnicity, gender, and cultural context, to create a model that is centered in the patient. Patient centeredness implies more than a focus on choice, values, and preferences, because patient characteristics are known to moderate the effects of interventions (APA, 2006). In mental health, in particular, patient characteristics (such as race, gender, ethnicity, sexual orientation, and so on, in addition to level of pathology, comorbidity, and other clinical concerns), and life context (such as socio-economic status, class, and culture) are extremely important. Although research on characteristics and context remains sparse, and we do not yet fully know the extent to which cross-diagnostic characteristics (including personality traits) affect the impact of our interventions, these factors must be incorporated into any effective treatment approach. The APA policy takes into account the evolving nature of science, and we expect the evidence to become clearer over time.

EBPP AND COUNSELING PSYCHOLOGY

The principles endorsed by the Society of Counseling Psychology are quite useful for understanding and interpreting the empirical foundation for various practice interventions and processes. Similarly, it may be helpful for counseling psychologists to consider the extent to which evidence-based practice approaches are consistent with the core values and principles of counseling psychology. These core principles (as adapted from Gelso & Fretz, 1986) include:

a. A focus on health and adaptation, building upon strengths, as opposed to an emphasis on psychopathology;
b. A focus on a developmental perspective and a life-span approach, which takes into account individual, group, and system needs, in order to foster growth;
c. A focus on social and cultural context, in order to enhance individual, group, and system environments, interactions and well-being, and an emphasis on multiculturalism and diversity,
d. A focus on brief interventions, insofar as they are effective and meet the needs of the person, group, or system;
e. A focus on healthy work relationships, behavior, and role fulfillment.

As noted previously, the two major approaches to evidence-based practice rely on (1) specific interventions or intervention strategies for specific diagnoses and treatment populations (diagnosed disorder) and (2) practice strategies that are relationally grounded and patient centered. Counseling psychologists feature prominently in the latter approach, and the principles espoused by the Society of Counseling Psychology are more consistent with the latter approach as well.

An approach to evidence-based practice that relies on specific intervention strategies for specific diagnoses and treatment populations is, necessarily, focused on pathology and a medical disease model, rather than on a health and adaptation model. A model based on health may be preventive, enhancing, or adaptive to chronic conditions, rather than solely focused on remediation. In addition, a health and adaptation model facilitates a client's positive strivings for growth and her or his recognition of changing needs and perspective across the life span. Furthermore, such an approach recognizes diversity and embraces individual differences, as well as complex group identity differences, which are increasingly important in a multicultural nation.

Current empirical evidence is limited for the application of strategies that are well researched on majority populations to minority populations, leaving it uncertain which strategies will apply. The need for additional evidence in this area is urgent, given that 33% of the United States is comprised of ethnic minorities and the proportion is growing (U.S. Census Bureau, 2007). We need to know more about what cultures we are reaching effectively and those we are not. There is a growing body of research on human diversity that includes culture and psychotherapy, which places psychology in a strong position to find ways to integrate research and clinical expertise with an understanding of the patient characteristics that are essential to EBPP (Zane, Hall, Sue, Young, & Nunez, 2004). Counseling psychology's strong emphasis on multiculturalism and valuing of individual differences is aligned with treatment approaches based on attention to health and adaptation, life-span perspective, diversity, individual and group differences, and role fulfillment.

Relational approaches, which begin with the client and proceed dynamically and fluidly according to the needs of the client, are certainly consistent with the values and principles of counseling psychology. An approach to evidence-based practice that begins with the client may arise from either an emphasis on psychopathology or an emphasis on health, enhancement, and prevention; although the latter is strongly part of counseling psychology's focus, an emphasis on psychopathology where it exists is not incompatible. A relational approach can proceed consonantly with development across the life span and take into account changing needs and changing life situations without requiring new treatment strategies.

Approaches that begin with the client are easily adaptable to individuals, groups, or systems representing varying identities, characteristics, and cultures. There is no requisite need for multiple studies on various population groups to norm each treatment strategy according to the different groups to which it may apply. At the same time, this does not mean empirical evidence about different population groups is irrelevant; quite the contrary, evidence about different population groups provides significant grounding for practice applications as that evidence is incorporated into the developing treatment process (see reviews by Chwalisz, 2003; Neville & Mobley, 2001; Ponterotto, 1998).

Clearly, relational approaches to evidence-based practice are consistent with counseling psychology values and with the "Principles of Empirically Supported Interventions" (Wampold et al., 2002). Another divide, however, also creates difficulties. It is the recurring science-practice split, which many psychologists attempt to bridge with the scientist-practitioner model. This divide reflects differences related to the ways in which researchers and practitioners understand the world, and the differing demands inherent in research and practice processes. The varying epistemologies that underlie the research foundation for practice and the clinical expertise required for practice endeavors are interconnected in some ways, but have distinct differences.

DIVERSE EPISTEMOLOGIES

The EBPP movement has been described as a "culture war" in which applied psychologists with differing worldviews battle over what treatment approaches to use and on what basis (Messer, 2004). Psychologists have a great deal of difficulty agreeing upon what science approaches to attend to and what the translation of science into practice should look like. Stated simply, there is a central tension between those who believe (Goodheart & Kazdin, 2006):

Either

- Best practice entails *starting with a diagnosed disorder* and applying an empirically based treatment package (EBT) with a central emphasis on techniques that have been demonstrated to be efficacious; other evidence is sought only when an EBT is not available or is not working; this may be characterized as the use of a hierarchical system of treatment, in line with the hierarchy of evidence.

Or

- Best practice entails *starting with the patient,* establishing a therapeutic relationship, and developing a treatment plan from research evidence on interventions, common factors, human development, psychopathology, individual and group differences, and other relevant research topics; this may be characterized as the use of a heterarchical system, in line with the need for multiple strands of research evidence and clinical information to tailor treatment to a particular client. (p. 8)

Differences in the underlying philosophies of science that guide the work of researchers and clinicians contribute significantly to this tension. It is important to understand these important distinctions in order to arrive at a rapprochement that advances both science and practice.

Definitions, Properties, and Choices

Epistemology is the branch of philosophy that studies the nature of knowledge, its structures, sources, and scope. In other words, how do we know what we know? What language do we use to describe it to others? What knowledge do we value? Where do we direct our energies to obtain new knowledge? How do we achieve harmony with psychologists who do not hold the same worldview? And how do we integrate science and clinical wisdom?

Logical positivism is the dominant epistemology of psychological science related to EBPP. It reflects a striving for advances in psychological treatment based on a hierarchy of scientific evidence. This epistemology assumes that the scientific method of controlled, internally valid, and replicable observation is the best way to understand the world and improve evidence-based practice. The viewpoint has well-described strengths and a logically consistent strategy for the discovery and verification of new knowledge.

There are, however, those who take exception to the dominance of this epistemology, especially when relied upon in isolation. The limitations of logical positivism have been pointed out by many authors and are summarized by Morowski (2005):

- The choice of quantification as the best way to classify and describe mental life and behavior leads to disregard for qualitative experience and methods.
- The choice of reductionism as the best explanatory mode leads to the neglect of holism, emergence, and a unified gestalt.
- The choice of the positivist scientific method as exclusively sufficient leads to the lack of measurement and integration of other valuable phenomena, such as those embraced by the physical sciences.
- The assumed abstract position of the observer standing outside the interaction leads to dehumanizing explanations.
- The assumed value-free position of science leads to ignoring the values and beliefs inherent in the choices made during the scientific process.
- The search for governing universal laws of human nature leads to a lack of consideration for the dynamic, temporal, and contextual aspects of human nature. (p. 3)

Alternative epistemologies exist within psychology that both challenge and augment the dominant focus on predictability, objectivity, determinism, and statistical regularity. Not surprisingly, in response to a nondiverse dominant epistemology, some of the alternative constructions have come from clinicians, women, ethnic minorities, and qualitative researchers with different worldviews.

Other epistemologies that provide a framework for the pursuit of knowledge relevant to both science and practice include: radical empiricism (e.g., ecological psychology is an outgrowth of this epistemology that espouses pragmatism, transformation, and engagement), the standpoint theories (e.g., these epistemologies seek a science not restricted to a singular perspective of human experience and are integral to the feminist and Black psychology movements, as well as other socioeconomic and historical conditions), constructivism (e.g., role theory, relational psychology, narrative psychology, and self-psychology are outgrowths of observations that people construct views of the self and the world through active social processes), and dynamic nominalism (e.g., feminist, ethnic minority, lesbian/gay/bisexual/transsexual, and some intervention research assumes a dynamic looping process of human change that changes the human sciences, in turn). These ways of knowing recognize the presence and force of uncertainty, indeterminism, pluralism, plasticity, and complexity in human beings (Morowski, 2005).

As we move science and practice forward, psychology benefits from enlarged epistemological frames of reference. Because of the nature of the therapeutic enterprise, practitioners rely on data from both nomothetic (attempts to discover general laws) and idiographic (attempts to understand a particular individual or event) processes, findings based on both quantitative and qualitative methods, and views based on both scientific and humanistic attitudes; these are psychology's dual heritage (Messer, 2004). Nevertheless, it remains a challenge to integrate the unique strengths of different approaches to knowledge in practical applications.

Differences Between Intervention Researchers and Clinicians

Ways of knowing are different for clinicians and researchers. There are between-group differences in worldview, incentives, personality, and role between researchers and clinicians.

First, practice and research are different endeavors with distinct purposes (Goodheart, 2006). The professional interests and objectives, the cultures and constraints of work settings, the work products, the rhythm of daily life, and even the kinds of questions posed differ for practitioners and researchers. There are different values placed on the kinds of evidence each group uses for its work. The presence of differing values affects the orientation toward treatment held by the two groups.

Second, researchers and practitioners differ in personality characteristics. They vary on the underlying continuum of egocentric–sociocentric views of the world and they hold different epistemological values, such as increasing knowledge versus improving the human condition. They often have differing theoretical orientations, cognitive strengths, and developmental influences (Conway, 1988; Dana, 1987; Frank, 1984; Zacher & Leong, 1992).

Third, role demands for researchers and practitioners differ (Goodheart, 2006). Researchers must show that a treatment works under specified conditions, but clinicians must do all they can to resolve the problem at hand. For the most part, researchers seek efficacy, internal validity, and reliability based on clinical trials, whereas practitioners seek effectiveness, external validity (utility), and feasibility (resources) for the particular patient, couple, family, or group in the room at the moment. Of course, it is important to remember that these are broad-stroke differences, and few individual psychologists fit neatly into these categories. Instead, psychologists span a continuum of traits.

Common Ground for Practitioners and Intervention Researchers

Despite these many differences, there are commonalities that offer opportunities for rapprochement among psychologists with epistemological differences. Although significant tensions remain for issues such as reductionism versus contextualism and acceptance versus rejection of the fact–value dichotomy, it is important to move beyond an oppositional approach to these differences (Russo, 2006). The whole really is greater than the sum of its parts. All psychologists are trained in scientific methods and attitudes, regardless of their eventual work setting and focus; all are committed to the improvement of patients' lives through good psychological research and practice; all agree upon the high priority of patient care, the need for high-quality professional training, and the importance of the scientific research foundation for practice; all recognize the importance of expertise and sensitivity to patient characteristics, culture, and preferences, and tailoring care to the person (Goodheart & Kazdin, 2006).

THE CURRENT STATE OF PRACTICE: CHALLENGES AND PROGRESS

The differences inherent in the debates about EBPP are real and substantial. Therefore, we face challenges in our attempts to reach closer agreement about the details of which evidence is most valuable and what constitutes clinical wisdom. But the field is advancing rapidly as both practitioners and researchers grapple with these issues.

Discussions about EBPP have evolved to take into account both the logical positivist approaches based on specific ingredients and the contextual approaches based on attention to the patient's subjective experience, the therapist's characteristics and activities, the therapeutic alliance, and the "betweenness" of patient and therapist. There is mounting evidence in favor of methodological pluralism (Norcross, 2006).

The Society of Clinical Psychology, Division 12 of the APA, has advocated for the primacy of logical positivism and an evidence hierarchy headed by randomized control clinical trials, since the formation of their Task Force on the Promotion and Dissemination of Psychological Procedures in 1993 (Chambless & Ollendick, 2001).

The Society of Counseling Psychology (Division 17) has a long tradition of consideration for the individual and understanding him or her in context. For example, Wampold and Bhati (2004) caution against the emphasis of the EBPP movement on treatment and the omission of the role of the psychologist and the subjective experience of the patient. They support alternative conceptualizations based on scientific rigor that focus on common factors and broader research perspectives, such as those recommended by the Society of Counseling Psychology (APA Division 17; Wampold et al., 2002) and Psychotherapy (APA Division 29; Norcross, 2002). Psychotherapy (and the delivery of other types of psychological intervention) will always be challenging because it is a highly complex interpersonal enterprise that takes place in an ever-changing context and is driven forward by a patient's pressing needs. Clinical expertise is needed to synthesize and integrate knowledge of the relevant science and knowledge of the patient, for the purpose of offering a coherent treatment tailored to the particular clinical situation. Thus, there is no successful application of clinical science without clinical expertise. It would seem to go almost without saying that two heads, that of the scientist and the clinician, are better than one.

Attempts to implement a one-way system of translation from science into practice seem to fail most of the time. For example, there has been continuing dismay in practitioner communities about the proliferating number of treatment manuals, most of which are cognitive-behavioral in orientation, are proprietary, and are not available from one source for ready comparison. Clinicians find that treatments conceived, designed, tested, and implemented under controlled conditions without consideration of their perspectives are of limited use in their world of patient and family complexity and different health care settings. A two-way mutual process is far superior. Practitioner input is necessary at the outset for a functional bidirectional approach. Based on sophisticated efforts to test treatments in practice settings, Weisz and Addis (2006) concluded:

> In our view, efforts to bring research-based treatments into practice can succeed only if they draw on the experience, expertise, and wisdom of practitioners, as well as their insights into what is possible in their work settings. (p. 185)
>
> Overall, team members found that clinic operations and research operations converged increasingly, creating an interactive process—a kind of research-practice tango—in which clinic staff and research staff learned to operate in ever-closer synchrony with one another. In the process, we learned more and more about each other's beliefs, perspectives, settings, and workplace. (p. 191)

Promising Avenues for Strengthening Practice

Researchers are encouraging practitioners to stay current with the research literature and to evaluate progress and outcomes. Practitioners are encouraging researchers to address therapeutic processes and mechanisms in more meaningful, useful, and accessible ways. Perhaps at least partially as a result, both groups are evolving into fresher promising directions.

It seems clear by this point in the evolution of EBPP discussions that the complexity of the psychotherapeutic enterprise requires conscientious psychologists to attend to patient, therapist, interpersonal, and methodological dimensions. Either-or conceptual distinctions between technical and contextual factors are not often useful in the field.

Core processes for integrative psychotherapy training have been identified and refined over the years. These processes include therapeutic communication, engagement, pattern search, facilitation of change, resolving misperceptions and conflicts enacted in the therapeutic dyad, and handling termination (Beitman, Soth, & Bumby, 2005; Good & Beitman, 2006). Core ingredients of the therapeutic alliance that contribute to positive outcomes have been identified as well: shared goals, consensus on the treatment approach and tasks, and an emotional bond (Bachelor & Horvath, 1999; Bordin, 1979; Horvath & Bedi, 2002; Miller, Duncan, & Hubble, 2005).

In psychotherapy research, there has been an increasing focus on: (a) identifying principles of change in psychotherapy across theoretical orientations (Castonguay & Beutler, 2006); (b) documenting issues of emotional regulation and negative affectivity across multiple diagnostic categories (Campbell-Sills & Barlow, 2007; Westen, Gabbard, & Blagov, 2006); and (c) using outcomes measures as a means of substantiating therapeutic gains across differing orientations, settings, and disorders (Lambert & Archer, 2006; Miller et al., 2005).

Principles

The review of the interdependent domains of participant, relationship, and technique factors by Castonguay and Beutler (2006) identified 61 principles of change, with some overlap. Twenty-six of the principles were found across the treatment of at least two different problem areas (dysphoria, anxiety, substance abuse, or personality disorders). Their findings underscore the interactions among the factors that contribute to therapeutic outcomes. Clinical experts use broad principles, some of them implicit, to make decisions and implement treatment strategies (Levitt, Neimeyer, and Williams, 2005; Williams & Levitt, 2007). Therefore, the attention paid to principles across therapy orientations holds promise for future research and guideposts for practitioners.

Function Across Diagnoses

Consistent with the values of counseling psychology, practicing psychologists typically work with a person's functional capacity and personality, as well as his or her life context, rather than simply a *DSM-IV* diagnostic category. All of the Axis I and Axis II mood and anxiety disorders share a common factor: negative affectivity or *internalizing* spectrum personality pathology (Brown, Chorpita, & Barlow, 1998; Krueger, 1999; Westen et al., 2006). Also related to negative affectivity, the presence of maladaptive efforts to regulate emotion is a common element across the diagnostic categories of anxiety and depression (Campbell-Sills & Barlow, 2007). This accounts for much of their co occurrence. Furthermore, there is a broad *externalizing* factor that underlies many other DSM category disorders such as substance abuse and antisocial personality disorders (Krueger et al., 2002). The growing volume of data on the relationship between dysfunction and personality supports the view that one cannot separate the symptom from the person (Westen et al., 2006). To the extent that practitioners can help patients to better handle their emotional valences and propensity to internalize or externalize beyond an adaptive range, there are potential gains not only in the reduction of symptoms, but also overall improved function and quality of life.

In addition to the *DSM-IV,* which has been criticized as sexist and insensitive to culture, ethnicity, and situational context (Becker, 2001; Lopez & Guarnaccia, 2000; Worell & Remer, 2003), there are other systems that may serve as helpful decision and categorization tools in the future. The *Psychodynamic Diagnostic Manual* (*PDM*) is intended to complement the

DSM-IV and fill a void by offering a diagnostic framework for a full range of functioning (PDM Task Force, 2006). It describes patterns of function, symptoms, healthy and disordered personalities, and their expression. The authors, who represent a collaborative effort by six psychoanalytic organizations, attempt to capture ". . . . depth as well as the surface of emotional, cognitive, and social patterns" (p. 1).

Another system related to health and mental health, also designed to assess and categorize function, is *The International Classification of Functioning, Disability, and Health* (*ICF;* World Health Organization [WHO], 2001). The *ICF* is derived from a biopsychosocial perspective and classifies function, not disease. It includes how people live with a health condition, classifies health and health-related domains and aspects of well being, and attends to personal, social, and environmental factors that affect function. Collaboration between the American Psychological Association and the World Health Organization led to the development of a prototype *ICF Procedural Manual* (APA, 2003). Further development will make this model more widely available for psychologists' use.

Outcomes

The measurement of baseline function, progress, and outcome is yet another focus that shows promise if used properly to assist practitioners and not used as a cost-cutting tool by third-party payers.

It has been demonstrated repeatedly that the outcomes of psychotherapy are substantial and are maintained; psychotherapy is relatively efficient across a range of interventions; and 75% of patients treated show a benefit (Lambert & Ogles, 2004). Yet some patients do not improve, and it is not always apparent why. The use of outcomes measurement to monitor progress and identify a stalled or deteriorating treatment is a promising step forward for practice.

The measurement of outcomes protects practitioners by documenting successful treatment that accomplishes the patient's goals; this will become increasingly useful for responding to accountability demands within the health care system. Miller et al. (2005, p. 98) have coined the term "practice-based evidence" to describe the value of outcome-informed psychotherapy. Theoretically, it should be possible to practice within any of the long-established legitimate and ethical treatment orientations or integrative combinations, as well as to adopt new emerging applications, so long as one can document appropriate progress and outcomes and meet ethical standards of care.

Blending

Practitioners are improving efforts to describe the dynamic interplay of science, clinical expertise and pattern recognition, the therapeutic relationship, theoretical pluralism, technical eclecticism, and cultural variation among patients and therapists, all of which affect their work (e.g., see Carter, 2006; Comas-Diaz, 2006; Goodheart, 2006). There are signs that the use of theory as a bridge between science and practice will improve science-practice integration (Murdock, 2006). And there is an ever-increasing amount of theoretical blending in treatment approaches (Barlow, 2004; Goodheart, 2006). The discipline of psychology does not stand still.

CONCLUDING THOUGHTS ABOUT EBPP AND COUNSELING PSYCHOLOGY

Based on the current state of knowledge about psychotherapy, we believe the APA policy adopted in 2005, and its accompanying report, provide a definition and focus of EBPP appropriate for counseling psychologists (APA, 2006). They provide guidance about the need to use evidence for the provision of effective services, and, in combination with the principles developed and endorsed by the Society of Counseling Psychology, offer valuable resources for the implementation of EBPP.

An essential point of the policy and report cannot be emphasized enough: *EBPP is an overarching conceptual approach to practice.* Unfortunately, acronyms change and become confusing. Thus, many psychologists do not understand the difference between empirically supported treatments (ESTs), which are interchangeably called evidence-based treatments (EBTs), and Evidence-Based Practice in Psychology (EBPP). The APA did not endorse ESTs/EBTs as a policy; instead it adopted a policy on Evidence-Based Practice in Psychology (EBPP) that is not prescriptive about treatments, which is consistent with the approach taken in the Society of Counseling Psychology's Principles. ESTs/EBTs are a part of EBPP, but they are not all of it. EBPP is the broader concept and subsumes ESTs/EBTs and other systems.

Some readers criticized the view of evidence in the task force report as being either too objective or too subjective, too hard or too soft, and their comments are valuable to the ongoing dialogue about EBPP (Hunsberger, 2007; Stuart & Lilienfeld, 2007; Wendt & Slife, 2007). However, it is important to clarify that the task force discussed the philosophy of science issues and intentionally did not define evidence as related only to objective measures; it did not select certain treatments as being privileged by certain forms of evidence; it did not recommend specific treatments for specific disorders;

and it did not endorse a disorder-specific approach as the best approach (Wampold, Goodheart, & Levant, 2007). By contrast, the task force did recognize that an evidence-based approach has an empirical philosophy of science foundation, and it did reiterate the APA's standing policy statement that, when compared to alternatives, "randomized controlled experiments represent a more stringent way to evaluate treatment efficacy because they are the most effective way to rule out threats to internal validity in a single experiment" (APA, 2002, p. 1054).

NEXT STEPS AND FUTURE DIRECTIONS

We support the integrationist view that five identified elements legitimately comprise the proper focus of EBBP: the individual therapist, the treatment method, the therapeutic relationship, the active patient, and principles of change (Norcross, 2006; Norcross, Beutler, & Levant, 2005). All of these factors need the attention of applied researchers and practitioners, because any of them, alone or in combination, may be particularly salient in a given therapeutic situation. Psychologists who offer evidence-based practice must take into account all five of these determinants and their optimal combinations or syntheses (APA TF, 2006; Norcross, 2006).

Considerable room remains for research in several areas. First, clinical expertise is one of the three main components of the APA definition of Evidence-Based Practice in Psychology and is the means through which integration of evidence into practice occurs. However, the body of research on clinical expertise remains spotty and would benefit from greater elaboration. Another area that would benefit from a strong research emphasis is the improved understanding of multiculturalism and the components of individual identity as they relate to practice applications.

The field would also benefit from more effective interaction and interplay between researchers and practitioners to enhance the questions that researchers are asking and to strengthen practitioners' use of research findings. In addition, ongoing development of resources that translate research findings into practitioner-friendly materials will facilitate practitioners' more effective use of research.

The EBPP movement has many concerned stakeholders: practitioners, researchers, patients and their families, payers, and health care policy makers. There are different ways to reach the common goal of improving practice. There is no reason to let epistemological differences lead to the Balkanization of psychology. In the end, progress involves a process of searching for a respectful fit between and among groups with differences. The strengths of both science and clinical skill are needed to serve the public well, and these are hallmarks of EBPP. In recognizing the necessary differences between the goals of science and practice, we must remember the shared goal is to solve problems in our society. Psychology has much to offer when we combine our efforts and resources to meet those needs. Only by acknowledging the importance of integrating multiple epistemologies, multiple sources of evidence, and multiple elements of the therapeutic encounter do we achieve the synergy of science and clinical wisdom.

ENDNOTE

1. Naomi Meara referred to psychotherapy as "the integration of possibility and probability" during a symposium in her honor sponsored by the Division 17 Section for the Promotion of Psychotherapy Science in 2006. It is a fitting description of our vision of evidence-based practice, and we use it in her memory.

BIBLIOGRAPHY

Ablon, J. S., & Marci, C. (2004). Psychotherapy process: The missing link: Comment on Westen, Novotny & Thompson-Brenner. *Psychological Bulletin, 130*, 664–668.

Ackerman, S. J., Benjamin, L. S., Beutler, L. E., Gelso, C. J., Goldfriend, M. R., Hill, C., et al. (2001). Empirically supported therapy relationships: Conclusions and recommendations of the Division 29 Task Force. *Psychotherapy: Theory, Research, Practice, Training, 38*, 495–497.

American Psychological Association. (1995). *Template for developing guidelines. Interventions for mental disorders and psychosocial aspects of physical disorders.* Washington, DC: Author.

American Psychological Association. (2002). Criteria for evaluating treatment guidelines. *American Psychologist, 57*, 1052–1059.

American Psychological Association. (2003). *Procedural manual and guide for a standardized application of the international classification of functioning disability and Health (ICF): A manual for health professionals. Sample and prototype.* Washington, DC: Author.

American Psychological Association. (2005). Policy statement on evidence-based practice in psychology. Retrieved March 9, 2007, from http://www2.apa.org/practice/ebpstatement.pdf

APA Presidential Task Force on Evidence-Based Practice. (2006). Evidence-based practice in psychology. *American Psychologist, 61*, 271–285.

Bachelor, A., & Horvath, A. (1999). The therapeutic relationship. In Hubble, M. A., Duncan, B. L., & Miller, S. D. (Eds.), *The heart and soul of change: What works in therapy* (pp. 133–178). Washington, DC: American Psychological Association.

Barlow, D. H. (2004). Psychological treatments. *American Psychologist, 59*(9), 869–878.

Becker, D. (2001). Diagnosis of psychological disorders: DSM and gender. In J. Worell (Ed.), *Encyclopedia of women and gender: Sex similarities and differences and the impact of society on gender* (Vol. 1, pp. 333–343). San Diego, CA: Academic Press.

Beitman, B. D., Soth, A. M., & Bumby, N. A. (2005). The future as an integrating force through the schools of psychotherapy. In J. C. Norcross & M. R. Goldfried, (Eds.), *Psychotherapy integration* (2nd ed.). New York: Oxford University Press.

Bordin, E. S. (1979). The generalizability of the psychoanalytic concept of the working alliance. *Psychotherapy: Theory, Research, and Practice, 16*, 252–260.

Brown, T. A., Chorpita, B. F., & Barlow, D. H. (1998). Structural relationships among dimensions of the DSM-IV anxiety and mood disorders and dimensions of negative affect, positive affect, and autonomic arousal. *Journal of Abnormal Psychology, 107*(2) 179–192.

Campbell-Sills, L., & Barlow, D. H. (2007). Incorporating emotion regulation into conceptualizations and treatments of anxiety and mood disorders. In J. J. Gross (Ed.), *Handbook of emotion regulation*. New York: Guilford.

Carter, J. A. (2006). Theoretical pluralism and technical eclecticism. In C. D. Goodheart, A. E. Kazdin, & R. J. Sternberg (Eds.), *Evidence-based psychotherapy: Where practice and research meet*. Washington, DC: APA Books.

Castonguay, L. G., & Beutler, L. E. (Eds.). (2006). *Principles of therapeutic change that work*. New York: Oxford.

Chambless, D. L., & Ollendick, T. H. (2001). Empirically supported psychological interventions: Controversies and evidence. *Annual Review of Psychology, 52*, 685–716.

Chambless, D. L., Sanderson, W. C., Shoham, V., Bennett-Johnson, S., Pope, K. S., Crits-Cristoph, P., et al. (1996). An update on empirically validated therapies. *The Clinical Psychologist, 49*, (2), 5–18.

Chambless, D. W., Baker, M. J., Baucom, D. H., Beutler, L. E., Calhoun, K. S., Daiuto, A., et al. (1998). Update on empirically validated therapies, II. *The Clinical Psychologist, 51*, 3–16.

Chwalisz, K. (2003). Evidence-based practice: A framework for twenty-first-century scientist-practitioner training. *The Counseling Psychologist, 31*(5), 497–528.

Comas-Diaz, L. (2006). Cultural variation in the therapeutic relationship. In C. D. Goodheart, A. E. Kazdin, & R. J. Sternberg (Eds.), *Evidence-based psychotherapy: Where practice and research meet*. Washington, DC: APA Books.

Conway, J. B. (1988). Differences among clinical psychologists: Scientists, practitioners, and scientist-practitioners. *Professional Psychology: Research and Practice, 19*, 642–655.

Crits-Christoph, P., Baranackie, K., Kurcias, J. S., Carroll, K., Luborsky, L., McLellan, T., et al. (1991). Meta-analysis of therapist effects in psychotherapy outcome studies. *Psychotherapy Research*, 1, 81–91.

Dana, R. H. (1987). Training for professional psychology: Science, practice, and identity. *Professional Psychology: Research and Practice, 18*, 9–16.

Frank, G. (1984). The Boulder Model: History, rationale, and critique. *Professional Psychology: Research and Practice, 1*, 417–435.

Gelso, C. J., & Fretz, B. F. (1986). *Introduction to counseling psychology*. New York: Wiley.

Good, G. E., & Beitman, B. D. (2006). *Counseling and psychotherapy essentials: Integrating theories, skills, and practices.* New York: Norton.

Goodheart, C. D. (2006). Evidence, endeavor, and expertise in psychology practice. In C. D. Goodheart, A. E. Kazdin, & R. J. Sternberg (Eds.), *Evidence-based psychotherapy: Where practice and research meet.* Washington, DC: APA Books.

Goodheart, C. D., & Kazdin, A. E. (2006). Introduction. In C. D. Goodheart, A. E. Kazdin, & R. J. Sternberg (Eds.), *Evidence-based psychotherapy: Where practice and research meet.* Washington, DC: APA Books.

Horvath, A. O., & Bedi, R. P. The alliance. In Norcross, J. C. (Ed.), *Psychotherapy relationships that work: Therapist contributions and responsiveness to patients* (pp. 37–69). New York, NY: Oxford University Press (2002).

Hoshmand, L. T. (2003). Applied epistemology and professional training in a science-based cultural enterprise. *The Counseling Psychologist, 31*(5), 529–538.

Hunsberger, B. (2007). Re-establishing clinical psychology's subjective core. *American Psychologist, 62*(5), 614–615.

Huppert, J. D., Bufka, L. F., Barlow, D. H., Gorman, J. M., Shear, M. K., & Woods, S. W. (2001). Therapists, therapist variables, and cognitive-behavioral therapy outcome in a multicenter trial for panic disorder. *Journal of Consulting and Clinical Psychology, 69*, 747–755.

Institute of Medicine. (2001). *Crossing the quality chasm: A new health system for the 21st century.* Washington, DC: National Academy of Sciences.

Kim, D. M., Wampold, B. E., & Bolt, D. M. (2006). Therapist effects in psychotherapy: A random effects modeling of the NIMH TDCRP data. *Psychotherapy Research, 16*, 161–172.

Krueger, R. F. (1999). The structure of common mental disorders. *Archives of General Psychiatry, 56*(10), 921–926.

Krueger, R. F., Hicks, B.M., Patrick, C.J., Carlson, S. R., Iacono, W. G., & McGue, M. (2002). Etiologic connections among substance dependence, antisocial behavior and personality: Modeling the externalizing spectrum. *Journal of Abnormal Psychology, 111*(3) 411–424.

Lambert, M. J., & Archer, A. (2006). Research findings on the effects of practice and their implications for practice. In C. D. Goodheart, A. E. Kazdin, & R. J. Sternberg (Eds.), *Evidence-based psychotherapy: Where practice and research meet.* Washington, DC: APA Books.

Lambert, M. J., & Ogles, B. M. (2004). The efficacy and effectiveness of psychotherapy. In M. J. Lambert (Ed.), *Bergin and Garfield's handbook of psychotherapy and behavior change* (pp. 139–193). New York: Wiley.

Levitt, H. M., Neimeyer, R. A., & Williams, D.C. (2005). Rules versus principles in psychotherapy: Implications of the quest for universal guidelines in the movement for empirically supported treatments. *Journal of Contemporary Psychotherapy, 35*, 117–129.

Lopez, S.R., & Guarnaccia, P.J.J. (2000). Cultural psychopathology: Uncovering the social world of mental illness. *Annual Review of Psychology, 51*, 571–598.

Messer, S. B. (2004). Evidence-based practice: Beyond empirically supported treatments. *Professional Psychology, 35*, 580–588.

Miller, S. D., Duncan, B. L., & Hubble, M. A. (2005). Outcome-informed clinical work. In J. C. Norcross & M. R. Goldfried (Eds.), *Psychotherapy integration*. New York: Oxford University Press.

Morowski, J. G. (2005). *Epistemological diversity in the history of modern psychology*. Paper presented at the Education Leadership Conference, American Psychological Association, Arlington, VA, September 17.

Murdock, N. L. (2006). On science-practice integration in everyday life: A plea for theory. *The Counseling Psychologist, 34*(4), 548–569.

Neville, H. A., & Mobley, M. (2001). Social identities in contexts: An ecological model of multicultural counseling psychology processes. *The Counseling Psychologist, 29*, 471–486.

Norcross, J. C. (Ed.). (2002). *Relationships that work*. New York: Oxford University Press.

Norcross, J. C. (2006, August). *What is the proper focus of EBPP? Five contenders*. Symposium presented at the annual convention of the American Psychological Association, New Orleans, LA.

Norcross, J. C., Beutler, L. E., & Levant, R. F. (Eds). (2005). *Evidence-based practices in mental health: Debate and dialogue on the fundamental questions*. Washington, DC: American Psychological Association.

PDM Task Force (2006). *Psychodynamic diagnostic manual*. Silver Spring, MD: Alliance of Psychoanalytic Organizations.

Ponterotto, J. G. (1998). Charting a course for research in multicultural counseling training. *The Counseling Psychologist, 26*, 43–68.

Reed, G. M., & Eisman, E. J. (2006). Uses and misuses of evidence: Managed care, treatment guidelines, and outcomes measurement in professional practice. In C. D. Goodheart, A. E. Kazdin, & R. J. Sternberg (Eds.), *Evidence-based psychotherapy: Where practice and research meet*. Washington, DC: APA Books.

Russo, N. F. (2006, August). *Clinical wisdom, science, and policy: Lessons from the front lines*. Paper presented at the annual convention of the American Psychological Association, New Orleans, LA.

Stuart, R. B., & Lilienfeld, S. O. (2007). The evidence missing from evidence-based practice. *American Psychologist, 62*(5), 615–616.

Task Force on Promotion and Dissemination of Psychological Procedures. (1995). Training in and dissemination of empirically-validated psychological treatments. *The Clinical Psychologist, 48*, 3–23.

U.S. Census Bureau. (2007). Minority population tops 100 million. http://census.gov/Press-Release/www/releases/archives/population/010048.html

Wampold, B. E., & Bhati, K. S. (2004). Attending to the omissions: A historical examinations of evidence based practice movements. *Professional Psychology: Research and Practice, 35*, 563–570.

Wampold, B. E., & Brown, G. (2005). Estimating therapist variability in outcomes attributable to therapists: A naturalistic study of outcomes in managed care. *Journal of Consulting and Clinical Psychology, 73*, 914–923.

Wampold, B. E., Goodheart, C. D., & Levant, R. F. (2007). Evidence-based practice in psychology: Clarification and elaboration. *American Psychologist, 62*(5), 616–618.

Wampold, B. E., Lichtenberg, J. W., & Waehler, C. A. (2002). Principles of empirically supported interventions in counseling psychology. *The Counseling Psychologist, 30*(2), 197–217.

Weisz, J. R., & Addis, M.E. (2006). The research-practice tango and other choreographic challenges: Using and testing evidence-based psychotherapies in clinical care settings. In C. D. Goodheart, A. E. Kazdin, & R. J. Sternberg (Eds.), *Evidence-based psychotherapy: Where practice and research meet.* Washington, DC: APA Books.

Wendt, D. C., & Slife, B. D. (2007). Is evidence-based practice diverse enough? Philosophy of science considerations. *American Psychologist, 62*(5), 613–614.

Westen, D., Gabbard, G., & Blagov, P. (2006). Back to the future: Personality structure as a context for psychopathology. In R. F. Krueger & J. L. Tackett (Eds.), *Personality and psychopathology.* New York: Guilford.

Williams, D. C., & Levitt, H. M. (2007). Principles for facilitating agency in psychotherapy. *Psychotherapy Research, 17*(1), 66–82.

Worell, J., & Remer, P. (2003). *Feminist perspectives in therapy: Empowering diverse women* (2nd ed.). New York: John Wiley & Sons.

World Health Organization (2001). *International classification of functioning, disability, and health* (ICF). Geneva, Switzerland: Author.

Zacher, P., & Leong, F. T. (1992). A probem of personality: Scientist and practioner differences in psychology. *Journal of Personality, 60,* 665–677

Zane, N., Hall, G. C. N., Sue, S., Young, K., & Nunez, J. (2004). Research on psychotherapy with culturally diverse populations. In M. J. Lambert (Ed.), *Bergin and Garfield's handbook of psychotherapy and behavior change.* New York: Wiley.

Chapter Four

Science and Practice in Supervision

An Evidence-Based Practice in Psychology Approach

Cal D. Stoltenberg
Terry M. Pace

The practice of psychology has been formally tied to psychological science in clinical psychology for over 50 years since the Boulder Conference (Raimy, 1950) and for counseling psychology for over 40 years since the Greyston Conference (Thompson & Super, 1964), which delineated the scientist-practitioner model as core to training. How science should influence practice, however, has not achieved consensus. Recently, a movement toward articulating principles of evidence-based practice has gained visibility in psychology with the Report of the 2005 Presidential Task Force on Evidence-Based Practice (American Psychological Association, 2005), which provided the definition, "Evidence-Based practice in psychology (EBPP) is the integration of the best available research with clinical expertise in the context of patient characteristics, culture, and preferences" (p. 5).

The present chapter is organized to briefly address each of the three major categories included in this definition as important in considering EBPP, with the focus on the domain of clinical supervision. These categories are (1) best available research evidence; (2) clinical expertise; and (3) supervisee characteristics, culture, and preferences. Of course, to adequately evaluate the process and outcome of supervision, attention must also be paid to the evaluation of the work of the supervisee. Considerable debate continues regarding what qualifies as evidence for EBPP as well as what constitutes research that can be used to evaluate effective practice (Norcross, Beutler, & Levant, 2006). Although a detailed treatment of these issues goes beyond the scope of our intent, we will address some of these concerns as space allows.

Best Available Research Evidence

> What research evidence exists for the impact of supervisory method, the characteristics of the individual supervisor and supervisee, and the supervisory relationship on effective supervision?

METHOD OF SUPERVISION

Surveys indicate that most clinical supervisors practice without specific education in supervision, training on how to conduct supervision, or supervision on their supervision of trainees (Scott, Ingram, Vitanza, & Smith, 2000). This occurs despite calls for the importance of competence in supervision (Falender et al., 2004; Stoltenberg et al., 2003). Consistent with our focus on evidence-based practice, Chambless and Hollon (1998) were interested in examining the training of clinical psychology students in effective therapies, which stimulated the development of criteria for categorizing treatment approaches as empirically validated (EVTs) and empirically supported (ESTs). They then surveyed clinical training programs to ascertain how many of these approaches were actually included in the training of students. Based on the premise that students should learn how to use effective treatments, the results were troubling.

We will address ESTs in more detail later, but we should note that the assumptive basis of the importance of ESTs to therapy practice has been challenged (Wampold, 2006, among others). The current emphasis has moved to evidence-based practice that includes more types of "evidence" for the impact of treatment on clients as well as a broader range of mechanisms for evaluating this evidence. Discussions of evidence-based practice in supervision must not only address what is taught, but also how supervisees are educated and trained in professional practice. Of course, the complexity of the approach to supervision and the factors that are considered will impact the focus of the process and the types of evidence that are considered in evaluating the process and outcome of training.

Discussions of supervision orientations often group approaches into broad categories (Bernard & Goodyear, 2004; Falender & Shafranske, 2004; Stoltenberg, in press). These categories provide some basis for conceptualizing the supervision process, although it is likely that most supervisors (as do therapists) probably rely on eclectic procedures and intuition while working with their supervisees.

Psychotherapy-Based Approaches

These approaches to supervision use particular orientations to therapy as models for how to conduct supervision. Thus, the therapy approach becomes the framework for the supervision process, and the supervisor is seen, to varying degrees, as engaging in a similar process as would the therapist working with a client (supervisee). Of course, other than relying on modeling as the primary mechanism for training (which may not be specifically addressed by nonsocial learning approaches), the effectiveness of these approaches lies in the assumption that the goals, processes, and roles of the supervisor and supervisee closely approximate those of the therapist and client. More generally, Bernard and Goodyear (2004) note that person-centered approaches have emphasized facilitative conditions (empathy, genuineness, warmth) that fit well with a focus on supervisee learning and growth. Pearson (2006) observes that the growth and change for clients that is the focus of psychotherapy-based models should also be helpful in eliciting growth and change in supervisees.

Critics, however, have argued that supervision is more educational and, of course, less psychotherapeutic than the goals of psychotherapy, which can lead to frustration in the supervisor working from these orientations (Bernard, 1992). Similarly, Bernard and Goodyear (2004) caution against an overreliance on therapeutic conceptualizations at the expense of education of the supervisee. Of additional concern is the potential for ethical problems with the risk that the supervisor will fall into the habit of psychotherapy with the supervisee and breach ethical guidelines (Stoltenberg, McNeill, & Delworth, 1998).

From an EBPP perspective, the utility of psychotherapy-based approaches would appear to be a function of the overlap between the goals and procedures of the psychotherapeutic orientation and the supervision process. For example, the concept of the working alliance in psychotherapy has been translated to the supervisory context (Bordin, 1979, 1983) with some success. Goodyear and Guzzardo (2000) note that supervision can positively affect therapist–client working alliances (Patton & Kivlighan, 1997), which, in turn, has been shown to positively affect therapeutic outcomes (Horvath & Symonds, 1991). This and related research has been reviewed by Bernard and Goodyear (2004). Pearson (2006) has suggested that the strengths of the psychotherapy-based approaches should be integrated with more specific supervision-based models.

Process-Based Approaches

These orientations to supervision focus on how the components of the supervision process (roles, tasks, and so on) are described and enable an understanding of events that occur in conducting supervision. Another term that has been applied to these models, and is useful in conceptualizing how they work, is social role models (Holloway, 1992). As Bernard and Goodyear (2004) have noted, many of these models have in common the description of various functions in supervision falling into the role categories of teacher, counselor/therapist, and consultant (e.g., Bernard, 1979; Hess, 1980), with others adding monitoring and/or evaluation functions (e.g., Carroll, 1996; Holloway, 1995; Williams, 1995). Although these role categories are conceptually useful in considering the various aspects of supervisor functioning, they have been viewed by some as approximations of what occurs rather than as comprehensive descriptors (see Douce, 1989). These approaches conceptualize the roles as broad mechanisms for engaging the supervisee to achieve specific objectives or goals within a specific supervision situation. Little specific research has been done on these models, with Bernard's Discrimination Model receiving the most attention with general support found for this framework for organizing useful components of the supervision process, particularly the teacher and counselor roles (Bernard & Goodyear, 2004). Research related to these models is probably best utilized within an EBPP framework when one examines the aspects of the various roles the supervisor can assume in response to particular situations in the supervision context. Essentially, when are teaching versus counseling orientations most useful in dealing with specific situations in supervision?

Competency-Based Approaches

An increased focus on competencies in professional practice has occurred in recent years that has been stimulated, to a degree, by accountability considerations. Delineating the competencies necessary for practice from adequacy through expert has been the focus of much of this recent work (Kaslow, 2004; Kaslow et al., 2004; Peterson, Peterson, Abrams, & Stricker, 1997; Rodolfa et al., 2005; Summerall, Lopez, & Oehlert, 2000). A number of areas of professional practice have become the focus of delineating and assessing competencies including psychological assessment (Krishnamurthy et al., 2004), psychological intervention (Spruill et al., 2004), as well as competencies tied directly to practicum training (Hatcher & Lassiter, 2005). Similarly, the competencies associated with training psychologists through clinical supervision have received attention (Falender et al., 2004; Milne & James, 2002; Stoltenberg et al., 2003).

These approaches can be viewed as an extension and updating of the skills training models that flourished in the late 1960s and 1970s (e.g.,

Hackney & Nye, 1973; Ivey, 1971, among others), where certain core communication skills were taught in focused training experiences. Methods for training in these skills were based largely on modeling of the skills by trainers or supervisors and teaching. Studies examining these approaches suggested that the skills could be effectively learned (Cormier, Hackney, & Segrist, 1974, among others), but that they may not generalize to other counseling contexts (Spooner & Stone, 1977), and may decay over time (Mahon & Altmann, 1977; McCarthy, Danish, & D'Augelli, 1977). More recently, Hill (2004) has reviewed empirical research relevant to her three-stage model of helping, which suggests that helping skills have a significant, though small, effect on impact in specific sessions, and that evidence also suggests that the skills are actually used, in various degrees, in counseling sessions.

Consistent, in part, with the focus of the skills training models, recent work on professional competencies has addressed specific knowledge and skills, with an additional focus on attitudes (Kaslow, 2004). These are examined across various foundational competencies (e.g., ethics, diversity issues, science of psychology) that impact the functional competencies (e.g., intervention, assessment, consultation, research) of professional practice (Rodolfa et al., 2005). Recent work in this area has expanded this focus to address specific benchmarks and methods of assessment of competencies (American Psychological Association, 2007). These efforts help delineate what competencies are to be expected for practicum training, internship, entry to practice, and advanced practice. They do not, however, directly address how the training should occur that produces these competencies and the empirical status of associated training approaches. As noted earlier, initial efforts toward guidelines for supervisor training and competence have been articulated (Falender et al., 2004), but at present these guidelines do not constitute a model of supervision.

Milne and James (2000, 2002) have proposed a circumplex model of experiential learning in supervision that is adapted from Kolb (1984). Based on limited related research in supervision, and other research on learning, the model posits competent supervision to be the balanced utilization of supervisory behaviors including supporting, managing, challenging, listening, and providing feedback. These, in turn, should impact the supervisee learning cycle of experiencing, reflecting, conceptualizing, planning, and experimenting, which also should be balanced. An initial study of one supervisor working with six supervisees indicated that the supervisor tended to not use a balance of supervisory behaviors, but in response to consultation (supervision of supervision), moved to a more balanced use of supervisory interventions. Supervisee satisfaction with supervision was only slightly affected by this balance of supervision, beginning as quite favorable with a slight increase in favorability over the training period and an increase in the balance of their own behaviors related to the posited learning cycle (Milne & James, 2002).

Although the focus on competencies has the potential to positively impact the training and supervision of professional psychologists by providing benchmarks for expected levels of performance at various stages of professional development, it says little about the ways one can facilitate this acquisition of competencies. Providing benchmarks for knowledge and skill acquisition and suggesting methods for assessment do not suggest how one teaches or learns them. To the degree that there is developing consensus on these competencies and their benchmarks, we may move to a "no professional psychologist left behind" framework that provides guidelines for establishing evidence for standards being met (akin to treatment objectives and goals), but limited guidance concerning how to achieve them (treatment planning).

Developmental Approaches

These models are more meta-theoretical in that they tend to view the process of supervision as a distinct professional activity that is, largely, independent in overall orientation of the therapeutic models used by the supervisor and supervisee. A number of these models have been proposed over the years (see Stoltenberg & Delworth, 1987, for a review of early models, and Bernard and Goodyear, 2004, for a recent update). One of the more detailed models is the Integrated Developmental Model (IDM; Stoltenberg, 2005; Stoltenberg et al., 1998), which posits supervisee development through three levels over time as evidenced by changes in self-other awareness, motivation, and autonomy. This development is conceptualized to occur within a number of domains of professional practice, noting that any given supervisee may be functioning at different levels for different domains at a particular point in time. Further, this view of developmental changes suggests particular supervision environments that will facilitate growth in the supervisee for specific levels. Logically, if a supervisee is functioning at different levels of development with respect to various domains of professional activity (e.g., individual counseling with depressed clients within a cognitive-behavioral orientation versus marital counseling from an emotion-focused orientation), different approaches to supervision would be suggested for each, even within a given supervision session. Considerable research relevant to some of these models has been conducted over the past few decades, which some have seen as broadly supportive of at least some aspects of the approach (Bernard & Goodyear, 2004; Stoltenberg, 2005), yet many of these studies have been criticized on methodological grounds and noting that specific predictions of the models have not been adequately tested (Ellis & Ladany, 1997).

Summary

Of these categories of supervision approaches, the developmental models have, arguably, stimulated the most theoretically based research. Although much of this research has significant methodological shortcomings, that criticism can be applied to supervision research in general and not just specifically to studies examining developmental constructs.

Clearly, insufficient support exists for one to select a particular approach to supervision based solely on the current state of empirical research specifically examining these orientations. Of course, with the exception of some specific problems, the same state of affairs exists in the practice of psychotherapy where a specific theoretical orientation has yet to emerge as superior to others (Wampold, 2001). Nonetheless, theory fills in where data is missing, and it is likely to be more effective to have a model for conducting supervision than merely "shooting from the hip." In addition, evidence-based practice guidelines provide mechanisms for making decisions based on specific circumstances that can allow the supervisor to evaluate the impact of supervisory processes for a given trainee and his or her clients.

INDIVIDUAL CHARACTERISTICS

Considerable research has been conducted that examines the individual characteristics of supervisees and, to a lesser extent, supervisors. Bernard and Goodyear (2004) have summarized much of this research and concluded that certain individual characteristics appear to have at least some impact on the supervision process. Some of the characteristics found to be influential, in at least some studies, include cognitive complexity (conceptual level), cognitive style (one's preferred way of learning or processing information), theoretical orientation (of supervisee and supervisor), gender (of the supervisee and supervisor), relevant experience (of supervisees and, to some extent, supervisors), and developmental level (specifically as related to professional development). There also appear to be differential reactions of supervisees to various supervision environments as provided by supervisors. Similarly, culture (often operationalized as differences in ethnicity) has been found in some studies to impact the supervision process. Goodyear and Bernard (2004) summarize this research as suggesting the most powerful influence may be the supervisor's willingness to "open the cultural door and walk through it with the supervisee" (p. 125). They go on to recognize that "all interactions are multicultural" (p. 134).

From an EBPP perspective, supervisors would benefit from enlightened self-awareness concerning their own personal characteristics and experiences, and how that has shaped their approach to supervision as well as to supervisees who are similar or dissimilar from them in various ways. Consistent with the traditional perspective of counseling psychology, attention to person-in-context considerations are important in understanding how interactions in supervision can affect the supervisor and the supervisee. It would be difficult, at best, to attempt to monitor or formally assess supervisees (or supervisors) on the array of individual characteristics that have been explored in supervision research. Nonetheless, sensitivity as well as process and outcome evaluation of supervision can alert us to the need for more specific and careful scrutiny of these variables for any given supervision relationship. We will discuss mechanisms for doing this later.

SUPERVISORY RELATIONSHIP

The relationship between the supervisor and the supervisee has been the focus of a number of studies over the years. Stoltenberg et al. (1998) summarized this research as suggesting that supervisees of various levels of training have differing needs and expectations for supervision, moving from a focus on didactic training and developing self-awareness for beginners, to learning to develop alternative conceptualizations, emphasizing personal development, and deriving a cohesive theory for intermediate trainees, whereas advanced therapists prefer a more complex examination of personal development, transference and countertransference, parallel process, and issues of defensiveness and resistance. They go on to note that "warmth, acceptance, respect, understanding, and trust" characterize good supervisory relationships and effective supervisors encourage an atmosphere of experimentation and appropriately self-disclose (p. 111).

Horvath (2001), among others, has concluded that the quality of the working alliance in therapy has been shown to have a consistently positive impact on therapy outcome. Bordin (1983) and later Efstation, Patton, and Kardash (1990) extrapolated the concept of therapeutic working alliance to the supervision relationship. Thus, when Patton and Kivlighan (1997) found evidence for the impact of supervision on enhancing trainee-client working alliances, Goodyear and Guzzardo (2000) concluded that this relationship, by inference, suggests a positive affect of supervision on client outcomes. However, more direct evidence of this relationship is lacking. In practicing supervision from an EBPP perspective, it is important to assess the impact of supervision on the effectiveness of the supervisee's counseling and psychotherapy with his or her clients as well as evidence for the learning and professional development of the supervisee.

Evidence for One's Own Effectiveness in Supervision

> How does one evaluate what is occurring (evidence) in a given supervision relationship, the impact on the supervisee, and the impact on the client?

Before we address issues related to how one evaluates effectiveness in clinical supervision, it is important to establish how we might judge the effectiveness of supervisees with their clients, and then move on to see how we might ascertain if and how supervision might positively influence this process. Ultimately, if, as supervisors, we are unaware of the impact of our supervisees on their clients, it is difficult to consider what should be emphasized in supervision beyond simply attending to the requests or reactions of the supervisees in supervision sessions, or professional development concerns that become apparent in our interactions with them.

Over a decade ago, clinical psychologists became interested in which approaches to psychological intervention and psychotherapy were being taught in training programs, which lead to the movement for identifying and listing empirically validated and supported treatments (EVTs, ESTs; Chambless et al., 1998; Chambless et al. 1996). Although this was quite informative concerning the lack of focus in many training programs at the time in training students in approaches defined by these criteria as empirically validated, the limitations of these criteria for selecting effective treatments were debated over the years, including the choice of standards for acceptable research (the types and number of studies required) and the focus on manualized treatments (and their limitations) that most closely fit the evaluation criteria (Addis & Cardemil, 2006; Duncan & Miller, 2006; Ollendick & King, 2006; Stricker, 2006; Wampold, 2006). Whether one sees EVTs or ESTs as the best mechanism for evaluation of therapeutic effectiveness or views them as rather reductionistic and simplistic (or anywhere in between), it is certainly useful for students to be exposed to the rationale for their use and become familiar with at least some manualized approaches. From an integration of science and practice perspective, it is also important that supervisees gain an understanding of efficacy and effectiveness research, or clinical significance, so they can assess issues of generalizability and portability of approaches (Jacobson & Christensen, 1996; Jacobson, Roberts, Berns, & McGlinchey, 1999).

The EBPP approach has been offered as a replacement for the unfulfilled promise of the scientist-practitioner model (Chwalisz, 2003) and as a more broad and inclusive framework for examining how we can evaluate therapeutic effectiveness (Norcross, Beutler, & Lavant, 2006). We argue that the EBPP approach is a viable expression of the scientist-practitioner orientation and not a substitute for it. As such, EBPP principles offer us a context in which to examine a number of research and evaluation approaches to clinical work and, therefore, add a useful dimension to scientist-practitioner training.

Although there is still disagreement regarding what constitutes "evidence" in EBPP (see Norcross, Beutler, & Levant, 2006, for discussion), consistent with the Presidential Task Force (American Psychological Association, 2005), Reed (2006) suggests integrating "best research evidence" along with clinical expertise and patient values. A number of approaches have been discussed as appropriate for determining evidence for effective practice; a few of these appear to fit rather well within the constraints of a supervisory relationship, while others (although offering considerable rigor) tend to be less easily adaptable to this context, at least for one's evaluation of his or her own work (e.g., effectiveness research, qualitative studies, and randomized clinical trials; see Norcross, Beutler, and Levant for detailed discussions of the pros and cons of various mechanisms for ascertaining "evidence"). Some of the more relevant approaches include single-participant or N = 1 research, change process research, and case studies. These mechanisms offer supervisees tools with which to examine their own work in therapy as well as their role as therapist, aspects of the therapeutic relationship, and relevant client variables. We have argued that a main goal of science and practice integration need not be the generation of published research, but rather to train supervisees to examine their work in a therapy context, as these are skills that will translate more directly into utilizing science for individuals primarily engaged in practice (Stoltenberg & Pace, 2007).

Useful mechanisms for accomplishing this include evaluating observations of one's own behavior and that of the client in therapy against a given theory (case studies), identifying and measuring process variables that are thought to have an impact on outcomes (process research), and/or identifying and measuring client behaviors before, during, and after interventions (N = 1 studies); (see Norcross, Beutler, & Levant, 2006, and Heppner, Kivlighan, & Wampold, 1999, for examples of these research approaches as they are used in counseling and therapy contexts). Consistent with an EBPP perspective is to ask supervisees "to investigate and use approaches/interventions that have some empirically established rationale (or, lacking that, strong theoretical grounding), and then assess how and why this approach works (or doesn't work) for them when implemented with a given client" (Stoltenberg & Pace, 2007). Others have noted, "The results of nomothetic research are to be complemented by idiographic research in which practitioners study their own outcomes" (Reed, Kihlstrom, & Messer, 2006, p. 44).

Consistent, then, with evidence-based decision-making, an attitude of self-evaluation is promoted along with the skills necessary to allow supervisees to assess their own effectiveness, rather than assume that approaches that have been supported in research by others will automatically translate to their own work with clients. This self-evaluation also encourages the supervisee to examine how effectively he or she has assessed client needs, selected interventions, and administered those interventions. Furthermore, this process should be one that supervisees can apply in other settings as they progress through their careers.

Depending on the developmental level of the supervisee, and the experience and breadth of knowledge of therapy and supervision of the supervisor, different approaches to the selection of therapeutic orientation and interventions may be pursued. With less experienced supervisees, the supervisor may prescribe, or at least suggest, an orientation and subsequent interventions to the supervisee and work closely with her or him to identify objectives and goals. With more experienced supervisees, rather than requiring a particular approach be taken with a given client, the supervisee might produce a rationale based on a relevant review of the literature or previously acquired knowledge. This process can be quite elaborate and consistent with standards for single subject research including multiple baseline A-B-C studies (Heppner et al., 1999) or more limited with a primary focus on particular process variables that are expected to be important for a particular phase of therapy within a given theoretical orientation (Stoltenberg & Pace, in press).

Evaluation of supervision should, by extension, include (but not be limited to) an evaluation of the effectiveness of the supervisee in working with clients. Indeed, as with psychotherapy, clinical supervision involves an interpersonal relationship with specific aims. Thus, as noted earlier, the qualities of the supervisor, the supervisee, prior supervision and clinically related experiences, stages of professional development of each, and the specific context and goals of the supervision relationship will all come into play in shaping the supervision process and, consequently, outcomes. Implementing a scientific model in approaching supervision means the use of assessment, planning, and evaluation. Thus, a three-stage scientist-practitioner approach to supervision includes: (1) assessment of modifying factors relevant to supervision process and goals (including ongoing evaluation of supervisee effectiveness), (2) formulation of a supervision plan, and (3) implementation and ongoing evaluation of supervision.

Assessment of Modifying Factors Relevant to Supervision

Goals and Developmental Stage

Clinical supervision should be purposeful in both processes and goals. If the goal is to monitor client well-being, then case review and monitoring methods need to be emphasized. By contrast, if the goal is to enhance supervisee development, then a focus on the specific dimensions of development that are most relevant to the supervisor and supervisee must be included. Of course, both of these foci should be present in most actual clinical supervision settings. Some degree of case review and monitoring to ensure client well-being is an ethical duty (American Psychological Association, 2002) and should be a part of the supervision plan. These methods commonly include review and discussion of the assessment of client symptoms, goals, background and risk factors, review of formal assessments, observation of actual counseling sessions (video or live), or actual supervisor interaction with the client. Although these methods may help to shape the feedback given to the supervisee in order to provide appropriate services, they do not directly address supervisee needs or educational goals.

For example, one might want to consider if the goals should be focused toward the development of basic skills and attitudes supported by the scientific and professional literature. If this is the case (which it commonly is for less experienced supervisees), then how might these goals best be pursued? Drawing upon the literature on the acquisition of expertise (Anderson, 2005), supervisors should ensure their supervisees have ample practice experiences, use modeling and direct coaching to enhance skill acquisition, and provide specific feedback regarding the supervisee's performance. If the goals are to enable the supervisee to develop advanced theoretical or critical thinking abilities, then, again, drawing on research from these areas (e.g., Westin & Weinberger, 2004), broad-based case presentations, literature reviews, discussions of theory, and case conferences might be the methods of choice with the effect of directing the supervisee's attention toward important concepts and data to impact his or her information processing. Finally, if the goals reflect a focus on self-awareness or the development of empathy and emotional competence (e.g., Goleman, 1995), then experiential methods such as service assignments in diverse contexts, multicultural awareness exercises, empathy training, exploration of personal life experiences, or referral for personal therapy may be most helpful.

A major factor in shaping the choice of goals and methods should usually include an assessment of the supervisee's stage of professional development (Stoltenberg et al., 1998). This perspective suggests that supervisees are more prepared to engage in specific developmental tasks at different times in their professional training. For example, it may be that too early of an emphasis on a single theoretical model or set of techniques may foster premature closure of exploration of alternatives, thus, effectively creating attitudinal and emotional blocks inhibiting supervisees from considering and exploring other perspectives. Rather, we would suggest that the literature argues for an early focus on fundamental skills and attitudes that have been demonstrated to underlie most approaches to therapy (Hill, 2004; Hubble, Duncan, & Miller, 1999).

Although gradual exposure to specific models and methods may be necessary to include in supervision, we believe that a focus on critical thinking and theoretical reflection is often very helpful as a secondary focus after basic skills have been reasonably mastered. This is consistent with Schön's (1987) concept of schema refinement through the process of "reflection-in-action" where we examine our "knowledge-in-action" or learned responses (in this case, fundamental skills) in situations where the interactions are inconsistent with our expectations. When these "on the fly" reflections on the process fail to yield adequate understanding or results, the process of reflection on action is useful, which can include the supervisee's own examination of what occurred in a specific session, as well as in supervision with the supervisor. Of course, a key requirement for this sequence to activate is the awareness of the supervisee of verbal and/or nonverbal cues from the client that indicate non-facilitative or unexpected reactions. If not recognized by the supervisee, then it becomes increasingly important that sufficiently close monitoring by the supervisor is occurring to allow her or him to become aware of these situations. Once recognized, this process often results in the need to focus on advanced techniques, specific theoretical models, and other evidence-based procedures to gain sufficient understanding and skill sets to refine and elaborate relevant schemata to enable the supervisee to handle more complexity in the clinical process.

Supervisee Qualities

A number of supervisee (learner) qualities are known to affect the acquisition of expertise (advanced, complex, critically examined knowledge and skills). Motivation or readiness for change are factors that affect learning across settings and domains and include issues of competence, relatedness, and autonomy (Ryan & Desi, 2000). Supervisees may vary from amotivation through extrinsic and to intrinsic motivation, reflecting a locus of causality in regard to their own behavior. The condition of amotivation, which we might expect in some supervisees with limited or no experience in a particular domain, suggests a lack of intention to act, which reflects seeing little or no value to an activity (skill, intervention) or a lack of perceived competence in performing it. Additionally, it may relate to not expecting a desired outcome from the action. Extrinsic motivation, which is more likely as experience increases from the neophyte level, includes a full range of regulation of behavior varying in degree of perceived autonomy, reflecting perceptions of locus of control from external through early internal. Finally, intrinsic motivation suggests a perceived internal locus of control, or the sense that the supervisee controls much of his or her own professional behavior. For example, in many cases, especially with early trainees, their goals may be overly narrow and simplistic based on prior experiences, confidence, or other factors. An effective supervisor would be able to accommodate such variations (within reason), encourage incremental change, and spend time building readiness (by engaging in practice to increase confidence, establishing trust, and enhancing knowledge) rather than focusing on quick and dramatic development.

One's life experiences play an important role in developing a worldview that can vary in terms of how well it can accommodate the perspectives reflected in the ethical and effective practice of psychology. A broader example of this same type of concern is cultural encapsulation (Ridley, Mendoza, Kanitz, Angermeier, & Zenk, 1994; Wrenn, 1962). Many, perhaps most, supervisees begin their professional development from a more or less encapsulated culture–worldview. Thus, a major goal in supervision is establishing sufficient rapport to be able to enter into and share in the supervisees' cultural experiences and then gradually be able to help them broaden their understanding and appreciation of diversity (consistent with the recommendations of Bernard & Goodyear, 2004). To do this, as in multicultural therapy, advanced self-, interpersonal-, and cultural awareness are needed by the supervisor as well as a willingness to be open to different cultural perspectives (American Psychological Association, 2003; Sue et al., 1998).

Another context for examining this process is reflected in recent efforts to broaden the scope of schema theory by incorporating sociocultural perspectives. McVee, Dunsmore, and Gavelek (2005) note three key points in their summary of this work:

> (1) Schema and other cognitive processes or structures are embodied—that is, who we are as biological beings determines our sensorial interactions with the world and thus the nature of the representations we construct; (2) knowledge is situated in the transaction between world and individual; and (3) these transactions are mediated by culturally and socially enacted practices carried out through material and ideal artifacts. (pp. 555–556)

Thus, the patterns of our understanding of the world, manner of interacting with others, and what we remember of these experiences influence our thoughts and behaviors, and are influenced by our continuing active experiences in the world. McVee et al. (2005) note that culture affects our development through culturally influenced knowledge or ideas, how we utilize this knowledge that is obtained through social interactions, and how we transform these ideas by personal thought and reflection, as well as sharing these perspectives with others. Thus, one's experiences are largely determined by the sociocultural contexts we have experienced and, therefore, are subject to expansion and alteration (broadening of schemata) through additional exposure and processing of experience.

Given variations in the sociocultural contexts that may have been experienced by supervisors and supervisees, these differences often need to be addressed in order for an effective learning environment and working alliance to be established in supervision. As noted earlier, some diversity factors have been explored in supervision research while others have yet to be examined. Relevant dimensions may include gender, race/ethnicity, SES, rural-urban backgrounds, relational and family status (marriage, children, etc.), sexual orientation, spiritual and/or religious differences, age, life stage, career stage, health, personality, and situational demands or stressors. Awareness of the potential impact of these dimensions on the interpersonal relationship and communication patterns and being open to exploring these differences are likely to set the stage for building an effective supervision relationship (Bernard & Goodyear, 2004).

Formulation of a Supervision Plan

As in most other realms of professional psychology, clinical supervision is a complex multidimensional, dynamic, contextually shaped interpersonal process. Thus, in order to account for this degree of variation and diversity, one must learn to think reflectively and purposefully about supervision. Just as there are many variations on case conceptualization and treatment plans for psychotherapy (e.g., Beutler & Clarkin, 1990; Eells, 2007; Hubble et al., 1999), there may be a range of useful approaches to formulation of a supervision plan. Within the IDM (Stoltenberg et al., 1998), a general framework exists that may be used to form an outline for supervision planning. Within this model, the plan first considers where the supervisee is functioning developmentally. Supervision goals and methods should be guided by such an assessment across domains of practice relevant to the supervisee's current professional activities, and varied according to the needs reflected in competencies attained. Second, drawing on a contextual and multicultural perspective, individual and situational factors (across supervisees, between supervisees and supervisor) should be added into the supervision formulation in order to thoughtfully, respectfully, and effectively engage each supervisee in relevant ways and draw on and expand their strengths and resources to aid their development and their clinical work.

A third level of planning should take into account the personal and professional beliefs, experiences, interests, strengths, characteristics, limitations and biases of the supervisor. Although this is implied in considering supervisee diversity, a clear articulation of these issues for the supervisor and, if relevant, the supervisor's supervisor to reflect upon is most desirable. This cultural self-assessment may help to prevent supervisors from acting from habit and comfort alone, may keep their interactions open and engaged in learning and development and thus more authentic and attuned to supervisee, client, and contextual needs. This effort may help supervisors to more appropriately time interventions with supervisees and to more openly, systematically, and scientifically help to ensure client well-being.

Finally, a comprehensive formulation should include important aspects of the clinical context of the supervisory relationship. Thus, specific client needs, agency or setting needs and policies, professional and ethical standards, legal considerations, limitations of competency or resources, and community needs and standards all may play a modifying role in shaping the content and process of supervision.

Educational tools and resources will of course affect supervision as well. For example, if video is available to use in supervision, both case assessment and specificity of supervisory focus may be better informed and development enhanced (Huhra, Yamokoski-Maynhart, & Prieto, in press). The effectiveness of supervision in part depends upon the quality and specificity of the information available to use in the process of supervision. As we are all in varying degrees biased observers of our own behaviors and their impact, we need solid external evidence to be able to see and understand ourselves as well as to guide our decision making (see Westin & Weinberger, 2004). Thus, supervision plans may need to actively consider and account for the available educational resources and quality of the information available and determine if, minimally, resources allow for adequate supervision.

Implementation and Ongoing Evaluation of Supervision

As a plan is formulated and implemented, evaluation should be a continuous part of the process. Essentially, all aspects of the plan should be evaluated in a self-corrective dynamic fashion, allowing for modification as specific needs are met and others emerge or conditions change. This requires an active, thoughtful approach to supervision rather than relying on habit or inertia. Evaluation should address supervisee developmental level across motivation, autonomy, and awareness (Stoltenberg et al., 1998) as well as the performance of the supervisor and supervisee. The supervisory alliance (Efstation et al., 1990) should be evaluated along with the unique cultural and contextual factors that may be impacting the supervision relationship, professional learning and development, and client needs and outcomes. Evaluation should usually consider the effects of processes and the outcomes of supervision, including the assessment of specific professional competencies (American Psychological Association, 2007) as well as client outcomes (Lambert & Hawkins, 2004). Finally, evaluation should consider the role and impact of various educational resources and conditions.

The methods of evaluation should be multiple. Self-reflection and reflection on the process by both supervisee and supervisor form a foundation, but are limited in terms of processes and impacts that can be assessed. Again, for reflection to be effective, certain processes need to be highlighted (Schön, 1987). Sitting and discussing perceptions week after week is a poor substitute for comprehensive monitoring and evaluation. Formal types of evaluation must be added to these reflective and interpersonal methods, such as the use of various rating forms tapping supervisee, supervisor, and client assessments of processes and outcomes. Work samples from the supervisee are also necessary and include videotape and/or live observation, case conceptualizations, assessments, and so on (Stoltenberg et al., 1998). A major implication of these considerations is that supervision is a serious, diverse, complex, resource-influenced and time-intensive professional activity that requires focal professional development and ongoing educational growth. Simplistic, overly assumptive, unsystematic approaches to supervision are not likely to be as successful or rewarding as specific and thoughtful professional approaches that are well integrated into work roles, training approaches, and professional identities.

Clinical Expertise

> How do we avoid bias or idiosyncratic interpretations, overgeneralizations, and so on in supervision?

The prior discussions on the role of sociocultural experiences and their impact on our schemata, and the cautions noted specifically about being sensitive to diversity issues in supervision, suggest some limitations or, at least, qualifications of how clinical expertise (or supervisor expertise) can be relied on in the supervision context. These issues have tended to be dealt with more directly as they impact clinical decision-making, but the relevance to supervision is equal. Chambless and Crits-Christoph (2006) note that little research has been conducted concerning therapists' decision-making process regarding psychotherapy, which is in contrast to work done in psychological assessments. They argue that, if relevant empirical research does not play a role in treatment selection, then one is likely to rely on clinical lore, personal preference, or other less empirical mechanisms for selection. They also argue that it is unlikely that clinicians can, by reflection or memory only, "be confident about which of their many behaviors are consistently related to the results of treatment for a particular type of client or problem" (p. 194). This becomes of even greater concern when one considers estimates that fewer than one-third of practicing clinicians monitor client outcomes (Lambert & Hawkins, 2004). Indeed, others have suggested that believing we are correct in our decision making is often not related to being correct (Gambrill, 1990; Garb, 1998; Nezu & Nezu, 1995).

The local clinical scientist model has been presented as a disciplined inquiry approach, utilizing a consideration of what one has learned, careful observation of clinically relevant behavior, and effective logical analysis that can form the basis of effective clinical expertise (Stricker & Treirweiler, 1995). We have maintained that this provides a useful framework, but that consideration of relevant nomothetic research is also important (Stoltenberg & Pace, 2007).

Westin and Weinberger (2004) have suggested that, although statistical prediction has typically been shown to be superior to clinical prediction (which, of course, directly relates to clinical decision-making), there are approaches to systematically aggregating and evaluating data that can give clinicians an edge. They state that clinicians are susceptible to the same biases as anyone unless they are aware of them. Consistent with research on the development of expertise (Anderson, 2005), Westin and Weinberger note that, "with increasing experience in a given domain, people are typically able to make more subtle discriminations, process information more efficiently, and automatize procedures that initially required conscious attention and hence consumed working memory resources" (p. 599). If we receive accurate and constructive feedback through the training process by supervisors and peers (from direct observation of behavior), we should develop more useful "clinical expertise," particularly if we remain open to feedback and actively collect evidence allowing us to evaluate our effectiveness. Without this process, however, we run the same risks as laypeople in misjudging our abilities and effectiveness.

As we have already noted, our understanding of clinical processes (schemata) can be refined and elaborated by reflection-in-process (r-i-p) and reflection-on-process (r-o-p) (Schön, 1987). Stoltenberg et al. (1998) have described the process of the counselor "pulling back" within a counseling session and processing current interactions, emotional and conceptual information, and accrued related knowledge that describes r-i-p. Processing events between sessions, including during supervision, constitutes r-o-p. Also in the supervision literature, suggestions have been made regarding techniques and processes that can encourage supervisees to engage productively in the reflective process (Griffith & Frieden, 2000; Neufeldt, 1999; Neufeldt, Karno, & Nelson, 1996), with the role of the supervisor varying but often serving to stimulate thinking. Of additional importance, however, to reflecting upon one's own reactions and experiences, getting feedback from supervisors and peers, processing client reactions, and so on is attending in a systematic manner to these sources of information with respect to broad empirical research and theory

CONCLUSION

We have argued that an EBPP perspective on clinical supervision can be useful in assisting supervisors' decision making regarding conducting and evaluating the process and outcomes. In order to effectively utilize the best available research evidence, clinical expertise, and understanding supervisee characteristics, culture, and preferences, supervisors need to become and remain current in our understanding of the research and models of clinical supervision. Specific training in supervision, and supervision of one's supervision, is necessary to set this process in motion. In addition, theories and research from other fields (e.g., learning, psychotherapy, human development) should be used to augment our understanding of key processes within the supervision environment. Finally, we should maintain a focus on the effects of supervisee behavior on clients and others in the professional environment as part of a comprehensive evaluation of supervision process and outcomes.

To us, there appear to be no simple prescriptions for an effective, scientist-practitioner approach to supervision. Although there are significant limitations in our empirical literature on supervision, considerable advancement has occurred over the past 30 or so years. Nonetheless, the nomothetic research literature must be enhanced by idiographic research conducted by practitioners (supervisors, supervisees) within their own practice to more fully inform the supervision process. Engaging in "best practices" (should we get to that point) is insufficient in assuring that optimum (or even acceptable) services are being rendered without an evaluation of one's personal effectiveness with various supervisees. Multiple mechanisms exist for this ongoing evaluation that can then impact the planning and implementation of supervision and the professional activities being supervised. Considerable thoughtful, informed, systematic, and effortful investment in the supervision process is necessary by all parties to enhance the growth and development of supervisees, and protect the welfare of their clients.

BIBLIOGRAPHY

Addis, M. E., & Cardemil, E. V. (2006). Psychotherapy manuals can improve outcomes. In J. C. Norcross, L. E. Beutler, & R. F. Levant (Eds.), *Evidence-based practices in mental health* (pp. 131–140). Washington, DC: American Psychological Association.

American Psychological Association. (2002). *Ethical principles of psychologists and code of conduct:* 2002. Washington, DC: Author.

American Psychological Association. (2003). Guidelines on multicultural education, training, research, practice, and organizational change for psychologists. *American Psychologist, 58,* 377–404.

American Psychological Association. (2005). Report of the 2005 Presidential Task Force on evidence-based practice (2005). Washington, DC: Author.

American Psychological Association. (2007). Assessment of competencies benchmarks work group: A developmental model for defining and measuring competencies in professional psychology. Washington, DC: Author.

Anderson, J. R. (2005). *Cognitive psychology and its implications* (6th ed.). New York: Worth Publishers.

Bernard, J. M. (1979). Supervisor training: A discrimination model. *Counselor Education and Supervision, 19,* 60–68.

Bernard, J. M. (1992). The challenge of psychotherapy-based supervision: Making the pieces fit. *Counselor Education and Supervision, 31,* 232–237.

Bernard, J. M., & Goodyear, R. K. (2004). *Fundamentals of clinical supervision* (3rd ed.). Boston: Allyn & Bacon.

Beutler L. E., & Clarkin, J. F. (1990). *Systematic treatment selection: Toward targeted therapeutic interventions.* New York: Bruner/Mazel.

Bordin, E. S. (1979). The generalizability of the psychodynamic concept of the working alliance. *Psychotherapy: Theory, Research, and Practice, 16,* 252–260.

Bordin, E. S. (1983). A working alliance model of supervision. *The Counseling Psychologist, 11,* 35–42.

Carroll, M. (1996). *Counseling supervision: Theory, skills, and practice.* London: Cassell.

Chambless, D. L., Baker, M. J., Baucom, D. H., Beutler, L. E., Calhoun, K. S., Daiuto, A., et al. (1998). Update on empirically validated therapies II. *The Clinical Psychologist, 51,* 3–16.

Chambless, D. L., & Crits-Christoph, P. (2006). The treatment method. In J. C. Norcross, L. E. Beutler, & R. F. Levant (Eds.), *Evidence-based practices in mental health* (pp. 191–200). Washington, DC: American Psychological Association.

Chambless, D. L., & Hollon, S. D. (1998). Defining empirically supported therapies. *Journal of Consulting and Clinical Psychology, 66,* 7–18.

Chambless, D. L., Sanderson, W. C., Shoham, V., Bennett-Johnson, S., Pope, K. S., & Crits-Christoph, P. (1996). An update on empirically validated therapies. *The Clinical Psychologist, 49,* 5–18.

Chwalisz, K. (2003). Evidence-based practice: A framework for twenty-first-century scientist-practitioner training. *The Counseling Psychologist, 31,* 497–528.

Cormier, L.S., Hackney, H., & Segrist, A. (1974). Three counselor training models: A comparative study. *Counselor Education and Supervision, 14,* 95–104.

Douce, L. (1989, August). *Classroom and experiential training in supervision.* Paper presented at the annual meeting of the American Psychological Association, New Orleans, LA.

Duncan, B. L., & Miller, S. D. (2006). Treatment manuals do not improve outcomes. In J. C. Norcross, L. E. Beutler, & R. F. Levant (Eds.), *Evidence-based practices in mental health* (pp. 140–149). Washington, DC: American Psychological Association.

Eells, T. D. (2007). *Handbook of psychotherapy case formulation* (2nd ed.). New York: Guilford.

Efstation, J. F., Patton, M. J., & Kardash, C. M. (1990). Measuring the working alliance in counselor supervision. *Journal of Counseling Psychology, 37,* 322–329.

Ellis, M. V., & Ladany, M. (1997). Inferences concerning supervisees and clients in clinical supervision: An integrative review. In C. E. Watkins, Jr. (Ed.), *Handbook of psychotherapy supervision* (pp. 447–507). New York: Wiley.

Falender, C. A., Cornish, J. A. E., Goodyear, R., Hatcher, R., Kaslow, N. J., Leventhal, G,. et al. (2004). Defining competencies in psychology supervision: A consensus statement. *Journal of Clinical Psychology, 60,* 771–785.

Falender, C. A., & Shafranske, E. P. (2004). *Clinical supervision: A competency-based approach.* Washington, DC: American Psychological Association.

Gambrill, E. (1990). *Critical thinking in clinical practice.* San Francisco: Jossey-Bass.

Garb, H. N. (1998). *Studying the clinician: Judgment research and psychological assessment.* Washington, DC: American Psychological Association.

Goleman, D. (1995). *Emotional intelligence.* New York: Bantam.

Goodyear, R. K., & Guzzardo, C. R. (2000). Psychotherapy supervision and training. In S. D. Brown & R. W. Lent (Eds.), *Handbook of counseling psychology* (3rd ed., pp. 83–108). New York: Wiley.

Griffith, B. A., & Frieden, G. (2000). Facilitating reflective thinking in counselor education. *Counselor Education and Supervision, 40,* 82–93.

Hackney, H., & Nye, L. S. (1973). *Counseling strategies and objectives.* Englewood Cliffs, NJ: Prentice Hall.

Hatcher, R. L., & Lassiter, K. D. (2005). Report on practicum competencies. www/adptc.org/public_files/cctcPracticumCompetenciesChartRevFeb2005.doc. Initial training in professional psychology: The practicum competancies outline. *Training and Education in Professional Psychology, 1,* 49–63.

Heppner, P. P., Kivlighan, D. M., Jr., & Wampold, B. E. (1999). *Research design in counseling* (2nd ed.). Belmont, CA: Wadsworth.

Hess, A. K. (1980). Training models and the nature of psychotherapy supervision. In A. K. Hess (Ed.), *Psychotherapy supervision: Theory, research and practice* (pp. 15–28). New York: John Wiley & Sons.

Hill, C. D. (2004). *Helping skills: Facilitating exploration, insight, and action* (2nd ed.). Washington, DC: American Psychological Association.

Holloway, E. L. (1992). Supervision: A way of teaching and learning. In S. D. Brown & R. W. Lent (Eds.), *Handbook of counseling psychology* (2nd ed., pp. 177–214). New York: Wiley.

Holloway, E. L. (1995). *Clinical supervision: A systems approach.* Thousand Oaks, CA: Sage.

Horvath, A. O. (2001). The alliance. *Psychotherapy, 38,* 365–372.

Horvath, A. O., & Symonds, D. B. (1991). Relationship between working alliance and outcome in psychotherapy: A meta-analysis. *Journal of Counseling Psychology, 38,* 139–149.

Hubble, M. A., Duncan, B. L., & Miller, S. D. (1999). *The heart and soul of change. What works in therapy.* Washington, DC: American Psychological Association, 1999.

Huhra, R. L., Yamokoski-Maynhart, C. A., & Prieto, L. R. (in press). Reviewing videotape in supervision: A developmental approach. *Journal of Counseling & Development.*

Ivey, A. E. (1971). *Microcounseling: Innovations in interviewing training.* Springfield, IL: Thomas.

Jacobson, N. S., & Christensen, A. (1996). Studying the effectiveness of psychotherapy: How well can clinical trials do the job? *American Psychologist, 51,* 1031–1039.

Jacobson, N. S., Roberts, L. J., Berns, S. B., & McGlinchey, J. B. (1999). Methods for defining and determining the clinical significance of treatment effects: Description, application, and alternatives. *Journal of Consulting and Clinical Psychology, 67,* 300–307.

Kaslow, N. J. (2004). Competencies in professional psychology. *American Psychologist, 59,* 774–781.

Kaslow, N. J., Borden, K. A., Collins, F. L., Forrest, L., Illfelder-Kaye, J., Nelson, P. D., et al. (2004). Competencies Conference: Future directions in education and credentialing in professional psychology. *Journal of Clinical Psychology, 80,* 699–712.

Kolb, D. A. (1984). *Experiential learning: Experience as the source of learning and development.* Englewood Cliffs, NJ: Prentice Hall.

Krishnamurthy, R., VandeCreek, L., Kaslow, M. J., Tazeau, Y. M., Milville, M. L., Kerns, R., et al. (2004). Achieving competency in psychological assessment: Directions for education and training. *Journal of Clinical Psychology, 80,* 725–740.

Lambert, M. J., & Hawkins, E. J. (2004). Measuring outcome in professional practice: Considerations in selecting and using brief outcome instruments. *Professional Psychology: Research and Practice, 35,* 492–499.

Mahon, B. R., & Altmann, H. A. (1977). Skill training: Cautions and recommendations. *Counselor Education and Supervision, 17,* 42–50.

McCarthy, P. R., Danish, S. J., & D'Augelli, A. R. (1977). A follow-up evaluation of helping skills training. *Counselor Education and Supervision, 17,* 29–35.

McVee, M. B., Dunsmore, K., & Gavelek, J. R. (2005). Schema theory revisited. *Review of Educational Research, 75*, 531–566.

Milne, D. L., & James, I. (2000). A systematic review of effective cognitive-behavioural supervision. *British Journal of Clinical Psychology, 39*, 111–129.

Milne, D., & James, I. (2002). The observed impact of training on competence in clinical supervision. *British Journal of Clinical Psychology, 41*, 55–72.

Neufeldt, S. A. (1999). Training in reflective processes in supervision. In E. Holloway, & M. Carroll (Eds.), *Training in counselling supervision* (pp. 92–105). London: Sage Publications, Inc.

Neufeldt, S. A., Karno, M. P., & Nelson, M. L. (1996). A qualitative analysis of experts' conceptualization of supervisee reflectivity. *Journal of Counseling Psychology, 42*, 3–9.

Nezu, C. M., & Nezu, A. M. (1995). Clinical decision making in everyday practice: The science in the art. *Cognitive and Behavioral Practice, 2*, 5–25.

Norcross, J. C., Beutler, L. E., & Levant, R. F. (2006), *Evidence-based practices in mental health*. Washington, DC: American Psychological Association.

Ollendick, T. H., & King, N. J. (2006). Empirically supported treatments typically produce outcomes superior to non-empirically supported treatment therapies. In J. C. Norcross, L. E. Beutler, & R. F. Levant (Eds.), *Evidence-based practices in mental health* (pp. 308–317). Washington, DC: American Psychological Association.

Patton, M. J., & Kivlighan, D. M. J. (1997). Relevance of the supervisory alliance to the counseling alliance and to treatment adherence in counselor training. *Journal of Counseling Psychology, 44*, 108–111.

Pearson, Q. M. (2006). Psychotherapy-drive supervision: Integrating counseling theories into role-based supervision. *Journal of Mental Health Counseling, 28*, 241–252.

Peterson, R. L., Peterson, D. R., Abrams, J. C., & Stricker, G. (1997). The National Council of Schools and Programs of Professional Psychology educational model. *Professional Psychology: Research and Practice, 28*, 373–386.

Raimy, V. C (Ed.). (1950). *Training in clinical psychology (Boulder Conference)*. New York: Prentice Hall.

Reed, G. M. (2006). Clinical expertise. In J. C. Norcross, L. E. Beutler, & R. F. Levant (Eds.), *Evidence-based practices in mental health* (pp. 13–23). Washington, DC: American Psychological Association.

Reed, G. M., Kihlstrom, J. F., & Messer, S. B. (2006). Dialogue: Convergence and contention. In J. C. Norcross, L. E. Beutler, & R. F. Levant (Eds.), *Evidence-based practices in mental health* (pp. 40–55). Washington, DC: American Psychological Association.

Ridley, C. R., Mendoza, D. W., Kanitz, B. E., Angermeier, L., & Zenk, R. (1994). Cultural sensitivity in multicultural counseling: A perceptual schema model. *Journal of Counseling Psychology, 41*, 125–136.

Rodolfa, E. R., Bent, R. J., Eisman, E., Nelson, P. D., Rehm, L., & Richie, P. (2005). A cube model for competency development: Implications for psychology educators and regulators. *Professional Psychology: Research and Practice, 36*, 347–354.

Ryan, R. M., & Desi, E. L. (2000). Self-determination theory and the facilitation of intrinsic motivation, social development, and well-being. *American Psychologist, 55*, 68–78.

Schön, D. A. (1987). *Educating the reflective practitioner.* San Francisco, CA: Jossey-Bass.

Scott, K. J., Ingram, K. M., Vitanza, S. A., & Smith, N. G. (2000). Training in supervision: A survey of current practices. *The Counseling Psychologist, 28,* 403–422.

Spooner, S. E., & Stone, S. C. (1977). Maintenance of specific counseling skills over time. *Journal of Counseling Psychology, 24,* 66–71.

Spruill, J., Rozensky, R. H., Stigall, T. T., Vasquez, M., Binghman, R. P., & Olivey, C. D. V. (2004). Becoming a competent clinician: Basic competencies in intervention. *Journal of Clinical Psychology, 80,* 741–754.

Stoltenberg, C. D. (2005). Enhancing professional competence through developmental approaches to supervision. *American Psychologist, 6,* 855–864.

Stoltenberg, C. D. (in press). Supervision. In E. Altmaier & B. D. Johnson (Series Eds.), *Encyclopedia of counseling: Volume One: Changes and challenges for counseling in the 21st century.* Thousand Oaks, CA: Sage.

Stoltenberg, C. D., & Delworth, U. (1987). *Supervising counselors and therapists: A developmental approach.* San Francisco, CA: Jossey-Bass.

Stoltenberg, C. D., Kaslow, N. J., Cornish, J., Felander, C., Bjorkman, A., Goodyear, R. K., et al. (2003, August). *Future directions in education and credentialing in clinical supervision.* Paper presented at the annual meeting of the American Psychological Association, Toronto, Canada.

Stoltenberg, C. D., McNeill, B. W., & Delworth, U. (1998). *IDM supervision: An integrated developmental model for supervising counselors and therapists.* San Francisco, CA: Jossey-Bass.

Stoltenberg, C. D., & Pace, T. M. (2007). The scientist–practitioner model: Now more than ever. *Journal of Contemporary Psychotherapy, 37,* 195–203.

Stricker, G. (2006). A poor fit between empirically supported treatments and psychotherapy integration. In J. C. Norcross, L. E. Beutler, & R. F. Levant (Eds.), *Evidence-based practices in mental health* (pp. 275–282). Washington, D.C.: American Psychological Association.

Stricker, G., & Treirweiler, S. J. (1995). The local clinical scientist: A bridge between science and practice. *American Psychologist, 50,* 995–1002.

Sue, D. W., Carter, R. T., Casa, J. M., Fouad, N. A., Ivey, A. E., Jensen, M., et al. (1998). *Multicultural counseling competencies: Individual and organizational development.* Thousand Oaks, CA: Sage.

Summerall, S., Lopez, S. J., & Oehlert, M. E. (2000). *Competency-based education and training in psychology.* Springfield, IL: Charles C Thomas.

Thompson, A. S., & Super, D. E. (Eds.). (1964). *The professional preparation of counseling psychologists: Report of the 1964 Greyston conference.* New York: Bureau of Publications, Teachers College, Columbia University.

Wampold, B. E. (2001). *The great psychotherapy debate: Models, methods, and findings.* Mahwah, NJ: Lawrence Erlbaum.

Wampold, B. E. (2006). Not a scintilla of evidence to support empirically supported treatments as more effective than other treatments. In J. C. Norcross, L. E. Beutler, & R. F. Levant (Eds.), *Evidence-based practices in mental health* (pp. 299–308). Washington, D.C.: American Psychological Association.

Westin, D., & Weinberger, J. (2004). When clinical descriptions becomes statistical prediction. *American Psychologist, 59,* 593–613.

Williams, A. (1995). *Visual and active supervision: Roles, focus, technique*. New York: Norton.

Wrenn, C. G. (1962). The culturally-encapsulated counselor. *Harvard Educational Review, 32*, 44–49.

Chapter Five

Multicultural Competence

Clinical Practice, Training and Supervision, and Research

Madonna G. Constantine
Jairo N. Fuertes[1]
Gargi Roysircar
Mai M. Kindaichi

Population estimates indicate that people of color (i.e., Black/African American, Asian/Asian American, Latino/a American, Native Hawaiian and other Pacific Islanders, and Native Americans) currently comprise about 35% of the population of the United States (U.S. Census Bureau, 2004). It is projected that by the year 2050, the percentage of individuals who self-identify as White American or Caucasian will decrease by over 10%, and the overall percentage of individuals who self-identify as Black, Latino/a, and Asian American will increase to about 50% of the population (U.S. Census Bureau, 2004). In light of the increased diversity of the U.S. population overall, and of the population of mental health service consumers specifically, counseling psychologists have studied and documented the significant and unmet mental health needs of racially and culturally diverse individuals (Constantine, 2007a).

The visibility of counseling psychologists in the field-wide advance of multicultural issues in psychology coincided with the publication of the Division 17 Position Paper (Sue et al., 1982), in which specific competencies in working with culturally diverse individuals were organized into three broad areas that addressed counselors' cultural attitudes/beliefs, knowledge, and skills to intervene effectively in practice. The initial presentation of the tripartite model of multicultural counseling competence, to be described in greater detail later, set in motion a wave of research pertaining to counseling psychologists' ability to provide culturally responsive counseling, as well as the development of several quantitative instruments that have been used extensively in research pertaining to multicultural counseling competence (see Constantine & Ladany, 2001; Ponterotto, Fuertes, & Chen, 2000, for reviews). Furthermore, numerous informative conceptual models have emerged in concert with research addressing the mental health concerns of people of color, therapeutic experiences of people of color, and the degree to which counseling psychologists can provide responsive care within a field that is bound by a historical base in Western, Eurocentric cultural values (Ridley, 2005).

In this chapter, models of multicultural counseling (i.e., frameworks that provide guidance regarding expectations of effective therapy, counselors' and clients' roles in therapy, and ways to understand dynamics that contribute to beneficial therapeutic processes and outcomes) are summarized. Although numerous models and frameworks have been presented in the literature, those summarized reflect examples of frameworks that address variables regarding the interplay of client and counselor cultural variables in multicultural counseling. In addition, this chapter discusses important considerations for therapists providing culturally competent mental health services to clients of color. The chapter also summarizes salient issues regarding multicultural training and supervision that have been addressed in the multicultural competence literature. Finally, the chapter reviews research in the area of multicultural counseling competence and identifies future research directions in this important area.

MODELS OF MULTICULTURAL COUNSELING

Tripartite Model of Multicultural Counseling

For nearly 25 years, the tripartite model of multicultural counseling, initially presented by Sue and his colleagues (1982) and subsequently reformulated (Sue, Arredondo, & McDavis, 1992; Sue et al., 1998), has been a critical part of research, training, and practice in multicultural counseling. In this model, multicultural counseling competence is characterized by three basic domains, namely (a) counselors' awareness of their culturally based beliefs, attitudes, and potential biases that might influence their therapeutic perceptions and subsequent therapeutic dynamics; (b) counselors' knowledge of the unique dimensions of clients' worldviews, the historical backgrounds of diverse cultural groups, and current sociopolitical influences on diverse groups; and (c) multicultural counseling skills, or counselors' ability to devise and implement prevention and intervention strategies that are relevant to clients' cultural values, beliefs, and expectations. The language of the tripartite model uses an inclusive definition of "diverse," such that differences and similarities across multiple social locations and cultural variables are considered (e.g., race, ethnicity, gender, sexual orientation, social class, religious orientation, age, and ability status).

The multicultural counseling competencies were conceptualized originally as 11 specified areas of professional attention with regard to working effectively with culturally diverse populations (Sue et al., 1982). A decade later, in response to advances in the literature and movements within counseling psychology organizations, Sue et al. (1992) expanded these 11 competencies to 31, while retaining the original tripartite model. In 1996, Arredondo and her colleagues clarified constructs that had not been explicated clearly in the 1992 article, such as "diversity" and "multicultural," and articulated competencies that had been vague. In the most recent iteration of the tripartite model (Sue et al., 1998), culturally competent counselors' ability to develop culturally sensitive organizations were included as part of the multicultural counseling competencies.

Although the tripartite model of multicultural competence explicates expected behaviors characteristic of counselors who are (a) culturally self-aware, (b) knowledgeable about diverse cultural groups' histories and present contexts, and (c) skillful in integrating their awareness and knowledge in formulating and implementing responsive care, limited reference is made explicitly to therapeutic processes, including clients' experiences of their therapists and the interplay of clients' and counselors' cultural identities in multicultural counseling. In years following Sue et al.'s (1982) initial tripartite model of multicultural counseling competence, several scholars offered conceptual models of multicultural counseling competence with regard to interpersonal processes in therapy. Several of these relevant models are summarized here.

Helms's (1984) Interactional Counseling Process Model

In an effort to describe and understand potential counseling dynamics that emerge from differences and similarities in individuals' racial consciousness, rather than race as a demographic variable, Helms (1984) proposed an interactional counseling process model. Counseling dyads are described in terms of the combination of the counselors' and clients' racial identity development (i.e., one's sense of collective identity with a given racial group, which informs cognitive and emotional processes about the self and racially different others over the course of time and circumstance; Helms, 1995). The interactional counseling process model relies on racial identity development models pertaining to White people and people of color, and the degree to which there is convergence or divergence in their relative development toward a transcendent, nonracist identity and their attitudes toward Whites and people of color.

Helms and Cook (1999) provided a summary of racial identity statuses relevant to people of color as they move from an externally defined cultural identity toward an appreciation of one's collective identities and connection with other marginalized groups: *conformity/pre-encounter* (i.e., cultural self-definition that is congruent with dominant White standards and devaluing), *dissonance/encounter* (i.e., confusion and ambivalence about one's cultural self-definition, sparked by a discrete interaction or the course of several interactions), *immersion* (i.e., idealization of one's racial reference group and denigration of that which is perceived to be associated with White culture), *emersion* (i.e., a sense of pride and solidarity that comes with surrounding oneself with racially similar others), *internalization* (i.e., positive commitment and acceptance of a positive racial self-definition), and *integrative awareness* (i.e., valuing multiple cultural and collective identities and empathy with other denigrated cultural groups).

Similarly, Helms and Cook (1999) summarized White racial identity statuses that described the movement from (a) passive acceptance and nonquestioning of the status quo that imbues White people with societal privileges because of their membership in the White racial group to (b) the capacity and willingness to relinquish such privileges in an effort toward adopting a nonracist identity. These statuses included: *contact* (i.e., obliviousness to one's role as a beneficiary and participant in the maintenance of White privilege), *disintegration* (i.e., anxiety brought about through confrontation with circumstances that speak to racial inequities), *reintegration* (i.e., idealization of one's racial group and associated behaviors and preferences), *pseudo-independence* (i.e., intellectualized interest and acknowledgement of racial inequities without affective ownership of one's role in perpetuating racism), *immersion* (i.e., search for a personal meaning of whiteness that is informed by affective restructuring), *emersion* (i.e., feeling positively about associating with progressive and committed White people), and *autonomy* (i.e., an adoption of a restructured definition of whiteness that is committed to nonparticipation in racist systems).

As mentioned, the descriptors used to characterize the counseling dyad reflect the degree of convergence or divergence in counselors' and clients' racial identity ego statuses, respective to the distribution of power in the dyad (namely that counselors are in a position of power relative to clients). Drawing from studies regarding supervisory dyads (Constantine, Warren, & Miville, 2005; Ladany, Brittan-Powell, & Pannu, 1997), as well as Helms's (1984) original description, interactional dyads may be categorized as: progressive (i.e., the counselor exhibits greater levels of racial-cultural self-and other-awareness than the client); regressive (i.e., the counselor exhibits less racial-cultural awareness than the client); parallel-high (i.e., both counselor and client are at comparable advanced levels of racial-cultural awareness); and parallel-low (i.e., both counselor and client are at similarly lower levels of racial-cultural awareness).

In their examination of cross-racial counseling dyads, Carter and Helms (1992) reported client and counselor reactions to parallel, progressive, and regressive interactions in which racial content was introduced. Both counselors and clients perceived parallel interactions as smooth, though it was suggested that mutual discomfort with racial content led to avoidance of racial issues. By contrast, racial content was addressed in dyads characterized as progressive and regressive dyads, such that counselors in progressive dyads appeared to provide an opportunity to explore racial attitudes safely, whereas clients in regressive dyads appeared frustrated with counselors' reactions (e.g., avoidance and blaming the client for her or his struggles). Therefore, in an effort to provide environments for culturally diverse clients to feel safe and heard when discussing race-related experiences and concerns, and to address racial dynamics that may evidence in the room, counselors and counseling psychologists benefit client care through their own active exploration of their racial identity.

Atkinson, Thompson, and Grant's Three-Dimensional Model

Atkinson, Thompson, and Grant (1993) formulated a three-dimensional model of multicultural counseling that was characterized by the consideration of three client-based characteristics: clients' level of acculturation (i.e., the degree to which clients adopt the beliefs, values, and customary behaviors associated with the majority or host culture); the extent to which the goal of counseling is preventative or remedial; and the perceived locus of the presenting concern, namely the extent to which a problem is externally derived (e.g., oppression or a toxic work environment) or internally based (e.g., poor impulse control or mood swings). Based on these three axes, helping professionals can determine which role(s) might be most effective in addressing clients' needs in the context of certain culturally relevant variables.

The three axes intersect at eight points to form a cube, wherein eight helping roles can be identified. Helping roles related to lower levels of client acculturation include adviser (e.g., the helper guides clients in navigating new environments that might be potentially stressful in the future), advocate (e.g., the helper intervenes on behalf of clients who have been discriminated against), facilitator of indigenous healing methods (e.g., the helper refers clients to an indigenous healer of their cultural background to aid them in remedying their inner conflicts), and facilitator of indigenous support systems (e.g., the helper can learn about culturally congruent groups with whom clients may affiliate in an effort to increase their social network).

For clients who appear more highly acculturated to dominant American cultural experiences, Atkinson et al. (1993) discussed four complimentary roles: consultant (e.g., the helper informs clients of potential external causes of distress in a new environment), change agent (e.g., a helper whose clientele includes a group of professional women who share similar encounters of discomfort at the workplace related to gender biases may contribute to social efforts to bring awareness to sexual harassment issues), counselor (e.g., a helper aids clients in preventing the onset of distresses that have an internal source, such as procrastination) and psychotherapist (e.g., the helper intervenes to aid clients as they are struggling with anxieties related to a heightened and persistent fear).

Although Atkinson et al.'s (1993) model has been well received generally, only one study (Atkinson, Kim, & Caldwell, 1998) has tested their model empirically. More specifically, Atkinson et al. (1998) presented eight vignettes to both psychologists and Asian American university students, each of whom separately rated the anticipated effectiveness of and preference for the eight different helping roles for each vignette. The surveyed psychologists demonstrated an ability to differentiate helping roles relative to client variables described in the vignettes as expected; however, the perceived helpfulness of the advisor role and advocate role did not receive empirical support. Surveyed university students provided higher ratings for the recommended roles of facilitator of indigenous support systems, consultant, and change agent, as expected by the researchers; that both psychologists and the university students endorsed the helpfulness of seemingly nontraditional helping roles (e.g., facilitator of indigenous support systems) appears to provide support for the importance of providing services that are culturally congruent with clients' acculturation levels.

Atkinson et al.'s (1993) model of multicultural counseling provides unique insights into how counselors might understand counseling dynamics in light of the influences of specific cultural variables (e.g., level of acculturation) on counseling processes and outcomes. More specifically, Atkinson et al.'s (1993) model identifies specific roles that counselors can adopt when considering the interplay of aspects of clients' cultural identity with the goals of care and perceived origin of the clients' concern. However, it can be argued that level of acculturation in isolation fails to encompass the multiple cultural exchanges that exist over the course of counseling.

The models of multicultural counseling presented by Fischer, Jome, and Atkinson (1998), Constantine and Ladany (2000), and Neville and Mobley (2001) provide frameworks that describe multicultural competence with reference to the development of a viable working relationship between counselors and clients in the context of cultural differences and similarities and the cultural characteristics of the counseling endeavor itself.

Fischer, Jome, and Atkinson's (1998) Common Factors Model

Fischer et al. (1998), in their extensive review of multicultural counseling literature, used a common factors approach to organize studies that examined different aspects of counseling processes within culturally specific frameworks. In essence, the common factors framework draws attention to core elements of helping that transcend theoretical orientation, and are conceptualized to be universal across helping and healing strategies among diverse cultures. The four universal healing contexts that Fischer et al. identified were (a) the therapeutic relationship (e.g., the bond, confidence, and safety shared between helpers and clients); (b) a shared worldview between helpers and clients (e.g., a common framework, way of making meaning, and setting expectations within the context of their relationship); (c) clients' expectations of the helpfulness of the given form of help; and (d) the rituals or interventions (e.g., helping techniques used to bring about relief and/or address clients' identified distress) that helpers enact in their positions.

Rather than suggesting a one-size-fits-all model of counseling and psychotherapy, Fischer et al. suggested that counselors and helpers need to evaluate how they can enhance the therapeutic relationship, encourage a convergence in worldviews, meet and raise clients' expectations, and use culturally relevant interventions in an effort to attend to clients' experiences holistically and effectively. In this respect, Fischer et al. asserted that "the skeleton of universal healing factors requires the flesh of cultural knowledge" (p. 525) in order for helping processes to be meaningful. Because it can be argued that all counseling is multicultural to some extent, Fischer et al.'s common factors model underscored the importance of clinicians' multicultural counseling competence to identify and attend to cultural considerations that shape the aforementioned helping processes with all clients. It appears that Fischer et al. provided a theory in which multicultural counseling competence is superordinate to general counseling skills.

In an application of the common factors framework, a counseling outreach prevention service (Roysircar, Gard, Hubbell, & Ortega, 2005) provided English as a Second Language (ESL) students in the schools with opportunities to talk, ask and answer questions, or otherwise actively engage in language learning. Specifically, counselors and ESL students in

10 individual sessions engaged in natural conversations on festivals, historical events, geographic locations, foods, and family events. Through these conversations, the counselors showed respect for and responsiveness to cultural and personal diversity. Counselors who were rated to have followed multicultural practice guidelines more closely and to have expressed less disconnection/distance from their ESL clients had clients who self-reported significantly higher persistence, satisfaction with services, well-being, and relationship scores than other ESL clients whose counselors were perceived to have provided less multiculturally competent service. The differences in effect size were large. In another outcome study (Roysircar, Pimpinella, Spanakis, & Vincent, 2006), observer ratings on the Cultural Diversity Observer Rating Scale (CDORS) improved for counselors' helping behaviors and counselors' barriers and frustrations at the end session, whereas perceptions of teachers' adaptive behaviors were higher for ESL students whose mentors received higher CDORS ratings than for those whose mentors received lower CDORS ratings.

Constantine and Ladany's (2001) Model of Multicultural Counseling Competence

Building on the tripartite model of multicultural counseling competence and Fischer et al.'s (1998) common factors model, Constantine and Ladany (2001) presented an expanded model of multicultural counseling competence. In their model, multicultural counseling competence is not considered an end state, but rather a commitment to ongoing enhancement of counselors' awareness, knowledge, and skills pertaining to helping culturally diverse clients. The six components of Constantine and Ladany's model reflect a focus on core processes, such as the development and continuance of a trusted relationship and belief in the efficacy of the means of helping, as well as counselor-based competencies. For example, *counselor self-awareness* involves the degree to which counselors can identify the influences of multiple cultural identities and socialization experiences on the lenses through which they perceive, evaluate, conceptualize, and treat clients. Counselors' *general knowledge about multicultural issues* encompasses counselors' investment in building their understanding about diverse psychological experiences relevant to living in a culturally pluralistic society. Drawing from empirical studies that had argued that self-report instruments designed to measure multicultural counseling competence may be subject to impression management effects and not related statistically to demonstrated cultural sensitivity (e.g., Constantine & Ladany, 2000), *multicultural counseling self-efficacy* was identified as an aspect of multicultural counseling competence;

multicultural counseling self-efficacy speaks to counselors' beliefs that they can enact skills and behaviors that contribute to effective treatment with diverse clients. Multiculturally competent counselors also are thought to possess an understanding of how *unique client variables,* such as personality style or family of origin dynamics, and situational factors may interact to affect clients' self-presentations and psychological experiences. The ability to co-construct and maintain effective *working alliances,* which refer to clients' and counselors' agreement about the goals and tasks of treatment and their interpersonal therapeutic bond, provides the foundation for culturally responsive care. Lastly, *multicultural counseling skills* includes counselors' abilities to address multicultural issues effectively, including their sensitivity in identifying cultural-related content and dynamics.

Neville and Mobley's (2001) Ecological Model of Multicultural Counseling Processes

Drawing from ecological models of human development, Neville and Mobley (2001) presented a nonlinear ecological model of multicultural counseling processes (EMMCCP) to illustrate various sociocultural influences on counseling processes. In the development of the EMMCCP, Neville and Mobley posed three assumptions: (a) personal characteristics influence individuals' encounters with their social environments; (b) culture necessarily influences human behavior; and (c) there are social hierarchies related to various demographic domains, including race, class, gender, and sexual identity, that inform our self- and other-perceptions. Thus, both counselors and clients enter the counseling relationship having unique positions socioculturally (i.e., their relative reference group identities) that inform their worldviews and their experiences of others. Further, the counseling dyad itself operates in the contexts of a given helping environment (e.g., counseling center, private practice, hospital, etc.) and systemwide policies and practices related to counseling (e.g., ongoing multicultural counseling training, provision of multilingual services, managed care concerns, etc.). Essentially, as both clients and counselors interact in the consultation office, both parties occupy, represent, and operate from various cultural reference groups that inform their dynamic relationship across social domains. Culturally competent counselors and helping professionals are charged with having a sophisticated appreciation for how cultural dynamics and experiences can shape the counseling relationship and therapeutic processes across multiple levels, and to consider how such dynamics can influence information gathering, assessment, case conceptualization, and treatment.

Summary

From different perspectives, the summarized models place both clients and counselors in larger cultural contexts, and they describe the salience of the interaction of helpers' and clients' cultural identities and what they may represent to each other. Although Helms's (1984) model focused on the interface of counselors' and clients' racial identity attitudes and Atkinson et al.'s (1993) model considered the relevance of clients' levels of acculturation, the models by Constantine and Ladany (2001), Fischer et al. (1998), and Neville and Mobley (2001) integrated the relevance of clients' and counselors' multiple sociocultural identities into broad conceptualizations of multicultural competence.

This is not to say that model specificity or breadth is more or less useful; instead, it can be argued that each of these models has specific explanatory use. For example, Helms's (1984) interactional model can clarify therapeutic disconnections can be experienced by clients who are relatively more racially conscious than their therapists. In addition, Atkinson et al.'s (1993) model can identify culturally relevant roles or approaches that mental health professionals can adopt in working with diverse clients and can address skill sets that helping professionals should be trained to develop in meeting the needs of diverse individuals. Specific multicultural competence training objectives can be extrapolated from Constantine and Ladany's model, while Neville and Mobley's ecological framework explicates levels of awareness that are essential in developing and enacting cultural competence. It also appears that, among these models, Neville and Mobley's and Constantine and Ladany's models speak broadly to how nuances of individual personality variables, cultural variables, and social structures shape therapeutic relationships and counseling; in effect, concepts evident in Fischer et al.'s (1998) articulation of the common factors framework appears to have informed both models. Thus, the "take home" message communicated by the synthesis of the aforementioned models can be that clinicians attend to the dynamic interplay of cultural variables, such as racial identity and acculturation status, as they shape the therapeutic working alliance, operate in clinical interviews and assessments, inform contemporaneous clinical determinations about problem etiology and treatment, and potentially mirror broader sociocultural hierarchies.

MULTICULTURAL COUNSELING PRACTICE

Sue and Zane (1987) recommended that cultural knowledge is made proximal to therapy when it is translated into clinical skills such as case conceptualization, strategies for problem resolution, and the formulation of counseling goals. Knowing how to appropriately categorize experiences as cultural, knowing when to generalize and be inclusive, and knowing when to individualize and be exclusive is a skill- and knowledge-based multicultural competency. For example, among immigrant clients, there might be a divergence from enculturated values, as people struggle to integrate what they learned throughout life and the new cultural information gathered from now living in a different society (Roysircar, 2004). Hence, it would be important that clinicians understand how immigrant clients identify with their cultural group (i.e., ethnic identification), are unconsciously influenced by their cultural socialization (i.e., enculturation), and consciously relate to the White dominant society in the United States (i.e., acculturation; Frey & Roysircar, 2006). In fact, several studies since the 1990s have investigated counseling processes and outcomes when therapists have used culturally responsive approaches.

Clinicians' awareness of diverse cultural values, and knowledge of how cultural values may shape the nature of counseling and helping, may affect therapist-client relationships and clinical treatment approaches in different ways. For instance, in a study on perceived counselor credibility (Sodowsky, 1991), participants of different nationalities viewed a tape of an Asian Indian college student expressing his concern about his desire to change his major from computer science to sociology and how his choice would conflict with his family's expectations for a technology-oriented career. Asian Indian respondents reported that the counselor who used culturally sensitive family- and community-oriented strategies was more expert-like and trustworthy. White Americans, however, gravitated toward the tape where the counselor used treatments consistent with American values of personal autonomy. This study suggested that White American counselors exercise caution not to assume that culturally diverse individuals perceive clinical interactions with the same lenses, or experience given interventions or approaches as equally helpful or meaningful. Similarly, Jencius and Duba (2002) suggested that family systems approaches that are guided by the belief that family members are "a collection of individuals that will eventually move toward individuation" (p. 412) may be incongruent with values characteristic of more collectivistic cultural groups.

Therapists' application of multicultural awareness and knowledge affects the course of therapy from the intake process through the eventual development of the therapeutic relationship. During the initial counseling intake process, clinicians are encouraged to ask clients questions about their cultural backgrounds to glean information about clients' experiences of culture and their senses of cultural identity (Roysircar, 2005). Clients' subjective cultural experiences, as understood through this inquiry, then may be synthesized with or compared to counselors' body of multicultural knowledge. The extent to which counselors possess and are perceived by clients to possess knowledge of diverse cultural experiences may shape these clients' perceptions of the strength of the therapeutic relationship and their personal investment in the helping process. For instance, Pope-Davis et al. (2002) reported that some clients of color accepted the cultural limitations of their therapists, but that they also blamed themselves if their counselors lacked information about people of color. Important pieces of information that these clients thought therapists should know included culture-specific knowledge about family structures and relationships, racism and other forms of discrimination, cultural beliefs about counseling, gender-role issues, communication styles, cultural identity issues, and cultural norms for behavior (Pope-Davis et al., 2002). Furthermore, Thompson, Worthington, and Atkinson (1994) reported that clients of color reported feeling more willing to self-disclose to counselors who addressed racial concerns, as compared to counselors who did not. Both studies suggested that clinicians' willingness to attend to racial and cultural issues can affect clients' perceptions of the safety of the working relationship and their counselors overall.

In the spirit of Helms's (1984) interactional model summarized earlier, Thompson and Jenal (1994) qualitatively examined quasi-counseling interaction between race-avoidant counselors and their clients. The interactional styles that emerged were described as *smooth* (e.g., conceding to counselor), *exasperated* (e.g., hastened, rapid-fire dialogue that would end abruptly), *disjunctive* (e.g., characterized by derailments from conversation or counselors' overexplanations), or *constricted* (e.g., characterized by silence, lack of self-disclosure, and awkward breaks in conversation) interactions. Interactional styles were suggested to be a related to clients' strategies to manage feelings related to race avoidance; for example, clients in smooth-type interactions may have been invested in ensuring harmonious exchanges, while the one client who exhibited the constricted type operated from resistance and possibly veiled hostility. The results of this study suggest that clients, particularly clients of color, react notably to counselors' avoidance of racial content, such that the helping relationship may be negatively affected, or experienced as non-genuine or harmful. Furthermore, Thompson and Jenal's study has implications for the interaction of counselors' and clients' racial identity attitudes, particularly to the extent that counselors who may minimize the importance of race and culture through a non-knowingness (e.g., contact [White racial identity status] or pre-encounter [person of color racial identity status]) or depersonalization (e.g., pseudo-independence [White racial identity status]) may alienate clients of color (c.f., Carter & Helms, 1992).

Over the past 20 years, researchers in counseling psychology have attended to influences of counselors' and clients' race-related attitudes and behaviors on expectations and perceptions of therapy. Many of these studies juxtaposed White counselors with Black clients, either in analogue or actual counseling contexts. For example, Watkins and Terrell (1988) showed that Black clients with higher cultural mistrust attitudes toward Whites expected less from counseling regardless of therapist race; however, they also rated White therapists lower on immediacy and likeability. Thompson et al. (1994) reported that low levels of mistrust were associated with clients sharing a greater number of disclosing statements to Black therapists, whereas high levels of mistrust were associated with a lesser number of disclosing statements to White therapists.

Constantine (2007b) examined the relationships between African American clients' perceptions of racial microaggressions (i.e., subtle and commonplace racial slights or messages) by White therapists, the working alliance, the counselor's general and multicultural competence, and counseling satisfaction. Some of the microaggressions by White therapists were characterized as colorblindness, over-identification with people of color, denial of personal or individual racism, minimization of racial–cultural issues, idealization, and patronization. Constantine (2007b) reported that perceived microaggressions were negatively associated with perceptions of the therapeutic working alliance and with therapists' general and multicultural competence. Because clients of color may be acutely aware of or sensitive to clinicians' behaviors with respect to race and culture, clinicians' awareness of the potential impact of their behaviors on clients is paramount. In an effort to develop cultural self- and other-awareness as a component of multicultural counseling competence, clinicians' commitment to examining the influences of their deliberate and nonconscious interactions with racially and culturally diverse clients is inherent in providing effective care.

Fuertes, Mueller, Chauhan, Walker, and Ladany (2002) qualitatively investigated White American therapists' impressions of their work with African American clients. Therapists reported they were aware of the privilege associated with being White in the United States, the historical legacy of White oppression, and of contemporary racism. Therapists stated they were aware of having been oppressed in some way themselves, of having been oppressors, of having a one-up position with their clients, and recognizing that racism and tension between White Americans and African Americans is reflected in the counseling hour. Facilitative skills they described with respect to their work with African American clients included being direct but sensitive to issues pertaining to race, conveying a sense of openness, and showing acceptance of the historic effects of racism. The therapists reported favorable therapeutic outcomes, including reduced depressive and anxious symptoms, and impressions of therapeutic processes, such as better rapport, increased intimacy, client self-disclosure, and overall improved client participation and involvement in therapy. The therapists also indicated they attended to race as intertwined with various sociocultural factors such as sexism, homophobia, and poverty.

Multiculturally competent practice entails adapting counseling and therapeutic interventions to be more congruent to the cultural values and orientations of non-European or non-White cultural groups. Griner and Smith (2006) performed a meta-analysis of quantitative studies examining mental health interventions that were culturally adapted; often, the studies compared a culturally adapted intervention to one developed from a Western perspective. Of the studies analyzed, 84% explicitly included cultural values and concepts in the intervention. Other interventions included: matching therapist and client based on ethnicity or language, collaborating with cultural experts, and providing extra services. Overall, culturally adapted interventions had a positive effect with a moderate (d = .45) magnitude. These interventions " . . . resulted in significant client improvement across a variety of conditions and outcome measures" (p. 541). The authors found that adaptations that were specific to a cultural group tended to be more effective than general cultural adaptations. The effect sizes also were greater for participants who were older and Hispanic/Latino/a, and for clients who were not matched ethnically with clinicians. However, clients who were matched to therapists based on language had twice as effective outcomes than those who did not, which speaks to the significance of bilingual competence.

Summary

Exercising multicultural competence in clinical practice entails balancing the application of etic cultural knowledge, attention to clients' uniquenesses, and an appreciation for within-group cultural heterogeneity, such that stereotypes derived from less complex descriptions of diverse cultures are avoided (Constantine & Ladany, 2001). Stuart (2004) stated, "There is a very fine line between sensitivity to the implications of a person's membership in a particular group and losing sight of that person's individuality" (p. 6). The studies above have illustrated that multiculturally competent clinical practice builds from multicultural knowledge, learning about clients' unique cultural identities, and recognizing dynamics that may emerge in cross-racial and cross-cultural therapeutic relationships. Furthermore, the research has suggested that multiculturally competent counselors address racial and cultural issues directly in an effort to foster therapeutic relationships where culture has value and relevance; moreover, clients' experiences of their counselors' ability to attend to cultural concerns and their multicultural competence is likely to be enhanced through counselors' willingness to bring culture into the therapeutic space. Finally, these studies have illustrated the complexities of clinicians' racial-cultural self-awareness, particularly regarding their awareness of racial microaggressions, in light of the multiple forces explicated in the ecological model of multicultural counseling put forth by Neville and Mobley (2001). The following section will address training efforts, including multicultural education and supervision, designed to strengthen clinicians' multicultural counseling skills.

MULTICULTURAL TRAINING AND SUPERVISION

Multicultural Training

Over the past few decades, the importance of multicultural training has been recognized within American Psychological Association (APA) and Council for Accreditation for Counseling and Related Educational Programs (CACREP) mandates (Speight, Thomas, Kennel, & Anderson, 1995). For example, in order to obtain APA accreditation, training institutions must demonstrate a cogent plan to provide trainees with knowledge about the roles of diversity in human experience (APA, 1994). Following APA's 1986 mandate to include multicultural education in accreditation requirements, applied psychology graduate programs have reported an increase in their inclusion of multicultural content (Smith, Constantine, Dunn, Dinehart, & Montoya, 2006). Multicultural training clearly has become increasingly acknowledged as an intrinsic factor of general professional training in counseling psychology.

Hills and Strozier (1992) found that nearly 90% of graduate programs in counseling offered at least one course in multicultural counseling content, and other programs offered such training through affiliations with other departments. However, Constantine (1997) noted that 70% of responding supervisors in her study reported they had never taken a multicultural or cross-cultural counseling course formally. As a result, it appears that supervisees may be more likely to have had exposure to multicultural counseling theory and practical experiences in addressing cultural issues than their supervisors (Hird, Cavalieri, Dulko, Felice, & Ho, 2001).

Although multicultural counseling training experiences (e.g., coursework) within counseling psychology programs have increased, the extent to which such experiences exist in practice settings is unclear.

The content and emphases of multicultural counseling training across counseling psychology programs have been found to be highly variable (Ponterotto, Alexander, & Grieger, 1995; Smith et al., 2006). For example, counseling training programs may vary to the degree to which they encourage trainees to adopt emic (i.e., culture-specific), etic (i.e., universalistic), autoplastic (i.e., focusing on the individual as the primary locus of change and intervention), alloplastic (i.e., focusing on the environment as the course of malady and target of change), prevention/ remediation, and idiographic (i.e., integrating and appreciating clients' culture-specific meaning-making strategies) approaches to becoming multiculturally competent (Ridley, Mendoza, & Kanitz, 1994). Therefore, compounding the challenge that training programs may have in identifying multiculturally competent supervisors, it is possible that multicultural training experiences may emphasize the development of multicultural knowledge more than skill development (Smith et al., 2006). It also has been argued that there is little empirical knowledge about how multicultural competence training modifies or enhances counselors' conceptual and intervention skills or even therapeutic outcomes (Ridley et al., 1994).

Smith et al. (2006) conducted a meta-analysis to evaluate the overall effect of multicultural education on trainees and mental health practitioners from both retrospective and outcome perspectives. Based on responses from 45 survey studies, the researchers found that individuals who had completed multicultural education reported higher multicultural competence than those who did not have such education [moderate effect size (d = .49)]. However, this result does not suggest that receiving multicultural education enhances or detracts from qualities of therapeutic processes or outcomes. Based on 37 outcome studies, wherein participants had experienced a multicultural training workshop, program, or semester-long class, the researchers found a large effect size (d = .89), which suggested that individuals who had undergone multicultural training were likely to report strong gains in multicultural competence. Furthermore, Smith et al. reported that multicultural educational interventions that had been designed on the basis of theory and research produced effect sizes nearly twice as large as those interventions that lacked theoretical grounding; in other words, individuals who had participated in theory-driven multicultural education tended to have higher multicultural competence than those who participated in atheoretical multicultural educational experiences. Thus, their study supported previous researchers' calls (e.g., Ridley et al., 1994) for theory-based curricula and programming in multicultural education.

Multicultural Supervision

Multicultural supervision can offer a unique training environment that serves as a primary means of multicultural counseling and therapy skill development (Chen, 2001; Constantine, 1997; Inman, 2006; Kiselica & Maben, 1999). Because the goals of supervision are to foster professional competence in trainees and to promote and protect client welfare, supervisors are charged with understanding and facilitating trainees' understanding of the interplay of culture in interpersonal and therapeutic processes. Counseling training has attended increasingly to multicultural concerns in supervision. Despite the growing literature on multicultural competence in supervision, including empirical research (e.g., Constantine et al., 2005; Inman, 2006; Ladany, Inman, Constantine, & Hofheinz, 1997), conceptual supervision models (Chen, 2001; Constantine, 1997), and informed practices (Miville, Rosa, & Constantine, 2005), formal multicultural training for supervisors is lacking (Constantine & Sue, 2007).

Facilitative components of culturally responsive supervision have been identified to include supervisors' awareness of their racial cultural values, openness, vulnerability and self-disclosure, sincere commitment to attending to and exploring cultural factors, and providing opportunities for multicultural activities (e.g., Fukuyama, 1994). In addition, qualitative studies have suggested supervisors initiate and address racial, cultural, and power-related concerns early and throughout supervisory relationships; inquire about supervisees' culture; and address cultural dynamics evidenced in the supervisory dyad (Constantine, 1997, 2003; Duan & Roehlke, 2001; Fukuyama, 1994; Hird et al., 2001). In a qualitative study examining multicultural supervision across diverse supervisory dyads, Toporek, Ortega-Villalobos, and Pope-Davis (2004) reported that supervisors and supervisees believed that critical incidents improved their multicultural awareness, skill set, confidence to discuss racial and cultural concerns, and exposure to personal experiences of cultural differences.

Multicultural supervisory experiences serve as models of supervisees to raise race- and culture-related concerns, which may shape ultimately how supervisees interact with their clients (Kiselica & Maben, 1999; Miville et al., 2005). Although fostering such discussions may contribute to trainees' cultural competence and responsive client care, it also is possible for supervisors to engage in behaviors that can influence supervisory experiences negatively. For example, some supervisors may inhibit supervisees' emotional processing of race- and culture-related concerns for their own fears of being perceived as insensitive or ignorant (e.g., Constantine, 1997; Toporek et al., 2004). In addition, supervisors may minimize the importance of addressing racial and cultural concerns within the client-trainee and trainee-supervisor dyads, thereby omitting potentially salient lenses through which individuals experience the world. Moreover, supervisors themselves who have not engaged in racial-cultural identity development activities (e.g., reflection, racial-cultural awareness, building their theoretical knowledge of mental health concerns across races, etc.) may inhibit their supervisees' multicultural competence.

Supervisors' journeys in exploring their racial identity and their awareness of racial issues can influence supervisees' experiences in supervision and supervisees' multicultural counseling competence. Ladany, Brittan-Powell, et al. (1997) found that supervisees' experiences of their working relationship with their supervisors were related positively to their perceptions of the racial identity attitudes of their supervisors. Furthermore, trainees who have received supervision addressing racial-cultural issues have been found to have higher rates of self-reported and demonstrated multicultural counseling competence (e.g., Constantine, 2001a; Ladany, Inman, et al., 1997). In addition, Constantine et al. (2005) reported that White supervisees whose White supervisors endorsed racial identity attitudes that were more mature or equally as mature as their supervisees obtained higher self-reported multicultural counseling competence and multicultural case conceptualization ability scores than did their peers whose supervisors had equally less developed racial identity attitudes.

Hird, Tao, and Gloria (2005) found that supervisors of color rated themselves higher on multicultural counseling competence than White supervisors, and that the former spent more time discussing cultural issues in supervision than the latter. They also found that White supervisors spent more time discussing cultural issues with their supervisees of color than with their White supervisees. Inman (2006) found that supervisees' ratings of their supervisors' multicultural counseling competence were positively associated with their ratings of the supervisory working alliance and satisfaction with supervision, but negatively associated with their multicultural case conceptualization of etiology. These last two studies presented are seminal in that they examine more directly, or in a more applied fashion, the effect of supervisors' and supervisees' multicultural counseling competence on the process and outcome of supervision, such as the time devoted in supervision to discussing multicultural issues, the effect on the supervisory alliance, and satisfaction.

Supervisors' multicultural competence and racial-cultural awareness have complex implications for supervisees' training experiences and the welfare of clients (Chen, 2001). Moreover, as one of many interpersonal experiences, the ways in which racial and cultural concerns are discussed may affect the parties involved on deeply personal levels. Recently, a qualitative study explored Black trainees' experiences of racial microaggressions in supervision (Constantine & Sue, 2007), suggesting that White supervisors may discount the importance of race-related factors and experiences, hesitate to provide feedback for fear of being racist, make stereotypic assumptions about supervisees and clients, focus on supervisees' weaknesses, or offer culturally insensitive treatment suggestions. This study exemplified the power of supervisors' multicultural competence, or limitations thereof, on supervisees' practical multicultural training experiences and, subsequently, clients' well-being.

Summary

Recent studies have underscored the power that multicultural didactic and clinical training experiences may have on applied psychology trainees' multicultural competence. As Smith et al. (2006) noted, trainees who reported having multicultural education were more likely to report higher levels of multicultural competence. Whereas multicultural education, particularly that which is held in the classroom, may enhance trainees' knowledge base of the historical and contemporary experiences of people of color, effective multicultural supervision can serve as a model for trainees to approach, address, and process issues related to race and culture in therapeutic relationships. Moreover, whereas multicultural education can foster knowledge and aspects of cultural self-awareness, effective multicultural supervision can foster therapeutic skill development and attention to cultural dynamics that can influence the therapeutic relationship, in essence, multicultural education and multicultural supervision can complement each other over the course of trainees' development and beyond. It appears that the research regarding multicultural supervision parallels many findings regarding multicultural counseling practice, particularly to the degree that supervisors' and clinicians' awareness of racial-cultural dynamics as they emerge in vivo and their willingness to address culture in a non-stereotyped manner may enhance the working relationship and growth in trainees and clients, respectively. Future research should address the supervisory triad and assess how *clients* experience specific gains through supervisors' and trainees' multicultural education and supervision (Chen, 2001).

MULTICULTURAL COUNSELING RESEARCH

This final section of the chapter summarizes empirical research in the area of multicultural competence and is organized into three areas: empirical studies on correlates of multicultural competence, studies that have examined the multicultural competencies directly with respect to counseling/therapy, and multicultural competence studies conducted specifically with school counselors. The relatively high number of articles in this area and space limitations for this chapter prevent a detailed review and critique of each article. Thus, the presentation that follows has been integrated into broad themes.

One area of research on this topic has concerned the examination of factors associated with such competence, most often with graduate students and professionals in counseling. For example, a consistent finding in the literature is that greater multicultural training and education are associated with higher levels of multicultural competence (see Arthur, 2000; Constantine, 2001b; Pope-Davis, Reynolds, Dings, & Ottavi, 1994; Sodowsky, Kuo-Jackson, Richardson, & Corey, 1998). That is, students, therapists, counselors, and psychologists who have had at least one course in multicultural issues tend to report higher levels of multicultural counseling competence. Another consistent theme appears to be the moderate association between self-reports of multicultural counseling competence and more confidence in working with culturally diverse clientele and higher levels of racial identity development (see Constantine, 2002b; Constantine, Juby, & Liang, 2001; Cumming-McCann & Accordino, 2005; Neville, Spanierman, & Doan, 2006; Ottavi, Pope-Davis, & Dings, 1994). Professionals who have achieved some level of multicultural counseling competence feel more efficacious and ready to work with clients who represent an array of human diversity. Research also has shown that students and professionals of color report greater interest and skill in multicultural counseling competence (see Bernal et al., 1999; Holcomb-McCoy & Myers, 1999; King & Howard-Hamilton, 2003; Sodowsky et al., 1998) than do their White counterparts. This finding indicates that multicultural counseling competence may be more of a challenge for White counselors, who happen to be represent the majority of mental health professionals; thus, more attention and resources need to be directed at their training.

A more tentative observation based on the literature is that self-reported multicultural counseling competence may be associated with socially desirable response patterns (Constantine & Ladany, 2000; Sodowsky et al., 1998; Worthington, Mobley, Franks, & Tan, 2000). This issue indicates that the topic of multicultural counseling competence fuels reactions of impression management and self-deception for mental health professionals. Single studies were found in potentially fruitful new areas. Worthington et al. (2000) found a slight positive relationship between self-perceived and observer-rated multicultural competence, and Constantine

(2001a) found that prior multicultural training predicted observer-rated competence. Also, Constantine (2000) reported a moderate relationship between multicultural competence and affective and cognitive empathy. Moore-Thomas (1998) found that therapists' self-ratings of multicultural counseling competence were positively associated with their ratings of general competence, and that multicultural awareness was positively associated with openness to experience.

In more nascent years, Liu, Sheu, and Williams (2004) reported that multicultural counseling competence, research training, and self-efficacy were associated significantly and positively with multicultural research self-efficacy; furthermore, they found that multicultural counseling competence was negatively associated with students' research anxiety as well as students' ratings of their programs as being more practice oriented than science or balanced science-practice. They also found that multicultural counseling competence was positively associated with valuing the utility of research and with their confidence in being able to conduct research. A tentative conclusion that may be derived from the bulk of this research is that the concept of multicultural counseling competence is valid, insofar as it has been found to be associated in theoretically expected ways with an array of measures. It also should be noted that there are several published measures of multicultural counseling competence in the literature now, all with good to excellent psychometric properties of reliability and validity (see Constantine, Gloria, & Ladany, 2002).

Another avenue of research has been the direct examination of multicultural competence in counseling relationships. Constantine (2002a) found a significant level of association between ethnic minority clients ratings of counselor general and multicultural competence and between their ratings of counselor multicultural counseling competence and satisfaction with treatment. Constantine's (2002a) results are consistent with those obtained by Fuertes and Brobst (2002), who found an association between clients' ratings of counselors' multicultural competencies and their ratings of counselors' general competence and empathy. This latter study also found that counselor general competence explained a significant amount of variance in clients' satisfaction with therapy. However, when comparisons were made between Euro-American and ethnic minority clients on satisfaction, counselor multicultural competence explained a large and significant amount of variance for the ethnic minority sample only, above and beyond counselor general competency and empathy. The overlap between multicultural counseling competence and general counseling competence also was evident in the study by Moore-Thomas (1998) cited earlier.

More recently, Fuertes et al. (2006) investigated the role of counselor multicultural competence among 51 therapy dyads in counseling. These authors examined the relationship between counselor multicultural competence and several indices of counseling, such as the working alliance, counselor empathy, counselor social influence, and client and counselor satisfaction. Fuertes et al. found that for counselors, their ratings of the working alliance, but not self-ratings of multicultural counseling competence, were significantly associated with their satisfaction, along with clients' ratings of them on social influence. For clients, ratings of counselor multicultural competence were associated with their satisfaction with counseling, as well as ratings of counselor empathy and of counselor social influence. Fuertes et al., however, did not find a significant association between therapist multicultural counseling competence and general competence. Taken as a whole, the findings from these studies indicate that there is some overlap between therapist competence, broadly defined, and multicultural counseling competence. Fuertes, Bartolomeo, and Nichols (2001) speculated about this latter association and suggested that multicultural counseling competence can only be properly integrated in therapy by therapists who have a solid foundation in general competence skills, such as listening, empathy, probing, and other basic skills.

Some studies have examined therapist multicultural competence using qualitative research methods. Fuertes, Mueller, Chauhan, Walker, and Ladany (2002) conducted interviews with nine European American counseling and clinical psychologists. These psychologists revealed that they generally attended to differences in race between themselves and clients directly and openly within the first two sessions of counseling. This was done generally to acknowledge this difference and to convey to the client comfort and trust; psychologists also intended to engender client trust and participation in therapy. The psychologists saw race as a central component to be discussed, and continually attended to establishing and maintaining a trusting and solid working relationship. They typically saw race-related issues as relevant to clients' concerns. Fuertes et al. found that, despite wide variability in participant theoretical orientation and in client-presenting problems, the psychologists typically reported using Rogerian core skills to engage the client and to establish the relationship. Additionally, they also typically reported using more culture-specific and sensitive interventions to *deepen and strengthen* the therapy relationship. These interventions included relying on their level of racial identity development to understand the client, being attuned to the client's racial identity development and worldview, and, very prominently, attending and effectively intervening to client reports of racism and oppression.

Pope-Davis et al. (2002) used grounded theory to account for clients' perspectives of multicultural counseling. Clients were 10 racially/ethnically diverse undergraduate students who had experienced individual counseling with a counselor who they deemed culturally different from them. The results indicated that clients' perceptions of multicultural counseling competence and counseling were contingent on clients' needs/issues in counseling, and that these needs were influenced by client characteristics (e.g., client expectations, role of family and support), the counseling relationship (e.g., equity and power in the relationship), client processes (e.g., salience of culture in relationships, educating the counselor), and client appraisals of the counseling experience. The author noted the importance of understanding client variables in counseling, for example, by noting that clients who did not see culture as influencing their interpersonal relationships placed less importance on counselor multicultural counseling competence. The authors underscored the importance of context for clients in order to truly understand the process and outcome of treatment for them. Findings from these two studies highlight the importance of therapist skill in the nuances of relating with their clients in sensitive and informed ways, and the importance of the discussion in therapy as being based on therapists' understanding of clients' needs, particularly with respect to the salience of race, culture, and racism in their everyday life and as a possible mediating factor of their problems.

We now turn to research on multicultural counseling competence in school guidance. Constantine et al. (2001) surveyed school counselors. Results from their study indicated that multicultural education was positively predictive of self-reported multicultural counseling knowledge, but not multicultural awareness, and that two aspects of universal-diverse orientation (i.e., individuals' concurrent ability to appreciate the similarities and differences among people), diversity of contact (i.e., exposure to culturally diverse others) and relativistic appreciation (i.e., having an appreciation for culturally diverse others), were significantly predictive of multicultural counseling knowledge, after controlling for prior multicultural education. Only diversity of contact was positively associated with multicultural awareness, above and beyond multicultural education.

Constantine (2002b), in a study of school counselors in training, found that attitudes about racism and counselors' White racial identity were negatively associated with self-rated multicultural counseling competence, after controlling for multicultural education. She also found that disintegration of racial identity attitudes was associated with lower ratings of multicultural counseling competence. Constantine and Yeh (2001) noted that both prior multicultural training and independent self-construal (i.e., an individual's sense of self in relation to others) were positively associated with self-reported multicultural competence for women, but not for men. In another study, Constantine (2001b) surveyed master's-level students in school counselor training programs regarding their self-reported multicultural competence, empathy, and multicultural education. Results indicated that empathy was significantly associated with multicultural counseling competence, above and beyond the significant associations of multicultural education and counselor theoretical orientation. These results are consistent with those observed with therapists, psychologists, and students, in that there seem to be solid associations for school counselors between multicultural counseling competence and previous training in multicultural counseling.

Holcomb-McCoy (2001) found that elementary school counselors reported high levels of multicultural counseling competence, particularly on dimensions of multicultural terminology and awareness, but less so on dimensions of racial identity and multicultural knowledge. Previous education and professional work experience were not significantly associated with multicultural competence. Holcomb-McCoy (2005) surveyed professional school counselors and found that the respondents were partly competent across domains of multicultural competence, particularly if they had an entry-level course in multicultural counseling. However, participants' sex, school setting, or years of professional experience were not significantly related to multicultural competence.

Future Research Directions

Future research in the area of multicultural counseling competence is warranted with regard to several vital issues. For example more applied, outcome-oriented research is needed in counseling and therapy (e.g., Roysircar et al., 2005), with the goal of advancing the knowledge base on multicultural counseling competence; data from such studies ultimately may show the value added to assessment, intervention, and education when professionals are proficient in multicultural counseling competence. In addition, research in this area could possibly inform the current state of theory development in multicultural counseling competence, as well as inform clinical practice. There also seems to be interest, but not much available research, on the part of health care professionals and funding agencies, in knowing how multicultural counseling competence may improve health care practices and address the irrefutable evidence showing there is racism in medicine and mental health (Department of Health and Human Services, 2001).

ENDNOTE

1. Because the second and third authors contributed equally to this chapter, their names appear alphabetically.

BIBLIOGRAPHY

American Psychological Association. (1994). *Guidelines and principles for accreditation of programs in professional psychology.* Washington, DC: Author.

American Psychological Association. (2003). Guidelines on multicultural education, training, research, practice, and organizational change for psychologists. *American Psychologist, 58,* 377–402.

Arredondo, P., Toporek, R., Brown, S. P., Jones, J., Locke, D. C., Sanchez, J., et al. (1996). Operationalization of the multicultural counseling competencies. *Journal of Multicultural Counseling and Development, 24,* 42–78.

Arthur, N. (2000, April). Predictive characteristics of multicultural counselling competence. Paper presented at the annual conference of the American Educational Research Association, New Orleans, LA.

Atkinson, D. R., Kim, B. S. K., & Caldwell, R. (1998). Ratings of helper roles by multicultural psychologists and Asian American students: Initial support for the three-dimensional model of multicultural counseling. *Journal of Counseling Psychology, 45,* 414–423.

Atkinson, D. R., Thompson, C. E., & Grant, S. K. (1993). A three-dimensional model for counseling racial/ethnic minorities. *The Counseling Psychologist, 21,* 257–277.

Bernal, M. E., Sirolli, A. A., Weisser, S. K., Ruiz, J. A., Chamberlain, V. J., & Knight, G. P. (1999). Relevance of multicultural training to students' applications to clinical psychology programs. *Cultural Diversity and Ethnic Minority Psychology, 5,* 43–55.

Carlson, M. H., Brack, C. J., Laygo, R., Cohen, R., & Kirkscey, M. (1998). An exploratory study of multicultural competence of counselors in training: Support for experiential skills building. *The Clinical Supervisor, 17,* 75–87.

Carter, R. T., & Helms, J. E. (1992). The counseling process as defined by relationship types: A test of Helms's interactional model. *Journal of Multicultural Counseling and Development, 20,* 181–201.

Chen, E. C. (2001). Multicultural counseling supervision: An interactional approach. In J. G. Ponterotto, J. M. Casas, L. A. Suzuki, & C. M. Alexander (Eds.), *Handbook of multicultural counseling* (2nd ed., pp. 801–824). Thousand Oaks, CA: Sage.

Constantine, M. G. (1997). Facilitating multicultural competency in counseling supervision: Operationalizing a practical framework. In D. B. Pope-Davis & H. L. K. Coleman (Eds.), *Multicultural counseling competencies: Assessment, education and training, and supervision* (pp. 310–324). Thousand Oaks, CA: Sage.

Constantine, M. G. (2000). Social desirability attitudes, sex, and affective and cognitive empathy as predictors of self-reported multicultural counseling competence. *The Counseling Psychologist, 28,* 857–872.

Constantine, M. G. (2001a). Predictors of observer ratings of multicultural counseling competence in Black, Latino, and White American trainees. *Journal of Counseling Psychology, 48*, 456–462.

Constantine, M. G. (2001b). Theoretical orientation, empathy, and multicultural counseling competence in school counselor trainees. *Professional School Counseling, 4*, 342–348.

Constantine, M. G. (2002a). Predictors of satisfaction with counseling: Racial and ethnic minority clients' attitudes toward counseling and ratings of their counselors' general and multicultural counseling competence. *Journal of Counseling Psychology, 49*, 255–263.

Constantine, M. G. (2002b). Racism attitudes, White racial identity attitudes, and multicultural counseling competence in school counselor trainees. *Counselor Education and Supervision, 41*, 162–174.

Constantine, M. G. (2003). Multicultural competence in supervision: Issues, processes, and outcomes. In D. B. Pope-Davis, H. L. K. Coleman, W. M. Liu, & R. L. Toporek (Eds.), *Handbook of multicultural competencies in counseling and psychology* (pp. 383–391). Thousand Oaks, CA: Sage.

Constantine, M. G. (Ed.). (2007a). *Clinical practice with people of color: A guide to becoming culturally competent*. New York: Teachers College Press.

Constantine, M. G. (2007b). Racial microaggressions against African American clients in cross-racial counseling relationships. *Journal of Counseling Psychology, 54*, 1–16.

Constantine, M. G., & Gainor, K. A. (2001). Emotional intelligence and empathy: Their relation to school counselors' multicultural knowledge and awareness. *Professional School Counseling, 5*, 131–137.

Constantine, M. G., & Ladany, N. (2000). Self-report multicultural counseling competence scales: Their relation to social desirability attitudes and multicultural case conceptualization ability. *Journal of Counseling Psychology, 47*, 155–164.

Constantine, M. G., & Ladany, N. (2001). New visions for defining and assessing multicultural counseling competence. In J. G. Ponterotto, J. M. Casas, L. A. Suzuki, & C. M. Alexander (Eds.). *Handbook of multicultural counseling* (2nd ed., pp. 482–498). Thousand Oaks, CA: Sage.

Constantine, M. G., & Sue, D. W. (2007). Perceptions of racial microaggressions among Black supervisees in cross-racial dyads. *Journal of Counseling Psychology, 54*, 142–153.

Constantine, M. G., & Yeh, C. J. (2001). Multicultural training, self-construals, and multicultural competence of school counselors. *Professional School Counseling, 4*, 202–207.

Constantine, M. G., Arorash, T. J., Barakett, M. D., Blackmon, S. M., Donnelly, P. C., & Edles, P. A. (2001). School counselors' universal-diverse orientation and aspects of their multicultural counseling competence. *Professional School Counseling, 5*, 13–18.

Constantine, M. G., Gloria, A. M., & Ladany, N. (2002). The factor structure underlying three self-report multicultural counseling competence scales. *Cultural Diversity and Ethnic Minority Psychology, 8*, 334–345.

Constantine, M. G., Juby, H. L., & Liang, J. J-C. (2001). Examining multicultural counseling competence and race-related attitudes among White marital and family therapists. *Journal of Marital and Family Therapy, 27*, 353–362.

Constantine, M. G., Warren, A. K., & Miville, M. L. (2005). White racial identity dyadic interactions in supervision: Implications for supervisees' multicultural counseling competence. *Journal of Counseling Psychology, 52*, 490–496.

Cumming-McCann, A., & Accordino, M. P. (2005). An investigation of rehabilitation counselor characteristics, White racial attitudes, and self-reported multicultural counseling competencies. *Rehabilitation Counseling Bulletin, 48*, 167–176.

D'Andrea, M., Daniels, J., & Heck, R. (1991). Evaluating the impact of multicultural counseling training. *Journal of Counseling and Development, 70*, 143–150.

Department of Health and Human Services (2001). *Mental health: Culture, race, and ethnicity: A supplement to mental health: A report of the surgeon general.* Retrieved February 26, 2007, from http://mentalhealth. samhsa.gov/cre/ch2_racism_discrimination_and_mental_health.asp

Diaz-Lazaro, C. M., & Cohen, B. B. (2001). Cross-cultural contact in counseling training. *Journal of Multicultural Counseling and Development, 29*, 41–56.

Duan, C., & Roehlke, H. A. (2001). A descriptive "snapshot" of cross-racial supervision in university counseling center internships. *Journal of Multicultural Counseling and Development, 29*, 131–146.

Evans, K. M., & Foster, V. A. (2000). Relationships among multicultural training, moral development, and racial identity development of White counseling students. *Counseling and Values, 45*, 39–48.

Fischer, A. R., Jome, L. M., & Atkinson, D. R. (1998). Reconceptualizing multicultural counseling: Universal healing conditions in a culturally specific context. *The Counseling Psychologist*, 26, 525–588.

Frey, M., & Roysircar, G. (2006). South and East Asian international students' perceived prejudice, acculturation, and frequency of help resource utilization. *Journal of Multicultural Counseling and Development*, 34, 208–222.

Fuertes, J. N., Bartolomeo, M., & Nichols, C. M. (2001). Future research directions in the study of counselor multicultural competencies. *Journal of Multicultural Counseling and Development, 29*, 3–12.

Fuertes, J. N., & Brobst, K. (2002). Clients' ratings of counselor multicultural competency. *Cultural Diversity and Ethnic Minority Psychology, 8*, 214–223.

Fuertes, J. N., Mueller, L. N., Chauhan, R. V., Walker, J. A., & Ladany, N. (2002). An investigation of Euro-American therapists' approach to counseling African-American clients. *The Counseling Psychologist, 30*, 763–788.

Fuertes, J. N., Stracuzzi, T. I., Bennett, J., Scheinholtz, J. Mislowack, A., Hersh, M., et al. (2006). Therapist multicultural competency: A study of therapy dyads. *Psychotherapy: Theory, Research, Practice, Training, 43*, 480–490.

Fukuyama, M. A. (1994). Critical incidents in multicultural counseling supervision: A phenomenological approach to supervision research. *Counselor Education and Supervision, 34*, 142–151.

Griner, D., & Smith, T. (2006). Culturally adapted mental health interventions: A meta-analytic review. *Psychotherapy: Theory, Research, Practice, Training, 43*, 531–548.

Helms, J. E. (1984). Toward a theoretical explanation of the effects of race on the counseling process: A Black-White model. *The Counseling Psychologist, 12*, 153–165.

Helms, J. E. (1995). An update of Helms's White and people of color racial identity models. In J. G. Ponterotto, J. M. Casas, L. A. Suzuki, & C. M. Alexander (Eds.), *Handbook of multicultural counseling* (pp. 181–198). Thousand Oaks, CA: Sage.

Helms, J. E., & Cook, D. A. (1999). *Using race and culture in counseling and psychotherapy: Theory and process*. Needham Heights, MA: Allyn & Bacon.

Hills, H. L., & Strozier, A. L. (1992). Multicultural training in APA-approved counseling psychology programs: A survey. *Professional Psychology: Research and Practice, 23*, 43–51.

Hird, J. S., Cavalieri, C. E., Dulko, J. P., Felice, A. A., & Ho, T. A. (2001). Visions and realities: Supervisee perspectives of multicultural supervision. *Journal of Multicultural Counseling and Development, 29*, 114–130.

Hird, J. S., Tao, K. W., & Gloria, A. M. (2005). Examining supervisors' multicultural competence in racially similar and different supervision dyads. *The Clinical Supervisor, 23*, 107–122.

Holcomb-McCoy, C. C. (2001). Exploring the self-perceived multicultural counseling competence of elementary school counselors. *Professional School Counseling, 4*, 195–201.

Holcomb-McCoy, C. C. (2005). Investigating school counselors' perceived multicultural competence. *Professional School Counseling, 8*, 414–423.

Holcomb-McCoy, C. C., & Myers, J. E. (1999). Multicultural competence and counselor training: A national survey. *Journal of Counseling and Development, 77*, 294–302.

Inman, A. G. (2006). Supervisor multicultural competence and its relation to supervisory process and outcome: *Journal of Marital and Family Therapy, 32*, 73–85.

Jencius, M., & Duba, J. D. (2002). Creating a multicultural family practice. *The Family Journal: Counseling and Therapy for Couples and Families, 10*, 410–414.

King, P. A., & Howard-Hamilton, M. (2003). An assessment of multicultural competence. *NASPA Journal, 40*, 119–133.

Kiselica, M. S., & Maben, P. (1999). Do multicultural education and diversity appreciation training reduce prejudice among counseling trainees? *Journal of Mental Health Counseling, 21*, 240–255.

Kitaoka, S. K. (2005). Multicultural counseling competencies: Lessons from assessment. *Journal of Multicultural Counseling and Development, 33*, 37–47.

Ladany, N., Brittan-Powell, C. S., & Pannu, R. K. (1997). The influence of supervisory racial identity interaction and racial matching on the supervisory working alliance and supervisee multicultural competence. *Counselor Education and Supervision, 36*, 285–305.

Ladany, N., Inman, A. G., Constantine, M. G., & Hofheinz, E. W. (1997). Supervisee multicultural case conceptualization ability and self-reported multicultural competence as functions of supervisee racial identity and supervisor focus. *Journal of Counseling Psychology, 44*, 284–293.

LaFromboise, T. D., Coleman, H. L. K., & Hernandez, A. (1991). Development and factor structure of the Cross-Cultural Counseling Inventory-Revised. *Professional Psychology: Research and Practice, 22*, 380–388.

Liu, W. M., Sheu, H. B., & Williams, K. (2004). Multicultural competency in research: Examining the relationships among multicultural competencies, research training and self-efficacy, and the multicultural environment. *Cultural Diversity and Ethnic Minority Psychology, 10,* 324–339.

Manese, J. E., Wu, J. T., & Nepomuceno, C. A. (2001). The effect of training on multicultural counseling competencies: An exploratory study over a ten-year period. *Journal of Multicultural Counseling and Development, 29,* 31–40.

Miville, M. L., Rosa, D., & Constantine, M. G. (2005). Building multicultural competence in clinical supervision. In M. G. Constantine & D. W. Sue (Eds.), *Strategies for building multicultural competence in mental health and educational settings* (pp. 192–211). Hoboken, NJ: Wiley.

Moore-Thomas, C. (1998). Master's-level counselors self-perceived multicultural competence: Relation to general counseling competence, conscientiousness, and openness to experience. *Dissertation Abstracts International Section A: Humanities and Social Sciences, 66*(8-A), 2831. (UMI No. 3186854)

Murphy, M. C., Wright, B. V., & Bellamy, D. E. (1995). Multicultural training in university counseling center predoctoral psychology internship programs: A survey. *Journal of Multicultural Counseling and Development, 23,* 170–180.

Neville, H. A., Heppner, M. J., Louie, C. E., Thompson, C. E., Brooks, L., & Baker, C. E. (1996). The impact of multicultural training on White racial identity attitudes and therapy competencies. *Professional Psychology: Research and Practice, 27,* 83–89.

Neville, H. A., & Mobley, M. (2001). Social identities in contexts: An ecological model of multicultural counseling psychology processes. *The Counseling Psychologist, 29,* 471–486.

Neville, H. A., Spanierman, L., & Doan, B-T. (2006). Exploring the association between color-blind racial ideology and multicultural counseling competencies. *Cultural Diversity and Ethnic Minority Psychology, 12,* 275–290.

Ottavi, T. M., Pope-Davis, D. B., & Dings, J. G. (1994). Relationship between White racial identity attitudes and self-reported multicultural counseling competencies. *Journal of Counseling Psychology, 41,* 149–154.

Parham, T., A., & Helms, J. E. (1985). Relation of racial identity attitudes to self-actualization and affective states of Black students. *Journal of Counseling Psychology, 32,* 431–440.

Parker, W. M., Moore, M. A., & Neimeyer, G. J. (1998). Altering White racial identity and interracial comfort through multicultural training. *Journal of Counseling and Development, 76,* 302–310.

Ponterotto, J. G., Alexander, C. M., & Grieger, I. (1995). A multicultural competency checklist for counseling training programs. *Journal of Multicultural Counseling and Development, 23,* 11–20.

Ponterotto, J. G., Fuertes, J. N., & Chen, E. C. (2000). Models of multicultural counseling. In S. D. Brown & R. W. Lent (Eds.), *Handbook of counseling psychology* (3rd ed., pp. 639–669). New York: Wiley.

Pope-Davis, D. B., Reynolds, A. L., Dings, J. G., & Ottavi, T. M. (1994). Multicultural competencies of doctoral interns at university counseling centers: An exploratory investigation. *Professional Psychology: Research and Practice, 25,* 466–470.

Pope-Davis, D. B., Toporek, R. L., Ortega-Villalobos, L., Ligiero, D. P., Brittan-Powell, C. S., Liu, W. M., et al. (2002). Client perspectives of multicultural counseling competence: A qualitative examination. *The Counseling Psychologist, 30,* 355–393.

Ridley, C. R. (2005). *Overcoming unintentional racism in counseling and therapy* (2nd ed.). Thousand Oaks, CA: Sage.

Ridley, C. R., Mendoza, D. W., & Kanitz, B. E. (1994). Multicultural training: reexamination, operationalization, and integration. *The Counseling Psychologist, 22,* 227–289.

Roysircar, G. (2004). Counseling and psychotherapy for acculturation and ethnic identity concerns with immigrants and international student clients. In T. B. Smith (Ed.), *Practicing multiculturalism: Affirming diversity in counseling and psychology* (pp. 248–268). Boston: Allyn & Bacon.

Roysircar, G. (2005). Culturally sensitive assessment, diagnosis, and guidelines. In M. G. Constantine & D. W. Sue (Eds.), *Strategies for building multicultural competence in mental health and educational settings* (pp. 19–38). Hoboken, NJ: Wiley.

Roysircar G., Gard, G., Hubbell R., & Ortega, M. (2005). Development of counseling trainees' multicultural awareness through mentoring ESL students. *Journal of Multicultural Counseling and Development, 33,* 17–36.

Roysircar G., Pimpinella, E., Spanakis, N, & Vincent, W. (2006). *Development of the Cultural Diversity Observer Rating Scale: A functional approach to assessing multicultural practice.* Unpublished manuscript.

Smith, T. B., Constantine, M. G., Dunn, T. W., Dinehart, J. M., & Montoya, J. A. (2006). Multicultural education in the mental health professions: A meta-analytic review. *Journal of Counseling Psychology, 53,* 132–145.

Sodowsky, G. R. (1991). Effects of culturally consistent counseling tasks on American and international student observers' perception of therapist credibility. *Journal of Counseling and Development, 69,* 253–256.

Sodowsky, G. R., Kuo-Jackson, P. Y., Richardson, M. F., & Corey, A. T. (1998). Correlates of self-reported multicultural competencies: Counselor multicultural social desirability, race, social inadequacy, locus of control racial ideology, and multicultural training. *Journal of Counseling Psychology, 45,* 256–264.

Sodowsky, G. R., Taffe, R. C., Gutkin, T. B., & Wise, S. L. (1994). Development of the Multicultural Counseling Inventory: A self-report measure of multicultural competencies. *Journal of Counseling Psychology, 41,* 137–148.

Speight, S. L., Thomas, A. J., Kennel, R. G., & Anderson, M. E. (1995). Operationalizing multicultural training in doctoral programs and internships. *Professional Psychology: Research and Practice, 26,* 401–406.

Stuart, R. B. (2004). Twelve practical strategies for achieving multicultural competence. *Professional Psychology: Research and Practice, 35,* 3–9.

Sue, D. W., Arredondo, P., & McDavis, R. J. (1992). Multicultural counseling competencies and standards: A call to the profession. *Journal of Multicultural Counseling and Development, 20,* 64–88.

Sue, D. W., Bernier, J. B., Durran, M., Feinberg, L. Pedersen, P. Smith, E., et al. (1982). Position paper: Cross-cultural counseling competencies. *The Counseling Psychologist, 10,* 45–52.

Sue, D. W., Carter, R. T., Casas, J. M., Fouad, N. A., Ivey, A. E., Jensen, M., et al. (1998). *Multicultural counseling competencies: Individual and organizational development*. Thousand Oaks, CA: Sage.

Sue, S., & Zane, N. (1987). The role of culture and cultural techniques in psychotherapy: A critique and reformulation. *American Psychologist, 42*, 37–45.

Thompson, C. E., & Jenal, S. T. (1994). Interracial and intraracial quasi-counseling interactions when therapists avoid discussing race. *Journal of Counseling Psychology, 41*, 484–491.

Thompson, C. E., Worthington, R., & Atkinson, D. R. (1994). Therapist content, orientation, therapist race, and Black women's cultural mistrust and self-disclosure. *Journal of Counseling Psychology, 41*, 155–161.

Toporek, R. L., Ortega-Villalobos, L., & Pope-Davis, D. B. (2004). Critical incidents in multicultural supervision: Exploring supervisees' and supervisors' experiences. *Journal of Multicultural Counseling Development, 32*, 66–83.

U.S. Census Bureau. (2004). U.S. interim projections by age, sex, race, and Hispanic origin. Retrieved on February 1, 2007, from http://www.census.gov/ipc/www/usinterimproj/

Watkins, C. E., & Terrell, F. (1988). Mistrust level and its effects on counseling expectations in Black-White therapist relationships: An analogue study. *Journal of Counseling Psychology, 35*, 194–197.

Worthington, R. L., Mobley, M., Franks, R. P., & Tan, J. A. (2000). Multicultural counseling competencies: Verbal content, counselor attributions, and social desirability. *Journal of Counseling Psychology, 47*, 460–468.

Chapter Six

Changing Face of Vocational Psychology

The Transforming World of Work

David L. Blustein
Nadya A. Fouad

Throughout the history of counseling psychology, vocational psychology has been, and continues as, a strong and vibrant field. Vocational psychology has contributed significantly to the identity of counseling psychology and to the development of a unique and important knowledge base (Brown & Lent, 2005; Fouad, 2007; Phillips & Imhoff, 1997; Walsh & Savickas, 2005). The fact that a chapter on vocational psychology is appearing in the inaugural issue of the *Biennial Review of Counseling Psychology* underscores the critical importance of the psychological study of working to the current status and future directions of counseling psychology.

Fouad (2007) noted that, over the past two decades, research in vocational psychology has focused on four main questions: What factors influence career choices? How do people make career decisions? How are clients effectively helped? and How does context influence career decisions? In this chapter, we will explore our perspectives on the research and conceptual frameworks on the last question. We will argue that it is critical to understand the contextual influences on career choices, within the world of work, which, itself, is undergoing a radical transformation (Blustein, 2006; Fouad, 2007; Friedman, 2005). Consistent with a fundamental core attribute of counseling psychology, we examine the shifting working environment in light of individual or intrapersonal experience, which is predicated on the assumption that individuals interact in complex and reciprocal ways with their context. The locus of intrapersonal experience that we examine in this chapter is the self, which has been a key construct in counseling psychology and continues to form a cornerstone for intellectual advances in theory, research, and practice (Blustein & Noumair, 1996; Guichard, 2005). In the following sections, we first present an argument for a contextual perspective on the role of the self in vocational psychology, review the literature on gender and race, and then discuss how the changes in the world of work are causing a major transformation in how we think about the role of the self in the career development process.

SELF-IN-RELATION AND VOCATIONAL PSYCHOLOGY

Throughout each of the major theories of career choice and development, constructs pertaining to the self, self-concept, or identity are prominent (cf. Brown, 2002; Brown & Lent, 2005). For example, in Holland's (1997) theory of career choice, the aspect of the individual that ostensibly is matched with the work context is the vocational identity, which refers to an individual's internal attributes such as values, beliefs, and attitudes. Similarly, the theory of work adjustment (Dawis, 2005) focuses on the complexities of the person-environment fit; in this conceptual model, the person dimensions are related to the historically important notion of traits and assume a significant role in this interactive model of career choice and adjustment behavior. Super's (e.g., 1957, 1980) theory and Savickas's (2005) recent extension of the developmental perspective of vocational behavior posit that individuals interact with the educational and occupational worlds via their self-concepts. Indeed, in Savickas's framework, decision makers ideally construct and optimize their options via their vocational personality. The contributions from social cognitive career theory (e.g., Lent, Brown, & Hackett, 2002) also include a focus on the self as a primary agent of movement and change. From the perspective of social cognitive career theory, individuals are viewed as active agents in their lives; moreover, the internal set of beliefs about one's ability to negotiate with the educational and occupational world has assumed considerable importance, generally falling under the rubric of self-efficacy. In sum, the existing major theoretical contributions in vocational psychology have conceptualized an internal construct; although each theory differs in the focus on specific aspects of individual's inner lives, they each hypothesize that internal constructs of the individual interact with the environment.

In recent years, considerations of the self have extended to explore the relationship between individual psychological experience and the context. Blustein and Noumair (1996) summarized this position as follows:

> One of the most recent advances in considerations of self and identity has to do with the increasingly apparent observation that any attempt at understanding intrapsychic experiences necessitates a corollary need to discern the context of a given individual. In relation to the emerging views of the self and identity, context attempts to capture a number of factors that are implicated in the formation and expression of both self and identity. More precisely, context can be operationalized to encompass contemporary as well as historical factors related to those familial, social, and economic influences that affect individuals throughout the life span. (Blustein, 1994; Vondracek, Lerner, & Schulenberg, 1986) (Blustein & Noumair, 1996, pp. 434–435)

This chapter follows the lead of Blustein and Noumair in considering the contextual aspects of the self within vocational psychology. In this chapter, we adopt the term "self-in-relation" to denote the reality that individuals exist in dynamic contexts of relationships, culture, and historical events (Blustein, 1994; Cushman, 1995; Jordan, Walker, & Hartling, 2004; Josselson, 1992). In short, we view the self as an intrapersonal and dynamic attribute of individuals that contains multiple dimensions. Consistent with the view articulated by Super, Starishevsky, Matlin, and Jordaan, 1963) and Harren (1979), we believe that the self contains a complex array of identity domains and affective domains. The identity domains pertain to the attributes that individuals use to define themselves (such as social, intelligent, honest, etc.). The affective domains pertain to the feelings and emotions that individuals have in relation to various identity attributes (cf. Swann, Chang-Schneider, & McLarty, 2007). For example, some people may value their own need for affiliation, whereas others may find that need to be less important. Moreover, the relationship between the identity domains and affective domains is linked to the context in many cases. Some situations may evoke greater reliance upon one's inner attributes, and other situations may pull for interpersonal behavior and feelings that are designed to help the individual manage a complex or challenging scenario.

One of the key debates in the literature on the self is the degree to which attributes of the self are stable and consistent over time and contexts. This debate, in many ways, cuts to the core of an ongoing and critical psychological debate between nature and nurture. A full review of this debate is beyond the scope of this chapter; however, a cursory review of this literature reveals that most scholars believe that the experience of the self is shaped to some degree by the context and to some degree by genetic predispositions and early childhood experiences (e.g., Leary & Tangney, 2002; Swann et al., 2007). The precise nature of this interaction is difficult to discern. However, the prevailing view within vocational psychology is that the self is embedded within a complex network of cultural, social, and relational influences that exists in a reciprocal relationship with each individual (e.g., Blustein & Noumair, 1996; Lent et al., 2002; Savickas, 2005; Vondracek et al., 1986).

Self-in-Relation and the Experience of Working

At the heart of the major career choice and development theories is a core assumption that individuals seek to implement their self-concepts in the world of work (Super, 1957, 1980; Super et al., 1963). In other words, most vocational theories assume that individuals engage in a process of understanding themselves and then finding work that fits that self-concept. In our view, this notion represents an ideal process grounded in freedom to choose an occupation that fits an individual's self-concept, which is certainly hard to refute. However, our premise is that the notion of self-concept implementation remains an aspiration but is not a reality for most people around the globe. As we have argued elsewhere (Blustein, 2006; Fouad, 2007), the notion of a career represents a dream for many individuals whose main objective in working is to simply survive. Most of the major career choice and development theories that guide research and practice have been predicated on the lives of relatively privileged European American and Western European men with access to education and social resources (Blustein, 2006; Richardson, 1993). However, the reality is that most people do not experience the sort of volition in their educational and occupational options as is presumed in the major career choice theories. (We explore this issue later in the chapter in presenting the psychology-of-working perspective.)

At the same time, the rapid changes in the world of work have reshaped the notion of career even for those who do have access to resources. Since the later part of the 20th century, career development specialists and management scholars have observed that the traditional notion of a hierarchical career that is connected to a singular organization or field is no longer the prevailing experience, even for highly educated professionals (Arthur & Rosseau, 1996; Hall, 1996, 2002). Within the past decade, scholars have used the terms *protean career* or *boundaryless career* to denote the impact that the rapidly changing occupational landscape has had on those with access to education and high-level professional skills. These terms are best understood as related but distinct constructs, as Briscoe and Hall (2006) noted here:

> The boundaryless career has many "meanings" (Arthur & Rousseau, 1996) but is typically associated with careers that transcend organi-

> zational boundaries. A boundaryless career might be either perceived by the individual subjectively or defined by others objectively. The protean career explicitly defines independence and self-directed career behavior (Hall, 1976). Such independence could be inferred by others, but the usual "test" for a protean career would be the subjective perception of the career actor. . . .
>
> Much of the power of these two career theories lies in their symbolism—in essence the sway they offer as metaphors. The boundaryless career is easy to visualize in the contemporary employment context where job descriptions, organizations, work–home boundaries, and other career features seem to be dissolving or reorganizing themselves continuously. The protean metaphor (based upon the Greek god Proteus) is a bit harder to literally picture (changing shape), but the need to define the shape of one's career through identifying and expressing values (Hall, Briscoe, & Kram, 1977) and directing career behavior (Hall & Associates, 1996) can be clearly seen as an adaptive response to the volatile, uncertain, and ambiguous work environment. (p. 1)

GLOBALIZATION

As reflected in the scholarship on the boundaryless career, the changes in the labor market are taking place at all levels, from unskilled work to highly skilled professions and trades. Many of these changes are a direct outgrowth of globalization, which represents an enormous shift in the nature of the market economy, with profound implications for the world of work and for career development. As Coutinho, Dam, and Blustein (in press) stated, "globalization as a product of human innovation and technology has been a long-developing process, which erupted with the rapid technological and information dissemination changes that occurred after World War II (International Monetary Fund, 2000). . . . The increased rate of connection and consequent interdependence manifests itself in a number of different arenas. National economies are increasingly interdependent and susceptible to events outside a country's borders (Suárez-Orozco & Qin-Hilliard, 2004); industries experience a higher level of mobility and the flexibility to move production without compromising quality (Friedman, 2006); and, people, ideas, and concepts travel at an increased speed, allowing for a greater degree of contact between cultures (Hermans & Kempen, 1998; Jenkins, 2004)" (pp. 5–6). A consequence of globalization is that the stability that defined the world of work for many middle-class and relatively well-educated individuals is no longer the norm. Moreover, globalization has introduced the free market economy to nearly all nations around the globe, with the result of increasing levels of competition in the world of work.

Amid the advent of globalization is a greater awareness that individuals are no longer as capable of navigating a straight career path that begins with a clearly delineated educational plan and culminates in lifelong employment in an organization or field that remains relatively stable during the course of the life span. In other words, few individuals choose a career at age 16, seek the education for that career, and stay in that career for their working lifetime. In fact, that scenario may describe a miniscule number of people in North America and Europe, much less workers in Africa, Asia, or South America. The changes that globalization has engendered in the world of work, in many ways, bring to the middle class the sort of instability in work that has long characterized the experiences of those without access to educational, financial, and career-related resources (Blustein, 2006). Moreover, the advent of globalization has encouraged our field to fully understand and incorporate the complex ways that the context affects individuals as they grapple with their educational and career development tasks. In the following sections, we review the literature on gender and race, which represents some of the most important research agendas in vocational psychology that have thoughtfully incorporated knowledge about the context of human development. Following this material, we then discuss how the changes in the world of work are causing a major transformation in how we think about the role of the self in the career development process.

A CONTEXTUAL PERSPECTIVE ON WORK

The field of vocational psychology has shifted dramatically in the past 50 years from assuming that all individuals make the same career choices to an understanding that individuals' career decisions are shaped, and often constrained, by their contexts. Crites's (1969) classic text *Vocational Psychology* exemplifies the historically one-dimensional view of career development in that there were just two mentions of women's careers, one of which was a comment that it is a "largely neglected area of research" (p. 10). There were no index terms for race, poverty, social class, sexual orientation, or culture. But nearly 50 years later, vocational psychologists have become much more attuned to the ways that context can shape career choices. As we argued earlier, it is critical to understand the role of context in shaping vocational identity and the development of self.

Although there is still a tremendous need for more empirical research on the role of context in career choice, it has become clear that vocational psychologists must increase their understanding of the contextual influences in career choice and development to effectively help individuals make decisions. Consider the career choices made by George, a European

American male who is born to an upper-class family in the northeastern United States. His choices will be shaped by different influences than the choices made by Bao, a first-generation Hmong woman living in northern Wisconsin. Both individuals may feel that their occupational choices are constrained by family obligations and expectations; both decisions may be shaped by access to resources, and the high school they attended. Both individuals might, indeed, pursue the same occupational goal, but a career counselor will be ineffective with either if s/he does not understand the context in which his or her decision is made.

Family expectations may play a role for both individuals, but the greater influence of collective goals in the Hmong culture may lead Bao to make a decision based on family obligations (Leong & Gupta, 2007). Both clients are influenced by the geographic region in which they reside, and the opportunities provided in that region. Both are influenced by the social class in which they were born. Social class helps to shape the resources an individual can access; these resources may be financial, emotional, or educational (Blustein, 2006; Blustein et al., 2002). Each individual's decision clearly is shaped by his or her gender, social class, culture, familial expectations, and perceptions of social obligations.

Studies have shown that women's and men's choices are shaped strongly by gender socialization, that race influences individuals' perceptions of barriers to career, and that individuals in varying social classes perceive the world of work, and their options to enter that world, differently (Fouad & Kantamneni, in press). Sexual orientation is also a contextual factor that influences career development (Fassinger, 1995; Prince, 1995). Identifying oneself as gay or a lesbian may occur as a process at the same time as the identification of occupational goals and aspirations. Thus, understanding one's sexual identity may impede career developmental tasks, may foreclose some career options (for fear of discrimination or homophobia), and may result in loss of parental and family support (Adams, Cahill, & Ackerlind, 2005; Boatwright, Gilbert, Forrest, & Ketzenberger, 1996; Long et al., 2005). Much more empirical work is needed to understand both the positive and challenging aspects of sexual identification in adolescence as well as in adulthood as it relates to individuals' development of personal and vocational identity.

This section will review selected empirical articles on the two areas of context that have been the most widely researched, gender and race. Although we will later argue the need to understand the intersecting dimensions of diversity (e.g., race and gender) that influence individuals' career choices, most studies have focused on one aspect of context, and, thus, we will review the research on gender and race separately. Space precludes an in-depth examination of the role of gender and race in career development;

we encourage readers to study more in-depth reviews by Betz (2005), Cook, Heppner, and O'Brien (2002), and Fassinger (2005) for more information on the role of gender in vocational psychology, and Worthington, Flores, Navarro Brown, and Lent (2005) and M. T. Brown, Yamini-Diouf, and Ruiz de Esparza (2005) for more information on the role of race/ethnicity in vocational psychology.

Gender

The role of gender in vocational choice was the first area of context examined in vocational psychology. Responding to the changing influences in the United States during the 1970s, vocational psychologists initially examined differences between women who did, or did not, work (e.g., Oliver, 1975; Tinsley & Faunce, 1978). These studies assumed that women who worked had a career orientation, and those who did not work had a homemaking orientation. Research focused on the differences between the two. By the 1980s, however, economic and social factors led to a dramatic increase in women's participation in the labor force and better explanations were needed to predict how, rather than whether, women made career decisions. Scholars also began to challenge the research in vocational psychology, postulating that women's career development was different from men's, and critiquing career development theories that assumed a male model fit for everyone. A controversy erupted over the charge that interest inventories were being used to limit women's career choices (Holland, Gottfredson, & Gottfredson, 1975; Prediger & Cole, 1975), spurred on by the use of different inventories with men and women, and the inclusion of a homemaking scale on the women's form of the Strong Vocational Interest Blank. Those working with academically oriented women were encouraged to use the male form with those women (Munley, Fretz, & Mills, 1973), reinforcing the perception that men's careers were the norm into which women should fit.

Theoretical advancements began to focus on women's career development separate from men's. For example, Betz and Hackett (1981) applied social cognitive theory (Bandura, 1986) to enhance understanding of women's avoidance of math and science careers. Astin (1984) proposed a separate model of women's career development, optimistically arguing that since the opportunity structure had become more equal, women would have more freedom in their career choices. Betz and Fitzgerald (1987) wrote a comprehensive review of the career psychology of women, documenting the structural barriers for women to choose freely, and highlighting the multiple roles for women that precluded their consideration of some careers.

Twenty years after Betz and Fitzgerald's (1987) seminal work, vocational psychologists have empirically demonstrated that, indeed, gender strongly influences career choices and development. Men and women differ in their career aspirations (Miller & Budd, 1999), differ in their self-efficacy to engage in different tasks (Betz, 2006), and, even when making the same career choices, differ in their reasons for the choice (Farmer, Wardrop, Anderson, & Risinger, 1995).

The influence of gender roles upon an individual's occupational preferences and choices starts early in one's development and is often insidious and subtle. Gender influences the types of occupations that children aspire, or dream, to do. This is in part due to different perceptions of the types of occupations that are appropriate for men and for women. These differences have been found as early as elementary school (Helwig, 2004), and clearly continue into high school. Armstrong and Crombie (2000) studied the aspirations of 8th and 10th graders, contrasting what they dreamed of doing with the occupation they expected to enter. They found that the gap between aspirations and expectations narrowed by 10th grade, most often toward more gender-traditional occupations. Although longitudinal studies have found that girls have higher educational aspirations than boys (e.g., Rojewski & Yang, 1997), studies have also shown that women seeking traditional jobs have more success in finding those jobs than women seeking nontraditional jobs (e.g., Levine & Zimmerman, 1995).

Girls and boys do, of course, sometimes make the same career choice, but often give different reasons for those choices. For example, Davey (2001) found that male high school seniors reported that they chose an occupational goal based on their interests, while the female seniors choosing the same goal indicated that their decision was based on altruism. Farmer et al. (1995) also found similar results in their longitudinal study of high school students who entered engineering. Although both boys and girls had Investigative interests, the second Holland code for their interests differed. The secondary area of interest was Realistic for men and Social for women. These findings highlight that men and women continue to have different patterns of vocational interests. Although the men's and women's forms of the Strong Vocational Interest Blank were merged in 1974, men continue to score higher, in general, than women in Realistic scales, and women score higher on Artistic scales. Fouad (2002) found that, in fact, gender differences in vocational interests were larger than differences among racial/ethnic groups or between students and professionals.

A significant portion of recent empirical research on the role of gender in career development has focused on ways to increase women's consideration of science, math, engineering or technical careers (see, for example, Fassinger, 2005). There is a concern that girls make choices to avoid coursework in math or science in high school, foreclosing their options to consider math and science careers (National Science Foundation [NSF], 2003). Women's consideration of math/science/technical careers decreases as women graduate from high school. Even those women who considered a technical or science career in high school were less likely than the males in their cohort to want a career in that area 10 years later (Farmer et al., 1995). Thus, currently, only 20% of engineering majors are women (NSF, 2003) and less than 10% of employed engineers are women (Bureau of Labor Statistics, 2006).

Because innate abilities of mathematical performance do not differ significantly between men and women (Hyde, 2005; NSF, 2003), scholars have investigated women's expectations of success (Eccles, 1994) or women's self-efficacy beliefs for math-related tasks (e.g., Farmer, Wardrop, & Rotella, 1999; Hackett, Betz, Casas, & Rocha-Singh, 1992; Lent, et al., 2000). Interventions focusing on increasing self-efficacy expectations have been successful. For example, Betz and Schifano (2000) demonstrated that a relatively brief (6-week) workshop could increase Realistic self-efficacy and interests for women. Anderson and Betz (2001) also were able to demonstrate an increase in Social theme self-efficacy for men, finding that direct learning experiences clustered together distinctly from the indirect experiences of role-modeling. The latter indicates support for the importance of performance accomplishments as a source of self-efficacy (Lopez, Lent, Brown, & Gore, 1997).

In the past 10 years, some researchers (e.g. Flores & O'Brien, 2002; Kenny, Blustein, Chaves, Grossman, & Gallagher, 2003) have focused more on the strength of career aspiration, regardless of area of occupational choice, using a measure developed by O'Brien (1992); most of these studies have examined factors in the strength of women's aspirations to lead within their career. Strength of aspirations for women has been found to be related to perceptions of social support, school engagement, academic self-efficacy, positive role models, and ability level (Flores & O'Brien, 2002; Kenny et al., 2003; Nauta, Epperson, & Kahn, 1998).

Some of these findings may be related to the relative influence of significant others on career decisions for girls. For example, Vincent, Peplau, and Hill (1998) found that girls' perceptions of their parents' and boyfriends' preferences for them (social pressures) predicted their career orientation more than gender role attitudes in college; in turn, career orientation predicted their career behavior 15 years later. O'Brien (1996) found that women whose mothers were involved in their daily life and who had some attachment to their mothers, who were emotionally close to their mothers, and who shared similar beliefs and attitudes with both parents had higher career self-efficacy and moderately strong career orientation and realism.

O'Brien observed, however, that the attachment variables failed to correlate significantly with career constructs when controlling for separation from mothers.

Although career development research has focused on male career development for many decades, more current research has begun to focus on the role of male gender role stereotyping in career choice. Jome and Tokar (1998) surveyed 100 undergraduate and graduate men, half in gender-traditional majors (e.g., engineering, computer science) and half in gender-nontraditional majors (e.g., nursing, social work). The groups differed in gender-traditional men scoring higher on antifeminine attitudes, higher attitudes toward traditional male gender identity, and two indicators of homophobic attitudes. Furthermore, Lease (2003) found boys choosing a nontraditional career had more liberal social attitudes.

In summary, gender influences both girls' and boys' career dreams and the career they expect to have. Gender influences individuals' perceptions of what careers might be appropriate, the self-efficacy both boys and girls have to enter nontraditional careers, and the interests that both girls and boys have for activities. Race and gender interact to influence career choice, such that in some racial/ethnic minority groups, women have very prescribed roles. Families have gender-related expectations of both boys and girls. Women have fewer socioeconomic resources and are disproportionately affected by inequities in the workforce. Gender influences individuals' perceptions of opportunities and options within the labor market. In short, at all levels, gender influences career development and choices.

Race/Ethnicity

It is axiomatic that the United States has become more racially and culturally diverse than ever. In the most recent census, one in three U.S. residents identified themselves as a member of a racial/ethnic minority (Census Bureau, 2007). In 2006, 12% of the U.S. population identified themselves as Black or African American, 1% identified themselves as Native American or American Indian, 13% identified themselves as Hispanic or Latino, and 4% identified themselves as Asian or Pacific Islander (Census Bureau, 2007).

If opportunities for occupational choice were equal, one might expect a relatively similar representation of racial/ethnic minority group members across all occupational groups. However, there is an underrepresentation of racial/ethnic minority group members in occupations that are higher paying and an overrepresentation in occupations that are lower paying (Census Bureau, 2007). For example, 8% and 6.4% of individuals in management, professional, or related occupations are African American or Hispanic/Latino, respectively. This includes psychologists (2.8% are African American, and 4.7% are Hispanic/Latino), lawyers (4.7% are African American, 3.5% are Hispanic/Latino), and chief executive officers (3% are African American, and 3.8% are Hispanic/Latino). On the other end of the occupational prestige and pay spectrum, African Americans and Hispanic/Latinos comprise 24% and 15.6%, respectively, of personal health aides, 18.3% and 27.3%, respectively, of janitors, and 29.3% and 35.7%, respectively, of garment and textile workers. These occupational differences are reflected in the median yearly earnings: Whites earn an average of $34,944, African Americans earn $27,040, and Hispanic/Latinos earn $24,492 a year.

Clearly the occupational context differs for members of racial/ethnic minority groups, and understanding and advocating for changes has been a focus for the past 20–30 years (cf. Smith, 1983). These disparities in occupational representation are not recent, and there is little evidence that they have diminished over the years (Bureau of Labor, 2007). Smith (1983) highlighted the differences in occupational choices across racial/ethnic groups nearly three decades ago, and became one of the first scholars to call for a focus on race and ethnicity in vocational psychology. However, most of the early research on the role of race/ethnicity in career development focused on the ways that "special populations" (e.g., racial/ethnic minorities) were different from the mainstream U.S. student or adult (e.g., Lee, 1984; Minatoya & Sedlacek, 1983). By the early 1990s, however, scholars began to urge vocational psychology to incorporate multicultural counseling principles and change the way that career counseling was conducted (e.g., Bowman, 1993; Fouad & Bingham, 1995; Leong, 1995; Okocha, 1994).

Researchers were encouraged to examine the context in which career decisions were made for racial/ethnic minority individuals, noting that some of the central assumptions about career in mainstream U.S. culture may not apply across populations (e.g., Cook et al., 2002; Helms & Cook, 1999). These assumptions include a linear progression of career, high value placed on individual decisions (vs. decisions shaped by family or cultural group), the central role that work plays in one's life, and the assumption that opportunities are open to all. These assumptions may not be valid for all racial/ethnic populations in the United States due to social oppression, discrimination, lack of educational parity among racial/ethnic groups, and differences in cultural values that place a higher value on collective (or family) decision making (Helms & Cook, 1999).

In the past 10 years, research on the context of career development for racial-ethnic minorities has focused on gaining a greater understanding of the role of perceptions of barriers and opportunities in career choice (Kenny et al., 2003; McWhirter, Hackett, & Bandalos, 1998). Scholars have also heeded a call to examine within-group differences, rather than conducting studies comparing one racial group to another (e.g., Jones, 1997; Juntunen et al., 2001; Pearson & Bieschke, 2001). Similar to research on career choices of women, scholars began to focus on the career aspirations of racial/ethnic minorities. A recent meta-analysis found very few differences among groups in the careers they hoped to do, but there were differences among racial/ethnic groups in the careers they expected to do (Fouad & Byars-Winston, 2005). This may be related to the perception of discrimination that might limit occupational choice. For example, a qualitative study by Cook et al. (1996) found that inner-city African American boys' discussion of their future careers replicated the structural inequities in occupational structure as early as second grade.

The barriers encountered by many racial/ethnic minority individuals clearly shape the educational opportunities for occupational preparation, the resources they might have to seek further occupational preparation, and the opportunities they might have to choose the career they desire. But, although these barriers are both real in the marketplace and in perceptions that preclude options for some individuals, other racial/ethnic minority individuals are seeking and achieving in the occupation of their choice. A recent group of studies has examined the construction of meaning for highly achieving members of racial/ethnic minorities. For example, Juntunen et al. (2001) conducted a qualitative study with 18 American Indians, and identified five themes in their analysis of the interviews. The first was the meaning of career for participants, which included incorporating traditional ways for Native American Indians. The second theme was success as a collective, rather than solely individual experience. The third theme included supportive factors in career achievement, such as family and a high value placed on education by the family. The fourth theme was the identified obstacles to achievement, such as discrimination, alienation from the tribe, and limits as a result of being on a reservation. Finally, the fifth theme was the perception of living in two worlds, the Native world and the mainstream world.

Other qualitative studies have focused on Latinas (Gomez et al., 2001) or African Americans (Jones, 1997; Pearson & Bieschke, 2001; Richie et al., 1997). Findings from these studies also highlighted a realistic appraisal of the obstacles to achievement and the mobilization of resources to overcome those barriers. These resources included the importance of family as a supportive factor in career achievement and a value placed on education. Many of the participants in these studies also mentioned the role that their culture played in their career decisions, as well.

In sum, the literature on race and gender in vocational psychology underscores the critical importance of the context in understanding and intervening in the lives of clients and students. In many ways, the discussion of race and gender in vocational psychology has foreshadowed and even led the conversation about how to understand the role of the environment in the educational and occupational lives of people (Blustein, 2006). One of the themes of this research is that the underlying notion of implementing the self-concept in the world of work, which has been a key assumption in existing theories, is not necessarily the modal experience, even within affluent and postindustrial nations like the United States and Canada. Gender and race often constrain the real options that people have, as well as the perceptions of choices they have. We next explore the theme of understanding how the self and the context intersect in the world of work by identifying potentially useful conceptual models that can enhance conceptualizations of the self in relation to the work context.

CONCEPTUAL MODELS IN INTEGRATING CONTEXT

As reflected by the literature on race and gender that we have reviewed, the impact of context on individual's experience of the self and the changing world of work is daunting and difficult to discern. How do race, gender, and environment interact with one another to shape the working life an individual considers, believes she or he might pursue, or takes to support herself or himself? We believe that new conceptual models are needed to help explain and predict the role of the self within the 21st-century landscape. Although numerous important theoretical and conceptual models have been developed to understand the interaction between the self and context (e.g., Fouad & Kantamneni, in press; Lent et al., 2002; Vondracek, Lerner & Schulenberg, 1986), we have chosen to highlight two specific conceptual initiatives. We believe that these two theoretical models have the potential to reshape how we think about the self in relation to contextual factors and the increasing instability that characterizes the work context of the 21st century.

Savickas's Career Construction Theory

As the material presented here indicates, the world of work is a very different place than it was when Super (1957; Super et al., 1963) developed his seminal theory of career development. Savickas's extension and expansion of Super's work has incorporated the reality of a fluid and dynamic occupational and educational context. As Savickas has proposed, "the process of career construction is essentially that of developing and implementing vocational self-concepts in work roles" (2005, p. 46). This premise, as we noted earlier, lies at the core of most major career development theories.

The implementation of the self-concept places the career decision-making process into a framework in which individuals' conceptions of themselves interact with and are shifted by the context.

Savickas (2005) offers a number of theoretical tools that may help to illuminate important new ways of understanding how individuals can navigate the new world of work. A key example is the importance of adaptability in career construction. According to Savickas, career adaptability represents an individual's coping resources (competencies) and readiness (attitudes) in the face of external work-related challenges and developmental tasks. Career adaptability is particularly relevant to the changing needs of the 21st-century workforce in that it offers a flexible rubric to describe self-concept dimensions that are manifested in the world of work. Career adaptability reflects the degree of resilience that an individual manifests in relation to the demands of work related tasks, transitions, and traumas (personal communication, Mark Savickas, May 4, 2007). In effect, career adaptability describes a psychosocial dimension of the self that relates to both the content and affective aspects of intrapersonal experience. An example of career adaptability functioning at its optimal level would be in the sort of planfulness, exploratory focus, continual skill development, and flexibility that a contemporary worker would employ in dealing with a work context that consistently shifts as a result of globalization and economic changes. The need for adaptability in developing optimal internal resources is clearly an asset in contemporary views of self-in-relation and, therefore, provides important ideas for future vocational psychological research.

Psychology of Working Perspective

In contrast to the prevailing models of career choice and development that have emphasized the challenges of crystallizing and implementing the self-concept in the world of work, Blustein has articulated a critique of existing paradigms and offered an expansive alternative. Building on the work of other scholars and critics of traditional career development theory (e.g., Fouad, 2007; Richardson, 1993; Smith, 1983), Blustein has argued that our field would benefit from a focus on working as opposed to the more circumscribed focus on career. A key dimension of the new psychology-of-working framework is that considerable variability exists in the degree to which individuals experience volition or choice in their work-related choices. Arguing that many poor and working-class individuals are faced with considerable obstacles in implementing a self-determined work life, Blustein has proposed that vocational and counseling psychologists ought to examine the entire spectrum of working experiences, including volitional careers as well as the work lives of individuals with little to no choices in their educational and work-related options.

Blustein has suggested that working may optimally fulfill three fundamental human needs, including the need for survival, need for relatedness, and need for self-determination. (See Blustein, 2006, and Blustein, Kenna, Gill, & DeVoy, in press, for further details on the psychology of working.) In addition to the fulfillment of human needs, the psychology-of-working framework has explicated the critical role of the context as a focal point for resources and barriers in vocational psychology. Consistent with much of the work emanating from feminist and multicultural perspectives, the psychology-of-working framework has detailed how social, political, and economic forces affect the world of work, often in ways that reinforce existing inequities.

The psychology-of-working perspective also has examined the extensive impact of the context on the work lives of people, with a particular focus on gender and race. One of the implications of the psychology-of-working framework for the present chapter is that the notion of the self may need to be revised and reframed to accommodate the challenges of the 21st century. In keeping with the previous discussions on the boundaryless career, the impact of race and gender, and the importance of career adaptability, we propose that new conceptual tools are needed to understand the self-in-relation to the changing context.

NEW DIRECTIONS IN UNDERSTANDING CONTEXT

Over a decade ago, Blustein and Noumair (1996) proposed the notion of the embedded self as a means of understanding the way in which individuals existed within a relational and cultural context. At this point, we suggest that further enhancements are needed in conceptualizing the self-in-relation to the context. Given the broader focus on working, as suggested by Blustein (2006), Fouad (2007), and others (e.g., Peterson & González, 2005), as well as the notion of career adaptability (Savickas, 2005), we believe that the political and economic context also needs to be infused in current conceptualizations of the self. The advent of globalization coupled with the growing knowledge about how various forms of social oppression serve to reinforce stereotypes and sustain privilege among the few, often at the cost of the many, creates a compelling argument for a reinvigorated perspective of self-in-relation. That broadened perspective needs to incorporate the dynamic intersections of the influence of race, gender, sexual orientation, and family on career development and choice, as well as the societal influences that constrain and shape those choices (Fouad & Kantamneni, in press).

The Role of Reciprocity in Self-in-Relation to the Changing Work Context

Another key attribute of a contemporary view of the self-in-relation to the changing occupational context is the importance of reciprocity in human interactions. As reflected in current conceptualizations of life-span development (Lerner, 2002; Vondracek et al., 1986), human behavior is inherently reciprocal. In short, the context is thought to affect individuals in a wide array of dimensions, and individuals also influence their context. In effect, a complex set of subtle and often more obvious interactions takes place in forming an individual's sense of self or identity; in turn, an individual's sense of self will affect her/his interactions with the context. As Skorikov and Vondracek (2007, p. 134) recently noted, "adolescent career development and the experience of schooling should be viewed as reciprocal influences: Career development affects the experience of schooling, and the experience of schooling affects career development (Stuart, 2003)."

Although these dimensions reflect more macro-level aspects of the context and individuals, a closer examination of the educational context–career development connection very likely includes complex self-in-relation interactions that are reciprocal. For example, high school students who have robust levels of career salience may lobby their high school counselors and administrators for courses and programs that more clearly connect school and work, thereby changing the context to some extent. This change in context may then lead to greater career planfulness among other students in the school, creating a complex web of events that affects both individuals' conceptions of themselves and the environment.

Given the complexity of causality between the self and the context, we advocate that the next generation of self-in-relation research needs to include a focus on delineating the way in which reciprocity is manifested in the development and expression of intrapersonal attributes in work-oriented situations. Some useful conceptual lenses to support this type of research may come from developmental-contextualism (Lerner, 2002; Vondracek et al., 1986), career constructivism (Savickas, 2005), and the three-dimensional model proposed by Fouad and Kantamneni (in press). The latter model highlights the dynamic and reciprocal intersections between group-level factors (e.g., gender, race/ethnicity, social class, family) and societal factors (e.g., acculturation, influences from majority culture). In addition to the needed focus on reciprocity, we also recommend that scholars consider enhancing the self-in-relation construct by exploring the social and political dimensions of the self and the context as summarized next.

The Social and Political Dimensions of Self-in-Relation to the Changing Work Context

One of the key themes of the literature reviewed thus far is that social and political factors play a major role in determining access to the resources that facilitate an adaptive work life (Blustein, 2006; Fouad, 2007; Helms & Cook, 1999; Richardson, 1993). As reflected in the prior discussion about race and gender, the world of work parallels the broader social world in replicating conditions of inequity, often based on appearance, culture, and other attributes of individuals that have no bearing on one's skills and ability to perform work tasks. We believe that the next generation of research on self-in-relation to the world of work will need to examine various intrapersonal dimensions of political and social values and knowledge. At the same time, an equally robust scholarly initiative is needed to understand how the social and political aspects of the context influence the full gamut of personal constructions of oneself. Two illustrative dimensions of the self-in-relation are reviewed here that foreshadow the rich knowledge that can be obtained in examining the social and political dimensions of intrapersonal experience.

Racial Identity Status

Helms and Cook (1999) as well as others (e.g., Carter & Constantine, 2000; Carter & Cook, 1992; Gainor & Lent, 1998) have explored the connection between racial identity statuses and various aspects of vocational functioning. Racial identity status represents conceptual differences in how people understand and react to the racial diversity that exists in society (Helms & Cook, 1999). Helms and Cook have argued that logical distinctions exist in how all people manage their phenotypic appearance in relation to others and in relation to social norms and implicit messages about race and culture. The available literature suggests that some logical connections exist between variations in racial identity status and specific aspects of career development, such as self-efficacy (Gainor & Lent, 1998) and vocational identity (Jackson & Neville, 1998). We believe that additional research, perhaps integrating race, culture, social class, and gender, can provide important insights into the complex nature of the self-in-relation to a world of work that regrettably serves in many cases to sustain inequitable conditions.

Critical Consciousness

Another promising variable that has implications for the context and for deepening our understanding of the self-in-relation construct is critical consciousness. Blustein defined "critical consciousness (as) encompass(ing) individuals' ability to reflect upon the broad structured aspects of the world and to take action on these observations" (2006, p. 280). Critical consciousness, which is derived from Friere's (1970/1993) work on liberation education, provides an optimal outcome for students and clients who can read and discern the nature of social policies and structures, thereby empowering them to engage in activities that can change aversive aspects of their context. Diemer and Blustein (2006) found that critical consciousness was associated with adaptive career attitudes and behaviors among a sample of inner-city high school students. Similarly, Chronister and McWhirter (2006) conducted an experimental treatment study using a career intervention for women who have experienced domestic violence. They found that the women who were exposed to the intervention that included a critical consciousness component made the most progress in achieving their goals. These studies, when considered collectively, point to the importance of considering internalized political dimensions of the self-in-relation to the world-of-work.

Closing Comments

The two new dimensions of the self-in-relation that have been reviewed provide a logical extension of the work of Blustein and Noumair (1996) and to the existing literature on the changing world of work. Although racial identity status and critical consciousness represent two promising constructs, we also are aware that other scholars may initiate additional innovative lines of inquiry to illuminate further the self-in-relation construct for the 21st century. What is clear, however, is that the notion of the embedded self, which reflects the contextual approach of the past decade, will need further enhancements to fully capture the depth, complexity, and challenges of a rapidly changing world of work.

CONCLUSION

The material that we have presented in this chapter reviews a number of fundamental issues in vocational psychology. Indeed, we believe that, in reviewing the changing landscape of the world of work in light of shifts in conceptualization of the self, we have provided readers with an exemplar of vocational psychology at its best—integrating the context with human experience to promote positive and satisfying lives. That said, we also want to acknowledge that the field of vocational psychology continues to be robust and is exploring a full array of issues that are central to the broader counseling psychology community (cf. Blustein, 2006; Brown

& Lent, 2005; Fouad, 2007; Walsh & Savickas, 2005). All of the central issues that have been so prominent in counseling psychology in recent years have been well represented or even began within the vocational psychology community, including many of the advances in feminist thinking, the focus on social and political contexts, and the importance of culture in human behavior. As the material in this chapter indicates, the study of work within our field forces us to reckon with implicit and explicit factors that have the potential to facilitate growth as well as inhibit our natural strivings for health and progress. We hope that our review has served to inspire readers to actively engage in an open and critical examination of the role of work in people's lives, which historically and currently serves as a central core component within the field of counseling psychology.

ACKNOWLEDGMENTS

We would like to thank Christine Catraio, Maria Coutinho, Neeta Kantamneni, and Kerri Murphy for their comments and assistance on earlier drafts of this chapter.

BIBLIOGRAPHY

Adams, E. M., Cahill, B. J., & Ackerlind, S. J. (2005). A qualitative study of Latino lesbian and gay youths' experiences with discrimination and the career development process. *Journal of Vocational Behavior, 66*, 199–218.

Anderson, S. L., & Betz, N. E. (2001). Sources of social self-efficacy expectations: Their measurement and relation to career development. *Journal of Vocational Behavior, 58*, 98–117.

Armstrong, P. I., & Crombie, G. (2000). Compromises in adolescents' occupational aspirations and expectations from grades 8 to 10. *Journal of Vocational Behavior, 56*, 82–98.

Arthur, M. B., & Rousseau, D. M. (Eds.). (1996). *The boundaryless career.* New York: Oxford University Press.

Astin, H. (1984). The meaning of work in women's lives: A sociopsychological model of career choice and work behavior. *The Counseling Psychologist, 12*, 117–126.

Bandura, A. (1986). *Social foundations of thought and action: A social cognitive theory.* Englewood Cliffs, NJ: Prentice Hall.

Betz, N. E. (2005). Women's career development. In S. D. Brown & R. W. Lent (Eds). *Career development and counseling: Putting theory and research to work* (pp.253–277). Hoboken, NJ: John Wiley & Sons, Inc.

Betz, N. (2006). Basic issues and concepts in the career development and counseling ofwomen. In W. B. Walsh, & M. J. Heppner, (Eds.), *Handbook of career counseling for women* (2nd ed., pp. 45–74). Mahwah, NJ: Lawrence Erlbaum Associates.

Betz, N. E., & Fitzgerald, L. F. (1987). *The career psychology of women.* San Diego, CA: Academic Press, Inc.

Betz, N. E., & Hackett, G. (1981). The relationship of career-related self-efficacy expectations to perceived career options in college women and men. *Journal of Counseling Psychology, 28,* 399–410.

Betz, N. E., & Schifano, R. S. (2000). Evaluation of an intervention to increase realistic self-efficacy and interests in college women. *Journal of Vocational Behavior, 56,* 35–52.

Blustein, D. L. (1994). "Who am I?": The question of self and identity in career development. In M. L. Savickas & R. W. Lent (Eds.), *Convergence in career development theories: Implications for science and practice* (pp. 139–154). Palo Alto, CA: CPP Books.

Blustein, D. L. (2006). *The psychology of working: A new perspective for career development counseling, and public policy.* Mahwah, NJ: Lawrence Erlbaum Associates.

Blustein, D. L., Chaves, A. P., Diemer, M. A., Gallagher, L. A., Marshall, K. G., Sirin, S., et al. (2002). Voices of the forgotten half: The role of social class in the school-to-work transition. *Journal of Counseling Psychology, 49,* 311–323.

Blustein, D. L., Kenna, A. C., Gill, N., & DeVoy, J. E. (in press). The psychology of working: A new framework for counseling practice and public policy. *Career Development Quarterly.*

Blustein, D. L., & Noumair, D. A. (1996). Self and identity in career development: Implications for theory and practice. *Journal of Counseling & Development, 745,* 433–441.

Boatwright, K., Gilbert, M., Forrest, L., & Ketzenberger, K. (1996). Impact of identity development upon career trajectory: Listening to the voices of lesbian women. *Journal of Vocational Behavior, 48,* 210–228.

Bowman, S. L. (1993). Career intervention strategies for ethnic minorities. *The Career Development Quarterly, 42,* 14–25.

Briscoe, J. P., & Hall, D. T. (2006). Special section on boundaryless and protean careers: Next steps in conceptualizing and measuring boundaryless and protean careers. *Journal of Vocational Behavior, 69,* 1–3.

Brown, D. (2002). (Ed.) *Career choice and development* (4th ed.). San Francisco: Jossey-Bass.

Brown, M. T., Yamini-Diouf, Y., & Ruiz de Esparza, C. (2005). Career interventions for racial/ethnic minority persons: A research agenda. In W. B. Walsh & M. L. Savickas (Eds.), *Handbook of vocational psychology* (3rd ed., pp. 227–244). Mahweh, NJ: Lawrence Erlbaum.

Brown, S. D., & Lent, R. W. (Eds.). (2005). *Career development and counseling: Putting theory and research to work.* Hoboken, NJ: John Wiley & Sons, Inc.

Bureau of Labor Statistics (BLS). (2006). Labor Force Statistics from the Current Population Survey. Retrieved March 26, 2008, from http://www.bls.gov/cps/cpsaat9.pdf

Carter, R. T., & Constantine, M. G. (2000). Career maturity, life role salience, and racial/ethnic identity among Black and Asian American college students. *Journal of Career Assessment, 8,* 173–187.

Carter, R. T., & Cook, D. A. (1992). A culturally relevant perspective for understanding the career paths of visible racial/ethnic group people. In H. D. Lea & Z. B. Leibowitz (Eds.), *Adult career development: Concepts, issues, and practice* (pp. 192–217). Alexandria, VA: National Career Development Association.

Census Bureau (2007). 2006. American Community Survey. Retrieved March 26, 2008 http://factfinder.census.gov/servlet/DTTable?_bm=y&-geo_id=01000US&-ds_name=ACS_2006_EST_G00_&-mt_name=ACS_2006_EST_G2000_B02001

Chronister, K. M., & McWhirter, E. H. (2006). An experimental examination of two career interventions for battered women. *Journal of Counseling Psychology, 53*, 151–164.

Cook, E. P., Heppner, M. J., & O'Brien, K. M. (2002). Career development of women of color and White women: Assumptions, conceptualization, and interventions from an ecological perspective. *Career Development Quarterly, 50*, 291–305.

Cook, T. D., Church, M. B., Ajanaku, S., Shadish, W. R., Kim, J., & Cohen, R. (1996). The development of occupational aspirations and expectations among inner-city boys. *Child Development, 67*, 3368–3385.

Coutinho, M. T., Dam, U. C., & Blustein, D. L. (in press). The psychology of working and globalization: A new perspective for a new era. *International Journal of Vocational and Educational Guidance.*

Crites, J. O. (1969). *Vocational psychology.* New York: McGraw Hill.

Cushman, P. (1995). *Constructing the self, constructing America: A cultural history of psychotherapy.* Reading, MA: Addison-Wesley.

Davey, F. H. (2001). The relationship between engineering and young women's occupational priorities. *Canadian Journal of Counseling, 35*, 221–228.

Dawis, R. V. (2005). The Minnesota theory of work adjustment. In S. D. Brown & R. W. Lent (Eds.), *Career development and counseling: Putting theory and research to work* (pp. 3–23). Hoboken, NJ: John Wiley & Sons, Inc.

Diemer, M. A., & Blustein, D. L. (2006). Critical consciousness and career development among urban youth. *Journal of Vocational Behavior, 68*, 220–232.

Eccles, J. S. (1994). Understanding women's educational and occupational choices: Applying the Eccles et al. model of achievement-related choices. *Psychology of Women Quarterly, 18*, 585–609.

Farmer, H. S., Wardrop, J. L., Anderson, M. Z., & Risinger, R. (1995). Women's career choices: Focus on science, math, and technology careers. *Journal of Counseling Psychology, 42*, 155–170.

Farmer, H. S., Wardrop, J. L., & Rotella, S. C. (1999). Antecedent factors differentiating women and men in science/nonscience careers. *Psychology of Women Quarterly, 23*, 763–780.

Fassinger, R. E. (1995). From invisibility to integration: Lesbian identity in the workplace. *Career Development Quarterly, 44*(2), 148–167.

Fassinger, R. E. (1996). Notes from the margins: Integrating lesbian experiences into the vocational psychology of women. *Journal of Vocational Behavior, 48*, 160–175.

Fassinger, R. E. (2005). Theoretical issues in the study of women's career development: Building bridges in a brave new world. In W. B. Walsh & M. L. Savickas (Eds.), *Handbook of vocational psychology* (3rd ed., pp. 85–124). Mahwah, NJ: Lawrence Erlbaum Associates.

Flores, L. Y., & O'Brien, K. M. (2002). The career development of Mexican American adolescent women: A test of social cognitive career theory. *Journal of Counseling Psychology, 49,* 14–27.

Fouad, N. A. (2002). Cross-cultural differences in vocational interests: Between-group differences on the Strong Interest Inventory. *Journal of Counseling Psychology, 49,* 283–289.

Fouad, N. A. (2007). Work and vocational psychology: Theory, research, and applications. *Annual review of psychology, 58,* 543–564.

Fouad, N. A., & Arrendondo, P. (2007). *Becoming culturally oriented: Practical advice for psychologists and educators.* Washington, DC: American Psychological Association.

Fouad, N. A., & Bingham, R. P. (1995). Career counseling with racial and ethnic minorities. In W. B. Walsh, & S. H. Osipow (Eds.), *Handbook of vocational psychology: Theory, research, and practice* (2nd ed., pp. 331–365). Hillsdale, NJ: Lawrence Erlbaum Associates.

Fouad, N. A., & Byars-Winston, A. M. (2005). Cultural context of career choice: Meta-analysis of race/ethnicity differences. *Career Development Quarterly, 53,* 223–233.

Fouad, N. A., & Kantamneni, N. (in press). Contextual influences in vocational choice: A three-dimensional model. In S. Brown & R. W. Lent (Eds.), *Handbook of counseling psychology* (4th ed.). New York: Wiley.

Freire, P. (1970/1993). *Pedagogy of the oppressed.* New York: The Continuum Publishing Company.

Friedman, R. L. (2005). *The world is flat: A brief history of the twenty-first century.* Waterville, ME: Thorndike Press.

Gainor, K. A., & Lent, R. W. (1998). Social cognitive expectations and racial identity attitudes in predicting the math choice intentions of Black college students. *Journal of Counseling Psychology, 45,* 403–413.

Gomez, M. J., Fassinger, R. E., Prosser, J., Cooke, K., Mejia, B., & Luna, J. (2001). Voces abriendo caminos (voices foraging paths): A qualitative study of the career development of notable Latinas. *Journal of Counseling Psychology, 48,* 286–300.

Guichard, J. (2005). Life-long self construction. *International Journal for Educational and Vocational Guidance, 5,* 111–124.

Hackett, G., Betz, N. E., Casas, J. M., & Rocha-Singh, I. A. (1992). Gender, ethnicity, and social cognitive factors predicting the academic achievement of students in engineering. *Journal of Counseling Psychology, 39,* 527–538.

Hall, D. T. (1996). *The career is dead—long live the career: A relational approach to careers.* San Francisco: Jossey-Bass.

Hall, D. T. (2002). *Careers in and out of organizations.* Thousand Oaks, CA: Sage Publications.

Hall, D. T., Briscoe, J. P., & Kram, K. E. (1977). Identity, values and learning in the protean career. In C. L. Cooper & S. E. Jackson (Eds.), *Creating tomorrow's organizations* (pp. 321–335). London: John Wiley.

Harren, V. A. (1979). A model of career decision making for college students. *Journal of Vocational Behavior, 14,* 119–133.

Helms, J. E., & Cook, D. A. (1999). *Using race and culture in counseling and psychotherapy: Theory and process.* Boston: Allyn & Bacon.

Helwig, A. A. (2004). A ten-year longitudinal study of the career development of students: Summary findings. *Journal of Counseling & Development, 82*, 49–57.

Hermans, H. J. M., & Kempen, H. J. G. (1998). Moving cultures: The perilous problems of cultural dichotomies in a globalizing society. *American Psychologist, 53*, 1111–1120.

Holland, J. L. (1997). *Making vocational choices: A theory of vocational personalities and work environments* (3rd ed.). Odessa, FL: PAR.

Holland, J. L., Gottfredson, G. D., & Gottfredson, L. S. (1975). Read our reports and examine the data: A response to Prediger and Cole. *Journal of Vocational Behavior, 7*, 253–259.

Holland, J. L., Gottfredson, D. C. & Power, P. G. (1980). Some diagnostic scales for research in decision making and personality: Identity, information and barriers. *Journal of Personality and Social Psychology, 39*(6), 1191–1200.

Hyde, J. S. (2005). The gender similarities hypothesis. *American Psychologist, 60*, 581–592.

International Monetary Fund (2000, April). Globalization: Threat or opportunity. Retrieved January 5, 2007, from http://www.imf.org/external/np/exr/ib/2000/041200.htm#II

Jackson, C. C., & Neville, H. A. (1998). Influence of racial identity attitudes on African American college students' vocational identity and hope. *Journal of Vocational Behavior, 53*, 97–113.

Jenkins, H. (2004). Pop cosmopolitanism: Mapping cultural flows in an age of media convergence. In M. M. Suárez-Orozco & D. B. Qin-Hilliard (Eds.), *Globalization: Culture and education in the new millennium* (pp. 114–140). Berkeley: University of California Press.

Jome, L. M., & Tokar, D. M. (1998). Dimensions of masculinity and major choice traditionality. *Journal of Vocational Behavior, 52*, 120–134.

Jones, S. R. (1997). Voices of identity and difference: A qualitative exploration of the multiple dimensions of identity development in women college students. *Journal of College Student Development, 38*, 376–386.

Jordan, J. V., Walker, M., & Hartling, L. M. (Eds.). (2004). *The complexity of connection: Writings from the Stone Center's Jean Baker Miller Training Institute.* New York: Guilford Press.

Josselson, R. (1992). *The space between us: Exploring the dimensions of human relationships.* San Francisco: Jossey-Bass.

Juntunen, C. L., Barraclough, D. J., Broneck, C. L., Seibel, G. A., Winrow, S. A., & Morin, P. M. (2001). American Indian perspectives on the career journey. *Journal of Counseling Psychology, 48*, 274–285.

Kenny, M. E., Blustein, D. L., Chaves, A., Grossman, J. M., & Gallagher, L. A. (2003). The role of perceived barriers and relational support in the educational and vocational lives of urban high school students. *Journal of Counseling Psychology, 50*, 142–155.

Leary, M. R., & Tangney, J. P. (Eds.). (2002). *Handbook of self and identity.* New York: Guilford Press.

Lease, S. H. (2003). Testing a model of men's nontraditional occupational choices. *Career Development Quarterly, 51*, 244–258.

Lee, C. C. (1984). Predicting the career choice attitudes of rural Black, White, and Native American high school students. *Vocational Guidance Quarterly, 32*, 177–184.

Lent, R. W., Brown, S. D., & Hackett, G. (2000). Contextual supports and barriers to career choice: A social cognitive analysis. *Journal of Counseling Psychology, 47*, 36–49.

Lent, R. W., Brown, S. D., & Hackett, G. (1994). Toward a unifying social cognitive theory of career and academic interest, choice, and performance. *Journal of Vocational Behavior, 45*, 79–122.

Lent, R. W., Brown, S. D., & Hackett, G. (2002). Social cognitive career theory. In D. Brown (Ed.). *Career choice and development* (pp. 255–311). San Francisco: Jossey-Bass.

Leong, F. T. L. (Ed.) (1995). *Career development and vocational behavior of racial and ethnic minorities.* Hillsdale, NJ: Lawrence Erlbaum Associates.

Leong, F. T. L., & Gupta, A. (2007). Career development and vocational behaviors of Asian Americans. In F. T. L. Leong, A. Ebreo, L. Kinoshita, A. G. Inman, L. H. Yang, et al. (Eds.), *Handbook of Asian American psychology: Second edition* (pp. 159–178). Thousand Oaks, CA: Sage Publications.

Lerner, R. (2002). *Concepts and theories of human development* (3rd ed.). Mahwah, NJ: Lawrence Erlbaum Associates.

Levine, P. B., & Zimmerman, D. J (1995). A comparison of the sex-type of occupational aspirations and subsequent achievement. *Work & Occupations, 22*, 73–84.

Long, L., Adams, R. S., & Tracey, T. J. G. (2005). Generalizability of interest structure to China: Application of the Personal Globe Inventory. *Journal of Vocational Behavior, 66*, 66–80.

Lopez, F. G., Lent, R. W., Brown, S. D., & Gore, P. A. (1997). Role of social-cognitive expectations in high school students' mathematics-related interest and performance. *Journal of Counseling Psychology, 44*, 44–52.

McWhirter, E. H., Hackett, G., & Bandalos, D. L. (1998). A causal model of the educational plans and career expectations of Mexican American high school girls. *Journal of Counseling Psychology, 45*, 166–181.

Miller, L., & Budd, J. (1999). The development of occupational sex-role stereotypes, occupational preferences and academic subject preferences in children at ages 8, 12, and 16. *Educational Psychology, 19*, 17–35.

Minatoya, L. Y., & Sedlacek, W. E. (1983). Assessing differential needs among university freshmen: A comparison among racial/ethnic subgroups. *Journal of Non-White Concerns in Personnel & Guidance, 11*, 126–132.

Munley, P. H., Fretz, B. R., & Mills, D. H. (1973). Female college students' scores on the men's and women's Strong Vocational Interest Blanks. *Journal of Counseling Psychology, 20*, 285–289.

National Science Foundation, Division of Science Resources Statistics. (2003). *Women, minorities, and persons with disabilities in science and engineering: 2002*, Arlington, VA: NSF 03–312. Retrieved from http://www.nsf.gov/sbe/srs/nsf03312/pdf/c01.pdf

Nauta, M. M., Epperson, D. L., & Kahn, J. H. (1998). A multiple-groups analysis of predictors of higher level career aspirations among women in mathematics, science, and engineering majors. *Journal of Counseling Psychology, 45*, 483–496.

O'Brien, K. (1992). *Career Aspirations Scale.* College Park: University of Maryland.

O'Brien, K. M. (1996). The influence of psychological separation and parental attachment on the career development of adolescent women. *Journal of Vocational Behavior, 48*, 257–274.

Okocha, A. A. G. (1994). Preparing racial ethnic minorities for the work force 2000. *Journal of Multicultural Counseling and Development, 22*, 106–114.

Oliver, L. W. (1975). The relationship of parental attitudes and parent identification to career and homemaking orientation in college women. *Journal of Vocational Behavior, 7*, 1–12.

Pearson, S. M., & Bieschke, K. J. (2001). Succeeding against the odds: An examination of familial influences on the career development of professional African American women. *Journal of Counseling Psychology, 48*, 301–309.

Peterson, N., & González, R. C. (2005). *The role of work in people's lives: Applied career counseling and vocational psychology* (2nd ed.). Belmont, CA: Brooks/Cole.

Phillips, S. D., & Imhoff, A. R. (1997). Women and career development: A decade of research. *Annual Review of Psychology, 48*, 31–59.

Prediger, D. J., & Cole, N. S. (1975). Sex-role socialization and employment realities: Implications for vocational interest measures. *Journal of Vocational Behavior, 7*, 239–251.

Prince, J. P. (1995). Influences on the career development of gay men. *The Career Development Quarterly, 44*, 168–177.

Richardson, M. S. (1993). Work in people's lives: A location for counseling psychologists. *Journal of Counseling Psychology, 40*, 425–433.

Richie, B. S., Fassinger, R. E., Linn, S. G., Johnson, J., Prosser, J., & Robinson, S. (1997). Persistence, connection, and passion: A qualitative study of the career development of highly achieving African American-Black and White women. *Journal of Counseling Psychology, 44*, 133–148.

Rojewski, J. W., & Yang, B. (1997). Longitudinal analysis of select influences on adolescents' occupational aspirations. *Journal of Vocational Behavior, 51*, 375–410.

Savickas, M. L. (2005). The theory and practice of career construction. In S. D. Brown & R. W. Lent (Eds.), *Career development and counseling: Putting theory and research to work* (pp. 42–70). Hoboken, NJ: John Wiley & Sons, Inc.

Skorikov, V., & Vondracek, F. W. (2007). Positive career orientation as an inhibitor of adolescent problem behaviour. *Journal of Adolescence, 30*, 131–146.

Smith, E. J. (1983). Issues in racial minorities' career behavior. In W. B. Walsh & S. H. Osipow (Eds.), *Handbook of vocational psychology: Vol. 1, Foundations* (pp. 161–222). Hillsdale, NJ: Lawrence Erlbaum Associates.

Stuart, S. K. (2003). Choice or chance: Career development of girls with emotional or behavioral disorders. *Behavioral Disorders, 28*, 150–161.

Suárez-Orozco, M. M., & Qin-Hilliard, D. B. (2004). Introduction. In M. M. Suárez-Orozco & D. B. Qin-Hilliard (Eds.), *Globalization: Culture and education in the new millennium* (pp. 1–37). Berkeley: University of California Press.

Super, D. E. (1957). *The psychology of careers*. New York: Harper & Row.

Super, D. E. (1980). A life-span, life-space, approach to career development. *Journal of Vocational Behavior, 13*, 282–298.

Super, D. E., Starishevsky, R, Matlin, N., & Jordaan, J. (1963). *Career development: Self-concept theory*. New York: College Entrance Examination Board.

Swann, W. R., Chang-Schneider, C., & McLarty, K. L. (2007). Do people's self-views matter? Self-concept and self-esteem in everyday life. *American Psychologist, 62*, 84–94.

Tinsley, D. J., & Faunce, P. S. (1978). Vocational interests of career and homemaker oriented women. *Journal of Vocational Behavior, 13*, 327–337.

Vincent, P. C., Peplau, L. A., & Hill, C. T. (1998). A longitudinal application of the theory of reasoned action to women's career behavior. *Journal of Applied Social Psychology, 28*, 761–778.

Vondracek, F. W., Lerner, R. M., & Schulenberg, J. E. (1986). *Career development: A life-span developmental approach.* Hillsdale, NJ: Lawrence Erlbaum Associates.

Walsh, W. B., & Savickas, M. L. (Eds.). (2005). *Handbook of vocational psychology: Theory, research and practice* (3rd ed.). Mahwah, NJ: Lawrence Erlbaum Associates.

Worthington, R. L., Flores, L. Y., Navarro, R. L., Brown, S. D., & Lent, R. W. (2005). Career development in context: Research with people of color. In S. D. Brown & R. W. Lent (Eds.), *Career development and counseling: Putting theory and research to work* (pp. 225–252). Hoboken, NJ: John Wiley & Sons.

Chapter Seven

Human Agency, Strengths-Based Development, and Well-Being

Jeana L. Magyar-Moe
Shane J. Lopez

INTRODUCTION

Focusing on the positive in psychology is a hallmark of those in the counseling psychology profession. Indeed, a distinctive feature and unifying theme of the work of counseling psychologists is the focus on client strengths, assets, and potentialities regardless of the degree of psychopathology (APA, 1999; Gelso & Fretz, 2001; Savickas, 2003). A brief review of the development of the counseling psychology specialty confirms this enduring philosophy and commitment to helping individuals to discover, develop, and utilize personal and social resources on a regular basis (see Lopez et al., 2006).

The counseling psychology discipline began to take form after the end of World War II when the field transitioned from an emphasis on vocational guidance to counseling psychology. Super (1955) pronounced at that time that the defining feature of the new specialty was "hygiology" or a focus on "the normalities of even abnormal persons" (p. 5). Indeed, counseling psychologists entered newly created positions in Veterans Administration (VA) hospitals, where they provided counseling services to general medical and surgical patients within the Division of Medicine and Neurology, in contrast to the Psychiatric Division, where clinical psychologists were typically employed. In these roles, counseling psychologists began to demonstrate to the public how counseling could be beneficial for all people, not just those with severe psychopathology (Gelso & Fretz, 2001). While new opportunities were taking shape in the VA system, colleges and universities across the nation were developing "counseling centers" that employed counseling psychologists whose primary roles were to assist veterans in adjusting to civilian life through addressing vocational and personal growth issues, with a focus on the identification of personal strengths and social resources of their clientele (Gelso & Fretz, 2001; Lopez et al., 2006).

During the 1960s, counseling psychologists continued to maintain their focus on the positive in psychology through creating a research base devoted to the discovery and promotion of matches between individuals (specifically, the personality strengths of these individuals) and their environments such that the environments that they were to work and live in would serve to highlight and capitalize on their personality traits. This focus on Person x Environment fit was an alternative to attempts by professionals in other disciplines to work on changing personality structure (Tyler, 1965). Likewise, research in the 1970s continued to focus on the concept of the healthy personality and ways in which practicing counseling psychologists could best help their clientele through realizing the needs, values, and interests of those with whom they worked (White, 1973). In the 1980s and 1990s, counseling psychologists continued this strengths-focus through highlighting the strengths, assets, and potentialities of people of all cultural backgrounds (APA, 1999; Lent, Lopez, Mikolaitis, Jones, & Bieschke, 1992).

In 2006, Lopez and colleagues conducted a content analysis of four major outlets of counseling psychology scholarship aimed at identifying the amount of research devoted to the study of human strengths, positive processes, and positive outcomes over the past 50 years. Results revealed that 29% of the research in counseling psychology guild and theme journals over the past 50 years was positive-focused. When broken down by decade, the percentage of positive-focused scholarship was at 23% or greater for the past 40 years, "indicating that counseling psychology's philosophical commitment to studying the best in people has resulted in a large scholarly base fairly consistent throughout the decades" (Lopez et al., 2006, p. 218).

Counseling psychology has a long track record of focusing on what is right in people and in environments. Our contributions to scholarship and practice have been rich and diverse. In the remainder of this chapter we highlight a body of scholarship on human agency that has shaped the thinking of researchers and change agents, and we summarize some of the latest work on strengths-based interventions that is being produced by counseling psychologists. Research on agency and development of strengths-enhancing strategies may be the most meaningful contributions we have made to the broader positive psychological literature and may serve as the lasting routes through which we could lead the discipline in discovery and application.

COUNSELING PSYCHOLOGY SCHOLARSHIP RELATED TO HUMAN AGENCY

In Bandura's view of human agency (1997; 2004), people are intentional (forming action plans and strategies for realizing them), future-minded (setting goals and finding motivation to aid in pursuit), self-regulatory (adopting personal standards and monitoring personal reactions and change), and self-reflective (reflecting on thoughts and actions and the meaning of goal pursuits, and making adjustments to thinking and behavior as necessary). Holding the primary assumption associated with human agency, that people are significant contributors to their life circumstances and not just products of them, counseling psychologists have embarked on a pursuit of new knowledge about how agentic forces lead to a better life. Indeed, counseling psychologists have made major contributions to the study of and promotion of human agency.

Human agency constructs such as self-efficacy (Bandura, 1977) and hope (Snyder, 1994) (which theoretically align with Bandura's four characteristics of agency) are *meaningful* as they are predictive of positive life outcomes, *measurable* via a brief scale or interview, *malleable* when the target of brief interventions, *multicultural* given that they often adequately describe what fuels the life pursuits of people of all backgrounds, and have been *mined* by counseling psychology scholars. Though other human agency constructs that are meaningful, measurable, malleable, multicultural, and mined by counseling psychologists might exist, we discuss these two because they have empirical links to positive outcomes that matter to counseling psychologists— academic and/or vocational success. We also discuss personal growth initiative (Robitschek, 1998), as it is the only human agency construct that was originally operationalized by a counseling psychologist and also appears to have great potential for predicting academic, vocational, and therapeutic outcome success.

Self-Efficacy

The examination of self-efficacy and its effects on (and relationships to) positive life outcomes accounts for a large portion of the strengths-focused research in counseling psychology (Lopez et al., 2006). Self-efficacy, "people's judgments about their capabilities to organize and execute courses of action required to attain designated types of performances" (Bandura, 1986, p. 391), is a central and pervasive aspect of human agency (Bandura, 1997) that has been positioned as the foundation of leading counseling psychologists' work on vocational development (e.g., Flores & O'Brien, 2002; Lent & Brown, 1996; Lent, Brown, & Hackett, 1994; O'Brien,

2003), dynamic change processes (e.g., Lent et al., 1992), and academic achievement (e.g., Gore, 2006; Lopez, Lent, Brown, & Gore, 1997; Multon, Brown, & Lent, 1991; Multon, Shortridge-Pearce, & Frey, 2005).

Given the current intense focus on accountability and learning outcomes in K–12 and higher education, Multon and colleagues' (Multon et al., 1991; Multon et al., 2005), meta-analytic work that revealed a moderate link between self-efficacy and academic performance (unbiased effect size estimate $r = .38$) and persistence (unbiased effect size estimate $r = .34$), may have particular societal relevance. Likewise, Gore's (2006) completion of two incremental validity studies to test whether self-efficacy beliefs accounted for a significant amount of variance in college success above and beyond that accounted for by standardized test scores is also quite relevant. Indeed, he found that self-efficacy seems to be a significant predictor of college academic outcomes, however, this relationship depends on when and what types of efficacy beliefs are measured. More specifically, academic self-efficacy beliefs measured at the end of one semester of college were significant predictors of college success, whereas academic self-efficacy beliefs measured at the beginning of the first semester of college were not. Additionally, differential results were found for two subscales on the College Self-Efficacy Inventory (Solberg, O'Brien, Villarreal, Kennel, & Davis, 1993), with course-related academic self-efficacy beliefs being more strongly related to grade point average and social self-efficacy beliefs being more strongly related to college persistence (Gore, 2006).

Regarding self-efficacy and vocational success, though the literature is replete with descriptions of studies and findings that link self-efficacy with other variables inherent to the career development process (see O'Brien, 2003, for a summary), there is much less empirical research that ties self-efficacy to vocational success (see Gainer, 2006, for a summary). Indeed, Betz and Hackett (2006) expressed concerns about current research efforts on career self-efficacy and have made several recommendations for improvement of such research, including a more careful focus on the theoretical underpinnings, conceptualization, and measurement of the self-efficacy construct. Lent and Brown (2006) provide further guidance on conceptualizing and assessing the core constructs of social cognitive *career* theory, including *self-efficacy*. In summary, they suggest a "list of five C's" that researchers should use as a guide in doing their work on self-efficacy. This list includes *contextualizing* measures, being *comprehensive* in sampling, making sure there is *compatibility* between predictors and criteria, and utilizing *challenging* tasks that are under the personal *control* of participants.

Notable exceptions to the lack of empirical research on self-efficacy and positive vocational outcomes include a longitudinal study in which Pinquart, Juang, and Silbereisen (2003) examined whether self-efficacy beliefs and school grades at ages 12 to 15 were associated with employment and job satisfaction at age 21. Indeed, the predictor variables were associated with gainful employment and job satisfaction. In an incremental validity study, Donnay and Borgen (1999) examined the explanatory power, beyond vocational interest, of vocational self-efficacy in identifying tenured and satisfied membership status of 1,105 employed women and men. Findings suggested that self-efficacy does have predictive value over and above interest.

Hope

Hope, another agentic life force, was defined by Snyder (1994) as a person's ability to conceptualize *goals,* develop specific strategies or *pathways* to reach those goals, and initiate and sustain the motivation or *agency* for using those strategies. People with high hope set more (and more challenging) goals than people with low hope, and they are able to reach goals more successfully because they are able to nimbly navigate around impediments (Snyder, 1994). Counseling psychologists have devoted research attention to the hope construct over the past 50 years (e.g., Edwards, Ong, & Lopez, 2007; Edwards, Rand, Lopez, & Snyder, 2007; Lopez et al., 2006), and some of this work has examined links between hope and well-being (Shogren, Lopez, Wehmeyer, Little, & Pressgrove, 2006) and has emphasized that hopeful thinking and related skills can be taught. For example, Worthington et al. (1997) examined the effects of a hope-based relationship enrichment program. Outcomes included enhancing and maintaining (at 3 weeks) partner satisfaction and quality of couple skills (Worthington et al., 1997) and increasing the ratio of positive to negative communications between couples (Ripley & Worthington, 2002). Regarding other approaches to hope enhancement across the life span, Lopez et al. (2004) identified numerous formal strategies (the core components of which are summarized in Table 7.1) and discussed the effectiveness data, where available, associated with these strategies.

Counseling psychologists and colleagues in clinical psychology also have examined the links between hope and educational outcomes (see Snyder, Lopez, Shorey, Rand, & Feldman, 2003). For example, in a 6-year longitudinal study, individual differences in hope scores of entering college freshmen predicted better overall grade point averages even after controlling for variance related to entrance examination scores. High- relative to the low-hope students also were more likely to have graduated and not to have

Table 7.1 Steps to Enhancing Hope in Adult Clients

I. Administration of the Adult Hope Scale (trait)

The first step in this process is the completion of the Adult Hope Scale. The therapist will then tally the total score and compute subscale scores for both pathway and agency.

II. Learning About Hope

Once a baseline hope score is determined, the therapist can then discuss hope theory with the client and its relevance to the therapy process and to positive outcomes.

III. Structuring Hope for the Client

In this step, the client will create a list of important life components, determine which areas are most important, and discuss the level of satisfaction within those areas.

IV. Creating Positive and Specific Goals

Using the important life components identified above, the client and therapist work together to create workable goals that are both positive and specific. These goals should be salient to the client and attainable. Additionally, the client will develop multiple pathways for each goal and identify agency thoughts for each goal.

V. Practice Makes Perfect

Once the client and therapist have agreed upon these goals, the client should visualize and verbalize the steps to reach his or her goals. With this practice, the client and therapist can collaborate on the most effective pathways and the agency behind the goals.

VI. Checking In

Clients will incorporate these goals, pathways, and agency into their life and report back to the therapist on the process of goal attainment. Again, collaboration can occur to adjust or modify any disparities in actions or thinking that may hinder the successful achievement of their desired goals.

This process is cyclical and requires continual assessment by both the client and the therapist. Once the client has grasped the concepts of hope theory, however, the client can then assume the bulk of responsibility in the implementation of hope theory to her or his unique experiences.

been dismissed over this 6-year period (Snyder et al., 2002). No studies linking Snyder's hope and vocational success appear in the literature, but promising scholarship is under way examining domain-specific work hope and its relationships with other agentic constructs (Juntunen & Wettersten, 2006).

Personal Growth Initiative

Personal growth initiative (Robitschek, 1998) is the active, intentional involvement in developing as a person. People with high personal growth initiative maintain a keen awareness of their growth opportunities and capitalize on them. They are also mindful of the environment, taking advantage of situations that would foster growth. Although Robitschek has completed considerable work on theory and instrument development and the introduction of the construct has sparked considerable dissertation research (with six studies cited in PsycInfo), there are no published papers linking personal growth initiative and academic success and only one peer-reviewed paper (Robitschek & Cook, 1999; initiative-predicted environmental exploration and vocational identity) connecting growth initiative and vocational development. Personal growth initiative has also been studied in the context of coping and therapy outcome. Findings suggest that personal growth initiative is positively correlated with problem-focused coping (Robitschek, 1998; Robitschek & Cook, 1999) and psychological well-being, and negatively correlated with psychological distress (Robitschek & Kashubeck, 1999). Indeed, when measuring therapy outcome in terms of increases in well-being experienced, personal growth was found to be a significant predictor, whereas when outcome was measured in terms of reduction of symptom distress, hope was the better predictor (Magyar-Moe, 2004). Finally, there is some evidence that counseling itself might enhance personal growth initiative (Magyar-Moe, 2006; Robitshek, 1999).

COUNSELING PSYCHOLOGY RESEARCH ON STRENGTHS-BASED DEVELOPMENT AND PRACTICES

Counseling psychologists have been developing practice methods in order to activate the human agency constructs of self-efficacy, hope, and personal growth initiative. Most current strengths-based practices (previously reviewed in Lopez & Edwards, 2008) encourage people to complete one of two comprehensive measures of strengths available online. One measure, the Values in Action Inventory of Strengths (VIA-IS; Peterson & Seligman, 2004), is based on the belief that strengths are the lived manifestations of virtues and are associated with well-being; it measures 24 character strengths. The other, the Clifton StrengthsFinder (CSF; Buckingham & Clifton, 2000; Lopez, Hodges, & Harter, 2005; Rath, 2007), is based on a platform of 34 talent themes that are prevalent in society and predictive of educational and vocational success. Three strengths-based approaches designed recently by counseling psychologists purportedly promote development, human agency, and well-being (Lopez, Tree, Bowers, & Burns, 2006; Smith, 2006; Wong, 2006). The three approaches were designed to be shared with individuals, rather than groups, and with people who are not symptomatic with a severe mental disorder. To date, these programs have not yet undergone empirical scrutiny.

In this section, we will briefly describe the development and psychometric characteristics of the VIA-IS and CSF and the stages of the three strengths-based practices.

Strengths Measures

The VIA-IS (Peterson & Seligman, 2004), originally commissioned by the Mayerson Foundation, measures 24 strengths, organized under six overarching virtues (wisdom and knowledge, courage, humanity, justice, temperance, and transcendence) thought to "emerge consensually across cultures and throughout time" (Peterson & Seligman, 2004, p. 29). The current iteration of the VIA-IS is available online (http://www.positivepsychology.org) and as a paper-and-pencil measure in English and several other languages. The 240 items (10 for each strength), answered along a 5-point Likert scale, can be completed in about 30 minutes.

All scales have produced satisfactory internal consistency and test-retest estimates over a 4-month period. In terms of validity, correlations among scales are higher than expected given that the inventory was designed to measure 24 unique constructs. However, more favorable validity evidence includes findings that (a) self-ratings correlate appropriately with ratings of the target individual by friends and family members, and (b) the majority of the scales correlate positively with measures of life satisfaction. Factor analytic findings suggest that the measure consists of five factors (strengths of restraint, intellectual strengths, interpersonal strengths, emotional strengths, theological strengths) instead of the six proposed virtues. Peterson and Seligman (2004) described studies comparing strengths across groups of people and argued that the VIA-IS can be used as an outcome measure for strengths-enhancing interventions. The researchers at the VIA Institute plan additional examinations of the psychometric properties of the measure.

Donald Clifton of the Gallup Organization identified personal talents using empirically based, semistructured interviews, which led to the creation of the CSF in the 1990s. Based on earlier interview data, Clifton identified 34 talent themes. The current CSF 2.0 presents, in an online format (http://www.strengthsfinder.com), 178 item pairs designed to measure 34 talent themes (Asplund, Lopez, Hodges, & Harter, 2007; Rath, 2007). It is appropriate for administration with adolescents and adults with reading levels of 10th grade or higher and is available in 17 languages. Although it is used to identify personal talents, the supporting materials are intended to help individuals discover how to build on their talents within particular life roles (e.g., Buckingham & Clifton, 2000; Clifton & Anderson, 2002; Clifton & Nelson, 1992).

The CSF 2.0 provides information on an individual's "Five Signature Themes," that is, the five themes on which he or she scored highest. Remaining themes are not rank ordered or shared with respondents. These data are provided to foster intrapersonal development. It should be noted, however, that this instrument is not designed or validated for use in employee selection or mental health screening. In addition, the CSF is not sensitive to change and, thus, should not be used as a pre-post measure of growth.

Extensive psychometric research on the CSF was conducted by Gallup researchers and summarized in a technical report by Asplund et al. (2007). Across samples, most scales (i.e., themes) have been found to yield acceptable internal consistency and test-retest reliability estimates over periods ranging from 3 weeks to 17 months. In a college student sample, the mean test-retest reliability estimate (with an 8- to 12-week interval) across the 34 themes was .70 (Schreiner, 2005). In terms of validity, intercorrelations among the themes suggest that they are relatively independent of one another. Preliminary construct validity evidence (Lopez et al., 2005; Schreiner, 2005) indicates that themes are related to expected Big Five personality constructs and scales on the 16PF (Cattell, 1993) and the California Personality Inventory-260 (Gough & Bradley, 1996).

Strengths-Centered Therapy

Strength-Centered Therapy (SCT; Wong, 2006) is a psychotherapeutic approach, grounded in social constructionism, designed to leverage character strengths and virtues (as defined by Peterson & Seligman, 2004) in the change process. Over the course of SCT, the counselor and client use social constructionist metastrategies (e.g., use of clients' interpersonal resources to expand the number of voices bearing on the clients' experiences, including their strengths), numerous solution-focused techniques, and provocative new mini-interventions to create a larger repertoire of personal strengths and their meaning in the client's life. With these meanings and a greater vocabulary of strengths, it is hypothesized that clients begin to attach their life experiences to that which is positive and adaptive. SCT employs weekly sessions during which clients are assumed to cycle and recycle through four phases (Explicitizing, Envisioning, Empowering, and Evolving) over the course of a few months.

In SCT, the process of naming the client's existing character strengths, which could be facilitated with the VIA-IS or strengths interviews, is termed Explicitizing. Reframing an apparent character flaw as a strength (Gelso & Woodhouse, 2003) also may prove to be an effective strategy for naming the best characteristics in people. Counseling creatively gifted individuals provides many opportunities for providing more appropriate labels for seemingly adaptive behavior that has been mischaracterized (e.g., highlighting how episodes of divergent thinking lead to discoveries in lieu of describing how such thinking is "off topic"). Next, clients identify the strengths they wish to develop through intentional use via Envisioning. The query "What strengths would you like to develop?" can provide the information needed, or previously identified therapeutic goals can be pursued through the development of particular strengths. During the Empowering phase, clients are assumed to experience a boost in agency as they begin to believe that using their strengths can positively affect their lives. This agency may be derived from the development of habits (e.g., writing weekly thank-you notes to cultivate gratitude) that lead to the effective use of strengths. Wong (2006) also recommended the use of metaphorical signposting during this phase to track therapeutic progress (e.g., Wong suggested the metaphor of a manual transmission and determining what promotes movement from second gear to third gear and all the way to fifth gear). Finally, the Evolving phase is most salient during the termination stage of psychotherapy and involves the process of making strengths-development a never-ending process that transcends the formal psychotherapeutic process. Progress should be reviewed and celebrated and considered successes to build on.

Strengths-Based Counseling for Adolescents

Strengths-Based Counseling for Adolescents (SBC; Smith, 2006) builds on the common factors of change and attempts to foster growth by helping clients use strengths to overcome some of life's problems. SBC guides the psychologist who "searches for what people have rather than what they do not have, what people can do rather than what they cannot do, and how they have been successful rather than how they have failed" (Smith, 2006, p. 38). Smith encourages building on the best in people by identifying character strengths with the VIA-IS and paying particular attention to how these strengths and others are manifested in a cultural context.

SBC involves 10 stages of counseling. Stage 1, Creating the Therapeutic Alliance, begins with discussion of the importance of personal strengths and honors personal struggles. Stage 2, Identifying Strengths, relies on narrative techniques to help clients discover and internalize their strengths. Stage 3, Assessing Presenting Problems, serves to clarify the client's concerns. In Stage 4, Encouraging and Instilling Hope, the strengths-based counselor provides the client with feedback on individual effort and improvement. Stage 5, Framing Solutions, relies heavily on Solution-Focused Strategies.

Stage 6, Building Strength and Competence, fosters the development of internal and external assets. Stages 7 through 9 (Empowering, Changing, Building Resilience) are designed to promote agency and facilitate goal pursuit. Finally, Stage 10, Evaluating and Terminating, allows the counselor and client to identify the strengths that were most valuable to the change process and to honor progress that has been made. Although this approach lacks specific strengths-enhancing techniques, it provides the counselor with a general guide for strengths-based counseling.

Strengths Mentoring

Strengths Mentoring (SM; Lopez, Tree, Bowers, & Burns, 2004; Lopez, Tree, et al., 2006) is a student development strategy designed to capitalize on the common factors of change and to boost academic self-efficacy (Bandura, 1977), hope (Snyder, 1994), and personal growth initiative (Robitschek, 1998). SM, a three-session manualized approach, promotes the intentional use of strengths, as measured by the Clifton Strengthsfinder, in students' daily lives. Over the course of SM, trained mentors and student mentees identify salient academic goals that could be attained over the course of a semester. Using microcounseling skills and narrative and hope-enhancing techniques, the mentor helps mentees move through three stages of strengths development (Naming, Nurturing, and Navigating).

In SM, students are assigned to mentors based on schedule availability. Before arriving for the Naming session, mentees complete the CSF and print out their feedback. During this structured first session, the mentor works to develop academic goals, to help the mentee understand the measure's feedback and how it relates to school-related goals, and to incorporate the five signature strengths into personal descriptions. The mentor walks the mentee through a Strengths Imagery toward the end of the session. As homework given at the end of the first session, mentees are asked to share their feedback with people close to them and to craft stories about how their strengths are used. In the Nurturing session, mentees are encouraged to complete narrative exercises designed to create a catalog of critical events that have been, or could be, resolved through intentional use of strengths or "doing what you do best." Nurturing homework involves completing additional storytelling exercises (that are e-mailed to the mentor upon completion) about using strengths to attain goals. During the last session, focused on Navigating, mentees are challenged to create pathways that could help resolve academic challenges or overcome real or perceived obstacles that might get in the way of academic success. Finally, the mentor and mentee discuss success experiences associated with using strengths and concerns about future strengths-development and academic pursuits.

WELL-BEING: A LIKELY OUTCOME OF STRENGTHS-BASED DEVELOPMENT

The promotion of self-efficacy, hope, and personal growth initiative via the aforementioned strengths-based development models may ultimately serve to promote well-being and human flourishing. Although much of the scholarship on well-being has been published in personality and social psychology journals (Lent, 2004), a number of counseling psychologists have provided important contributions to the literature on the assessment of well-being and the reconceptualization of therapy outcome (Brown, Ryan, & McPartland, 1996; Fordyce, 1977, 1983; Keyes & Lopez, 2001; Keyes & Magyar-Moe, 2003; Lightsey, 1996; Lopez, Snyder, & Rasmussen, 2003; Robbins & Kliewer, 2000). These contributions are highlighted in the following sections.

Reconceptualizing and Measuring Outcome: Balancing Symptom Distress and Well-Being

Traditionally, psychological treatment has been conceptualized as the practice of remediating illness (Keyes & Lopez, 2001). As such, much of the psychotherapy effectiveness and efficacy research to date has focused on measuring the therapeutic goals of symptom relief and improved functioning in life (Seligman, 1995). Indeed, a preponderance of therapy outcome measures are geared toward the evaluation of negative symptom alleviation.

More recently, a broader conceptualization of psychological treatment has been proposed that goes beyond mere symptom reduction (Keyes & Lopez, 2001; Keyes & Magyar-Moe, 2003; Lopez, et al., 2003). According to the complete state model of mental health and mental illness, mental health is defined as "a complete state consisting of the absence of mental illness and the presence of high-level well-being" (Keyes & Lopez, 2001, p. 48). This definition of mental health allows and encourages practitioners and clients to set therapeutic goals over and above mere attainment of baseline-level functioning, whereby clients are indeed free from disorder and poor functioning, yet not experiencing joy and well-being (Keyes & Lopez, 2001). From this perspective, in order to help clients flourish at levels of functioning beyond the baseline, attention must be given to symptoms of well-being.

Therapy outcome measures designed to assess growth and improvement beyond symptom relief are available, including the MacArthur Foundation's Successful Midlife Development Scale of Subjective Well-Being (MIDUS) (Brim, Ryff, & Kessler, 2004; Keyes, 1998; Mroczek & Kolarz, 1998). The MIDUS is a comprehensive self-report measure of subjective well-being, consisting of three major domains, namely, emotional, psychological, and social well-being (Keyes & Magyar-Moe, 2003). Emotional well-being consists of perceptions of avowed happiness and satisfaction with life, and the balance of positive to negative affects. (Sample items tapping this domain on the MIDUS include: *During the last 30 days, how much of the time did you feel cheerful; full of life; nervous; hopeless; satisfied? Overall, these days, how happy are you with your life?*). Psychological well-being consists of six wellness dimensions that include positive evaluation of oneself and one's past life, a sense of continued growth and development as a person, the belief that one's life is purposeful and meaningful, the possession of quality relations with others, the capacity to manage effectively one's life and surrounding world, and a sense of self-determination (Ryff & Keyes, 1995). (Sample psychological well-being MIDUS items include: *I think it is important to have new experiences that challenge how I think about myself and the world. I have confidence in my own opinions, even if they are different from the way most other people think.*) Finally, social well-being consists of five elements that, together, indicate whether and to what degree individuals are functioning well in their social world (e.g., as neighbors, as coworkers, and as citizens) (Keyes, 1998; Keyes & Shapiro, in press). (Sample social well-being items on the MIDUS include: *The world is becoming a better place for everyone. I have something valuable to give to the world.*)

Indeed, the three components of subjective well-being, as measured by the MIDUS, fit very well with the definition of complete mental health, which has also been described as "the syndrome that combines high levels of symptoms of emotional well-being, psychological well-being, and social well-being, and includes the absence of recent mental illness" (Keyes & Lopez, 2001, p. 49). (See Keyes & Lopez, 2001, for definitions and more information on the four states of complete and incomplete mental health and mental illness.)

Conceptualizing Well-Being in Normative and Restorative Terms

Perhaps the most comprehensive scholarship on well-being by a counseling psychologist to date is the unifying theoretical model of well-being developed by Lent (2004). Through an extensive review of the various scholarly definitions of well-being, as well as the many hypothesized predictors of well-being in a therapeutic context (i.e., demographic, personality, cognitive, and social-relational variables), Lent developed a two-pronged yet interwoven theory of well-being. From this theoretical perspective, well-being can be promoted under normative life circumstances (normative well-being) as well as under conditions of adversity (restorative well-being). More specifically, clients who define well-being in terms of the restorative approach see the ultimate goal of therapy to be the restoration of previous levels of well-being through the remediation of problems and stress so that they can be happy (i.e., hedonic subjective well-being). Clients who define well-being in terms of the normative approach will expect to work hard and challenge themselves to grow and develop in order to find meaning and purpose (i.e., eudaimonic psychological well-being). For many, it is the combination of these perspectives of well-being that defines their desired therapeutic outcome.

Lent's (2004) well-being framework equips practitioners to conceptualize well-being in client-friendly terms. In other words, practitioners can meet clients where they are and work with them toward whichever well-being outcome they may desire, rather than imposing therapist-generated perspectives of well-being on the clients. Indeed, Lent provides suggestions for practitioners to consider when working to enhance client well-being via these normative and restorative routes. For example, he suggests that the promotion of well-being may be achieved and enhanced through getting clients successfully involved in activities that are consistent with their value systems. Furthermore, goal-focused interventions designed to assist clients to develop and then make progress on key life goals is warranted. It is apparent that the human agency constructs of self-efficacy and hope come into play in the process of such counseling interventions as "people ordinarily chose to pursue courses of action for which they possess a sufficient sense of self-efficacy and for which positive outcomes are anticipated. Environmental (e.g., social) supports and coping skills serve to inform self-efficacy beliefs, promote goal progress, and enhance satisfaction with life task participation" (p. 497). We believe that the previously described strengths-based development and therapy interventions can also facilitate movement down the normative and restorative paths of well-being.

Lent (2004) also suggests lines of future research for counseling psychologists to pursue in order to strengthen our understanding of well-being and counseling. Among these are recommendations for developing and refining well-being measures, clarifying causal processes among well-being variables, and creating and testing interventions to promote well-being (such as strengths mentoring and strengths-centered therapy) utilizing measures of symptom well-being (rather than the alleviation of symptom distress).

COUNSELING PSYCHOLOGISTS FOCUS ON THE POSITIVE IN PSYCHOLOGY

Counseling psychology's philosophical and practical commitment to focusing on the positive in psychology is to be celebrated; however, counseling psychologists must not rest on their laurels. Indeed, Lopez, Magyar-Moe, and colleagues (2006) have put forth multiple recommendations to counseling psychology practitioners and scholars that may serve to further enhance and solidify the identity of the discipline and to make strengths-based practice more applicable to all people, while also contributing significantly to the science of positive psychology within psychology at large.

In addition to the aforementioned work being done by counseling psychologists on human agency, strengths-based development, and well-being outcomes, there are several other signs pointing to the commitment of counseling psychologists to play a significant role in promoting positive psychology. For example, in 2005, the Positive Psychology Section of the Society of Counseling Psychology within the American Psychological Association was officially recognized, and, as of May 2007, there were 108 official members of the section (http://www.div17pospsych.com/members.htm). Many of the members of this group are also in the process of conducting research on positive psychology topics, teaching positive psychology courses at various universities and colleges, as well as providing counseling, psychoeducational workshops, and outreach programming grounded in positive psychology on their campuses and in their communities (see Naming and Nurturing E-newsletters of the Positive Psychology Section, issues 1–4, http://www.div17pospsych.com/news.htm).

Counseling psychologists are in a prime position to be major players in developing and promoting the positive in psychology and, in recent years, have been stepping up to the challenge to do more of the work that truly serves as a foundation of the profession. We believe this trend will continue in the years ahead, and we look forward to seeing how capitalizing on a strength of our profession will help individuals and communities to utilize their strengths as well.

BIBLIOGRAPHY

American Psychological Association. (1999). Archival description of counseling psychology. *The Counseling Psychologist, 27,* 589–592.

Asplund, J., Lopez, S. J., Hodges, T., & Harter, J. (2007). *Technical report: Development and validation of the Clifton StrengthsFinder 2.0.* Omaha, NE: The Gallup Organization.

Bandura, A. (1977). Self-efficacy: Toward a unifying theory of behavioral change. *Psychological Review, 84,* 191–215.

Bandura, A. (1986). *Social foundations of thought and action.* New York: Prentice Hall.

Bandura, A. (1997). *Self-efficacy: The exercise of control.* New York: Freeman.

Bandura, A. (2004). *An agentic perspective on positive psychology.* Presented at the Third Gallup International Positive Psychology Summit Washington, D.C.

Betz, N. E., & Hackett, G. (2006). Career self-efficacy theory: Back to the future. *Journal of Career Assessment, 14,* 3–11.

Brim, O. G., Ryff, C. D., & Kessler, R. C. (2004). *How healthy are we? A national study of well-being at midlife.* Chicago: University of Chicago Press.

Brown, S. D., Ryan, N. E., & McPartland, E. B. (1996). Why are so many people happy and what do we do for those who aren't? A reaction to Lightsey. *The Counseling Psychologist, 24,* 751–757.

Buckingham, M., & Clifton, D. O. (2000). *Now, discover your strengths.* New York: Free Press.

Cattell, R. B. (1993). *The 16PF fifth edition.* Champagne, IL: Institute for Personality and Ability Testing, Inc.

Clifton, D. O., & Anderson, E. (2002). *Strengths quest: Discover and develop your strengths in academics, career, and beyond.* New York: Gallup Press.

Clifton, D. O., & Nelson, P. (1992). *Soar with your strengths.* New York: Delacorte Press.

Donnay, D. A. C., & Borgen, F. H. (1999). The incremental validity of vocational self-efficacy: An examination of interest, self-efficacy, and occupation. *Journal of Counseling Psychology, 46,* 432–447.

Edwards, L. M., Ong, A., & Lopez, S. J. (2007). Hope measurement in Mexican American youth. *Hispanic Journal of Behavioral Sciences, 29,* 225–241.

Edwards, L. M., Rand, K., Lopez, S. J., & Snyder, C. R. (2007). Understanding hope: A review of measurement and construct validity research. In A. Ong & M. van Dulmen (Eds.), *Handbook of methods in positive psychology* (pp. 83–95). New York: Oxford Press.

Flores, L. Y., & O'Brien, K. M. (2002). The career development of Mexican American adolescent women: A test of social cognitive career theory. *Journal of Counseling Psychology, 49,* 14–27.

Fordyce, M. W. (1977). Development of a program to increase personal happiness. *Journal of Counseling Psychology, 24,* 511–521.

Fordyce, M. W. (1983). A program to increase happiness: Further studies. *Journal of Counseling Psychology, 30,* 483–498.

Gainer, K. A. (2006). Twenty-five years of self-efficacy in career assessment and practice. *Journal of Career Assessment, 14,* 161–178.

Gelso, C. J., & Fretz, B. (2001). *Counseling psychology* (2nd ed). Ft. Worth, TX: Harcourt.

Gelso, C. J., & Woodhouse, S. (2003). Toward a positive psychotherapy: Focusing on human strengths. In W. B. Walsh (Ed.), *Counseling psychology and optimal human functioning* (pp. 344–369). New York: Erlbaum.

Gore, P. A. (2006). Academic self-efficacy as a predictor of college outcomes: Two incremental validity studies. *Journal of Career Assessment, 14,* 92–115.

Gough, H., & Bradley, P. (1996). *CPI™ manual* (3rd ed.). Palo Alto, CA: CPP, Inc.

Juntunen, C. L., & Wettersten, K. B. (2006). Work hope: Development and initial validation of a measure. *Journal of Counseling Psychology, 53,* 94–106.

Keyes, C. L. M. (1998). Social well-being. *Social Psychology Quarterly, 61,* 121–140.

Keyes, C. L. M., & Lopez, S. J. (2001). Toward a science of mental health: Positive directions in diagnosis and intervention. In C. R. Snyder & S. J. Lopez (Eds.), *Handbook of positive psychology* (pp. 45–59). New York: Oxford University Press.

Keyes, C. L. M., & Magyar-Moe, J. L. (2003). The measurement and utility of adult subjective well-being. In S. J. Lopez & C. R. Snyder (Eds.), *Positive psychological assessment: A handbook of models and measures* (pp. 411–425). Washington, DC: American Psychological Association.

Keyes, C. L. M., & Shapiro, A. (in press). Social well-being in the United States: A descriptive epidemiology. In C. D. Ryff, R. C. Kessler, & O. G. Brim, Jr. (Eds.), *A portrait of midlife in the United States*. Chicago: University of Chicago Press.

Lent, R. W. (2004). Toward a unifying theoretical and practical perspective on well-being and psychosocial adjustment. *Journal of Counseling Psychology, 51*, 482–509.

Lent, R. W, & Brown, S. D. (1996). Social cognitive approach to career development: An overview. *Career Development Quarterly, 44*, 310–321.

Lent, R. W., & Brown, S. D. (2006). On conceptualizing and assessing social cognitive constructs in career research: A measurement guide. *Journal of Career Assessment, 14*, 12–35.

Lent, R. W., Brown, S. D., & Hackett, G. (1994). Toward a unifying social cognitive theory of career and academic interest, choice, and performance [Monograph]. *Journal of Vocational Behavior, 45*, 79–122.

Lent, R. W., Lopez, F. G., Mikolaitis, N. L., Jones, L., & Bieschke, K. J. (1992). Social cognitive mechanisms in the client recovery process: Revisiting hygiology. *Journal of Mental Health Counseling, 14*, 196–207.

Lightsey, O. R. (1996). What leads to wellness? The role of psychological resources in well-being. *The Counseling Psychologist, 24*, 589–735.

Lopez, F. G., Lent, R. W., Brown, S. D., & Gore, P. A. (1997). Role of social-cognitive expectations in high school students' mathematics-related interest and academic performance. *Journal of Counseling Psychology, 44*, 44–52.

Lopez, S. J., & Edwards, L. M. (2008). The interface of counseling psychology and positive psychology: Assessing and promoting human strengths. In S. D. Brown & R. W. Lent (Eds.), *Handbook of counseling psychology*. New York: John Wiley and Sons.

Lopez, S. J., Hodges, T., & Harter, J. (2005). Technical report: Development and validation of the Clifton StrengthsFinder. Omaha, NE: The Gallup Organization.

Lopez, S. J., Magyar-Moe, J. L., Petersen, S. E., Ryder, J. A., Krieshok, T. S., Lichtenberg, J. W., et al. (2006). Counseling psychology's focus on positive aspects of human functioning: A major contribution. *The Counseling Psychologist, 34*, 205–227.

Lopez, S. J., & Snyder, C. R. (Eds.). (2003). *Positive psychological assessment: A handbook of models and measures*. Washington, DC: American Psychological Association.

Lopez, S. J., Snyder, C. R., Magyar-Moe, J., Edwards, L. M., Pedrotti, J. T., Janowski, K., et al. (2004). Strategies for accentuating hope. In P. A. Linley & S. Joseph, (Eds.), *Positive psychology in practice* (pp. 388–404). Hoboken, NJ: John Wiley & Sons.

Lopez, S. J., Snyder, C. R, & Rasmussen, H. N. (2003). Striking a vital balance: Developing a complementary focus on human weakness and strength through positive psychological assessment. In S. J. Lopez & C. R. Snyder (Eds.), *Positive psychological assessment: A handbook of models and measures* (pp. 3–20). Washington, DC: American Psychological Association.

Lopez, S. J., Tree, H., Bowers, K., & Burns, M. E. (2004). KU Strengths Mentoring Protocol. Unpublished mentoring protocol, University of Kansas, Lawrence.

Lopez, S. J., Tree, H., Bowers, K., & Burns, M. E. (2006, October). *Positive psychology on campus: Discovering students' strengths.* In S. J. Lopez's (Chair) Symposium: Positive psychology on campus. Presented at the 5th Gallup International Positive Psychology Summit Washington, DC.

Magyar-Moe, J. L. (2004, August). *Predictors of therapy outcome: A focus on personal growth initiative.* Paper presented at the 112th Annual Convention of the American Psychological Association.

Magyar-Moe, J. L. (2006, August). *Changes in therapy outcome predictor variables from intake to session three.* Poster presented at the 114th Annual Convention of the American Psychological Association.

Mroczek, D. K., & Kolarz, C. M. (1998). The effect of age on positive and negative affect: A developmental perspective on happiness. *Journal of Personality and Social Psychology, 75*, 1333–1349.

Multon, K. D., Brown, S. D., & Lent, R. W. (1991). Relation of self-efficacy beliefs to academic outcomes: A meta-analytic investigation. *Journal of Counseling Psychology, 38*, 30–38.

Multon, K. D., Shortridge-Pearce, B., & Frey, B. B. (2005, August). *Relation of self-efficacy beliefs and academic outcomes: An update.* Poster presented at the Annual Convention of the American Psychological Association.

O'Brien, K. M. (2003). Measuring career self-efficacy: Promoting confidence and happiness at work. In S. J. Lopez & C. R. Snyder (Eds.), *Positive psychological assessment: A handbook of models and measures* (pp. 109–126). Washington, DC: American Psychological Association.

Peterson, C., & Seligman, M. E. P. (2004). *Character strengths and virtues: A handbook and classification.* New York: Oxford University Press.

Pinquart, M., Juang, L. P., & Silbereisen, K. (2003). Self-efficacy and successful school-to-work transition: A longitudinal study. *Journal of Vocational Behavior, 63*, 329–346.

Rath, T. (2007). *StrengthsFinder 2.0.* New York: Gallup Press.

Ripley, J. S., & Worthington, E. L. (2002). Hope-focused and forgiveness-based group interventions to promote marital enrichment. *Journal of Counseling and Development, 80*, 452–463.

Robbins, S. B., & Kliewer, W. L. (2000). Advances in theory and research on subjective well-being. In S. D. Brown & R. W. Lent (Eds.), *Handbook of counseling psychology* (pp. 310–345). Hoboken, NJ: John Wiley & Sons, Inc.

Robitschek, C. (1998). Personal growth initiative: The construct and its measure. *Measurement and Evaluation in Counseling and Development, 30*, 183–198.

Robitschek, C. (1999). Further validation of the Personal Growth Initiative Scale. *Measurement and Evaluation in Counseling and Development, 31*, 197–210.

Robitschek, C., & Cook, S. W. (1999). The influence of personal growth initiative and coping styles on career exploration and vocational identity. *Journal of Vocational Behavior, 54*, 127–141.

Robitschek, C., & Kashubeck, S. (1999). A structural model of family functioning and psychological health: The mediating effects of hardiness and personal growth orientation. *Journal of Counseling Psychology, 46*, 159–172.

Ryff, C. D., & Keyes, C. L. M. (1995). The structure of psychological well-being revisited. *Journal of Personality and Social Psychology, 69*, 719–727.

Savickas, M. L. (2003). Toward a taxonomy of human strengths: Career counseling's contribution to positive psychology. In W. B. Walsh (Ed.), *Counseling psychology and optimal human functioning* (pp. 229–249). Mahwah, NJ: Lawrence Erlbaum Associates.

Schreiner, L. (2005). *A technical report of the Clifton StrengthsFinder with college students.* Omaha, NE: The Gallup Organization.

Seligman, M. E. P. (1995). The effectiveness of psychotherapy: The Consumer Reports Study. *American Psychologist, 50*, 965–974.

Shogren, K., Lopez, S. J., Wehmeyer, M., Little, T., & Pressgrove, C. (2006). The role of positive constructs in predicting life satisfaction in adolescents with and without cognitive disabilities: An exploratory study. *The Journal of Positive Psychology, 1*, 37–52.

Smith, E. (2006). The strengths-based counseling model. *The Counseling Psychologist, 34*, 13–79.

Snyder, C. R. (1994). *The psychology of hope: You can get there from here.* New York: Free Press.

Snyder, C. R., & Lopez, S. J. (2002). *Handbook of positive psychology.* New York: Oxford University Press.

Snyder, C. R., Lopez, S. J., Shorey, H. L., Rand, K. L., & Feldman, D. B. (2003). Hope theory, measurements, and applications to school psychology. *School Psychology Quarterly, 18*, 122–139.

Snyder, C. R., Shorey, H. S., Cheavens, J., Pulvers, K. M., Adams, V. H., & Wiklund, C. (2002). Hope and academic success in college. *Journal of Educational Psychology, 94*, 820–826.

Solberg, V. S., O'Brien, K., Villarreal, P., Kennel, R., & Davis, B. (1993). Self-efficacy and Hispanic college students: Validation of the College Self-Efficacy Instrument. *Hispanic Journal of Behavioral Sciences, 15*, 80–95.

Super, D. E. (1955). Transition: From vocational guidance to counseling psychology. *Journal of Counseling Psychology, 2*, 3–9.

Tyler, L. E. (1965). *The psychology of individual differences* (3rd ed.). New York: Meredith.

Tyler, L. E. (1973). Design for a hopeful psychology. *American Psychologist, 28*, 1021–1029.

White, R. W. (1973). The concept of healthy personality: What do we really mean? *The Counseling Psychologist, 4*(2), 3–12.

Wong, J. (2006). Strengths-Centered Therapy: A social constructionist, virtue-based psychotherapy. *Psychotherapy: Theory, Research, Practice, and Training, 43*, 133–146.

Worthington, E. L., Jr., Hight, T. L., Ripley, J. S., Perrone, K. M., Kurusu, T. A., & Jones D. R. (1997). Strategic hope-focused relationship-enrichment counseling with individual couples. *Journal of Counseling Psychology, 44*(4), 381–389.

Chapter Eight

Intersecting Identities of Gender-Transgressive Sexual Minorities

Toward a New Paradigm of Affirmative Psychology

Kathleen J. Bieschke
Jennifer A. Hardy
Ruth E. Fassinger
James M. Croteau

The scholarship that fosters the development of lesbian, gay, bisexual, transgender, and queer (LGBTQ) psychology is in the midst of a paradigm shift, one in which research incorporates a multiplicity of experiences and contexts, including increased cultural sensitivity as well as more explicit inclusion of bisexual, transgender, and other marginalized identities (e.g., queer) along the sexual minority continuum (Croteau, Bieschke, Fassinger, & Manning, in press). This new paradigm recognizes that, to fully understand sexual orientation, it must be explored in conjunction with gender, race, ethnicity, religion, class, disability, and other aspects of social or cultural location. Counseling psychologists are uniquely positioned by their history, values, and training to take the lead in creating this truly inclusive LGBTQ affirmative psychology (Croteau et al., in press).

In this chapter, our goal is to foster understanding of how the cultural location of LGBTQ individuals influences their personal, interpersonal, social, and sociopolitical experience as sexual minorities. We ground our discussion in Fassinger and Arseneau's (2007) model of identity enactment of gender-transgressive sexual minorities. After briefly describing this model, we turn our attention to reviewing the small but growing body of recent (2000 and later) empirical literature focused on the intersection of cultural location with sexual orientation. We conclude the chapter by briefly highlighting the implications of this nascent literature for research and practice.

MODEL OF IDENTITY ENACTMENT OF GENDER-TRANSGRESSIVE SEXUAL MINORITIES

Fassinger and Arseneau's (2007) model of identity enactment takes a social constructionist and critical theory perspective that centralizes the contexts in which identity is enacted (Croteau et al., in press). This model articulates a view of sexual minority identity as transgressive of gender expectations both in terms of the gender of an individual's sexual or romantic partners and in terms of an individual's gender-related expression. Thus, the model is inclusive of both common and varying experiences across such identities as lesbian, gay, queer, bisexual, and transgender.

In the Fassinger and Arseneau (2007) model, three interrelated aspects of orientation to identity must be considered: (a) *gender orientation,* or a sense of self in reference to male/female or masculine/feminine; (b) *sexual orientation,* or a sense of self in reference to sexuality and relational intimacy; and (c) *cultural orientation,* or a sense of self in reference to multicultural dimensions such as race, ethnicity, religion, disability status, and social class. This tripartite structure of orientation dimensions interacts within a context of *temporal influences* that include both the historical milieu of the cohort of LGBTQ people to which an individual belongs and the immediate context created by an individual's actual chronological age. Gender-transgressive sexual minorities enact their contextualized identities within four developmental arenas that include mental and physical health, relationships and families, education and work, and legal and political rights. This model allows infinite variation in how gender-transgressive sexual identity is formed and expressed across many life arenas, and represents a broad mapping of contexts that may influence identity enactment for gender-transgressive people in a variety of social locations related to gender, race, ethnicity, religion, age, disability, and other sociodemographic variables (Croteau et al., in press).

Bieschke, Perez, and DeBord (2007) describe the model as a "bold" attempt to attend to the "complexities that separate lesbian, gay, bisexual and transgender communities" while still asserting the commonality of gender transgression (p. 15). Perez (2007) points out that prior identity models have failed to take into account historical and community contexts and complexities, while this theoretical perspective "challenges therapists to question existing notions of identity construction and to begin considering the multiple constructions, layers, and methods through which LGBTQ identities (and even non-LGBTQ identities) are enacted" (p. 404). We use this model to frame our discussion because of its explicit delineation of the ways in which sexual orientation is inextricably linked to gender and culture. It thus both embodies and advances the new paradigm of an inclusive LGBTQ psychology that we wish to promote in this chapter. In the following sections, we use the model as an organizer of our discussion. We begin with age/cohort issues of gender-transgressive sexual minorities and then present various dimensions of cultural orientation (disability, race/ethnicity, social class, religion) as they relate to sexual and gender orientation.

Although this intersectional literature clearly is in its infancy, we present it here because we hope that it serves a heuristic function in stimulating future research consistent with the new paradigm of LGBTQ affirmative psychology that we are promoting in this chapter. Furthermore, because this literature is so small, we do not limit our attention to work done by counseling psychologists, although our lens highlights individual strengths and issues of social justice in this existing knowledge base. Finally, we note that, for all of the dimensions of cultural orientation presented here, the most salient contextual reality at the current time continues to be that of pervasive invisibility related to social stigma. Invisible identities carry with them a host of related problems: isolation, limited resources, constrained experiences, lack of modeling, biased or inaccurate information, stereotyping, stress and compromised coping, disrupted or inauthentic interpersonal relationships, and profound silence from helping professionals. These are the overarching contextual realities that shape the experiences of gender-transgressive sexual minorities across a broad range of cultural orientations, and all of the information presented in this chapter must be understood within that context of invisibility and stigmatization.

SEXUAL ORIENTATION AND AGE

We begin our discussion with age because it occupies a complicated place in the literature as both a contextual variable through its historical operation as captured in cohort effects, and as a dimension of cultural location through its function as a delineator of a particular reference group related to chronological age (i.e., youth, aged). A developmental perspective would suggest that there are important and unique age-related issues for sexual minority individuals at all points along the developmental continuum, from birth until death. Moreover, developmentalists would argue that individuals become increasingly differentiated as they age—physically, behaviorally, emotionally and psychologically, intellectually and cognitively—that is, 60-year-olds are far more different from one another than are 6-year-olds. Finally, development is shaped importantly by contextual forces, and thus is bound by the particular historical period in which it occurs (i.e., a 6-year-old in 2007 experiences a very different world from that of someone who was 6 years old in 1937 or 1967). The study of development, therefore, is always temporally and societally bound, and commonly used research methods further constrain what we know—for example, sampling a variety of differently aged people at the same point in time and in the same place, querying them for retrospective accounts of presumably accurately recalled complex developmental events. To further confound the study of age-related factors, there is little common agreement regarding the labels one uses to identify particular age groups; the term "older," for example, may refer to people in their 50s, 60s, 70s, or 80s depending on who is doing the labeling. Furthermore, within subpopulations, there may be more specific norms held in common, for example, the phenomenon of "accelerated aging" among gay males, in which men identify as old prematurely in relation to their actual chronological age, presumably a response to the youth-focused norms in gay male communities (Friend, 1987, cited in Barón & Cramer, 2000).

Given these complicated aspects of age-related development and research, it is virtually impossible to describe with certainty the particular developmental tasks and strategies of any specific age group, except within very broad parameters. However, particular age groups gain visibility in society because they represent patterns that signal some sort of need for a social or political response. Thus, in the contemporary United States, the aging have garnered attention because they are a population that is growing rapidly and creating needs for expanded goods and services as they age. As a subgroup of this population, aging people who also are sexual minorities suddenly have become a focus of attention in the lay, research, and practice literatures. In this section we briefly review some of the issues that older (i.e., 60 and above) LGBTQ people face.

Common themes for LGBTQ elders have begun to emerge from the literature, and they include (within a context of invisibility and stigma) issues related to social support, health (mental and physical) and health care, coupled relationships, and public policy. It is critical to note the generational or cohort effects of the current population of aging sexual minority people (Barón & Cramer, 2000; Kimmel, Rose, & David, 2006). Many who came out in their younger years did so within a context of much greater stigma and oppression than is reflected in the contemporary United

States (persistent and pervasive homonegativity notwithstanding), and the relationship patterns, identity management strategies, responses to health care providers, and ambivalence about social services evident in some older LGBTQ people are consistent with this experience. In addition, many LGBTQ people reaching old age at the current time are the first generation to be affected profoundly by the incalculable loss of loved ones from HIV/AIDS; in a recent study of 416 older lesbian, gay, and bisexual individuals (Grossman, D'Augelli, & O'Connell, 2003), 90% knew at least one person and 47% knew three or more people who had died from HIV/AIDS. It is unclear how living with constant death and loss over time as well as the obliteration of extensive social networks have affected this cohort of aging LGBTQ people (gay men in particular), both individually and across sexual minority communities. Indeed, there is some concern about growing rates of HIV infection among midlife gay men (Cox & Kellerhouse, 2007), and speculation that lack of social support, which consistently is found to be an important factor in positive mental and physical health and successful aging (see Barón & Cramer, 2000; Kimmel et al., 2006), may be negatively affecting gay men who are approaching old age. One recent study of 233 older gay men, for example, found 90% of them reporting at least fair health and moderate life satisfaction, but 30% also reported feelings of depression (Shippy, Cantor, & Brennan, 2004).

The Grossman et al. study (2003; noted above) investigated the mental and physical health and social support networks of 416 individuals (71% males, 29% females, mostly White, and generally well educated) accessed nationally through 19 sites providing social, recreational, and support services to older sexual minorities. Results indicated that (contrary to stereotypes of aging) almost all reported fair to excellent mental health, with higher income, less victimization, and having a live-in partner predictive of better mental health. Generally high reported levels of self-esteem and low levels of internalized homophobia were affected by age in that older individuals reported both decreased self-esteem and increased levels of internalized homophobia. Most reported that their physical health was fair to excellent, with very low levels of alcohol and drug abuse. More than one-quarter reported feeling lonely, but those respondents most satisfied with their social support networks reported the lowest levels of loneliness. Similar to Shippy et al. (2004), most reported social support by friends and partners (followed by relatives), with most respondents significantly older than those in their networks, and women indicating more extensive support networks than men. The most important factor in satisfaction with social support was the knowledge of their sexual orientation by that support network member.

Interestingly, almost two-thirds of this sample had experienced victimization based on sexual orientation, and yet the high levels of reported self-esteem and mental health suggest competent coping with stress. Indeed, one theory of LGBTQ aging (Friend, 1990) has suggested that sexual minority people develop "crisis competence" in the process of coming out within a context of stigma, and that this competence prepares them to deal successfully with the inevitable developmental tasks of aging (losing support networks, accessing services, dealing with bias in health care, coping with threats to coupled relationships). Similarly, Meyer (2007) notes in his application of the minority stress model to LGBTQ experience that, although minority status often involves stressors related to stigma and marginalization, it may also confer benefits of group solidarity and cohesiveness that protect individuals from those stressors. An empirical example is provided by Hall and Fine (2005), whose narrative study of two aging Black lesbians found evidence of "positive marginality"—that is, strengths developed from living both inside and outside the mainstream culture.

As is true for coupled gender-transgressive sexual minorities of any age, the lack of legal and fiscal support for coupled and family relationships intensifies the normal stresses of aging in same-sex couples—dealing with physical and mental health declines as well as increased interaction with medical and health care systems, facing the eventuality of death, shifting relationships with children and other family members, and losing loved ones. Lack of spousal insurance benefits and access to Social Security benefits for same-sex partners, for example, increases financial strain on a couple already facing increased medical costs associated with the common diseases of older age (e.g., heart disease, cancer). Moreover, being barred from medical discussions, decisions, and even hospital visitation with a sick partner, as well as facing insensitive and biased health care providers, places inordinate strain on both partners interacting with health care systems, and even may force disclosures of identity by individuals who previously had chosen to keep their sexual identities and intimate relationships hidden (see Barón & Cramer, 2000; Patterson, 2007, for fuller discussion).

For transgender people in particular, the health care issues of aging are extraordinarily difficult. It has been noted (Cooke-Daniels, 2006) that recent increased visibility of transgender treatment options has led to a substantial proportion of older transgender people electing surgical transition procedures. Transitioning in older age, however, brings with it greater difficulties as a result of other health problems related to aging, more deeply ingrained social roles, increased dating difficulties as a result of limited pools of age-appropriate partners (particularly for heterosexual male-to-females (MTFs), for whom gender differences in mortality create a dearth of available male partners) as well as physiological functional limitations, legal issues, and employment discrimination (Cooke-Daniels, 2006). Moreover, negative attitudes of health care professionals often produce overt discrimination against those with "noncongruent" bodies, and financial barriers abound as most insurance plans do not cover gender-related surgeries or cross-gender hormone treatments (Cooke-Daniels, 2006). These problems are compounded by the fact that, in most states, sex reassignment surgeries must be demonstrated in order to gain permission to change gender identity on legal documents, forcing medical responses to gender-identity issues that might otherwise be addressed in alternative ways (Lombardi, 2001, cited in Fassinger & Arseneau, 2007).

The increasing health issues that accompany normal aging for gender-transgressive sexual minorities may result in short- or long-term disability. Thus, concerns relevant to LGBTQ individuals with disabilities may apply to sexual minority elders as well. The following section highlights several issues related to the intersection of sexual orientation with disability.

SEXUAL ORIENTATION AND DISABILITY

As is true of the intersections of sexual orientation with other marginalized statuses discussed in this chapter, people with disabilities who also are gender-transgressive sexual minorities face shared as well as unique challenges in living their lives. It has been pointed out (e.g., Greene, 2003; Olkin, 1999) that people with disabilities and sexual minority people share in common the experience of being reared in families where their minority identity status often is not shared, and they learn about their minority group from others outside their families; this compromises the intergenerational transmission of knowledge and also highlights the deleterious effects on development of the lack of a visible, accessible community of mentors and peers. Moreover, the movement of the individual from the family to an outside group to obtain support may threaten and disrupt family relationships—in terms of disability, this may stem from family members' beliefs (sometimes realistic) that the individual cannot navigate such involvement without help, and in terms of sexual orientation, this may be rooted in family homonegativity and denial of sexuality.

When a gender-transgressive sexual minority individual with a disability does attempt to form ties to one or more communities, complex difficulties may arise. Venues that are architecturally inaccessible (e.g., no handicap-accessible bathrooms) or communicationally non-accommodating (e.g., no ASL translators) present obvious barriers to many people with disabilities. However, there are more specific accessibility issues for

LGBTQ people with disabilities. For example, given the well-documented tendency of able-bodied people to ignore, look away from, or otherwise avoid social and physical contact with people with disabilities (Olkin, 1999), the subtle visual and verbal cues used by sexual minority people to find and recognize one another in their communities may be inaccessible to LGBTQ people with disabilities when they attempt to enter such communities. Similarly, communicating comfortably with other sexual minority people in ASL necessitates learning specific expressions and words particular to LGBTQ experience, and lack of knowledge may hinder interpersonal interactions, not only with able-bodied peers but also with others with disabilities (Mona, Fraley, Theodore, Ballan, Cameron, & Crisp, in press).

It can be assumed that at least some sexual minority people with disabilities seek out communities with the expectation that they may find sexual and/or romantic partners through those involvements. A particularly troublesome aspect of the intersection of sexual orientation and disability identities is the clash between possessing a *sexual minority* identity that is overly sexualized in society, and, at the same time, a *disability* identity that is almost completely desexualized by society (Greene, 2003; Mona et al., in press), a confluence of expectations that surely must be perplexing to others if not also to the disabled LGBTQ individual him- or herself. It has been documented that health care workers rarely inquire about the sexual needs of people with disabilities, and social taboos against recognizing the sexual needs of people with disabilities may be most strongly maintained in relation to those with intellectual or developmental disabilities (Bennett & Coyle, 2007). One qualitative study of 10 gay men with intellectual disabilities, for example, found much difficulty expressed by participants in accessing and entering gay-friendly social venues due both to homonegative attitudes on the part of caregivers and to antidisability attitudes from within the gay community (Bennett & Coyle, 2007).

A number of issues have been identified (see Mona et al., in press) as possible complications for LGBTQ people with disabilities when they attempt to form intimate or sexual relationships: (a) poor body image based on narrow societal definitions of attractiveness and fitness (sometimes intensified in sexual minority communities, especially for men); (b) a view of people with disabilities as incapable of performing certain common sexual behaviors (e.g., anal sex); (c) lack of relevant medical information regarding sexuality, sexual health, and sexual activity in the context of disability (e.g., only heterosexually oriented educational videos and pamphlets); (d) libido compromised by medical (e.g., HIV medications) or physiological conditions (e.g., pain, fatigue due to disability) as well as by psychological factors (e.g., frustration with disability, fear of transmitting HIV disease); (e) reluctance to disclose sexual minority identity for fear of losing necessary social support regarding disability (e.g., family, medical professionals, legal guardians, personal care assistants); and (f) inaccessibility of facilitative resources (e.g., assistive devices and aids, sexual surrogates, sex workers, personal assistance services, and the Internet).

It is worth noting that coupled relationships for LGBTQ people with disabilities are formed under diverse circumstances—before or after the onset of a disability, prior to or after a change in gender or sexual identification, with a partner who is able-bodied or one who is not, with or without children, and across age differences, ranges of identity comfort and disclosure, social classes, and a host of other defining variables. How a sexual minority couple incorporates disability into their relationship also varies, although one important predictor of successful functioning appears to be the extent to which the couple openly discusses and co-owns the disability (Olkin, 1999). This is, of course, true for all couples in which at least one partner has a disability, but it is more difficult for sexual minority couples because heterosexist and homonegative attitudes on the part of family members, medical professionals, and health care providers may continually exclude or ignore the same-sex partner in discussions, decisions, and treatment-planning for the partner with the disability. Moreover, as for all sexual minority couples, legal and financial supports (e.g., insurance coverage, hospital visitation rights, child custody) almost always are absent, so that when one partner has a disability (with the concomitant threats to sustained employment and health), this absence is considerably more dangerous to the security of the coupled relationship (Greene, 2003; Olkin, 1999). When combined with socioeconomic issues (e.g., limited resources for health care), racial and ethnic prejudice (e.g., insensitive or inappropriate behavior from medical professionals), and socialized gender roles (e.g., expectations that women, not men, are caregivers), it is easy to imagine a vast array of relationship permutations and problems for sexual minority couples in which at least one partner has a disability. However, there are positive aspects of the intersection of sexual orientation and disability for coupled relationships. We would argue that the "normative creativity" (Brown, 1989) required to live one's life as a sexual minority also applies to people living with disabilities—one has to create norms, habits, and self-direction where none exist. For a couple in which both of these forms of creativity can be accessed to benefit the relationship, the capacity to imagine different ways of being together, of relating emotionally and sexually, is enhanced considerably.

SEXUAL ORIENTATION AND RACE/ETHNICITY

The term "culture" typically is invoked to explain the experiences and worldviews of people of color, the implicit assumption permeating the literature that the experience of White people is normative, and only experiences different from that norm bear scrutiny. This clearly is problematic because it not only excuses White people from interrogating their own cultural experiences, but it potentially distorts identity research on both Whites and people of color. That is, it foregrounds sexual minority status among Whites—not only may this be the only minority status that they hold consciously, but they also may have less experience managing stigma (Russell & Truong, 2001)—and it implicitly both highlights and marginalizes the cultural experiences of people of color. These paradoxes notwithstanding, it is important to examine the unique issues faced by LGBTQ people of color because they represent a nondominant racial/ethnic experience that risks being rendered invisible in the absence of directed attention. Thus, although it is not our intention to further the myth that only people of color have "culture," we do wish to foreground the cultural experiences of people of color so that they are not lost in professional discourse—an intellectual and social justice conundrum that we acknowledge.

In this section, we review the recent empirical literature focused on LGBTQ people of color. We organize this discussion around each of the four racial/ethnic communities most commonly delineated in the literature (African Americans, Asian Americans, Latino/a Americans, and Native Americans). Although we recognize the wide range of within-group experiences, we use these groupings for several reasons. First, LGBTQ people of color typically are raised by individuals who share their racial identity but not their sexual identity. As a result, strategies for dealing with racism are modeled from an early age by parents and may be applied later to heterosexism (Garnets, 2002; Wilson & Miller, 2002), producing unique cultural values and worldviews that vary by racial/ethnic group and strongly influence individual identity. Second, the definition and ramifications of sexual orientation are established by a person's cultural community (Fukuyama & Ferguson, 2000), and cultural norms vary in terms of how sexuality is defined and what behaviors are stigmatized (Zea, Reisen, & Díaz, 2003); for example, the Latino culture places less stigma on men who fulfill the insertive role in anal sex as compared to men who are receivers (Muóoz-Laboy, 2004). Third, identities vary in salience and visibility within different racial/ethnic communities (Fukuyama & Ferguson, 2000). For LGBTQ people of color, sexual orientation may be an identity for which some level of invisibility or silence is chosen as a means to lessen discrimination or alienation from within one's racial/ethnic community (Bridges, Selvidge, & Matthews, 2003; Liddle, 2007). Fourth, the few studies in this area are largely independent of one another and rarely build explicitly upon previous findings, rendering these literatures quite separate.

African Americans

The importance of extended family and a strong religious/spiritual orientation are hallmarks of traditional African American culture (Savage & Harley, 2005). Despite the positive support that these systems provide, African American gender-transgressive sexual minorities often find that their sexual identity runs counter to cultural expectations such as marriage and child-bearing (Savage & Harley). Prevalent homophobia often is legitimized by religious beliefs, leaving LGBTQ individuals feeling largely unsupported within their ethnic communities (Greene, 2000). For example, the family may choose to maintain the invisibility of the individual's sexual orientation, referring to partners in culturally accepted terms like "sister" (Bridges et al., 2003), and successful coming out may be judged by the level of acceptance ("bringing in"; Greene, 2003) of one's partner in the family, whether or not sexual minority labels are used (Liddle, 2007). Although this response may seem less than fully accepting to some observers, in the context of intersecting identities it is a legitimate way for some African American sexual minorities to maintain the salience of central relationships in their lives.

Two empirical studies were identified in the recent literature (Bowleg, Huang, Brooks, Black, & Burkholder, 2003; Bowleg, Craig, & Burkholder, 2004) that focused on African American bisexual and lesbian women, and both studies provide unique information regarding minority stress and resiliency factors. Bowleg et al. (2003) utilized a grounded theory approach to explore the experience and management of multiple minority statuses of 14 highly educated women attending a Black lesbian retreat. Participants described racist experiences as their most stressful, emotionally laden experiences in contrast to sexist experiences, which typically were viewed as annoyances. Struggles with heterosexism often were described in terms of difficulties with identity management, self-monitoring, and self-silencing across various environments (e.g., family, work, and friends). Several characteristics of internal resilience were identified by participants, including spirituality, feeling unique, self-esteem, social competencies, and an attitude of happiness and optimism. Furthermore, participants cited the importance of supportive relationships as a means to buffer stress. Although most participants identified at least one supportive family member, nearly all described this support as conditional upon the invisibility of their sexual orientation.

Bowleg et al. (2004) further sought to examine contributors to active coping in Black lesbians. A larger sample (N = 92) from the same retreat completed questionnaires regarding self-esteem, racial and sexual minority identification, social support, and sexual minority resources. Regression analyses of internal factors (self-esteem, sexual minority and race identifications) and external factors (social support, access to sexual minority resources) indicated that only lesbian identification was significantly related to active coping (the authors suggested that measurement issues may have factored into the insignificant findings).

Two empirical studies were identified in the recent literature (Crawford, Allison, Zamboni, & Soto, 2002; Wilson & Miller, 2002) that focused on African American gay and bisexual men. Crawford et al. examined the relationship between dual-identity management and psychosocial functioning in a sample of 174 men. Results indicated that participants who expressed positive identification as both African American and gay reported significantly higher self-esteem, higher life satisfaction, stronger social support, and lower levels of psychological symptoms compared to other groups.

Wilson and Miller (2002) utilized a grounded theory approach to examine heterosexism management in a sample of 37 African American gay and bisexual men. Five approaches to sexual identity management were identified. In non–gay friendly contexts, participants reported gender role-flexing, reliance on spiritual faith, openly confronting heterosexism, and abstinence from homosexual behaviors as strategies for either avoiding/buffering stigma or creating social change. Participants also described creating a "gay space" where they did not have to utilize identity management techniques (p. 383). In both gay-friendly and -unfriendly environments, participants identified self-acceptance as an important coping strategy. Overall, this study suggests that a variety of identity management strategies are implemented depending on the context.

Asian Americans

With a multiplicity of cultures represented in this category, it is difficult to generalize across all those considered to be Asian American. Most Asian cultures value traditional gender roles and filial piety (Bridges et al., 2003). For example, in an Australian qualitative study of 19 Asian gay men, participants described family and cultural issues as central in their lives, significantly influencing their choice of partners (Mao, McCormick, & Van de Ven, 2002). The influences of Christianity, Confucianism, Taoism, and

Buddhism vary by cultural group, impacting how each culture defines gender and sexuality (Kimmel & Yi, 2004). For instance, the influence of Christianity in South Korea has resulted in a conservative social culture that stigmatizes sexual minorities (Kimmel & Yi). In contrast, Japanese culture is considerably freer of religious prohibitions of same-sex behavior (Kimmel & Yi). Finally, Asian Americans often view terms such as *bisexuality* and *lesbianism* as Western concepts that do not apply to their cultural group (Bridges et al., 2003).

Only one recent study was identified (Kimmel & Yi, 2004) that specifically sampled LGBTQ Asians and Asian Americans, with samples from South Korea, China, Japan, and the United States. The results of this study indicated a sample that was quite open with their sexual orientation (including to family members) and sexually active overall. Differences were found between Korean, Japanese, and Chinese participants, but the authors did not make specific comparisons between ethnic groups within the United States. Korean participants were generally more conservative and secretive regarding their sexual orientation compared to participants from Japan and the United States (less open to family members, fewer gay friends). In contrast, the small Chinese sample (N = 10) was more open at work than Japanese and Korean participants. The fact that ethnic differences were found cross-nationally in this study suggests the value of more nuanced sampling of Asian subgroups within the United States in future studies.

Latino/a Americans

Latino culture is quite diverse but often is characterized by the centrality of the family, strict gender roles, and strong religious influence, with heterosexism common (Bridges et al., 2003; Colon, 2001). Similar to the family experiences of African Americans, the loyalty present in families often results in tolerance of LGBTQ family members as long as they are silent about their sexual orientation (Bridges et al., 2003).

Comparison research has been conducted between the Latino LGBTQ population and other ethnic minority groups, identifying issues unique to Latinos as well as the general influence of racism on identity development. First, Rosario, Schrimshaw, and Hunter (2004) examined differences in LGB milestone completion between African American, Latino, and Caucasian adolescent participants (N = 145). The results suggested that Latino participants were significantly more comfortable with others knowing their sexual orientation when compared to African American participants, but they reported significantly less disclosure than Caucasian participants. Adams, Cahill, and Ackerlind (2005) conducted a focus group with eight Latino lesbian and gay adolescents to examine how discrimination had affected their career development. Themes identified included: feeling different from peers, negative stereotypes toward Mexicans, feeling unrestricted in terms of career choice, resilience, and intersections between career development and other relationships. Also, the authors noted that the individuals seemed to use minimization as a way to cope with discrimination, which often resulted in contradictory expectations about their future work environments. In sum, these participants were navigating between identity development and discrimination management, suggesting that Latino/a LGBTQ individuals experience stress related to their multiple minority statuses but also possess positive coping mechanisms to help moderate the stress of discrimination.

No recent empirical studies were found that sampled Latina lesbian and bisexual women exclusively. A few studies, however, were found that included Latinas in their samples (Grov, Bimbi, Nanín, & Parsons, 2006; Parks, Hughes, & Matthews, 2004). In the Grov et al. study of 80 Latina lesbian and bisexual women, participants reported coming out to their parents significantly later than either Caucasians or African Americans, and significantly earlier initiation of same-gender sex as compared to Caucasians. Parks et al. (2004) examined data on 448 lesbians from the Chicago Health and Life Experiences of Women study, and found that Latina and African American lesbians reported completing identity milestones significantly earlier than Caucasian participants.

Cultural scripts create a unique interplay between sexual identity, sexual behavior, and gender roles; thus, Latino gay men may identify themselves as straight when with family but as gay in other environments (Zea et al., 2003). Furthermore, as noted previously, men's roles in anal sex have implications for gender and sexual identity (with anal-receptive partners seen as gay and assuming a female role; Zea et al., 2003). Muóoz-Laboy (2004) interviewed 18 Latino men who reported sex with both women and men in the preceding 2 years. Four broad types of bisexual Latino men were defined, with varying desires for hetero and homoerotic relationships over time; the author concluded that sexual desire in these men was tied complexly to partner gender, the eroticization of gender differences and similarities, and socially constructed roles for women and men. Similarly, in a study by Díaz, Bein, and Ayala (2006), many of the 293 gay and bisexual Latino men described living "double lives," shifting the visibility of their sexual orientation contingent on context (p. 212).

Some research has focused on the ways in which Latino gay and bisexual men experience multiple minority stress that may make them vulnerable to psychological distress. In Díaz et al.'s (2006) study, many reported experiences of discrimination, racism, and violence, including some racism and sexual objectification within the gay community itself. Díaz, Ayala, Bein, Henne, and Marin (2001) conducted a large study (N = 912) to address the impact of multiple minority stress on mental health as manifested in: social isolation and low self-esteem; experiences of homophobia, racism, and poverty; and resiliency in the face of stress. Based on their findings, the authors concluded that the psychological symptoms reported by participants were "deeply connected to a lifelong history and current experiences of social discrimination owing to sexual orientation and racial/ethnic diversity, as well as to high levels of financial hardship due to severe unemployment and poverty" (p. 931; note that socioeconomic status is discussed in a later section of this chapter).

Native Americans

Traditionally, the Native American or American Indian community has a fairly fluid conceptualization of gender and sexuality, with sexual identity seen as complex and ever-changing (Tafoya, 1997). Because tribal languages often do not translate well into English, Tafoya noted that it is difficult to fully describe the complexity and fluidity of concepts such as gender and sexual orientation among Native Americans. Consequently, these gender-transgressive sexual minorities may feel uncomfortable categorizing themselves using common LGBTQ labels, rather choosing to identify as "two-spirited." Despite affirmative traditions, the Native American community has experienced centuries of oppression and forced assimilation by European settlers, rendering contemporary Native American culture rife with a varying mix of heterosexism and homophobia (Walters, Simoni, & Horwath, 2001). As a result, two-spirited individuals may not feel accepted by their American Indian community, particularly the 60% who live in metropolitan areas and are likely to experience greater influence of non-American Indian culture (Garrett & Barret, 2003).

Walters et al. (2001) conducted eight focus groups consisting of 27 two-spirited American Indian participants and four service providers. Several participants identified invisibility as a barrier to receiving social support but also as an opportunity to anonymously explore sexual identity. Experiences with racism both in general society and in the LGBTQ community, as well as homophobia within the American Indian community, often were cited as significant stressors. Finally, nearly all of the respondents reported a history of trauma and violence, a finding consistent with a recent quantitative study (Balsam, Huang, Fieland, Simoni & Walters, 2004) which found higher rates of childhood physical abuse reported by urban Indian and Alaska Native sexual minority adults when compared to their heterosexual counterparts. Similarly, Morris and Balsam (2003) found that Native American sexual minority women reported significantly higher levels of trauma than African American, Latina, Asian American, and White women. Overall, these studies suggest that American Indian two-spirited people may experience significant stressors based on their sexual minority status. It is difficult to determine, however, the extent to which these difficulties are a result of sexuality or are a reflection of problems endemic to poverty, racism, substance abuse, and other realities of contemporary American Indian life.

Transgender People of Color

Lombardi (2007) pointed out two stereotypes of transgender people related to race/ethnicity: one is the White, middle-class, older transwoman and the other is the younger transwoman of color involved in sex work. These stereotypes have focused much of the transgender research on MTFs, and much of it in the health arena (also see Fassinger & Arseneau, 2006). For example, a high prevalence of HIV/AIDS in transwomen has been identified, with even higher rates (as high as 60%) reported for transwomen of color, particularly African Americans. The differential health status of transgender people across racial/ethnic groups highlights the pernicious effects of racism, poverty, geographic disadvantage, and cultural oppression in limiting access to adequate health care, and makes clear the need for increased attention to structural barriers in the health care system.

In terms of research on identity, however, the dearth of empirical research with transgender people of color is evidenced by locating only one study in the recent literature. This study (Gutierrez, 2004) sampled four male-to-female transgender adolescents of color identified through an alternative school for LGBTQ students. All four of the participants rejected the identity label *transgender* as incongruent with their holistic conceptualization of their multiple identities, consistent with the discussion of labeling by Fassinger and Arseneau (2007) in constructing their model of gender-transgressive sexual minority identity.

Summary of Sexual Orientation in Relation to Race/Ethnicity

Even with the limited empirical research available, the impact of multiple minority stress is apparent for sexual minority people of color. For many, their culture and family serve as powerful resources, but support may depend on some masking of their sexual identity. The salience of ethnic identity appears consistently throughout the literature, whereas sexual identity is more varied in its effects. For example, one large study comparing adolescents of different ethnic backgrounds (N = 13,205) found that ethnicity and gender were more predictive of depression and self-esteem than was sexual orientation (Consolacion, Russell, & Sue, 2004). Recognizing the varying levels of importance attached to aspects of identity within different contexts, Croteau and Constantine (2005) assert that "an individual can be fully understood only in a holistic manner that includes understanding the influences and interactions of the individual's multiple sociodemographic groups, some or all of which may be salient 'identities' for the individual" (p.162). The limited research generated thus far speaks to the richness and complexities of multiple identities for LGBTQ people of color.

SEXUAL ORIENTATION AND SOCIAL CLASS/SOCIOECONOMIC STATUS

Our consideration of social class and socioeconomic status (SES) focuses on LGBTQ individuals of lower SES and social class, in part to bring attention to socioeconomic issues, as relatively affluent individuals characterize much of the existing empirical literature. Furthermore, our review is focused on those studies that specifically addressed lower social class as a main variable of interest. Few recent studies were identified that specifically addressed the intersection between social class and sexual orientation; thus, information regarding the impact of shared membership in these two marginalized groups is quite limited.

Socioeconomic status can have a profound effect on one's social experiences and mental health status. Several ethnographic accounts have suggested that a tension exists between lower and higher social class LGBTQ individuals (Appleby, 2001a, 2001b; Ward, 2003). Specifically, working-class individuals expressed resentment and antagonism toward the middle class sexual minority community (Appleby, 2001a, 2001b). Furthermore, middle- and upper-class sexual minority individuals seemed to perceive lower-class members as less professional and competent (Ward, 2003). Thus, not only are working-class individuals impacted by LGBTQ community tensions, but they also experience the discrimination from the broader culture as well. Relative to mental health status, Díaz et al. (2001) found that experiences of financial hardship had a significant relationship with the presence of suicidal ideation in their sample of gay and bisexual Latino men.

Barrett and Pollack (2005) sought to identify the impact of social class on self-labeling and community involvement in gay men and, specifically, whether low-SES gay men could have access to "middle-class gay culture" (Barrett & Pollack, 2005, p. 439). Participants (N = 2605) were a subsample of the Urban Men's Health Study. Results indicated that: (a) social class was positively related to the likelihood of self-identifying as gay; (b) higher education was inversely related to the likelihood that time between age of first homosexual activity and coming out was more than 3 years; (c) nonminority ethnic status was significantly related to increased likelihood of self-labeling as gay and decreased likelihood of a disclosure gap of more than 3 years; and (d) level of openness was not related to social class in this sample. With regard to community involvement, higher social class was significantly related to increased likelihood of residence in a predominantly gay neighborhood, and nonminority ethnic status was significantly related to residence. Although the study's purpose was to identify the role of social class on participation in gay culture and self-expression, the measurement of social class was weak, with only educational attainment and income level reported and a definition of social class that did not include differential access to resources and privilege (see Liu et al., 2004, for further discussion of this issue).

McDermott (2006) used qualitative interviews to examine the relationship between social class, psychological health, and workplace lesbian identity in a sample of 24 participants representing a wide range of socioeconomic statuses. Regardless of social class, all of the participants cited workplace homophobia as a significant concern, though each also attempted to challenge heterosexist norms. Class differences were apparent. Middle-class participants were much more open about their sexual identity at work, often due to a more accepting workplace or to jobs with the power and authority to offset discrimination; this seemed to mediate the psychological impact of navigating their identity in the workplace. In contrast, working-class participants experienced considerable strain, with some choosing to have coworkers assume that they were heterosexual. This decision was the result of anxiety and fear related to disclosure and often was seen as their only option; that is, with limited power, these working-class women had to choose between openness and employment.

In our review of the recent literature, we were unable to identify any studies that specifically examined the intersection between social class and bisexuality. One could speculate, however, that some individuals from the previously discussed samples were bisexual but labeled as lesbian or gay based on their current same-sex relationship. Moreover, it could be hypothesized that at least some of the significant findings could be applied to bisexual women and men. For example, higher social class was found to increase the likelihood of living in gay communities (Barrett & Pollack, 2005). Financial resources may play a similar role in accessing community resources in the lives of bisexual women and men just as it does for other sexual minority populations.

No studies were found that examined the socioeconomic elements of social class and gender variance. Certainly, financial resources affect a transgender individual's access to sexual reassignment surgery and other critical components of transgender health care (e.g., hormone treatments; Lev, 2007). Furthermore, financial barriers also may impact an individual's ability to access support from online communities, an important resource for transgender people who otherwise may be quite isolated from similar others (Lev, 2007). In terms of employment issues, Pepper and Lorah (in press) highlighted the career concerns for individuals in transition, who must decide whether to transition at their current place of employment (with the concomitant emotional and financial stability that decision confers) but may face a more difficult adjustment process due to unsupportive coworkers. In contrast, individuals may not have to "out" themselves in a new employment situation but may sacrifice financial stability and support from previous collegial relationships. Moreover, there is anecdotal evidence that gender-based workplace discrimination plays out in the lives of transgender people quite distinctly. MTFs report marked decreases in salary and respect in the workplace post-transition, whereas female-to-males (FTMs) report increases in worker status (see Lev, 2004). Recently, media attention revealed the case of Ben Barres, a well-regarded Stanford biologist, who reported that, after transitioning 10 years ago from being a woman, his reputation and respect in the highly sexist scientific community were bolstered considerably by becoming a man (Vedantam, 2006).

Clearly, research is limited regarding the relationship between sexual minority identity and social class. From this limited review, however, it is apparent that social class does impact the ability of LGBTQ individuals not only to access elements of sexual minority culture (i.e., neighborhoods) but also to have the social capital to balance the marginalization of their sexual identity. Blackwell and Dziegielewski (2005) cited the potential negative impact of public policy changes for low-SES LGBTQ individuals. The Personal Responsibility and Work Opportunity Reconciliation Act (PRWORA), for example, permits religious organizations to compete for federal and state social service funding. As these organizations are permitted, based on religious tenets, to distinguish between who can and cannot access their services, many low-SES sexual minority individuals may be denied much-needed assistance.

Finally, there are methodological complexities associated with research focused on LGBTQ individuals who represent low or working-class socioeconomic status. McDermott (2004) and Taylor (2005) both addressed the impact of social class on the qualitative data collection process within lesbian samples. Both noted that participants who were working-class or of low SES displayed less confidence and more reticence when sharing their experiences, and required more reassurance and follow-up questions from the researchers. Taylor (2005) speculated that, because low social class has been stigmatized, researchers are presented with the task of creating a safe environment for these participants. Moreover, the measurement of social class is difficult and not widely agreed upon (Liu et al., 2004), and social class is a dynamic variable, with social class mobility possible over an individual's lifetime due to changes in educational status, income, and access to resources (Ward, 2003). Despite these methodological concerns, social class is an important contextual element in understanding the experiences of LGBTQ individuals and should be integrated more intentionally into future research.

SEXUAL ORIENTATION AND RELIGION

Within the context of multiple identities, few topics are more hotly debated than the intersection between religion and sexual orientation. The stance of professional psychology regarding sexual orientation is clearly affirmative and prohibits the provision of treatment aimed at changing sexual orientation. Yet there has been much discussion of the extent to which such a stance discriminates against those with strong religious identities. Most frequently, these discussions center on whether it is ethical to provide conversion or so-called "reparative" therapy to sexual minority clients (e.g., Fischer & DeBord, 2007; Greene, 2007; Haldeman, 2004; Morrow & Beckstead, 2004; Yarhouse, Burkett, & Kreeft, 2002). Recently, however, there has been some research that examined religious conflicts experienced by sexual minority individuals apart from the context of conversion therapy. We begin by describing the limited empirical research documenting religious conflict, and we then turn to a discussion of studies specifically examining conversion therapy.

Studies Focused on the Conflict Between Religion and Sexual Orientation

Consistent with anecdotal reports, the few recent empirical studies that examine the responses of sexual minority (specifically, LGB) individuals to religion confirm the distress that LGB individuals experience in regard to this conflict. Both Goodwill (2000) and Schuck and Liddle (2001) established that LGB individuals experience a conflict between their religion and sexual orientation, results similar to those found in relation to conversion therapy (e.g., Beckstead & Morrow, 2004; Nicolosi, Byrd, & Potts, 2000; Shidlo & Schroeder, 2002; Spitzer, 2003; Tozer & Hayes, 2004). Goodwill conducted 1- to 2-hour interviews with five highly educated gay men from

Mormon backgrounds. Results of the study document the extent to which identifying as gay conflicts with the Mormon Church; participants articulated church messages that clearly document gayness as negative, and four of the five viewed gay identity as incompatible with the Mormon Church (though not incompatible with spirituality more generally). Schuck and Liddle (2001) surveyed 66 LGB individuals, and two-thirds of respondents reported a conflict at the time of coming out between religion and sexual orientation. Results indicated both cognitive and emotional consequence of this conflict (e.g., fear that they would go to hell or that God had rejected them; feeling judged by their religious communities; depression, self-loathing, suicidal ideation; guilt and shame), and participants resolved these conflicts in a variety of ways, including withdrawing from their religion, maintaining their religion privately, or attending affirming congregations. Interestingly, some participants identified positive outcomes that emerged from this conflict, including identifying with gay-affirmative congregations and internal resolution of conflicts that led to deeper spirituality.

The results of another study (Lease, Horne, & Noffsinger-Frazier, 2005) documented the impact of affirming faith experiences on physical well-being, particularly in ameliorating the negative influence of internalized homophobia on physical health and via their positive associations with spirituality. Lease et al. collected data from 583 LGB individuals currently affiliated with a faith group, and their results indicated that affirmative faith group experiences were indirectly related to psychological health through internalized homophobia and spirituality (the latter of which were negatively and positively related to psychological health, respectively). This is an important result because it demonstrates that LGB individuals' relationship to religion and spirituality need not always be negative, despite that common assumption.

Exploring Conversion Therapy

Conversion therapy is any professional or peer-group attempt to change an individual's same-sex sexual orientation. Conversion therapy also has been termed "reparative therapy" or "reorientation therapy." We choose to use the term "conversion therapy" because both of the other terms imply that the individual's sexual orientation is faulty and in need of repair.

Religion commonly serves as the motivator for clients seeking to change their sexual orientation. A large proportion of conversion therapy participants have been individuals who were religious at the time they pursued treatment, and their religious beliefs were experienced as incongruent with the acceptance of a sexual minority identity (Beckstead & Morrow, 2004; Nicolosi et al., 2000; Ponticelli, 1996, 1999; Schaeffer, Nottebaum,

Smith, Dech, & Krawczyk, 1999; Schaeffer, Hyde, Kroencke, McCormick, & Nottebaum, 2000; Shidlo & Schroeder, 2002; Spitzer, 2003; Tozer & Hayes, 2004). For example, a study by Tozer and Hayes revealed that participants who held homonegative beliefs, whose intrinsic religious identities were central and organizing identities, and who were in the early phases of lesbian or gay identity development were inclined to view conversion therapy as an option for treatment.

Many individuals who seek conversion therapy have pursued treatment through Christian ministry organizations (Yarhouse et al., 2002). Schaeffer and her colleagues (1999, 2000) conducted initial and follow-up survey research of paraprofessional conversion treatment outcomes. In these studies, positive mental health variables were associated with self-reported behavior that was "more heterosexual" at the time of the survey administration than it had been in the past. Self-defined "success" in sexual orientation change was positively correlated with frequent and continuing religious service attendance. Participants who were described as highly religiously motivated were found to be more likely than other participants to have avoided same-sex intimate *behavior* over time. Researchers found, however, that paraprofessional conversion therapy was not effective in helping participants change sexual *orientation.* Ponticelli (1999) conducted a study that focused on 15 self-described ex-lesbians in one paraprofessional conversion ministry. She observed that individuals in this sample communicated in a common discourse, and the language and behaviors that were presented as appropriate by the conversion group were mirrored in the participants' narratives.

All three of the published studies that explicitly inquired about negative effects support the conclusion that conversion therapy can be harmful (i.e., Beckstead & Morrow, 2004; Nicolosi et al., 2000; Shidlo & Schroeder, 2002). For example, in Shidlo and Schroeder's (2002) qualitative study, 87% of the 202 consumers of professional and paraprofessional interventions reported failure, and many found conversion therapy to be harmful. In the Beckstead and Morrow (2004) study, of the 42 participants interviewed who had participated in conversion therapy, 22 described primarily negative outcomes such as increased discrimination, relational difficulties, hopelessness, self-hatred, and, for some, suicide attempts or completions. Interestingly, some participants who reported negative effects of conversion treatment in both of these studies also described their conversion therapy experiences as useful, including determining that conversion was not possible (Shidlo & Schroeder, 2002), experiencing some short-term relief (e.g., learning that they were not alone), and the opportunity to both explore being "ex-gay" as well as accepting themselves as lesbian, gay, or bisexual (Beckstead & Morrow, 2004).

Overall, it is unclear that conversion therapy can change sexual orientation. Spitzer (2003) and Nicolosi et al. (2000) conclude that complete change is possible for at least some individuals who participate in conversion therapy. Spitzer claimed complete change for 11% of the males and 37% of the females in his study, while Nicolosi et al. claimed complete change for 17.6% of their sample. Nicolosi et al. acknowledge that complete change is an "often difficult and lengthy process" (p. 1084), and Spitzer concludes that complete change "may be a rare or uncommon occurrence" (p. 413). Shidlo and Schroeder (2002, noted earlier) reported that eight of their participants viewed conversion therapy as helpful in shifting of sexual orientation (seven of those reported currently serving as conversion counselors). Thus, evidence suggests that conversion therapy is useful primarily to manage same-sex behavior but has little long-lasting influence on sexual orientation (Beckstead & Morrow, 2004; Schaeffer et al., 1999; Schaeffer et al., 2000; Shidlo & Schroeder, 2002).

Interestingly, although the evidence suggests that conversion therapy can be harmful, all four of the studies also concluded that at least some participants found conversion therapy helpful (Beckstead & Morrow, 2004; Nicolosi et al., 2000; Shidlo & Schroeder, 2002; Spitzer, 2003), although perceptions of helpfulness ranged widely. While Nicolosi et al. (2000) and Spitzer (2003) reported that participants retrospectively reported decreased engagement in homosexual thoughts, behaviors, and feelings after conversion therapy, in both the Shidlo and Schroeder (2002) and Beckstead and Morrow (2004) studies, the vast majority of those who found treatment to be helpful were still "struggling" with their orientations, although participants in both studies found cognitive and behavioral strategies for managing same-sex behavior to be useful.

Overall, the intersection of sexual orientation with religion suggests complex effects. Clearly, conversion therapy has produced mixed results, with some impact on same-sex behavior but little effect on actual sexual orientation, and the positive effects seem primarily derived from helping individuals to clarify and accept their orientation (regardless of what they decide to do behaviorally). Research also suggests that LGBTQ-affirmative faith-based activities and environments can exert much impact in ameliorating the negative impact on sexual minority individuals of homonegative religious teachings and institutions.

IMPLICATIONS OF THE INTERSECTIONAL LITERATURE FOR RESEARCH AND PRACTICE

As is evident from this review, there is limited empirical research available regarding the intersection or integration of cultural identity variables with sexual orientation, and the existing knowledge base is built on very few studies. For example, in the arena of race/ethnicity (the largest of the small literatures we review in this chapter), research on LGBTQ populations typically is conducted with Caucasian participants, ignoring race and ethnicity as cultural variables (Bieschke, Paul, & Blasko, 2007; Soto, 1997), whereas research on people of color largely ignores sexual orientation (for more detailed discussion, see Greene, 2000, 2003). Thus, the capacity to generalize empirical knowledge from either body of literature to describe in an integrated way the experiences of LGBTQ people of color is limited (Harper, Jernewall, & Zea, 2004). This separation of literatures applies not just to the cultural dimension of race/ethnicity but also to all of the cultural variables reviewed here.

Moreover, what little has been written about intersecting identities has been conceptualized from a bifurcated and additive point of view: One basic identity with its attendant oppression is centralized (e.g., lesbian), and then another identity with its oppressive elements (e.g., race/ethnicity) is added, producing an identity that is a sum total of those victim statuses; for example, a lesbian who is a woman of color is viewed as subject to all of the stigma related to sexual orientation plus the additional stigma related to race/ethnicity (with other aspects of social location such as class and age rarely addressed). The obvious problem with this approach (besides the fact that it highlights victimization and is extraordinarily discouraging) is that intersections of identity are much more complex than an additive model suggests. Family structures, cultural norms, available resources, geographic location, historical time period, involvement in communities organized around identities, and sociopolitical realities all are likely to influence the way in which the identities merge and are expressed. These intersecting minority statuses also influence the individual's membership within the LGBTQ community, the racial/ethnic community, as well as society in general (Collins, 2004; Garnets, 2002; Liddle, 2007; Miville & Ferguson, 2006). Both research and clinical practice need to produce approaches to understanding intersecting identities that fully expose their myriad aspects and expressions, and that present strengths-based perspectives on these identities.

Furthermore, the small knowledge base on intersectional identities is subject to a host of methodological limitations that plague the general literature on LGBTQ issues (e.g., sampling restrictions, questionable applicability of theories and measures, lack of generalizability; see Croteau et al., in press), including assumptive foundations that incorporate much of the bias present in psychological research more generally. For example, in an analysis of several studies on LGBTQ people of color, Riggs (2007) has demonstrated how dominant discourses in psychology render invisible the race of White LGBTQ individuals even as they centralize racial/ethnic experience for LGBTQ people of color, creating a literature of "psycolonization" (p. 62) in which White experience is positioned as normative, and the experience of people of color is relegated to consideration of extraneous but overdetermining "cultural" influences.

These complex epistemological, conceptual, and methodological issues notwithstanding, this chapter presented some recent empirical findings and broad generalizations applicable to the intersection of sexual and gender orientation with a range of cultural orientations (i.e., age, disability, race/ethnicity, social class, religion). All warrant critical attention clinically, sustained study empirically, and deconstruction of the hidden assumptions and biases that likely pervade this literature. Although such an agenda is challenging, pursuing research and clinical work from a complex and comprehensive framework will enable counseling psychologists to provide services and conduct research that is truly reflective of the lives of diverse LGBTQ people.

BIBLIOGRAPHY

Adams, E. M., Cahill, B. J., & Ackerlind, S. J. (2005). A qualitative study of Latino lesbian and gay youths' experiences with discrimination and the career development process. *Journal of Vocational Behavior, 66,* 199–218.

Appleby, G. A. (2001a). Framework for practice with working-class gay and bisexual men. *Journal of Gay & Lesbian Social Services, 12*(3/4), 5–46.

Appleby, G. A. (2001b). Ethnographic study of gay and bisexual working-class men in the United States. *Journal of Gay & Lesbian Social Services, 12*(3/4), 51–62.

Balsam, K. F., Huang, B., Fieland, K. C., Simoni, J. M., & Walters, K. L. (2004). Culture, trauma, and wellness: A comparison of heterosexual and lesbian, gay, bisexual, and Two-Spirit Native Americans. *Cultural Diversity and Ethnic Minority Psychology, 10,* 287–301.

Barón, A., & Cramer, D. W. (2000). Potential counseling concerns of aging lesbian, gay, and bisexual clients. In R. M. Perez, K. A. DeBord, & K. J. Bieschke (Eds.), *Handbook of counseling and psychotherapy with lesbian, gay, and bisexual clients* (pp. 207–224). Washington, DC: American Psychological Association.

Barrett, D. C., & Pollack, L. M. (2005). Whose gay community? Social class, sexual self-expression, and gay community involvement. *The Sociological Quarterly, 46,* 437–456.

Beckstead, A. L., & ,Morrow, S. L. (2004). Mormon clients' experiences of conversion therapy: The need for a new treatment approach. *The Counseling Psychologist, 32,* 651–691.

Bennett, C., & Coyle, A. (2007). A minority within a minority: Experiences of gay men with intellectual disabilities. In V. Clarke & E. Peel (Eds.), *Out in psychology: Lesbian, gay, bisexual, trans, and queer perspectives* (pp. 120–124). West Sussex, England: John Wiley and Sons, Inc.

Bieschke, K. J., Paul, P. L., & Blasko, K. A. (2007). Review of empirical research focused on the experience of lesbian, gay, and bisexual clients in counseling and psychotherapy. In K.Bieschke, R. Perez, & K. DeBord (Eds.), *Handbook of counseling and psychotherapy with lesbian, gay, bisexual, and transgender clients* (2nd ed., pp. 293–316). Washington, DC: American Psychological Association.

Bieschke, K. J., Perez, R. M., & DeBord, K. A. (2007). Introduction: The challenge of providing affirmative psychotherapy while honoring diverse contexts. In K. Bieschke, R. Perez, & K. DeBord (Eds.), *Handbook of counseling and psychotherapy with lesbian, gay, bisexual, and transgender clients* (2nd ed., pp. 3–10). Washington, DC: American Psychological Association.

Blackwell, C. W., & Dziegielewski, S. F. (2005). The privatization of social services from public to sectarian: Negative consequences for America's gays and lesbians. *Journal of Human Behavior in the Social Environment, 11*(2), 25–41.

Bowleg, L., Craig, M. L., & Burkholder, G. (2004). Rising and surviving: A conceptual model of active coping among Black lesbians. *Cultural Diversity and Ethnic Minority Psychology, 10*, 229–240.

Bowleg, L., Huang, J., Brooks, K., Black, A., & Burkholder, G. (2003). Triple jeopardy and beyond: Multiple minority stress and resilience among Black lesbians. *Journal of Lesbian Studies, 7*(4), 87–108.

Bridges, S. K., Selvidge, M. M. D., & Matthews, C. R. (2003). Lesbian women of color: Therapeutic issues and challenges. *Journal of Multicultural Counseling and Development, 31*, 113–130.

Brown, L. S. (1989). New voices, new visions: Toward a lesbian/gay paradigm for psychology. *Psychology of Women Quarterly, 13*, 445–458.

Collins, J. F. (2004). The intersection of race and bisexuality: A critical overview of the literature and past, present, and future directions of the "borderlands." *Journal of Bisexuality, 4*, 99–116.

Colon, E. (2001). An ethnographic study of six Latino gay and bisexual men. *Journal of Gay & Lesbian Social Services, 12*(3/4), 77–92.

Consolacion, T. B., Russell, S. T., & Sue, S. (2004). Sex, race/ethnicity, and romantic attractions: Multiple minority status adolescents and mental health. *Cultural Diversity and Ethnic Minority Psychology, 10*, 200–214.

Cooke-Daniels, L. (2006). Trans aging. In D. Kimmel, T. Rose, & S. David (Eds.), *Lesbian, gay, bisexual, and transgender aging* (pp. 20–35). New York: Columbia University Press.

Cox, S., & Kellerhouse, B. (2007, March 15). Why are so many mid-life gay men getting HIV? In *Gay City News*, New York; http://www.gaycitynews.com/site/news.cfm (Accessed February 15, 2008.)

Crawford, I., Allison, K. W., Zamboni, B. D., & Soto, T. (2002). The influence of dual-identity development on the psychosocial functioning of African-American gay and bisexual men. *The Journal of Sex Research, 39*(3), 179–189.

Croteau, J. M., & Constantine, M. G. (2005). Race and sexual orientation in multicultural counseling: Navigating rough waters. In J. M. Croteau, J. S. Lark, M. A. Lidderdale, & Y. B. Chung (Eds.), *Deconstructing heterosexism in the counseling professions: A narrative approach* (pp. 159–185). Thousand Oaks, CA: Sage Publications.

Croteau, J. M., Bieschke, K. J., Fassinger, R. F., & Manning, J. L. (in press). Counseling psychology and sexual orientation: History, selective trends, and future directions. In S. Brown & R. Lent (Eds.), *Handbook of counseling psychology* (4th ed.). New York: Wiley.

Díaz, R. M., Ayala, G., Bein, E., Henne, J., & Marin, B. V. (2001). The impact of homophobia, poverty, and racism on the mental health of gay and bisexual Latino men: Findings from 3 U.S. cities. *American Journal of Public Health, 91*, 927–932.

Díaz, R. M., Bein, E., & Ayala, G. (2006). Homophobia, poverty, and racism: Triple oppression and mental health outcomes in Latino gay men. In A. M. Omoto & H. S. Kurtzman (Eds.), *Contemporary perspectives on lesbian, gay and bisexual psychology* (pp. 207–224). Washington, DC: American Psychological Association.

Fassinger, R. E., & Arseneau, J. R. (2007). "I'd rather get wet than be under that umbrella": Differentiating the experiences and identities of lesbian, gay, bisexual, and transgender people. In K. Bieschke, R. Perez, & K. DeBord (Eds.), *Handbook of counseling and psychotherapy with lesbian, gay, bisexual, and transgender clients* (2nd ed., pp. 19–50). Washington, DC: American Psychological Association.

Fischer, A. R., & DeBord, K. A. (2007). Perceived conflicts between affirmation of religious diversity and affirmation of sexual diversity: That's perceived. In K. Bieschke, R. Perez, & K. DeBord (Eds.), *Handbook of counseling and psychotherapy with lesbian, gay, bisexual, and transgender clients* (2nd ed., pp. 317–340). Washington, DC: American Psychological Association.

Friend, R. A. (1990). Older lesbian and gay people: A theory of successful aging. *Journal of Homosexuality, 20*(3–4), 99–118.

Fukuyama, M. A., & Ferguson, A. D. (2000). Lesbian, gay, and bisexual people of color: Understanding cultural complexity and managing multiple oppressions. In R. M. Perez, K. A. DeBord, & K. J. Bieschke (Eds.), *Handbook of counseling and psychotherapy with lesbian, gay, bisexual, and transgender clients* (pp. 81–105). Washington, DC: American Psychological Association.

Garnets, L. D. (2002). Sexual orientations in perspective. *Cultural Diversity and Ethnic Minority Psychology, 8*, 115–129.

Garrett, M. T., & Barret, B. (2003). Two Spirit: Counseling Native American gay, lesbian, and bisexual people. *Journal of Multicultural Counseling and Development, 31*, 131–142.

Goodwill, K. A. (2000). Religion and the spiritual needs of gay Mormon men. *Journal of Gay & Lesbian Social Services, 11*, 23–37.

Greene, B. (2000). African American lesbian and bisexual women. *Journal of Social Issues, 56*, 239–249.

Greene, B. (2003). Beyond heterosexism and across the cultural divide—Developing an inclusive lesbian, gay, and bisexual psychology: A look to the future. In L. D. Garnets and D. C. Kimmel (Eds.), *Psychological perspectives on lesbian, gay, and bisexual experiences* (pp. 457–401). New York: Columbia University Press.

Greene, B. (2007). Delivering ethical psychological services to lesbian, gay, and bisexual clients. In K.Bieschke, R. Perez, & K. DeBord (Eds.), *Handbook of counseling and psychotherapy with lesbian, gay, bisexual, and transgender clients* (2nd ed., pp. 181–200). Washington DC: American Psychological Association.

Grossman, A. H., D'Augelli, A. R., & O'Connell, T. S. (2003). Being lesbian, gay, bisexual, and sixty or older in North America. In L. D. Garnets & D. C. Kimmel (Eds.), *Psychological perspectives on lesbian, gay, and bisexual experiences* (pp. 629–646). New York: Columbia University Press.

Grov, C., Bimbi, D. S., Nanín, J. E., & Parsons, J. T. (2006). Race, ethnicity, gender, and generational factors associated with the coming-out process among gay, lesbian, bisexual individuals. *The Journal of Sex Research, 43,* 115–121.

Gutierrez, N. (2004). Resisting fragmentation, living whole: Four female transgender students of color speak about school. *Journal of Gay & Lesbian Social Services, 16*(3/4), 69–79.

Haldeman, D. (2004). When sexual and religious orientation collide: Considerations in working with conflicted same-sex attracted male clients. *The Counseling Psychologist, 32,* 691–715.

Hall, R. L., & Fine, M. (2005). The stories we tell: The lives and friendship of two older Black lesbians. *Psychology of Women Quarterly, 29,* 177–187.

Harper, G. W., Jernewall, N., & Zea, M. C. (2004). Giving voice to emerging science and theory for lesbian, gay, and bisexual people of color. *Cultural Diversity and Ethnic Minority Psychology, 10*(3), 187–199.

Kimmel, D. C., & Yi, H. (2004). Characteristics of gay, lesbian, and bisexual Asians, Asian Americans, and immigrants from Asia to the USA. *Journal of Homosexuality, 47,* 143–172.

Kimmel, D., Rose. T., & David, S. (Eds.). (2006). *Lesbian, gay, bisexual, and transgender aging: Research and clinical perspectives.* New York: Columbia University Press.

Lease, S. H., Horne, S. G., & Noffsinger-Frazier, N. (2005). Affirming faith experiences and psychological health for Caucasian lesbian, gay, and bisexual individuals. *Journal of Counseling Psychology, 52,* 378–388.

Lev, A. I. (2004). *Transgender emergence. Therapeutic guidelines for working with gender-variant people and their families.* New York: Haworth Press.

Lev, A. I. (2007). Transgender communities: Developing identity through connection. In K. J. Bieschke, R. M. Perez, & K. A. DeBord (Eds.), *Handbook of counseling and psychotherapy with lesbian, gay, bisexual, and transgender clients* (2nd ed. pp. 147–175). Washington, DC: American Psychological Association.

Liddle, B. J. (2007). The challenge of understanding LGBTQ lives and experiences. In V. Clarke and E. Peel (Eds.), *Out in psychology: Lesbian, gay, bisexual, trans, and queer perspectives* (pp. 120–124). West Sussex, England: John Wiley and Sons, Inc.

Liu, W. M., Ali, S. R., Soleck, G., Hopps, J., Dunston, K., & Pickett, T. Jr., (2004). Using social class in counseling psychology research. *Journal of Counseling Psychology, 51,* 3–18.

Lombardi, E. (2001). Enhancing transgender health care. *American Journal of Public Health, 91,* 859–872.

Lombardi, E. (2007). Public health and trans-people: Barriers to care and strategies to improve treatment. In I. H. Meyer & M. E. Northridge (Eds.), *The health of sexual minorities* (p. 638). New York: Springer.

Mao, L., McCormick, J., & Van de Ven, P. (2002). Ethnic and gay identification: Gay Asian men dealing with the divide. *Culture, Health, & Sexuality, 4,* 419–430.

McDermott, E. (2004). Telling lesbian stories: Interviewing and the class dynamics of "talk." *Women's Studies International Forum, 27*(3), 177–187.

McDermott, E. (2006). Surviving in dangerous places: Lesbian identity performances in the workplace, social class and psychological health. *Feminism & Psychology, 16*(2), 193–211.

Meyer, I. H. (2007). Prejudice and discrimination as social stressors. In I. H. Meyer and M. E. Northridge (Eds.), *The health of sexual minorities* (pp. 242–267). New York: Springer.

Miville, M. L., & Ferguson, A. D. (2006). Intersections of sexism and heterosexism with racism: Therapeutic implications. In M. G. Constantine & D. W. Sue (Eds.), *Addressing racism: Facilitating cultural competence in mental health and educational settings* (pp. 87–103). Hoboken, NJ: Wiley & Sons.

Mona, L. R., Fraley, S. S., Theodore, P. S., Ballan, M. S., Cameron, R. P., & Crisp, C. C. (in press). Sexual expression among lesbian, gay, and bisexual people with disabilities. In S. Morrow & R. Fassinger (Eds.), *Sex in the margins: Erotic lives of sexual minority people.* Washington, DC: American Psychological Association.

Morris, J. F., & Balsam, K. F. (2003). Lesbian and bisexual women's experiences of victimization: Mental health, revictimization, and sexual identity development. *Journal of Lesbian Studies,* 7(4), 67–85.

Morrow, S., & Beckstead, A. (2004). Conversion therapies for same-sex attracted clients in religious conflict: Context, predisposing factors, experiences, and implications for therapy. *The Counseling Psychologist, 32,* 641–650.

Muòoz-Laboy, M. A. (2004). Beyond "MSM": Sexual desire among bisexually-active Latino men in New York City. *Sexualities, 7,* 55–80.

Nicolosi, J. (1993). *Healing homosexuality: Case stories of reparative therapy.* Northvale, NJ: Jason Aronson.

Nicolosi, J., Byrd, A. D., & Potts, R. W. (2000). Retrospective self reports of changes in homosexual orientation: A consumer survey of conversion therapy clients. *Psychological Reports, 86,* 1071–1088.

Olkin, R. (1999). *What psychotherapists should know about disability.* New York: Guilford Press.

Parks, C. A., Hughes, T. L., & Matthews, A. K. (2004). Race/ethnicity and sexual orientation: Intersecting identities. *Cultural Diversity and Ethnic Minority Psychology, 10,* 241–254.

Patterson, C. (2007). Lesbian and gay family issues in the context of changing legal and social policy environments. In K. J. Bieschke, R. M. Perez, & K. A. DeBord (Eds.), *Handbook of counseling and psychotherapy with lesbian, gay, bisexual, and transgender clients* (2nd ed., pp. 359–378). Washington, DC: American Psychological Association.

Pepper, S. M., & Lorah, P. (in press). Career issues and workplace considerations for the transsexual community: Bridging a gap of knowledge for career counselors and mental health care providers. *Career Development Quarterly.*

Perez, R. M. (2007). The "boring" state of research and psychotherapy with lesbian, gay, bisexual, and transgender clients: Revisiting Barón (1991). In K. Bieschke, R. Perez, & K. DeBord (Eds.), *Handbook of counseling and psychotherapy with lesbian, gay, bisexual, and transgender clients* (2nd ed., pp. 399–418). Washington, DC: American Psychological Association.

Ponticelli, C. M. (1996). The spiritual warfare of Exodus: A postpositivist research adventure. *Qualitative Inquiry,* 2(2), 198–219.

Ponticelli, C. M. (1999). Crafting stories of sexual identity reconstruction. *Social Psychology Quarterly,* 62(2), 157–172.

Riggs, D. W. (2007). Recognizing race in LGBTQ psychology: Power, privilege, and complicity. In V. Clarke & E. Peel (Eds.), *Out in psychology: Lesbian, gay, bisexual, trans, and queer perspectives* (pp. 120–124). West Sussex, England: John Wiley and Sons, Inc.

Rosario, M., Schrimshaw, E. W., & Hunter, J. (2004). Ethnic/racial differences in the coming-out process of lesbian, gay, and bisexual youths: A comparison of sexual identity development over time. *Cultural Diversity and Ethnic Minority Psychology, 10*, 215–228.

Russell, S. T., & Truong N. L. (2001). Adolescent sexual orientation, race and ethnicity, and school environments: A national survey of sexual minority youth of color. In K. K. Kumashiro (Ed.), *Troubling intersections of race and sexuality: Queer students of color and anti-oppressive education* (pp. 113–130). Lanham, MD: Rowman & Littlefield Publishers.

Savage, T. A., & Harley, D. A. (2005). African American lesbian, gay, and bisexual persons. In D. A. Harley & J. M. Dillard (Eds.), *Contemporary mental health issues among African Americans* (pp. 91–105). Alexandria, VA: American Counseling Association.

Schaeffer, K. W., Hyde, R. A., Kroencke, T., McCormick, B., & Nottebaum, L. (2000). Religiously-motivated sexual orientation change. *Journal of Psychology and Christianity, 19*(1), 61–70.

Schaeffer, K. W., Nottebaum, L., Smith, P., Dech, K., & Krawczyk, J. (1999). Religiously-motivated sexual orientation change: A follow-up study. *Journal of Psychology and Theology, 27*(4), 329–337.

Schuck, K. D., & Liddle, B. J. (2001). Religious conflicts experienced by lesbian, gay, and bisexual individuals. *Journal of Gay & Lesbian Psychotherapy, 5*, 63–82.

Shidlo, A., & Schroeder, M. (2002). Changing sexual orientation: A consumers' report. *Professional Psychology: Research and Practice, 33*, 249–259.

Shippy, R. A., Cantor, M. H., & Brennan, M. (2004). Social networks of aging gay men. *The Journal of Men's Studies, 13*(1), 107–120.

Soto, T. A. (1997). Ethnic minority gay, lesbian, and bisexual publications: A 10-year review. *Division 44 Newsletter, 13*, 13–14.

Spitzer, R. L. (2003). Can some gay men and lesbians change their sexual orientation? 200 participants reporting a change from homosexual to heterosexual orientation. *Archives of Sexual Behavior, 32*, 403–417.

Tafoya, T. (1997). Native gay and lesbian issues: The two-spirited. In B. Greene (Ed.), *Ethnic and cultural diversity among lesbians and gay men* (pp. 1–10). Thousand Oaks, CA: Sage Publications.

Taylor, Y. (2005). Classed in a classless climate: Me and my associates. . . . *Feminism & Psychology, 15*, 491–500.

Tozer, E. E., & Hayes, J. A. (2004). Why do individuals seek conversion therapy? *The Counseling Psychologist, 32*, 716–741.

Vedantam, S. (2006, July 13). Male scientist writes of life as female scientist. *Washington Post*. http://www.washingtonpost.com/wp-dyn/content/article/2006/07/12/AR2006071201883.html (Retrieved February 15, 2008.)

Walters, K. L., Simoni, J. M., & Horwath, P. F. (2001). Sexual orientation bias experiences and services needs of gay, lesbian, bisexual, transgendered, and two-spirited American Indians. *Journal of Gay & Lesbian Social Services, 13*, 133–149.

Ward, J. (2003). Producing "pride" in West Hollywood: A queer cultural capital for queers with cultural capital. *Sexualities, 6*, 65–94.

Wilson, B. D. M., & Miller, R. L. (2002). Strategies for managing heterosexism used among African-American gay and bisexual men. *Journal of Black Psychology, 28,* 371–391.

Yarhouse, M. A., Burkett, L. A., & Kreeft, E. M. (2002). Paraprofessional Christian ministries for sexual behavior and same-sex identity concerns. *Journal of Psychology and Theology, 30*(3), 209–228.

Zea, M. C., Reisen, C. A., & Díaz, R. M. (2003). Methodological issues in research on sexual behavior with Latino gay and bisexual men. *American Journal of Community Psychology, 31,* 281–291.

Chapter Nine

College Counseling and Mental Health Services

A 20-Year Perspective of Issues and Challenges

Stewart E. Cooper
Jaquelyn Liss Resnick
Emil Rodolfa
Louise Douce

The book *College of the Overwhelmed: The Campus Mental Health Crisis and What to Do About It*, by Kadison and DiGeronimo (2004), has enjoyed great popularity with a diverse range of audiences including parents, students, counseling center directors, and student affairs professionals. The authors' smoothly written narrative style richly captured a major transition in the general level of mental health issues and problems of the current generation of college students along with addressing a variety of important related issues. The authors conclude that there is a crisis on campus leaving people feeling hopeless and helpless. They question what colleges are doing about the crisis and what more should be done.

The book is divided in two parts—"the problems" and "the solution." Part I presents the typical developmental concerns college students face along with many of today's common stressors such as peer pressure, academic competition, cultural adjustment, and financial worries and social fears. Part II emphasizes what students, parents, and student affairs staff can do to address student mental health issues that can involve depression, sleep disorders, substance abuse, anxiety, financial stress, eating disorders, impulsive disorders, and a range of impulsive behaviors such as self-mutilation. The book provides an extensive list of mental health resources and a "Check List for College Counseling Centers" to help guide a self-assessment of services. However, Kadison and DiGeronimo's book was not the first time that the topic of challenges and issues to college mental health services has been articulated. The goal of this chapter is to present a longitudinal view of the changing, yet consistent, world of college counseling from the late 1980s to today. This chapter seeks to provide a historical picture by summarizing, in a time-sequenced manner, some of the major writings examining counseling center practice.

College counseling centers were founded in the 1950s to provide career counseling to veterans and other students. The field of college counseling has evolved through different stages of development during the course of its existence. Changes before 1990 are documented by several authors (see Archer & Cooper, 1998; Heppner & Neal, 1983; Stone & Archer, 1990). The 1970s through the early 1980s was viewed as a time when counseling centers become broader in scope (e.g., expanding diagnosis and assessment, increasing severity of clinical service, psychoeducational outreach and prevention, campus consultation) while facing constricted budgets, a theme that resonates among most college mental health services providers today. Since then, changes have been more evolutionary than revolutionary.

In 1990, The Counseling Psychologist (TCP) published Stone and Archer's article, "College and University Counseling Centers in the 1990s." The piece, which was based on reviews of journal articles, information from the counseling center databank, and a survey sent to 20 directors of college counseling centers, was recognized as a seminal work in the field. Stone and Archer based their writings on three assumptions: (1) the ethnic, racial, national, and experiential background of students will change; (2) the psychological, health, safety, and financial needs of students will increase; and (3) competition for resources in higher education will increase. Hindsight shows that their assumptions were and continue to be accurate, and, in fact, each one of these factors has increased in intensity. Stone and Archer emphasized six areas of college counseling center function—Clinical Services, Outreach and Consultation Services, Training, Staff Development, Research, and Administration. They articulated the challenges in each area, the current environmental changes contributing to those challenges, and recommendations to address them.

Within Clinical Services, the first challenge was to cope with the increased numbers of students with serious psychological problems. The second challenge was to continue to engage in career development and counseling work in the face of prioritizing clinical services and increasing careerism pressures that contributed to the formation of separate formal career centers on campus. The changes in student characteristics were accompanied by a decreased interest in career development and counseling among counseling center psychologists and staff. A third challenge was providing counseling services to a rapidly increasing number of diverse and nontraditional students plus serving as a significant positive force on campus for improved ethnic, racial, and other minority issues. All three of these challenges to clinical services remain relevant today.

The shift in providing career services from counseling centers to career centers has taken place on most college campuses, with the exception being those that still have joint or integrated counseling/career centers. Two streams of action support this conclusion. The first is that there has been a significant move within the majority of institutions of higher education to expand job planning and placement centers into career centers offering career counseling and a number of other career development activities and materials. Most such offices are now labeled "university career centers." The second stream of evidence is the significant reduction in the number of joint counseling/career services centers on campus, while simultaneously a very significant increase in the number of joint counseling/health services.

Within Outreach and Consultation Services, the first challenge was to respond to the need for such services during a period of high demand for individual and group counseling services. A second challenge was to provide outreach and consultation efforts directed toward personal and educational growth. A third challenge was to offer, promote, and facilitate effective self-help programs. All three of these challenges to outreach and prevention remain relevant today. With the first of the above challenges, the expression "doing more with less" has become the watchword of the decade with a predictable result that levels of staff burnout due to increased work and role overload appears higher. In regard to promoting growth and providing self-help programs, the effects of the technological revolution on the transmission of information could not have been foretold in 1990. Today, most students who seek assistance from campus mental health services first obtained information on these services from the Web, and countless more students who seek counseling services privately obtain mental health promotion information from the Web and other psycho-educational sources rather than seeking counseling services.

Within the Training area, Stone and Archer articulated several challenges: (1) the promotion of intern diversity; (2) dealing with intern impairment; (3) defining the training agenda; and (4) negotiating the increasing competition for applicants and resources. Although some aspects of all four of these challenges remain today, significant progress has occurred on the first three. Greater numbers of students from increasingly diverse backgrounds have enabled greater diversity among the trainees in many internship sites. This can be seen especially in the increasing numbers of international students entering graduate psychology programs and becoming part of the counseling center internship pool. The number of interns from ethnic/racial minority groups, those that identify as gay, lesbian, and bisexual or transgender, and those with disability have increased as well, but this number is increasing less rapidly, and pipeline issues remain in the field. There is less gender diversity, as psychology is a field being increasingly studied by women as opposed to men. The most recent number from the Association of Psychology Postdoctoral and Internship Centers (APPIC) indicates that approximately 77% of students seeking internship are women (APPIC, 2007).

The generous nature of training directors and training sites sharing resources in the field has not eliminated the problem of intern impairment, but policies and procedures for dealing with it are more broadly disseminated and widely discussed, especially within APPIC and the Association of Counseling Center Training Agencies (ACCTA). Both the ACCTA Web site (http://www.accta.net) and the APPIC Web site (http://www.appic.org) contain detailed examples of procedures to use with students experiencing significant professional and/or personal problems that interfere with their delivery of services. The research has also expanded in this area, limiting the use of impairment and focusing on professional problems, addressing remediation and corrective action, expanding competency definitions and models, and providing new methods to assess competency (Forrest, Elman, & Gizara, 1999; Kaslow, 2004; Miller, 1977).

Although now focused on problematic behavior, the 1987 definition of trainee impairment developed by Lamb et al. is used by many in the field. Specifically, these authors define trainee impairment as:

> an interference in professional functioning that is reflected in one or more of the following ways: (a) an inability and/or unwillingness to acquire and integrate professional standards into one's repertoire of professional behavior; (b) an inability to acquire professional skills to reach an acceptable level of competency; (c) an inability to control personal stress, psychological dysfunction and/or excessive emotional reactions that interfere with professional functioning. (p. 598)

A reasonable perspective on the supervisor's responsibilities to assess and respond to trainee impairment is stated in the Association for Counselor Education and Supervision (ACES, 1993) Ethical Code Standard 2.12:

> Supervisors, through ongoing supervisee assessment and evaluation, should be aware of any personal or professional limitations of supervisees which are likely to impede future professional performance.

> Supervisors have the responsibility of recommending remedial assistance to the supervisee and of screening from the training program, applied counseling setting, or state licensure those supervisees who are unable to provide competent professional services. These recommendations should be clearly and professionally explained in writing to the supervisees who are so evaluated.

The issue of an insufficient number of internship slots for the number of intern applicants results in rigorous competition for these slots as well as intense competition for high-quality interns. Maintaining funding for counseling center training programs is becoming increasingly difficult as institutions of higher education face growing economic challenges and reductions in financial support. Although federal funding through the Graduate Psychology Education (GPE) program was awarded to some psychology training programs, university counseling center sites were not eligible to access these funds.

In the area of Staff Development, Stone and Archer (1990) viewed limited career staff advancement as one major challenge. A second challenge they identified was that counseling centers needed to develop effective means to counter the stress and potential burnout of staff members. Providing training opportunities for staff to keep up with the latest research and practice related to students and treatment approaches was a third factor. These three challenges not only are active today but are increasingly relevant to staff practice and experience. For example, lack of upward mobility for center staff and the bifurcation between academic faculty and center staff in relation to access to teaching and academic rank is increasing. Indications are that staff stress and burnout may be increasing. Finally, pressures exist to obtain licensure-mandated continuing education in a growing number of content areas without accompanying resources to support such activities.

In regard to Research, Stone and Archer (1990) noted the challenge to develop, implement, and sustain a research program. The creation of the National College Counseling Center Research Consortium, and the emergence of the Center for the Study of College Student Mental Health, facilitate large sample, multicampus studies. The Association for University and College Counseling Centers (AUCCCD) Directors' Survey provides a single source of data collection regarding current status of counseling centers on a broad array of topics including client demographics, utilization, and professional staffing. However, decreased available time and lack of dedicated resources for conducting research is having a marked adverse affect on developing, implementing, and maintaining individual counseling center research programs, leading to a significant barrier in the amount of research being conducted by those who work in these settings.

Administration was the final area that Stone and Archer (1990) addressed. They identified three major challenges: (1) to balance resources and demands; (2) to incorporate new technologies into counseling center service and management systems; and (3) to identify and confront ethical and professional issues. The challenge for directors to balance resources and demands has intensified greatly given the growth in student population, and the accompanying increases in the number of students seeking help and the students with complex problems and/or severe psychopathology. The demand for outreach and consultation services has also increased, especially in relation to anticipating and managing crisis on campus. Unfortunately, these pressures on service delivery have generally occurred without commensurate increases in staff size or funding allocation. With technology, there is no question that sweeping technological advances have simplified a good deal of the work done by staff in college counseling centers but at the same time have significantly raised the bar for the amount and nature of the work to be accomplished. The release of the 2002 Ethical Principles of Psychologists and Code of Conduct from the American Psychological Association (APA) has assisted in staff focus on ethical and professional issues (and has raised the bar for ethical behaviors). Dealing with distressed or problematic staff is another sensitive administrative issue. The comprehensive monograph "Advancing Colleague Assistance in Professional Psychology" provides an understanding of the nature and extent of competence problems within a developmental context as well as prevention and intervention strategies (APA, 2006).

A major source of change for college mental health–related policies and procedures has been highly publicized lawsuits involving the role of counseling center and other health service providers and student affairs administrations and professionals. One of the recent cases was a suit brought against MIT by the Shin family, who sought financial compensation after the alleged suicide of their daughter by immolation. The importance of this case was that the administrators were sued for receiving numerous reports of self-destructive behavior, her plan to commit suicide on the date she died, and their failure to exercise reasonable care to protect this student from harm. The Massachusetts Superior Court did not support MIT's Motion for Summary Judgment on these charges, meaning they were not summarily dismissed (Hoover, 2005). The two phrases in the Shin case that emerge from the summary judgment are that the administration had a "special relationship" with Elizabeth Shin and that her death was "reasonably foreseeable and imminently probable." Three important takeaways emerge:

1. Coordination of care among providers and service settings must be established. In the facts of the case, the community providers, counselors, and psychiatrists often acted independently without establishing continuity and coordination of care.
2. Publications should be reviewed to minimize contract claim issues.
3. Swift action must be taken once a determination for hospitalization or in-patient care is needed. Elizabeth died in the time between an administrative decision for hospitalization and implementation of that decision. This ruling has had significant implications for treating mental health issues on campus. Unfortunately, the case was settled out of court, so the merits of the case and definitive evaluation of conduct or culpability were never established as case law.

Other case law such as *Jain vs. Iowa* (2000), which was upheld in *Mahoney vs. Allegheny College* (2005), found that "the act of suicide is considered a deliberate, intentional and intervening act that precludes another's responsibility for the harm." The *Allegheny* judgment found "no legal duty on the part of the university, including no duty to notify parents."

Another important consideration in policy decisions regarding the potential for suicidal or homicidal behavior is the American Disabilities Act, Section 504, which prohibits discrimination based on physical or mental impairment that substantially limits one or more major life activities (i.e., a disability). One implication of the passage of the ADA is that many universities have added a psychologist to the staff at the student disability services to assess and determine reasonable accommodations for students with mental disabilities.

This tension between appropriate action to prevent harm to self or others and to prevent discrimination based on a mental disorder (i.e., 504 compliance) is difficult to negotiate. Counseling centers are currently challenged to enhance their protocols for "direct threat analysis" in line with their state statutes in the arena of "duty to protect."

Subsequent to Stone and Archer's (1990) TCP article, a number of books and articles were published that touched upon the issues and challenges faced by college counseling centers. In 1998, Archer and Cooper wrote the first comprehensive book on college counseling centers entitled *College Mental Health Services on Campus: A Handbook of Contemporary Practices and Challenges.* In their preface and introduction, they wrote about the effects on college students and on universities of rapidly changing economic and social levels, changing family structures, increased health problems, growing student and institutional diversity, and an increasingly violent and politically unstable world. All of these remain as current pressures, exacerbated by the terrifying and traumatic national events, such as 9/11, Hurricane Katrina, and, most recently, the mass murder at Virginia Tech. Effective campus crisis management is expected in times of traumatic events and disaster, with counseling centers expected to play essential roles in planning, prevention, response, and recovery phases (Zdziarski, Dunkel, Rollo, & Associates, 2007). These domains interplay with the ambivalence of the appropriate roles for college counseling centers, as neither administrators nor faculty members have ever agreed on the scope of counseling in higher education, in particular how much of the college experience should involve personal and character development. This uncertainty has been compounded since 1998 by dramatic reductions in the level of federal and state financial support for institutions of higher education and the consequent examination of where costs can be reduced.

The Archer and Cooper (1998) book is divided into three parts. Part I focuses on meeting the basic counseling services needs of students and includes chapters on individual counseling; brief therapy; group counseling as a treatment of choice; utilization of faculty, students, and other helpers; alternatives and adjuncts to counseling; meeting the needs of students with serious and developmental problems; and counseling students from special populations. Part II focuses on strategies for outreach and systemic interventions. Chapters in this section include promoting prevention through outreach and consultation, counselors as initiators and catalysts for change, supporting faculty and student development, education and preventive responses to public health issues, and promoting campus diversity and multiculturalism. Part III focuses on administrative and professional issues including evaluation and research, ethical and legal requirements for practice, professional training and accreditation, options for the organization of delivery of counseling services, and providing leadership for quality in campus counseling.

A series of articles related to issues and challenges facing college counseling centers then appeared in the literature. Bishop, Gallagher, and Cohen (2000) found that 85% of counseling center directors reported seeing more students with serious mental health problems than in the previous 5 years. Not all authors agree, however, and posit bias in self-report by the directors (Schwartz, 2006).

The ACHA-NCHA national research survey organized by the American College Health Association now routinely provides the largest known comprehensive data set on the health of college students to date (ACHA, 2006). The spring 2003 survey asked students the level to which certain illnesses or mental health situations negatively impacted their academic performance. Available responses ranged from not affecting academic performance to receiving a lower grade on an exam, receiving a lower grade in the course, or receiving an incomplete or dropping the course. The conditions reportedly having a negative academic impact for 15% or more of the population were as follows: Stress (32.0%), Cold/flu/sore throat (25.3%), Sleep difficulties (24.0%), Concern for troubled friend or family member (18.4%), Relationship difficulty (15.9%), and Depression/anxiety disorder/SAD (14.6%). All but one of these was a mental health issue, and research would suggest that vulnerability to illness is stress mediated for many (Straub, 2006).

The spring 2006 survey obtained information from 97,357 respondents attending 123 universities and colleges. The majority of items on the survey inquired about physical health concerns, but there were subsections that focused on mental health and on lifestyle variables. A number of the findings from these mental health subsections have relevance to college counseling. For example, 17.8% of the students reported depression and 8.1% seasonal affective disorder, 12.4% reported anxiety, 3.4% reported a substance abuse problem and 4.8% some type of STD, and 4.2% reported either bulimia or anorexia. Associated with these summary figures, 34.5% were currently on a diet and 48.8% had engaged in sexual intercourse in the past 30 days; 27.7% stated they were feeling overwhelmed by all they had to do and 27.2% felt exhausted; 62.2% of students felt that "things were hopeless" at some time in the past year, 43.8% reported feeling "so depressed it was difficult to function, 9.3% reported seriously considering suicide, and 1.1% reported making a suicide attempt in the last year.

A frequently cited quantitative investigation by Benton, Robertson, Tseng, Newton, and Benton (2003) studied the clinical issues of several hundred counseling center clients. The investigation reported increases in 14 different clinical problems over a 13-year period of time. Some of these increases, such as depression, personality disorders, and suicidal intent, are indicative of increases in severe psychopathology among students. Other categories of noted increase, including situational problems, relationship concerns, and developmental issues, are less severe and more traditional issues but nonetheless contribute to an increased demand for services. Rudd (2004) suggested that the changes observed were due to changes in the student bodies more so than in any increased psychopathology among similar student bodies across time. Benton, Benton, Newton, Benton, and Robertson (2004) suggested a number of other plausible options, but, regardless of the cause, the effect has resulted in an increased student demand for counseling services presenting problems, concerns, and disorders with increased difficulty and challenge.

A recent study (Soet & Sevig, 2006) studied the mental health issues among college students who were and were not in counseling over the past 3 years. The study supported the findings of both of these studies. They found virtually the same rates of depression, anxiety, eating disorders, and substance abuse as the ACHA study. Of perhaps greater significance, Soet and Sevig found that one-third of the college students reported having received counseling, with 20% currently in therapy. This is compared to 9.7% of the population that seeks mental health services. Similarly, approximately 15% of students reported that they had taken psychotropic medication at some time, with 7% currently taking such medications. This latter figure is consistent with the national average for adults of 7.7% current or in the past year.

A number of popular press articles on college student psychological dynamics and mental health have also been published on the Internet and in the press. For example, Hara Estroff Marano wrote "A Nation of Wimps," which first appeared on the online version of *Psychology Today* in 2004. Marano (2007) recently published a book examining her thesis that an over-focus on children, adolescents, and young adults by parents and an overdependence on parents by young adults was ill preparing the next generation. "Parents are going to ridiculous lengths to take the bumps out of life for their children. However, parental hyper-concern has the net effect of making kids more fragile; that may be why they are breaking down in record numbers." Another illustration, in 2004 the *Harvard Crimson*, an online newsletter, featured an article entitled "College Faces Mental Health Crisis." The central theme of the piece was that many students face significant personal issues and that campuses do not have sufficient resources to meet these needs. The numerous articles related to the MIT Shin lawsuit focus on the institution's responsibilities for the mental well-being of its students and have sparked a rash of strong reactions, some of which have led to other lawsuits for overreactions such as the dismissal of a student for conveying he had suicidal thoughts.

The tragic shooting of 32 students at Virginia Tech University by a student with a history of problematic behavior and contact with the mental health system occurred soon after the state passed a law that forbids students from being dismissed from college for mental health reasons. But after the events at Virginia Tech, the state may once again review its recent decision and the pendulum may swing the other way.

Attention to college mental health continues to increase. In 2006, two books were published that covered a broad range of topics germane to university counseling centers and their work. Grayson and Meilman (2006) edited *College Mental Health Practice*. The opening line by Grayson in the introduction reads "Any clinician that comes to work at a college counseling center soon discovers that college mental health is a world unto itself" (Grayson & Meilman, 2006, p. 1). He goes on to assert, "In addition to their more conventional role as counselors or psychotherapists, college clinicians are variously called on to do triage; manage referrals; provide reassurance, feedback, and information; serve as long term supports and patient advocates; conduct consultations; and handle crisis. . . . College clinicians must handle tricky phone calls from parents and deans, balance patient's needs against the community welfare, and judge when to make exceptions to therapeutic neutrality and confidentiality. Political acumen is an asset when one works on a campus" (Grayson & Meilman, 2006, p. 1).

Grayson and Meilman's book uses patient problems as the basis for the edited chapters and is written mainly for mental health providers. The book begins with chapters on current legal and ethical regulations and pressures and an overview of the developmental nature of most college student psychological problems. One chapter covers each of the following areas: medication, family problems, relationship issues, depression and anxiety, stress, issues of diversity, academic difficulties, substance abuse, sexual concerns, sexual victimization, eating disorders, personality disorders, suicide, and suicidal behaviors.

Although the book is clinically focused, material in most of the chapters includes mention of the issues and challenges to the center that serving such clients creates. Additionally, the overview articulates four factors that distinguish the campus context for mental health services (Grayson & Meilman, 2006). The first of these factors is the individual student and the community, particularly the disruption that a student with significant psychopathology can cause and the related complex issues surrounding criteria for possible dismissal from the university. A second factor is the mental health service and the community. Justification for the existence of campus counseling services is rarely questioned, but the level of support and ability to demonstrate positive effects varies considerably. The latter is particularly difficult because showing that something bad did not happen (e.g., avoiding disruptions and tragedies) is significantly harder than showing that something good happened. Decision-making power is the third factor and emphasizes the ethical and other issues related to the roles that college counselors have when making decisions about student's lives, such as entry into a special program or special residential unit. The fourth factor is the challenge of maintaining professional confidentiality in a campus culture that stresses collaboration for the benefit of students. In general, counseling center staff members are required to protect client confidentiality, whereas others in the university assume an ethic of good intentions in sharing information.

In elaboration of this fourth factor, the tension in when to or not to disclose involves the interpretation of the APA Ethical Principles of Psychologists and Code of Conduct Ethical Standard 4.05 *Disclosures:*

> (a) Psychologists may disclose confidential information with the appropriate consent of the organizational client, the individual client/patient, or another legally authorized person on behalf of the client/patient unless prohibited by law. (b) Psychologists disclose confidential information without the consent of the individual only as mandated by law, or where permitted by law for a valid purpose such as to (1) provide needed professional services; (2) obtain appropriate professional consultations; (3) protect the client/patient, psychologist, or others from harm; or (4) obtain payment for services from a client/patient, in which instance disclosure is limited to the minimum that is necessary to achieve the purpose. (APA, 2003, p. 1066)

Counseling center staff, in line with other ethical standards regarding confidentiality and informed consent, generally take a very conservative stance on releasing confidential information during consultations, whereas others in offices like residence life, campus security, and so on, who also may be engaging in efforts to assist a student in need, have less constraints on their communications within the system and greater expectation that such communications should take place (Archer & Cooper, 1998).

Benton and Benton (2006) targeted a different audience—student affairs professionals, especially student affairs administrators. The book *College Student Mental Health: Effective Services and Strategies Across Campus* was published by the National Association of Student Personnel Administrators (NASPA). Chapters within the book cover a diverse range of topics in the mental health field including distressed and distressing students; legal issues for campus administrators, faculty, and staff; key issues for faculty regarding college student mental health; mental health consultation for urgent and emergent campus issues; counseling and mental health services; support services for students with mental health disabilities; contributing to college student mental health through health promotion and clinical health services; and college student mental health and special populations.

Most of these chapters examine some aspect of issues and challenges facing college counseling centers. The introductory chapter emphasizes some of the current contextual changes that are affecting students and colleges as well as the mental health services requested and provided in these settings. The authors mention changes in the relationship between the student and the institution, changes in societal expectations of the institutions due to university liability and lawsuits, and changes in the public's expectation of access to information. Students, too, have changed significantly—current students are more ethnically diverse, more often are women, more are first generation, more are foreign born, and more are of nontraditional age. Additionally, changes in the means by which families communicate using new technologies and the accompanying changes in the family are profound.

The chapter on counseling and mental health services by Cooper (2006) in the Benton and Benton book specifically focuses on the current issues and challenges facing college counseling centers. In consultation with Benton, Cooper developed a set of themes that touched on various factors affecting mental health services on campus. He then sent out these themes as a survey and solicited feedback from a number of experienced directors of college counseling center directors. The resulting themes were then organized into four domains: (1) increased demand for services, (2) the structure of services, (3) counseling center staff, and (4) changing legal and ethical contexts.

There were eight issues identified that fit into the first domain—Demand for Clinical Services:

- Issue 1: In the face of increasing severity, complexity, and quantity of mental health cases, counseling center staff have experienced NO growth in resources or have experienced a reduction in center budgets.
- Issue 2: Due to a combination of highly publicized litigation and the heightened involvement of many parents, college and university counseling centers are dealing with increasing liabilities and responsibilities for stabilizing students with severe emotional disabilities. Simultaneously, pressure is escalating to assist others who live in close community with such students as well as to reduce risks to the institution in general. The response to the above pressures often involves adding more services to manage the ongoing acting-in or acting-out behavior of the individual.
- Issue 3: College and university counseling centers are facing the challenges of incorporating and using newly emerging technologies while simultaneously protecting students' confidentiality.
- Issue 4: Today's students typically work part-time while pursuing a college degree and face pressures to acquire more academic minors and majors and to accrue extracurricular involvements, the combination of which make it difficult for campus mental health centers to schedule groups.

- Issue 5: The availability of increasingly focused medications for mental health problems, along with more marketing by the pharmaceutical industry, has increased demands for counseling centers to offer combined treatment (i.e., counseling plus medication). This is especially true for arriving students who are already on one or more medications or who have already received counseling and medication earlier in their lives.
- Issue 6: Because of the increasing diversity of the student body, accompanied by the need for targeted services and service providers, college and university counseling centers are under greater pressure to provide culturally informed services to an increasingly diverse campus population. Individuals who provide such services must be sensitive to students from a variety of cultures with divergent worldviews, who may favor differing domains of interventions
- Issue 7: Because of legal and media pressures, counseling centers are facing ongoing pressure to provide specialized services for difficult campus issues such as substance abuse, eating disorders, dating violence, academic failure, and so forth.
- Issue 8: Because of globalization and other world changes, college and university counseling centers face increased pressure to help students deal with a future that contains much greater job and economic uncertainty and much less safety than students from previous decades.

There were four issues identified that fit into the second domain—Structure of Services:

- Issue 9: Choosing what type of counseling center model to follow that best fits the campus and the needs of the students (i.e., clinical vs. developmental; short-term and refer out vs. moderate or longer-term care that responds to most student mental health needs; primary focus on individual vs. group therapy; balance of treatment/tertiary prevention vs. secondary prevention vs. primary prevention).
- Issue 10: College counseling centers face challenges in developing referral networks.
- Issue 11: Deciding how much direct involvement faculty, staff, and/or students should have in delivering or collaborating on mental health services.
- Issue 12: Deciding the nature and level of resources to put into counseling center and student mental health evaluation and research activities.

There were three issues identified that fit into the third domain—Staffing:

- Issue 13: Responding to counselor burnout.
- Issue 14: Dealing with the issue of low salaries and lack of career advancement opportunities.
- Issue 15: Providing training and development for those going into administrative roles.

There were two issues identified that fit into the fourth domain—Changing Ethical and Legal Contexts:

- Issue 16: Increasing fears of litigation
- Issue 17: Increasing regulatory control over actions clinical staff must take to obtain and maintain professional certification or licensure (adapted from Cooper, 2006, pp. 151–167).

The clinical services domains are related and reflect the increased demand for counseling center services without commensurate increases in staff size and difficulty managing this demand through the structure of services. The challenges identified include: (a) choosing what type of counseling center model to follow that best fits the campus and the needs of the students (i.e., clinical vs. developmental; short-term and refer out vs. moderate or longer-term care; focus on individual vs. group therapy; balance of treatment/tertiary prevention vs. secondary prevention vs. primary prevention); (b) developing referral networks; (c) deciding how much direct involvement faculty, staff, and/or students should have in delivering or collaborating on mental health services; and (d) deciding the level of resources to put into evaluation and research activities.

Domain 3 concerns issues related to the continued development and job satisfaction of counseling center staff. Domain 4 considers the increasingly litigious environment and the impact state law and regulation have on the practice of psychology in general and counseling center practice specifically.

THE LONGITUDINAL AND FUTURE VIEW: CONSISTENCIES AND CHANGES ACROSS 20 YEARS

This chapter has presented a 20-year view of issues and challenges facing college counseling centers beginning with Stone and Archer's (1990) seminal work. Their three primary assumptions—(1) the ethnic, racial, national, and experiential background of students will change; (2) the psychological, health, safety, and financial needs of students will increase; and (3) the competition for resources in higher education will increase—have been validated. Many of the issues they identified have intensified as current challenges for college counseling centers today. This is especially true with regard to the growing discrepancy between the pressure to offer more services and the lack of increasing staff and other resources to respond. Some issues and challenges, such as having greater diversity among trainees and having procedures to deal with problematic trainees, are less intense today because the profession has gained a better understanding of the issues involved. Still other issues—for example, those related to responding to the suicidal client or to the use of emerging technologies for dissemination of psychoeducation, information, or self-assessment—reflect current contextual and zeitgeist factors.

Formal accreditation of college and university counseling programs is conducted by the International Association of Counseling Services, Inc. (IACS). Over the past 20 years, the IACS accreditation guidelines for university and college counseling centers have undergone two revisions (Boyd et al., 2003; Kiracofe et al., 1994). The changes reflect the evolving role, functions, and changes in professional practice, with the most recent revision to the standards-added provisions on counseling services merged with other campus units (e.g., health services) and on the ethical use of technology in counseling services (Boyd et al., 2003). The accreditation process now evaluates six areas: (1) relationship of the counseling center to the university or college community, (2) counseling services roles and functions, (3) ethical standards, (4) counseling service personnel, (5) related guidelines (e.g., professional development, staffing size and practices, workload, etc.), and (6) special concerns/issues affecting counseling center mergers.

The recommendations to create strong mental health service centers have remarkable consistency. For example, Kadison and DiGeronimo (2004) mention the following aspects: providing student education to promote prevention, funding adequate staffing, emphasizing campus community outreach, providing follow-up care, and ensuring off-campus resources and continuity of care—a very stable listing, albeit potentially modernized through the development of innovative ideas for service delivery and incorporation of Web-based interventions.

Mental health service delivery utilizing Web-based communications is in its earliest stages and bound to grow. *The Counseling Psychologist* devoted a major section to "Online Counseling: Challenges for the Information Era"; Mallen and Vogel (2005) describe the possibilities for computer-mediated distance communication, including e-mail, synchronous chat (real time with both/all parties present), and videoconferencing. As counseling centers are being challenged to provide services to distance learners and study-abroad students, online counseling provides a potential mode for delivery. On many campuses, on-site students often take at least some Web-based classes or even enroll in distance learning classes. Student preference for accessing information and assistance through the Web on a 24/7 basis has transformed the way counseling centers reach out to students, with nearly all centers developing an extensive Web site presence and many having incorporated interactive self-assessment and self-help modules. Some counseling centers use e-mail and Internet chat rooms for consultations, information, and referral, and/or have included online counseling (in addition to telephone) as the way to continue service provision in case of a flu pandemic. Students also are communicating extensively through online social networking Web sites such as Facebook, which has millions of registered users among college-focused sites. For instance, at the time of the Virginia Tech tragedy, students reached out to each other using a specially created Facebook page, which received more than 100,000 hits in the first 24 hours, many from students across the country who expressed grief, fear, and worry (http://mystudentbody.com).

The past 20 years have been marked by an increasing awareness of multicultural issues in counseling centers. The "Guidelines on Multicultural Education, Training, Research, Practice and Organizational Change for Psychologists" (MC Guidelines) (APA, 2003) parallel this time frame, reflecting a 22-year development process. The MC Guidelines refer to interactions between individuals from minority ethnic and racial groups in the United States and the dominant European American culture, and also address interactions with individuals from other nations, including international students and immigrants (APA, 2003, p. 278). Diversity is steadily increasing on campuses, whereas the majority of counseling center practitioners are White. The MC Guidelines articulate principles that promote multicultural competency. They affirm that people are cultural beings with attitudes and beliefs that influence perceptions and affect interactions with others that can be detrimental, so that the process of learning about oneself and others is an integral part of the process (p. 382). The MC Guidelines are intended to facilitate a high level of professional practice and match well with the broad-based functions of university and college counseling centers.

Full implementation of the MC Guidelines is aspirational and means that multicultural perspectives must be infused into all counseling center transactions (Resnick, 2006). This implementation is a long-term process, including the initial assessment phase and incorporation of the MC Guidelines into practice, outreach and consultation, professional training, evaluation and research, and counseling center organizational change. Regular assessment, opportunity to make modifications, and ongoing commitment are essential. Sue and Sue (2003) note that it is not sufficient to have multicultural counselors on staff; to be a culturally competent agency, the counseling center itself will need to develop a "multicultural culture" (p. 450). This transformative process can occur within a system that does not place as high a value on multicultural competence. In order to thrive and be successful agents of change, counseling centers must contextualize their activities and be aware of institutional expectations and priorities.

Not only will the MC Guidelines influence future practice, the field of psychology is refining its treatment techniques through evidence-based practice (EBP). EBP in psychology is the careful, precise, and prudent use of the current best evidence in making decisions about the care of patients and clients (adapted from Sackett, Rosenberg, Gray, Haynes, & Richardson, 1996). EBP means integrating individual clinical expertise with the best available research-based clinical evidence. Although not specific to counseling center practice, EBP is being incorporated into the training guidelines and principles (APA, 2005) and emphasized in the practice of psychotherapy.

Counseling center directors have the opportunity to use their leadership position to promote a multicultural culture through hiring practices, policies and procedures, staff development, decision making, resource allocation, and accountability (Resnick, 2006, p. 18). Leadership also occurs on the part of staff members and trainees, many of whom have more advanced knowledge and experience in this area than their supervisors. Arredondo (1996) notes that motivation rarely emanates from one source, and in the best-case scenario, there is a synergistic effect in an organizational climate where everyone believes his or her voice will be heard. To best serve the needs of students and the campus community, counseling centers must move toward multicultural competency at all levels, presenting a challenging process. Reynolds and Pope (2003), developers of a useful assessment tool, the "Template for a Multicultural Counseling Center," caution that it is not possible for counseling centers to become multicultural overnight. Douce (2002) has pointed out "that paradigm change is difficult, sometimes painful and always confusing, and that no one gives up privilege willingly or with ease."

Stone and Archer (1990) predicted that "counseling center staff will be called upon to play a greater role in working with the entire campus community to fight racial, ethnic, and other prejudice and discrimination" (p. 555). Counseling centers have effectively expanded psychological practice beyond the office through outreach, consultation, and advocacy activities enabling campus-wide prevention and macro-level intervention (Resnick, 2006). Counseling centers have been leaders, often in collaboration with other stakeholders, to promote a healthy, inclusive, and caring campus community. Typical issues that have been addressed broadly include sexual harassment; sexual assault/abuse; lesbian, gay, bisexual, transgender issues; concerns for students with disabilities; international student concerns; ethnic/racial/cultural stereotyping; and bullying.

It is difficult to accurately predict the issues and challenges for the future, but based on where we have been and our understanding of where counseling centers are and appear to be going, we can state:

1. Counseling centers will continue to be under increased pressure to prevent mental health–influenced violence to self or others from occurring.
2. Counseling center staff will experience increased demands to provide crisis and postcrisis support for students and their collaterals.
3. Counseling centers will simultaneously remain under pressure to continue to provide a broad range of counseling, crisis, consultation, outreach, and research services to serve a diversity of stakeholders and constituents in and outside the campus environment.
4. The projected demographic changes toward increasing ethnic/racial/cultural diversity on campus will require that counselors are multiculturally competent and that counseling centers provide culturally sensitive services.
5. The increasingly technological world will provide opportunity and challenge for counseling centers to keep up with advances and use technology to enhance service delivery.
6. The bifurcation of work of psychologists and other mental health services providers between academically focused and applied counseling center work will continue, so many professionals will experience a limiting of their behavioral flexibility and increased difficulty in transferring employment from one side to the other.
7. The level of scholarship produced by those working in college counseling centers may be reduced due to the demands for other services. However, there are increasing examples of multicampus investigations of student mental health (i.e., the recent formation of the Center for the Study of College Student Mental Health at Pennsylvania State University).
8. Until campuses acknowledge the need to adequately fund mental health services, counseling center services will struggle to provide the breadth of services required by students.
9. Because of the increasing complexity and severity of student presenting problems, counseling centers will continue to increase the collaborative consultations with other student affairs units, in particular, housing, judicial affairs, and the university police.

10. Because of the continual influence of state and federal law on the practice of psychology, counseling center staff will have increasing contact with campus counsel, and their work will be increasingly dictated by concerns over limiting legal liability.

BIBLIOGRAPHY

American College Health Association. (2006). ACHA-NCHA Reference Group Executive Summary Spring 2006. Retrieved May 12, 2007, from http://www.acha-ncha.org/pubs_rpts.html

American Psychological Association. (2002). Ethical principles of psychologists and code of conduct. *American Psychologist, 57,* 1060–1073.

American Psychological Association. (2003). Guidelines on multicultural education, training, research, practice, and organizational change for psychologists. *American Psychologist, 58,* 377–402.

American Psychological Association. (2005). Report of the 2005 Presidential Task Force on Evidence-Based Practice. Retrieved on April 6, 2008, from http://www.apa.org/practice/ebpreport.pdf

American Psychological Association. (2006, February 10). *Advancing colleague assistance in professional psychology.* Retrieved June 15, 2007, from http://www.apa.org/practice/acca_monograph.pdf

Archer, J. A., & Cooper, S. E. (1998). *Counseling and mental health services in college contexts: A handbook of contemporary practices and challenges.* San Francisco: Jossey-Bass.

Arredondo, P. (1996). *Successful diversity management initiatives: A blue-print for planning and implementation.* Thousand Oaks, CA: Sage.

Association for Counselor Education and Supervision. (1993). *ACES Ethical Guidelines for Counseling Supervisors.* Washington, DC: Author.

Association of Psychology Postdoctoral and Internship Centers (APPIC). (2007). Retrieved on June 21, 2007 from http://www.appic.org/

Benton, S. A., & Benton, S. L. (Eds.). (2006). *College student mental health: Effective services and strategies across campus.* Washington, DC: NASPA, Student Affairs Administrators in Higher Education.

Benton, S. A., Benton, S. L., Newton, F., Benton, K. L., & Robertson, J. M. (2004). Changes in client problems: Contributions and limitations from a 13-year study. *Professional Psychology: Research and Practice,* 35, 317–319.

Benton, S. A., Robertson, J. M., Tseng, W. C., Newton, F. B., & Benton, S. L. (2003). Changes in counseling center client problems across 13 years. *Professional Psychology: Research and Practice, 34,* 66–72.

Bishop, J. B., Gallagher, R. P., & Cohen, D. (2000). College students' problems: Status, trends, and research. In D. C. Davis & K. H. Humphrey (Eds.), *College counseling: Issues and strategies for a new millennium* (pp. 89–110). Alexandria, VA: American Counseling Association.

Boyd, V., Hattauer, E., Brandel, I. W., Buckles, N., Davidshofer, C., Deakin, S., et al. (2003). Accreditation standards for university and college counseling centers. *Journal of Counseling and Development, 81,* 168–177.

Cooper, S. E. (2006). Counseling and mental health services. In S. A. Benton & S. L. Benton (Eds.), *College student mental health: Effective services and strategies across campus*. Washington, DC: NASPA, Student Affairs Administrators in Higher Education.

Douce, L. (2002, November). *Integrating diversity discussion into the fabric of the center.* Paper presented at the meeting of the Association for University and College Counseling Center Directors, Honolulu, HI.

Forrest, L., Elman, N., & Gizara, S. (1999). Trainee impairment: A review of identification, remediation, dismissal, and legal issues. *The Counseling Psychologist, 27*, 627–686

Grayson, P. A. (2006). Introduction. In P. A. Grayson & P. W. Meilman (Eds.), *College mental health practice*. New York: Brunner-Routledge.

Grayson, P. A., & Meilman, P. W. (Eds.). (2006). *College mental health practice.* New York: Brunner-Routledge.

Heppner, P. P., & Neal, G. W. (1983). Holding up the mirror: Research on the roles and functions of counseling centers in higher education. *The Counseling Psychologist, 11*, 81–98.

Hoover, E. (2005). Judge rules suicide against MIT can proceed. *The Chronicle of Higher Education, 51*, 49.

Jain v. State of Iowa, 617 N.W.2d 293 (Iowa 2000).

Kadison, R., & DiGeronimo, T. F. (2004). *College of the overwhelmed: The campus mental health crisis and what to do about it.* San Francisco: Jossey-Bass.

Kaplan, K. A. (2004). College faces mental health crisis. The Harvard Crimson. Retrieved on April 6, 2008, from http://www.thecrimson.com/article.aspx?ref=357023

Kaslow, N. J. (2004). Competencies in professional psychology. *American Psychologist, 59*, 774–781.

Kiracofe, N. M., Donn, P. A., Grant, C. O., Podolnick, E. E., Bingham, R. P., Bolland, H. R., et al. (1994). Accreditation standards for university and college counseling centers. *Journal of Counseling and Development, 73*, 38–43.

Lamb, D. H., Presser, N. R., Pfost, K. S., Baum, M. C., Jackson, V. R., & Jarvis, P. A. (1987). Confronting professional impairment during the internship: Identification, due process, and remediation. *Professional Psychology: Research and Practice, 18*, 597–603.

Mahoney v. Allegheny College, 2005 AD 892-2003.

Mallen, M. J., & Vogel, D. L. (2005). Introduction to the major contribution: Counseling psychology and online counseling. *The Counseling Psychologist, 33*, 761–775.

Marano, H. E. (2004, November/December). A nation of wimps. *Psychology Today.* Retrieved April 18, 2006, http://psychologytoday.com/articles/pto-3584.html

Marano, H. E. (2007). *A nation of wimps: The high cost of invasive parenting.* New York: Random House.

Meilman, P., & Cooper, S. E. (2006). Depression and anxiety. In P. Meilman & P. Grayson (Eds.), *College mental health practice.* New York: Brunner-Routledge.

Miller, P. M. (1977). Evaluation of trainee performance in psychology internship programs. *Clinical Psychologist, 30*, 2–5.

Resnick, J. L. (2006). Strategies for implementation of the Multicultural Guidelines in university and college counseling centers. *Professional Psychology: Research and Practice, 37*, 14–20.

Reynolds, A. L., & Pope, R. L. (2003). Multicultural competence in counseling centers. In D. B. Pope-Davis, H. L. K. Coleman, W. M. Liu, & R. L. Toporek (Eds.), *Handbook of multicultural competencies in psychology* (pp. 365–382). Thousand Oaks, CA: Sage.

Rudd, D. M. (2004). University counseling centers: Looking more and more like community clinics. *Professional Psychology: Research and Practice, 35*, 316–317.

Sackett D. L, Rosenberg W. M. C., Gray J. A. M., Haynes R. B., & Richardson W. S. (1996). Evidence based medicine: What it is and what it isn't. *British Medical Journal, 312*(7023), 71–72.

Schwartz, A. J. (2006, May/June). Are college students more disturbed today? Stability in the acuity and qualitative character of psychopathology of college counseling center clients: 1992–1993 through 2001–2002. *Journal of American College Health, 54*, 327–337.

Soet, J., & Sevig, T. (2006). Mental health issues facing a diverse sample of college students: Results from the college student mental health survey. *NASPA Journal, 43*, 410–429.

Stone, G. L., & Archer, J. A., Jr. (1990). College and university counseling centers in the 1990s: Challenges and limits. *The Counseling Psychologist, 18*, 539–607.

Straub, R. O. (2006). *Health psychology: A biopsychosocial approach*. New York: Worth.

Sue, D. W., & Sue, D. (2003). *Counseling the culturally diverse: Theory and practice* (4th ed.). New York: Wiley.

Zdziarski, E. L., Dunkel, N. W., Rollo, J. M., & Associates. (2007). *Campus crisis management: A comprehensive guide to planning, prevention, response, and recovery*. San Francisco: Jossey-Bass.

Chapter Ten

Counseling Within a Changing World

Meeting the Psychological Needs of Societies and the World

P. Paul Heppner
Frederick T. L. Leong
Lawrence H. Gerstein

The profession of counseling in the United States has a rich history dating back to the beginning of the 20th century (e.g., Blocher, 2000; Heppner, Casas, Carter, & Stone, 2000: Whitely, 1984). During the first 50 years of its existence, the profession was shaped by an interest in providing vocational services in the schools and community, a desire to develop and employ a variety of psychometrically sound psychological measures and assessment strategies, and a commitment to offer counseling to individuals in need. Since the 1960s, the counseling profession in the United States has expanded its focus to offer a wide variety of preventive, psycho-educational, and remedial services (e.g., counseling, consultation, assessment, policy development and implementation, training) to a highly diverse clientele (e.g., individuals, families, groups, communities, organizations). In the early 1980s, the profession broadened its perspective even further by recognizing the need to design and implement culturally sensitive counseling delivery models and strategies to effectively assist persons from different ethnic, racial, and socioeconomic backgrounds, individuals with physical disabilities, and persons representing diverse sexual orientations (Ponterotto, Casas, Suzuki, & Alexander, 2001; Sue & Sue, 2003). This multicultural perspective has become a major force and hallmark of the profession. In recent years, significant steps have also been taken to internationalize the U.S. counseling profession (Heppner, Leong, & Chiao, in press).

In essence, the profession evolved from the late–19th-century vocational guidance movement into a broad, strong, vibrant, and multicultural specialty within the discipline of psychology. Sometimes it may seem like counseling psychology has been an almost uniquely American discipline. But one should not be mislead by this limited perspective (Heppner et al., in press). As Pedersen (2005) noted, "The functions of counseling have been practiced for thousands of years and are not merely an invention of the last century or two" (p. xi); these counseling functions have been practiced around the world in a wide array of forms. Today, the counseling profession is active worldwide. However, there are many differences in the identity of counseling psychologists, the roles and functions of counselors and counseling psychologists, the credentials to function as such professionals, and the presence and infrastructure of associations that represent this occupational group.

The purpose of this chapter is to introduce the reader to the counseling profession around the globe. Given the breadth and variability of the counseling profession worldwide, it is impossible to summarize the profession in a single chapter. Rather, the chapter will focus on some individual countries as well as more encompassing international structures that promote the counseling profession. The first section of the chapter provides a brief description of counseling professions in nine countries across seven continents. Each of these country descriptions provide an overview of its counseling profession by discussing the professional structures that help organize the profession, such as their professional organizations, publication outlets, credentialing bodies and licensure regulations, and training regulations. In addition, each country description discusses the role of counselors, services provided, employment opportunities, the role of research, challenges, and how counselors are addressing important societal needs in their countries.

The world is undergoing rapid change and, in essence, becoming a global village with increased interdependence, communication, travel, migration, and trade around the world. These changes dictate a greater need for counselors to learn from each other and collaborate around the world. The second section articulates an array of cross-cultural competencies that will become increasingly important around the world for the counseling profession. In the past, it has been functional for people to be interdependent at the local level. With the shrinking of time and space (Friedman, 2005), there is an increasing need for collaboration across countries with specific cross-cultural or cross-national knowledge, awareness, and skills. The chapter concludes with some challenges and opportunities for growth in international psychology; in particular, we strongly encourage the profession to more fully articulate the full array of cross-cultural competencies, including knowledge of indigenous ways of healing.

THE COUNSELING PROFESSION IN AUSTRALIA

ROBERT G. L. PRYOR, AUSTRALIAN CATHOLIC UNIVERSITY, AUSTRALIA

Vocational guidance services commenced in New South Wales in 1927 (Richardson, 1977). However, the development of a recognizably modern set of counseling services in Australia began in the post–World War II period with the establishment of child welfare, educational development, career choice, personnel, and clinical services (O'Neil, 1987; Nixon & Taft 1977). Influential figures in this development were David Mace (relationship counseling), Clive Williams (student counseling), and Ted Rose (careers counseling). At present, there are a bewildering number of counselor organizations. The major ones include the Australian Society for Rehabilitation Counsellors (http://www.asorc.org.au), the Australian Counselling Association (http://www.theaca.net.au), the Psychotherapy and Counselling Federation of Australia (http://www.pacfa.org.au), the Australian Guidance and Counselling Association (http://www.agca.com.au), and the Australian Association of Career Counsellors (http://www.aacc.org.au). Additionally, the Australian Psychological Association (http://www.psychology.org.au) has a College of Counselling that overlaps in scope with other colleges for educational, clinical, organizational, health, and sports psychology. The leading counseling journals are the *Australian Journal of Career Development, Australian Journal of Rehabilitation Counselling, Australian Journal of Counselling Psychology, Australian Journal of Guidance and Counselling,* and *Australian Counselling Association Journal.*

Entry standards for the profession range from employment in a counseling-related organization to postgraduate qualifications. Most associations require at least a bachelor's degree for entry and practicum. However, there is no national credentialing body for counseling, although psychologist registration is mandated on a state-by-state basis. Counselor training is conducted in private agencies and tertiary institutions. Although the scientist-practitioner model is generally espoused, private agencies emphasize practical skills, whereas tertiary institutions such as universities focus more on the science and theory of counseling.

Counselors in Australia provide assistance to individuals, families, groups, and organizations. Their range of services continues to expand as the perceived relevance of counseling increases. Traditional counseling areas like relationship difficulties, career choice, rehabilitation, mental health, educational adjustment, and staff development are now supplemented by needs associated with drug and alcohol abuse, gambling addiction, blended families, gender identity, elite performance stress, trauma or abuse, reactions to change, unemployment, combat veterans, cross-cultural (including Aboriginal) issues, attention deficit, outplacement, chronic pain, anger, communication problems, and previously unrecognized depression.

Traditionally, counselors have been employed in government departments and educational institutions or charitable organizations (e.g., churches and community welfare groups). However, there has been a trend for larger organizations to hire counselors as a form of employer welfare and retention. Furthermore, there has been a recent trend for counselors to go into private practice as a sole practitioner or part of a consultancy (Patton, 2005).

Although there is general acceptance of the worth of counseling by the Australian community, it is typically seen as a palliative for a crisis rather than as a means of personal and relationship development. Counseling is perceived as a reactive activity rather than as a proactive contribution. Broadening this perception of counseling is one of the challenges facing the profession along with: (a) the development of national standards of training and accreditation, (b) the need to adapt practice to the ethnic diversity of the Australian community, (c) the uncritical acceptance of techniques and trends from overseas, (d) the increasing complexity of presenting problems, and (e) increasing constraints on time and funds to address such needs.

With respect to ongoing societal needs, counseling in Australia has the potential to contribute significantly in areas like: (a) adjustment for an aging population; (b) redressing the disadvantage of Aboriginal people; (c) relationship dissolution; (d) community insecurity in response to change and threat of terrorism; and (e) provision of services outside major population centers.

CAREER COUNSELING IN ITALY

SALVATORE SORESI AND LAURA NOTA,
UNIVERSITY OF PADUA, ITALY

Although some pioneer career counseling services existed in Italy in the 1930s, it was only after World War II that specific services were started by various governmental branches, initially only sporadically but later all over the country. Toward the end of the 1960s, a group of vocational guidance professionals founded the UNIO (Italian National Association for Vocational Guidance), which brought interested professionals together as well as drew attention to and requested specific legislation for career counseling. Early vocational guidance pioneers were Gemelli (1947), Meschieri (1961), and Scarpellini (1960). See Scarpellini and Strologo (1976) for documentation regarding the history of vocational guidance.

The S.I.Co. (Società Italiana di Counseling/Italian Society of Counseling) was founded in 1993 to bring together all counselors and counseling organizations as well as promote research and the diffusion of professional counseling. It has about 700 members. The minimum membership requirement is a 3-year postgraduate certificate issued by a university or an accredited body. Because there are no national laws specifying training competencies, vocational guidance is provided by diverse professional people who only rarely have in-depth specific training (e.g., teachers, psychologists, economists). The lack of specialization is a result of the following: (a) the absence of any specific legislation on the training of career service providers; (b) the lack of any requirements to be a member of any professional association in order to provide career services; and (c) only recently has there been discussion/debate on the training of career service providers.

In 2004, professionals specifically interested in promoting vocational guidance as well as establishing career counseling training requirements founded the SIO (Italian Society of Vocational Guidance). Its members (around 300) must have specific postgraduate training in career counseling granted by an Italian university or equally valid credentials (today, master's courses of 1,500 hours, at least 350 of which are devoted to doing career practice at universities). The courses examine a number of career models, all developed in the United States. The primary journal for scholars in the SIO is the *Giornale Italiano di Psicologia dell'Orientamento* (*Italian Journal of Vocational Psychology*).

SIO professionals operate in schools, vocational guidance centers, private practices, and job centers; they work with individuals seeking help to solve issues of indecision about their future and professional problems, with the aim of boosting self-determination, increasing the range of options to be considered, professional self-efficacy, problem-solving and social abilities, and enhancing available support and resources.

The need for career counseling in Italy is a result of: (a) the increase over time of diversified training opportunities; (b) the increase in dropping out of school and resulting in inadequate career choices; (c) the increase of instability in the world of work as well as the flexibility that the world of work requires; and (d) new legislation on the work inclusion of individuals with special needs.

The biggest challenges are connected to increasing the professionalism of the career service providers who do not have specific training (who are still the majority), and who often work with individuals at great risk (e.g., persons with disabilities, low income, immigrants). Their interventions tend to be superficial, aimed at giving information or promoting an equally superficial person-environment match. In addition to negatively affecting the professional self-efficacy beliefs of career service providers (Soresi, Nota, & Lent, 2004), this situation promotes the notion that vocational guidance is not important. Experts are very worried about clients at risk for maladjustment, and for nonadvantageous and unsatisfying career choices (e.g., Soresi, Nota, & Ferrari, 2005). Another challenge is to foster research, and to close the gap between research and application. Vocational guidance psychology is definitely weaker than other psychological specialties, and seems to suffer from an inferiority complex; it seems neither to fully benefit from contributions from other psychological specialties, nor to put itself forward as a promising and autonomous new sector of investigation and intervention.

COUNSELING IN PERU

INES V. BUSTAMANTE, UNIVERSIDAD PERUANA CAYETANO HEREDIA, PERU[2]

In Peru, psychological counseling is a relatively new and growing field. Given this fact, the structures mainly depend on the professional organizational bodies linked with psychology. The ethical conduct of psychologists is regulated by the Peruvian College of Psychologists (*Colegio de Psicólogos del Perú*), whereas the National Assembly of Chancellors accredits the training of psychologists. Currently, there are no professional organizations exclusively representing counseling psychologists.

Counseling is a required course in the preparation of psychologists, and further training can be obtained by attending certificate and master's programs that offer some advanced counseling courses. These classes cover counseling theories or conceptual models such as behavioral and cognitive theory, systems theory, and humanistic theory. They also address issues related to counseling techniques and practice. The career of psychology requires a study period of 5 to 6 years. There are a few Peruvian counselors who obtained certificates or master's degrees in counseling in the United States. There is no predominating training model to prepare counseling psychologists.

Research on counseling is very scarce. There are, however, some books and articles about psychological counseling related to specific topics such as the secondary prevention of drug abuse. There are no scholarly journals devoted exclusively to counseling.

Counseling is usually performed by psychologists in private educational settings (e.g., schools, universities) and less often in private practice and in nongovernmental organizations. Counseling is prevention oriented and focuses on people in crisis or with psychological problems. Also, counselors provide academic advice and assistance with career choice.

At the macro level, counseling in Peru is challenged by restrictions in economic resources within a cultural context where practice is valued and research is not a priority. At an intermediate level, a challenge counselors face is the need for creating their own field so as to have the same status as psychotherapists. The latter professionals are recognized because of their specialization and membership in scientific societies of psychotherapy. By contrast, counselors must reduce the stigma associated with seeking help from clinical psychologists or psychotherapists by demonstrating that their focus is not related to psychopathology or a deep psychological conflict to be resolved.

Finally, within educational settings and the workplace, there are many opportunities for the future development of the counseling specialty. Counselors are needed to provide orientation and support to people who have psychological problems caused by family difficulties, economical stress, violence, migration, unemployment, and prejudice against cultural and ethnic diversity.

Interestingly, the Peruvian population perceives counseling in two ways. First, there is a stigma associated with psychopathology and the treatment of mental disease. This raises the importance of helping Peruvians to differentiate between the counseling psychology profession and other disciplines of psychology and psychiatry. And, second, the population expects counselors to provide good advice including a solution in the form of a "recipe" rather than empowering them to find their own solutions in a participatory counselor-client relationship.

COUNSELING IN SOUTH AFRICA

ANTHONY NAIDOO AND ASHRAF KAGEE,
STELLENBOSCH UNIVERSITY, SOUTH AFRICA

Psychology as a discipline in South Africa has undergone a substantial change following the transition from apartheid to democracy (Anonymous, 1986; Cooper, Nicholas, Seedat, & Statman, 1990; Hickson & Kriegler, 1991; Holdstock, 1981; Nicholas & Cooper, 1990; Stead, 2004; Swartz & Gibson, 2001). Counseling psychology is one of five areas of specialization leading to registration (equivalent of licensing) following completion of an accredited master's program and a one-year approved internship. Accredited master's programs in counseling psychology are offered at eight universities.

The credentialing of psychologists is vetted by the Board of Psychology. The Psychological Society of South Africa (PsySSA) established in 1994 is the guild organization of psychologists, similar to the American Psychological Association. It has 10 divisions, including Counseling Psychology, which is one of the largest. The Society of Student Counseling also provides a professional forum for counselors working at universities and colleges. For a population of 45 million people, there are approximately 6,256 licensed psychologists, with 1367 (22%) registered as counseling psychologists. The majority of psychologists are White, largely serving White, middle-class clients (Naidoo, Shabalala, & Bawa, 2003). Two major journals serve the profession: *The South African Journal of Psychology* and *Psychology in Society*. For more details, see http://www.hpcsa.co.za/hpcsa/default.aspx, http://www.psyssa.com/, and http://www.sscsa.org.za/mission.html.

There have been several developments affecting training and the focus of psychology:

1. A new lower-level qualification, the 4-year bachelor of psychology degree, was introduced at several universities to train registered counselors for community grassroots work. However, several difficulties have emerged, including poor employment opportunities for these graduates in the health system.
2. The Board of Psychology has required students wishing to register as clinical psychologists to do a compulsory community service year before registering. Clinical positions are available in public health for this purpose. That this requirement was only made for clinical psychologists has fueled the old turf debates between various psychologists.
3. Counseling psychology programs emphasize community psychology as a growing discipline more attuned to the local psychosocial issues and context (Stead & Watson, 2006). These new programs draw heavily from counseling psychology philosophy and practice.

Some universities have elected to combine once separate clinical and counseling psychology programs to integrate the emphases of both subdisciplines. For example, the new master's program at Stellenbosch University in clinical psychology and community counseling provides training to psychologists to work with individuals, families, groups, and communities. In a country faced with problems such as poverty, unemployment, crime, and HIV/AIDS, the growing need for developing relevant interventions in different contexts for different populations has superseded the clinical versus counseling debates of the past.

Counseling psychology continues to be a specialization at a few universities, but it does not enjoy a distinctive identity. Among the pioneers of the counseling profession are Bodley van der Westhuisen, Neil Broekman, Dap Louw, Anthony Naidoo, and Lionel Nicholas. Although counseling has shifted from the one-on-one model, there continues to be some stigma associated with seeking mental health services. However, some specialized counseling services continue to flourish (e.g., HIV counseling, trauma counseling). Most counselors offer a range of services, including individual and family counseling, community consultation, and advocacy and lobbying, as well as administration and consultation in governmental and nongovernmental organizations. Counselors often address a variety of societal needs like psychological adjustment, physical health, education (e.g., health literacy, learning difficulties), and career assistance. The multicultural nature of South African society creates a dynamic relationship between the cultural context and work of counselors. Research is mainly conducted by professionals at universities, parastatal research organizations (e.g., Human Sciences Research Council, Medical Research Council), and other research organizations.

THE COUNSELING PROFESSION IN SOUTH KOREA

HYUN-JOO PARK, DONGGUK UNIVERSITY, KOREA

DONG-GWI LEE, YONSEI UNIVERSITY, KOREA

The advancement of counseling psychology as a profession in Korea is traced back to the establishment of the Korean Counseling Psychological Association (KCPA) in 1964 as a division of the Korean Psychological Association. Initially the KCPA and the Korean Clinical Psychology Association were housed as one division. In 1987, the KCPA separated itself as an independent division keeping counseling/psychotherapy as the primary focus. Currently, the KCPA has approximately 6,005 members, including 1,435 professional counselors. Recent presidents of the KCPA were Drs. Kwang-Woong Kim and Kyu Mee Lee. Recently, another counseling-related organization, the Korea Counseling Association, was launched, encompassing various modes of counseling (e.g., family counseling, group counseling, spiritual counseling), which diversifies the field of counseling in Korea. Lee (2005) provided a detailed documentation of the history and development of the counseling profession in Korea.

The *Korean Journal of Counseling and Psychotherapy* and the *Korean Journal of Counseling* are two major counseling journals in Korea. Although several credentialing systems for counselors exist in Korea (e.g., the youth counselor, the counseling teachers), the counselor certification system conferred by the KCPA is considered the flagship one. As of February 26, 2007, 403 counseling psychologists and 1,032 certified counselors hold this professional credential.

Counselors in Korea provide a variety of services (e.g., individual counseling, group counseling, assessment, outreach, and consultation) across settings such as university counseling centers, independent practice, secondary schools, and government-affiliated institutions. These settings offer employment opportunities for Korean counselors in training. Although general awareness of and interest in the counseling profession have consistently increased, the public's attitudes toward seeking counseling services are still far from being positive. Some researchers (e.g., Yoo, 2005) reported that adults and women in Korea have more positive attitudes toward counseling, and suggested that collectivism and Asian values (e.g., saving face, avoiding family shame) might affect Koreans' attitudes toward help-seeking.

Rapid industrialization and Westernization in the past decade in Korea has put forth societal challenges in mental health, such as depression, suicide, increasing divorce rate, bullying at schools, and maladjustment in the military services, where counselors play critical roles. The Korean government and society have begun to respond to these societal demands by employing mandatory counseling systems at divorce courts and military services. In addition, Korean counseling psychologists have actively engaged in research with topics including personality and adjustment, counseling process and outcome, career development, and scale construction (Cho, 2003). Current challenges in the Korean counseling profession involve: (a) the governmental approval of the counselor certification system, (b) development of systematic and quality training models for counselors tailored to Korean culture (Choi & Kim, 2006), (c) increasing collaboration and communication with professionals in other countries, (d) establishment of liability insurance systems for counselors, and (e) generating job opportunities for counselors in accordance with the societal demands.

COUNSELING PSYCHOLOGY DEVELOPMENT IN TAIWAN: ROOTED IN THE SCHOOLS

LI-FEI WANG, NATIONAL TAIWAN NORMAL UNIVERSITY, TAIWAN

HUNG CHIAO, UNIVERSITY OF MISSOURI-COLUMBIA

Although counseling psychology in Taiwan seems to be a relatively new profession, school guidance and counseling have been implemented since the 1950s (e.g., Chen, 1999). The first guidance institute was implemented in National Overseas Chinese High School and Taipei Municipal Zhong Shan Girls High School in 1960 (Chung & Wu, 1999). Later, guidance and counseling services were implemented in all school systems. Since then, the development of counseling and counseling psychology have been intertwined and profoundly influenced by educational policies and school cultures. For example, when the government developed the Six-Year National Development Plan in 1991, the school guidance and counseling projects were designed as the first and also the most important plan in national education policies (e.g., Chen, 1999). Today, more than 78% of counseling psychologists are employed in school settings and university counseling centers (Lin, 2005). Although they provide similar counseling services to U.S. psychologists, the majority of counseling psychologists in Taiwan call themselves "counseling teacher." Similarly, clients view themselves as "receiving counseling" in the manner of "going to class," which means they receive "education" rather than "treatment" in counseling.

The national licensure statute for psychologists for both clinical and counseling psychologists was established by the Taiwanese legislature in 2001; this statute was the first national licensing system for counseling psychologists in Asia. Licensure had a very significant impact on the professional identity, training of counseling psychologists, and even the client populations in Taiwan (Wang & Hwang, 2006). For example, the client population has been extended from schools into the community, and even some hospitals.

In addition, professional organizations (e.g., Chinese Guidance Association [CGA], and now Chinese Guidance and Counseling Association in Taiwan), journals (e.g., *Chinese Annual Report of Guidance and Counseling, Bulletin of Educational Psychology*) and pioneers (e.g., Jian-bai Jiang) have dramatically shaped the development of counseling psychology in Taiwan. For example, the first pioneer, Dr. Jian-bai Jiang, holding two important positions in Taiwan's central government and the first president of CGA, established guidance and counseling systems in the schools (e.g., Chen, 1999).

A continuous challenge for counseling psychology has been the general public view of counseling services as "Western imports" (e.g., Jin, 1999). Thus, the goodness of fit of counseling psychology into Taiwanese culture has been questioned (e.g., Yee, 2005). Some Taiwanese scholars attempted to build indigenous counseling theories and models from empirical studies (e.g., Chen, 2005; Wang, Tu, & Chao, in review; Yee, 2005). For example, Chen (2005) developed an indigenous model by integrating Western theories with Chinese cultural factors. Wang and her colleagues examined the performance of counseling psychologist in Taipei elementary schools. They found that, when counseling psychologists applied the concept of differential orders (which is the core factor of interpersonal interactions in Chinese societies; Huang, 2001) to build a culturally sensitive ecological model for practice, their counseling services became more efficacious (Chao, Wang, & Yang, 2006; Wang et al., in review).

In sum, as Taiwan grows into a developed country and more severe mental health and societal problems have been reported, the needs for the counseling profession in Taiwan have been growing. Counseling psychologists not only work in schools but also now have spread in varying degrees to communities and hospitals. Our counseling theories and models are also in the process of transformation from Western perspectives into indigenous counseling models that are culturally sensitive to more adequately meet the needs of Taiwanese people. Hopefully, such development could contribute to enhance the effectiveness of global counseling psychology in the future.

THE COUNSELING PROFESSION IN TWO ARAB COUNTRIES

FATIMA R. AL-DARMAKI, UNITED ARAB EMIRATES UNIVERSITY, UAE

S. M. A. SULAIMAN, SULTAN QABOOS UNIVERSITY, OMAN

The counseling profession in the United Arab Emirates (UAE) and Oman is relatively new. Counseling has not been seen as a valuable method of mental health treatment due to cultural and social factors in the past (e.g., viewing mental illness within the medical model, stigma of mental illness, family interference, and acceptability of traditional methods of healing). More recently, there has been a growing need for counseling primarily due to globalization, diversity, and rapid technological, social, economic, and cultural changes; huge gaps between generations; and growing family problems such as divorces, polygamous marriages, and female employment (Al-Damen & Sulaiman, 2004; Al-Darmaki, 2004; Al-Darmaki & Sayed, 2005).

United Arab Emirates

In the UAE, counseling is provided within educational settings, hospitals, and community mental health agencies. Help providers are mainly social workers and psychology paraprofessionals (Al-Darmaki & Sayed, 2005; Sayed, 2003), with some of them receiving supervision from well-trained practitioners. Usually well-trained psychologists/counselors practice within a hospital setting or hold academic or administrator positions. They were mostly educated in Western countries. Counselors are trained at the bachelor level because of the increasing need for counseling (personal, career, school, family), which creates job opportunities for counselors in various settings, and the unavailability of graduate programs in counseling (Al-Darmaki, 2004). Graduates of these programs typically work in schools, hospitals, social support services, and university counseling centers; services may involve individual/group therapy, career counseling, couples counseling, and other psychological help. Clients are seen for issues such as psychological concerns, academic difficulties, family-related issues, and career concerns.

Counseling research has focused on issues such as counseling training (e.g., Al-Darmaki, 2004), attitudes toward seeking professional help (e.g., Al-Darmaki, 2003), and other counseling-related issues (e.g., Al-Darmaki, Al-Etir, & Nassar, 2004; Al-Darmaki & Sayed, 2005). There is not a specialized counseling journal in UAE and, to our knowledge, the counseling services we have established at the UAE University in 1999 represent the first such pioneering counseling agencies (Al-Darmaki, 2003). These services were developed according to the U.S. model of college counseling centers following the procedures and the ethical standards of APA for delivering counseling services (Al-Darmaki, 1999, in press).

There have been some initial steps toward establishing a professional counseling organization. Although the counseling profession in the UAE is promising, it faces many challenges such as a shortage of professionally and culturally competent practitioners. The absence of a licensure board, accreditation bodies, standards of practice, and a professional association to regulate the provision of counseling services seems to contribute to malpractice and to the negative attitudes toward seeking professional psychological help (see Al-Darmaki & Sayed, 2005, for more discussion).

Oman

The Sultan Qaboos University (SQU) was established in 1986 as a first government University in Oman. Many students sought counseling help from the counseling faculty members at the department of psychology, but the academic advisors lacked the experience and the qualification to deal with their psychological problems (Al-Damen & Sulaiman, 2004). The counseling profession started in Oman through SQU when the Student Counseling Center (SCC) was established in 1999 according to a U.S. model of college counseling centers (Sulaiman, 2006). Today the counseling center consists of seven staff, all of whom hold a counseling degree, and five of whom hold a doctorate degree and serve more than 1,000 student yearly.

The Student Counseling Center has played a major role in the development of the counseling profession in Oman by providing awareness about counseling services that are available to the university students (Sulaiman, 2004) through research papers, presentations, newspaper articles, and radio and television programs. The SCC provides the students with developmental, prevention, and remedial counseling services. The developmental and prevention counseling services include developmental guidance programs, electronic consultation, workshops, and training courses. The remedial counseling services are provided to SQU students through individual and group counseling.

The Ministry of Higher Education Oman has now established counselor positions in all of its educational and technical colleges, resulting in an increase in job opportunities in the counseling field. In addition, many newly established private universities (e.g., Oman Medical College, Suhar University) have either established counseling centers or appointed professional counselors, as well as established a graduate program in counseling psychology. The Ministry of Education has a strategic plan to appoint a career guidance counselor in each school. Graduate programs in career guidance and counseling are planned to start by September 2007 at SQU.

To prevent possible malpractice, professional counseling standards, the ethical codes of the American Psychological Association and the American Counseling Association, were translated in Arabic and modified to adapt to the Arabic and Omani culture.

There is a bright future for the counseling profession in Oman; in the near future a professional counseling association will be established when there are enough counselors.

COUNSELING PSYCHOLOGY IN THE UNITED STATES

STEWART COOPER, VALPARAISO UNIVERSITY, INDIANA

The counseling profession in the United States, in particular counseling psychology, has a long and distinguished history. Many scholars have documented and analyzed the developments within various time periods (e.g.,

Blocher, 2000; Whitely, 1984). Sources cite the founding of the Division of Personnel and Guidance in 1944 (e.g., Scott, 1980; now the Society of Counseling Psychology with 2,974 members), the founding of major counseling journals such as the *Journal of Counseling Psychology* and *The Counseling Psychologist* (e.g., Whitely, 1999; Wrenn, 1966), the marked change in research patterns over time (e.g., Borgen, 1984), and the development of professional organizations within counseling psychology (e.g., Heppner et al., 2000). Moreover, through the use of oral histories, scholars have documented the stories and perceptions of some of the major pioneers and leaders (e.g., E. G. Williamson, G. Wrenn; see Heppner, 1990; Heppner, Fouad, & Hansen, 2002).

The development of the counseling psychology profession within the last 50 years has been particularly striking. These years have witnessed the creation of over 70 doctoral-level training programs (predominately through a scientist-practitioner training model) accredited through the American Psychological Association, and the credentialing of thousands of members to function as mental health professionals through state regulatory bodies. Scholars generate an impressive body of knowledge published in volumes of empirical and qualitative research. The infrastructures of professional organizations associated with counseling psychology continue to develop and the scope of their influence to expand.

The current role of counseling psychologists and the services they provide in the United States is broad and varied, including teaching, research, psychotherapeutic and counseling practice, career development, assessment, supervision, and consultation. Interventions focus on prevention, development, and adjustment across the life span, brief or long-term, often problem specific and goal directed, and guided by a philosophy that values individual differences and diversity.

Counseling psychologists are employed in a variety of settings, such as: (a) colleges and universities as teachers, supervisors, researchers, and service providers; (b) independent practice providing counseling, psychotherapy, assessment, and consultation services to individuals, families, groups, and organizations; and (c) community mental health centers, Veterans Administration Medical Centers, health maintenance organizations, rehabilitation agencies, business and industrial organizations, and consulting firms (for more details, see http://www.div17.org).

Public perception of the importance and benefits of counseling has strengthened in recent years, though significant barriers as a result of stigma continue to exist (Corregan, 2004). Moreover, there is a growing congruence between the capability of counseling to address a wide range of societal concerns and the culture's support for use of it for that purpose. However, adequate funding for counseling from the federal and state governments and from private insurance remains a highly problematic issue with a considerable body of research documenting the unmet needs of many, especially the economically disadvantaged and most racial and ethnic minority groups (Lewis, Lewis, Daniels, & D'Andrea, 2003). Serving the latter represents a growing area of employment for counseling psychologists. Other growing areas of employment for counseling psychologists are in health, with children and schools, and in organizations. Finally, the influence of legal issues on the field continues to grow and become more formalized as set into both ethical codes and legal statutes. Fear of lawsuits is a factor contributing to the development of many processes and procedures currently recognized as issue-specific standards of practice in the United States.

DEVELOPING INTERNATIONAL COMPETENCIES

Cross-Cultural Competence Movement in Counseling Psychology

Over two decades ago, the cross-cultural competence movement in psychology was launched in the United States when Allen Ivey, president of the American Psychological Association's Division of Counseling Psychology, appointed Derald Sue to chair a task force to develop a position paper on the topic. That position paper on cross-cultural counseling competencies, which was published in 1982 (Sue et al., 1982), has served as the foundation for the current movement toward cultural competence in mental health services in the United States. Within the American Psychological Association, the culmination of that movement was the passage of the Guidelines on Multicultural Education, Training, Research, Practice, and Organizational Change for Psychologists in August 2002.

Despite the accomplishments associated with the passage of the multicultural guidelines, it is quite clear that mainstream psychology in the United States has been slow in attending to multiculturalism. For example, even though the Division 17 position paper on cross-cultural competencies was published in 1982, it took another 20 years before it became official policy within APA. Furthermore, divisions within the American Psychological Association have been developed and numbered chronologically; the division devoted to racial ethnic minority issues was not formed until 1986 when it became Division 45. Additionally, the APA division devoted to international and cross-cultural issues was not developed until 1997, when it became Division 52! Yet, much of the interest and research in cross-cultural competence for the last two decades has been from the domestic perspective in the United States. With the increasing globalization of the economy and the aftermath of 9/11, there has been a surge of interest in international aspects of multiculturalism that has begun to parallel the interest in domestic aspects of multiculturalism.

In the movement toward developing greater cross-cultural competence in working across national boundaries, various groups within the American Psychological Association spearheaded by Division 52 (International Psychology) and the Committee on International Relations in Psychology have provided a resolution similar to the multicultural guidelines but focused on international aspects of psychology. This APA Resolution on Culture and Gender Awareness in International Psychology is serving as the current blueprint for psychologists interested in promoting international perspectives in our theory, research, and service.

This APA resolution clearly calls for the development of a multicultural mindset and increasing our cross-cultural competence in the international arena. The resolution includes recommendations to (a) advocate for more research on the role that cultural ideologies have in the experience of women and men across and within countries on the basis of sex, gender identity, gender expression, ethnicity, social class, age, disabilities, and religion, (b) advocate for more collaborative research partnerships with colleagues from diverse cultures and countries leading to mutually beneficial dialogues and learning opportunities, and (c) encourage more attention to a critical examination of international cultural, gender, gender identity, age, and disability perspectives in psychological theory, practice, and research at all levels of psychological education and training curricula.

International Competencies

Based on the cross-cultural counseling competencies outlined in the Division 17 position paper (Sue et al., 1982) and as an extension to the APA Resolution on Culture and Gender Awareness in International Psychology, we would like to present a model for developing international competencies in counseling psychology. The basic purpose of this model is to provide a preliminary conceptual framework for guiding the increasing internationalization of counseling psychology in the United States. As more counseling psychologists engage in international collaboration, whether through research, exchange programs, participating in international conferences, serving as invited speakers or consultants, training graduate students from abroad, or counseling international students, there is a need to develop a set of competencies for undertaking these tasks.

We would like to propose that the development of international or cross-cultural competencies in counseling psychology should begin with a multicultural mind-set (Leong & Hartung, 2000) that includes a deep understanding of the contextual basis of human behavior that requires a cross-cultural and comparative perspective. The tripartite model of cross-cultural knowledge, awareness, and skills is an essential part of this model. The opposite of such a stance is ethnocentrism where we assume that our culture's way of thinking, feeling, and behaving is the best and correct one regardless of context. It is also important to note that ethnocentrism is a common and natural human tendency and therefore requires mindful efforts at overcoming such a tendency. Given the importance of understanding cultural contexts in developing international competencies, we would like to propose the use of Bronfenbrenner's (1977, 1979) classic bio-ecological systems model of human development as the guiding theoretical framework for these competencies.

In his model, Bronfenbrenner (1977, 1979) identified five major interrelated subsystems influencing human behavior: (a) the microsystem, which consists of the interpersonal relations and settings in which an individual lives, including family, peers, school, neighborhood; (b) the mesosystem, which consists of interactions between two or more microsystem environments, such as the relations between an individual's school and family environments and between peers and family, etc.; (c) the exosystem, which involves linkages between subsystems that indirectly influence individuals, such as the health care systems and grandparents or between a parent's job stress and child's extramural activities; (d) the macrosystem, which consists of the ideological components of a given society such as norms and values, e.g., Judeo-Christian ethic and democratic ideals that dominate the U.S. culture; and (e) the chronosystem, which integrates the temporal dimension and is concerned with the patterning of environmental events and transitions over the life course and effects created by time or critical periods in development.

Bronfenbrenner's ecological model is especially important in its suppositions that all behavior is an act-in-context. Understanding that all human behavior happens within systems and subsystems helps us think about cross-cultural situations and individuals in a systematic way—examining the unique contexts of human life in other cultures all the way from the broad contexts of life to the individual microsystems. The ecological model thus provides a useful way of organizing the myriad of competencies needed as we work toward cross-cultural competence.

Indeed, Bronfenbrenner's (1977, 1979) model has already been applied to the field of multicultural counseling. For example, Neville and Mobley (2001) have used it in the development of their ecological model of multicultural counseling psychology processes (EMMCPP). They provide a rich and well-articulated integration of the ecological perspective into multicultural counseling processes. The application of Bronfenbrenner's (1977, 1979) model to multicultural counseling makes a great deal of sense given its emphasis on the ecological perspective and the role of cultural contexts and systems variables. However, the Neville and Mobley (2001) application is primarily a country-specific application (i.e., its value for guiding multicultural counseling in the United States). What is unique in our current use of this model is that it is for development of cross-cultural international competencies, which involves a cross-cultural and comparative perspective (e.g., how is the macrosystem in the United States different from the macrosystem in Saudi Arabia in its influence on the way that psychologists in each of these countries deal with psychotherapy with gay and lesbian clients?).

Based on Bronfenbrenner's (1977, 1979) model, we will present six propositions that outline a basic set of cross-cultural or international competencies for counseling psychologists who plan to engage in international activities. It is important to note that this model of international competencies and the associated propositions is meant to be only a starting point for us to explore and formulate how counseling psychologists can develop the key competencies to work in the international arena.

Proposition 1: The internationally competent counseling psychologist uses an ecological model such as that of Bronfenbrenner's (1977, 1979) in order to understand the influence of cultural contexts in human development.

Proposition 2: The internationally competent counseling psychologist studies and acquires knowledge about the microsystem, mesosystem, exosystem, macrosystem, and chronosystem (Bronfenbrenner, 1977, 1979) of his or her own culture or country and recognizes such as culture-specific knowledge.

Proposition 3: The internationally competent counseling psychologist understands that the microsystem, mesosystem, exosystem, macrosystem, and chronosystem (Bronfenbrenner, 1977, 1979) influencing the human development of ethnic minority populations in his or her own country may be significantly different from those of the majority population. He or she also recognizes that the nature and influence of these subsystems may also vary across gender, sexual orientation, social class, religion, and national origins.

Proposition 4: The internationally competent counseling psychologist seeks to acquire the knowledge, skills, and abilities of a cross-cultural psychologist by studying the microsystem, mesosystem, exosystem, macrosystem, and chronosystem (Bronfenbrenner, 1977, 1979) that influence the human development of persons from other cultures or countries in a comparative perspective.

Proposition 5: The internationally competent counseling psychologist applies these cross-cultural knowledge, skills, and abilities regarding the differential microsystem, mesosystem, exosystem, macrosystem, and chronosystem (Bronfenbrenner, 1977, 1979) that influence the human development of persons from other cultures or countries when engaged in international activities.

Proposition 6: The internationally competent counseling psychologist uses the cross-cultural knowledge, skills, and abilities related to differential contexts and ecologies in order to culturally accommodate for significant differences that would otherwise limit or hinder the relevance and effectiveness of his or her international activities.

In order to illustrate the application of these international competencies, we will provide a highly abbreviated and simplified example regarding a hypothetical case of a counseling psychology professor who is in the process of collaborating with colleagues in Taiwan on a number of professional projects (e.g., research, teaching, training, consultation). First, this counseling psychologist needs to understand the history and development of the United States and Taiwan in general, as well as the history of counseling and counseling psychology in both the United States and Taiwan (chronosystem). For example, counseling psychology in Taiwan is rooted in the schools (see Wang & Chiao in this chapter). Next, in a comparative analysis of the macrosystem, the counseling psychologist needs to understand the complex system of norms (e.g., differential order of interpersonal relationships), values (e.g., filial piety, collectivism, fate, emotional control), and religious/spiritual beliefs (e.g., Buddhism, Taoism, folk) in the Taiwanese culture, relative to the U.S. culture. Within these values, it is essential to understand how one may be initially perceived by another from the other culture, and why that may be the case. Moreover, it would be important to understand various cultural perspectives within Taiwan about education, mental health, physical health, indigenous ways of physical and mental healing, as well as counseling and psychotherapy.

Moving down to the exosystem, it would be important for the counseling psychologist to become familiar with the governmental, educational, and school regulations in Taiwan, and how these systems affect people's behavior throughout the life span. In terms of the mesosystem, what are the significant variations between the interplay of different contexts and between relations of family experiences to school experiences, school to temple, family to peers? For example, how should Taiwanese counselors be trained to work in school systems to apply the differential order of interpersonal relations in understanding expectations among the roles of counselors, teachers, students, parents, school administrators, and external university consultants?

Finally, the counseling psychologist will have to pay considerable attention to the microsystem of the individual client or counselor in Taiwan in terms of their roles and expectations within their families, peers, school, and neighborhood or community. Throughout this process, the counseling psychologist needs to be aware of the potential biases inherent in her or his Western worldviews and models of counseling that may be useful as well as inappropriate or insensitive within Taiwan culture.

One area in which U.S. counseling psychologists have considerable experience in developing international competencies is in counseling international students. A review of the counseling literature will reveal a steady stream of theoretical and empirical articles on the challenges of providing counseling to international students in the United States. This program of research has been driven by a pragmatic demand given the large number of international students that have come to pursue their higher education in the United States. Overviews of this literature can be found in the comprehensive reviews provided by Pedersen (1991) and Leong and Chou (1996, 2002). What is needed now is the development of a parallel set of literature on international competencies when counseling psychologists venture to other countries and cultures.

CONCLUSION

Most U.S. counseling psychology students and faculty have not been exposed to the development and current status of counseling professions around the world, thereby promoting a cultural and professional encapsulation within our country and culture (see Heppner, 2006; Heppner et al., 2000; Leong & Ponterotto, 2003; Leung, 2003). For example, "researchers and practitioners continue to rely solely on the U.S. literature . . . graduate students could receive a doctoral degree in counseling psychology without ever reading an article about counseling published outside the United States. Models and paradigms . . . continue to display an ethnocentric bias" (Leung, 2003, pp. 413–414). Many of our U.S. students and faculty have not lived abroad, and few are familiar with mental health issues in another country. In short, for the most part, U.S. counseling psychologists have not looked past our national borders in much depth except for brief vacations. This limitation greatly restricts U.S. counseling psychologists' understanding of the complexity of mental health issues embedded within different cultural contexts. Thus, a major challenge for U.S. counseling professionals remains "recognizing other countries' and other cultures' innovations and developments" (Heppner et al., 2000, p. 39) in promoting mental health within the counseling profession around the globe.

The brief descriptions of various counseling professions in this chapter and elsewhere (e.g., Ægisdóttir & Gerstein, 2005; Gerstein, 2005; Gerstein & Ægisdóttir, 2005) clearly indicate that there are many growing, strong, vibrant, and growing counseling professions around the globe. The professional structures (e.g., professional organizations) that help organize the field differ across countries, as is evident in the descriptions of counseling provided in this chapter. Similarly the functions (roles and services provided) and work settings of counselors differ across countries, as do the challenges facing the counseling profession in each country. Thus, these descriptions indicate that the term and conceptualization of counseling have different cultural meanings that have developed in different historical, cultural, social, and political contexts across the globe; it is important to note that such differences are not inferior or superior per se, just differences across different cultural contexts. In sum, the profession of counseling is evolving and changing worldwide, and is much bigger than any one country.

A profession cannot survive if it cannot demonstrate its utility to address important societal needs, not only in a specific country but also across the world. The counseling descriptions in this chapter and elsewhere (e.g., Ægisdóttir & Gerstein, 2005; Gerstein, 2005; Gerstein & Ægisdóttir, 2005) document how counseling professionals are addressing societal needs around the globe. Counselors in various roles and settings around the globe address depression, anxiety, stress, addictions, academic achievement, social development, interpersonal conflict and violence, loneliness, alienation, poverty, trauma, oppression, vocational uncertainty and dissatisfaction, and the desire to be a part of healthy, functional, and productive communities and organizations. Likewise, counseling professionals from many countries are involved in large-scale institutional and societal changes. It is clear that the counseling profession is meeting a very wide array of societal needs around the globe. As long as the profession of counseling is responsive to societal needs and cultural changes, the profession will be valued and thrive.

The world is shrinking in time and space (Friedman, 2005), and subsequently, the world around the counseling profession is changing, and resulting in new societal and cultural demands that must be addressed. Such challenges are not new for the counseling profession. In 1962, C. Gilbert Wrenn published a book titled *The Counselor in a Changing World;* in short, Wrenn maintained that our society continually faces a complex of new situations and intensified changes. He maintained that the competencies needed for counselors will change over the years to meet changing societal needs.

In order to effectively address an array of old and new societal needs in a rapidly changing world, it will be incumbent on U.S. counseling psychologists to expand our knowledge of how the cultural context around the world affects human behavior. However, counseling psychology students are not being systematically trained to acquire cross-cultural competencies related to promoting mental health, such as immigrants' mental health, academic achievement, acculturative stress, racism, and resilience, as well as intergroup conflict in the workplace and community. It is incumbent on the counseling psychology profession to promote the development of cross-cultural competencies, including the ability to develop cross-national collaborative and mutually beneficial partnerships. In essence, a broader array of cross-cultural competencies will be essential to facilitate change at the individual, institutional, and societal level to provide more culturally sensitive services to address the needs of an increasingly diverse population from around the world, not only in the United States but also in many other countries.

Although we have focused on professional counseling contexts in this chapter, it is important to note that people in all countries use resources other than counseling to cope with stressful life events and various mental health issues. Thus, it will be important for future counseling professionals to also be knowledgeable of a broad array of culture-specific and culturally sanctioned coping strategies in general, other than or in addition to seeking professional counseling.

In this chapter, we depicted some of the cross-cultural competencies needed within the counseling profession. The suggestions in this chapter for enhancing cross-cultural competencies are only the tip of the iceberg; we strongly encourage the profession to more fully articulate the full array of cross cultural competencies, including knowledge of indigenous ways of healing. It took over 20 years to develop the Multicultural Competency Guidelines (see Heppner et al., 2000), which most would agree was much too long. Almost 50 years ago, Wrenn (1962) called for changes in our training to enhance the cross-cultural competencies of the next generation of U.S. counselors. The counseling profession's response to Wrenn's call is long overdue, and is most apparent now as the demands greatly increase for cross-cultural competencies in our counseling graduates.

Endnotes

1. We kindly thank the following for their useful feedback in the development of this chapter: Chiao, Hung; He, Yuhong; Hsieh, Catherine, and Lin, Yi-Jiun.
2. Acknowledgment: Andreas Muhlbach.

BIBLIOGRAPHY

Ægisdóttir, S., & Gerstein, L.H. (2005). Reaching out: Mental health delivery outside the box. *Journal of Mental Health Counseling, 27*, 221–224.

Al-Damen, M., & Sulaiman, S. M. A. (2004). School counseling and guidance: Do we need them at our schools? *Egyptian Journal of Psychological Studies, 45*, 1–18.

Al-Darmaki, F. (1999, January). Establishing a Counseling Services Unit at the UAE University. A project submitted to UAE University.

Al-Darmaki, F. (2003). *Handbook of the Counseling Services Unit at UAE University*. UAE University Press (in Arabic).

Al-Darmaki, F. (2004). Counselor training, anxiety, and counseling self-efficacy: Implications for training of psychology students from the United Arab Emirates University. *Social Behavior & Personality: An International Journal, 32* (5), 429–440.

Al-Darmaki, F. (in press). *Counseling psychology*. UAE University Press (in Arabic).

Al-Darmaki, F., Al-Etir, F., & Nassar, K. (2004). Adolescents' problems in Abu Dhabi Emirate in the United Arab Emirates. *Journal of Humanities and Social Sciences, 20*(1), 108–145.

Al-Darmaki, F., & Sayed, M. (2005, August 18–21). *Mental health services in the UAE: In search for a paradigm*. Symposium conducted at the 113th Annual meeting of the American Psychological Association, Washington, DC.

Anonymous (1986). Some thoughts on a more relevant or indigenous counselling psychology in South Africa: Discovering the socio-political context of the oppressed. *Psychology in Society, 5*, 81–89.

Blocher, D. H. (2000). *The evolution of counseling psychology*. New York: Springer.

Borgen, F. H. (1984). Counseling psychology. In M. R. Rosenzweig, & L. W. Porter (Eds.), *Annual review of psychology, 35*, 579–604.

Bronfenbrenner, U. (1977). Toward an experimental ecology of human development. *American Psychologist, 32*, 513–531.

Bronfenbrenner, U. (1979). *The ecology of human development: Experiments by nature and design*. Cambridge, MA: Harvard University Press.

Chao, H., Wang, L., & Yang, K. (2006). The program evaluation of counseling psychology services in elementary schools. *Bulletin of Educational Psychology, 37*(4), 345–365.

Chen, P. H. (1999). Towards professionalism: The development of counseling in Taiwan. *Asian Journal of Counseling, 6*, 21–48.

Chen, P. H. (2005, August). *The self-relation in situation coordination counseling model for clients with interpersonal conflicts in Chinese communities*. Paper presented at the Annual Conference of the American Psychological Association, Washington, DC.

Cho, S. H. (2003). Analysis of research in the *Korean Journal of Counseling and Psychotherapy* (1988–2003). *Korean Journal of Counseling and Psychotherapy, 15*, 811–832.

Choi, H. R., & Kim, Y. H. (2006). A study on the graduate curriculum for the counselor education and training programs in Korea. *Korean Journal of Counseling and Psychotherapy, 18*, 713–729.

Chung, Z., & Wu, Z. (1999). The early functions and contributions of Chinese Guidance Association. In *The major trends of guidance and counseling* (pp. 3–23). Taipei: Psychological Publishing Co., Ltd.

Cooper, S., Nicholas, L., Seedat, M., & Statman, J. (1990). Psychology and apartheid: The struggle for psychology in South Africa. In L. J. Nicholas & S. Cooper (Eds.), *Psychology and apartheid* (pp. 1–21). Cape Town: Vision/Madiba Publication.

Corregan, P. (2004). How stigma interferes with mental health care. *American Psychologist, 59*, 614–625.

Friedman, T. L. (2005). *The world is flat: A brief history of the twenty-first century*. New York: Farrar, Straus & Giroux.

Gemelli, A. (1947). *L'orientamento professionale dei giovani nelle scuole* [Vocational guidance for young people in schools]. Milano: Vitae Pensiero.

Gerstein, L. H. (2005). Counseling psychologists as international social architects. In R. L. Toporek, L. H. Gerstein, N. A. Fouad, G. Roysircar-Sodowsky, & T. Israel (Eds.), *Handbook for social justice in counseling psychology: Leadership, vision, and action* (pp. 377–387). Thousand Oaks, CA: Sage Publications.

Gerstein, L. H., & Ægisdóttir, S. (2005). A trip around the world: A counseling travelogue! *Journal of Mental Health Counseling, 27*, 95–103.

Heppner, P. P. (Ed.). (1990). *Pioneers in counseling and human development: Personal and professional perspectives*. Washington, DC: AACD.

Heppner, P. P. (2006). The benefits and challenges of becoming cross-culturally competent counseling psychologists. *The Counseling Psychologist, 34*, 147–172.

Heppner, P. P., Casas, J. M., Carter, J., & Stone, G. L. (2000). The maturation of counseling psychology: Multifaceted perspectives from 1978–1998. In S. D. Brown & R. W. Lent (Eds.), *Handbook of counseling psychology* (3rd ed., pp. 3–49). New York: Wiley.

Heppner, P. P., Fouad, N. A., & Hansen, N. (Eds.). (2002). *First and second generation pioneers in the counseling profession: Personal and professional perspectives*. Columbia, MO: MU Custom Publishing.

Heppner, P. P., Leong, F. T. L., & Chiao, H. (in press). The growing internationalization of counseling psychology. In S. D. Brown & R. W. Lent (Eds.), *Handbook of counseling psychology* (4th ed.). New York: Wiley.

Hickson, J., & Kriegler, S. (1991). The mission and role of psychology in a traumatised and changing society: The case of South Africa. *International Journal of Psychology, 26*, 783–793.

Holdstock, T. L. (1981). Psychology in South Africa belongs to the colonial era: Arrogance or ignorance? *South African Journal of Psychology, 11*, 123–129.

Hwang, K. (2001). The theoretical construction of Confucian relationalism and its philosophical foundation. *Formosan Education and Society, 2*, 1–33.

Jin, S. (1999). The reflections and future visions of counseling psychology. In Chinese Guidance Association (Ed.), *The major trends of guidance and counseling* (pp. 53–72). Taipei: Psychological Publishing Co., Ltd.

Lee, C. H. (2005). *Counseling psychology* (4th ed.). Seoul: Park Young Press.

Leong, F. T. L., & Chou, E. L. (1996). Counseling international students. In P. B. Pedersen, J. G. Draguns, W. J. Lonner, & J. E. Trimble (Eds.), *Counseling across cultures* (4th ed., pp. 210–242). Beverly Hills, CA: Sage.

Leong, F. T. L., & Chou, E. L. (2002). Counseling international students and sojourners. In P. B. Pedersen, J. G. Draguns, W. J. Lonner, & J. E. Trimble (Eds.), *Counseling across cultures* (5th ed., pp. 185–207). Beverly Hills, CA: Sage.

Leong, F. T. L., & Hartung, P. (2000). Adapting to the changing multicultural context of career. In A. Collin & R. A. Young (Eds.), *The future of career* (pp. 212–227). Cambridge, UK: Cambridge University Press.

Leong, F. T. L., & Lee, S. H. (2006). A cultural accommodation model of psychotherapy: Illustrated with the case of Asian-Americans. *Psychotherapy: Theory, Research, Practice, and Training, 43*, 410–423.

Leong, F. T. L., & Ponterotto, J. G. (2003). A proposal for internationalizing counseling psychology in the United States: Rationale, recommendations, and challenges. *The Counseling Psychologist, 31*, 381–395.

Leung, S. A. (2003). A journey worth traveling: Globalization of counseling psychology. *The Counseling Psychologist, 31*, 412–419.

Lewis, J. A., Lewis, M. D., Daniels, J. A., & D'Andrea, M. J. (2003). *Community counseling: Empowerment strategies for a diverse society*. Pacific Grove, CA: Brooks/Cole-Thompson Learning.

Lin, J. (2005). *A manpower supply and demand study of counseling psychologists*. Unpublished manuscript.

Meschieri, I. (1961). *Caratteristiche, problemi e risultati dell'orientamento professionale* [Characteristics, problems and results of vocational guidance]. Roma: Atena.

Naidoo, A. V., Shabalala, N. J., & Bawa, U. (2003). Community psychology. In L. Nicholas (Ed.), *Introduction to psychology* (pp. 423–456). Cape Town: UCT Press.

Neville, H. A., & Mobley, M. (2001). Social identities in contexts: An ecological model of multicultural counseling psychology processes. *The Counseling Psychologist, 29*, 471–486.

Nicholas, L. J. (Ed.). (1993). *Psychology and oppression*. Johannesburg: Skotaville Publishers.

Nicholas, L. J., & S. Cooper (Eds.). (1990). *Psychology and apartheid*. Cape Town: Vision/Madiba Publication.

Nixon, M.C., & Taft, R. (Eds.) (1977). *Psychology in Australia: Achievements and prospects*. Sydney: Pergamon.

O'Neil, W.M. (1987). *A century of psychology in Australia*. Sydney: Sydney University Press.

Patton, W. (2005). Coming of age? Overview of career guidance policy and practice in Australia. *International Journal of Educational and Vocational Guidance, 5*(2), 217–227.

Pedersen, P. B. (1991). Counseling international students. *The Counseling Psychologist, 19*(1), 10–58.

Pedersen, P. (2005). Foreword. In R. Moodley & W.West (Eds.) *Integrating traditional healing practices into counseling and psychotherapy* (pp. xi–xii). Thousand Oaks, CA: Sage.

Ponterotto, J. G., Casas, J. M., Suzuki, L. A., & Alexander, C. M. (Eds.). (2001). *Handbook of multicultural counseling* (2nd ed). Thousand Oaks, CA: Sage.

Richardson, B. (1977). The history of vocational guidance in New South Wales. In B. Richardson (Ed.), *Celebrating fifty years of vocational counselling in Australia* (pp. 4–23). Sydney: NSW Department of Labour and Industry.

Sayed, M.A. (2003). Conceptualization of mental illness within Arab cultures: Meeting challenges in cross-cultural settings. *Social Behavior and Personality: An International Journal, 31*, 333–342.

Scarpellini, C. (1960). *La stima delle professioni nella scuola media* [Job estimation in middle school]. *Rivista di Psicologia Sociale, 9*, 83–91.

Scarpellini, C., & Strologo, E. (1976). *L'orientamento: problemi teorici e metodi operativi* [Vocational guidance: Theoretical issues and operational methods]. Brescia: Editrice La Scuola.

Scott, C. W. (1980). History of the division of counseling psychology: 1945–1963. In J. M. Whiteley (Ed.), *The history of counseling psychology* (pp. 25–40). Monterey, CA: Brooks/Cole.

Soresi, S., Nota, L., & Ferrari, L. (2005). Counseling for adolescents and children at risk in Italy. *Journal of Mental Health Counseling, 27*, 249–265.

Soresi, S., Nota, L., & Lent, R. (2004). Relation of type and amount of training to career counseling self-efficacy in Italy. *The Career Development Quarterly, 52*, 194–201.

Stead, G. B. (2004). Psychology in South Africa. In D. Wedding & M. J. Stevens (Eds.), *The handbook of international psychology* (pp. 59–74). New York: Brunner-Routledge.

Stead, G. B., & Watson, M.B. (Eds.). (2006). *Career psychology in the South African context* (pp. 214–225). Pretoria: J. L. Van Schaik.

Sue, D. W., Bernier, J. E., Durran, A., Feinberg, L., Pedersen, P., Smith, E., et al. (1982). Position paper: cross-cultural counseling competencies. *The Counseling Psychologist, 10*, 45–52.

Sue, D. W., Carter, R. T., Casas, J. M., Fouad, N. A., Ivey, A. E., Jensen, M., et al. (1998). *Multicultural counseling competencies: Individual and organizational development*. Thousand Oaks, CA: Sage Publications.

Sue, D. W., & Sue, D. (2003). *Counseling the culturally diverse: Theory and practice*. New York: John Wiley & Sons.

Sulaiman, S. M. A. (2004, February 15–16). *The role of counseling centers in institutions of higher education: The role of the student counseling center at SQU*. Counseling Psychology in Higher Education Symposium conducted by the Ministry of Higher Education, Rustaq College, Rustaq, Sultanate of Oman.

Sulaiman, S. M. A. (2006, May 13–15). *Student counseling center as a model for counseling centers in higher education*. Symposium conducted at the first meeting of Career Guidance, Ministry of Education, Muscat, Sultanate of Oman.

Swartz, L., & Gibson, K. (2001). The "old" versus the "new" in South African community psychology: The request for appropriate change. In M. Seedat, N. Duncan, & S. Lazarus (Eds.), *Community psychology: Theory, method and practice* (pp. 3–14). Cape Town: Oxford University Press.

Wang, L., & Huang, S. (2006, August). Counseling psychology licensure in Taiwan: Professional identity and employment issues. In P. P. Heppner & L. Wang (Cochairs), *Current licensure issues in three countries: Commonalities and challenges*. Symposium conducted at the 2006 Meeting of the American Psychological Association, New Orleans.

Wang, L., Tu, S., & Chiao, H. (in review). *An exploratory investigation of effective counseling frameworks for counseling psychologists working in elementary schools*. Bulletin of Educational Psychology.

Whiteley, J. M. (1984). *Counseling psychology: A historical perspective*. Schenectady, NY: Character Research Press.

Whiteley, J. M. (1999). The paradigms of counseling psychology. *The Counseling Psychologist*, 27, 14–31.

Wrenn, C. G. (1962). *The counselor in a changing world.* Washington, DC: American Personnel and Guidance Association.

Wrenn, C. G. (1966). Birth and early childhood of a journal. *Journal of Counseling Psychology, 13,* 485–488.

Yee, D. (2005). Ethical intervention and spiritual well-being as cultural therapeutics: Compound psychological healing in culturally Chinese societies. *Indigenous Psychological Research in Chinese Societies, 24,* 7–48.

Yoo, S. K. (2005). Korean college students' attitudes toward counseling, psychotherapy, and psychiatric help. *Korean Journal of Counseling and Psychotherapy, 17,* 617–632.

Chapter Eleven

Psychosocial Issues and Psychotherapeutic Treatment Considerations With Recent Immigrants

Azara L. Santiago-Rivera
Michele R. Guzmán

INTRODUCTION

Current census reports indicate that the immigrant population in the United States, both legal and undocumented, has reached an all-time high of 35 million, constituting about 12% of the total population (Camarota, 2005). Often described as a "nation of immigrants," the United States is by far one of the most culturally and ethnically diverse countries in the world, and its economic and political strength is a direct result of the enormous contributions made by immigrants (Marsella & Ring, 2003). Ironically, however, the current climate centers on a growing public concern that recent immigrants are becoming a burden to the U.S. economy. Moreover, the uneasiness often focuses on the steady growth of the undocumented immigrant population, which is estimated to be at nearly 10 million (Camarota, 2005).

In a recent report by the Pew Hispanic Center (2006), 53% of approximately 6,000 people surveyed said that the undocumented immigrants should return to their countries of origin, whereas 43% indicated that they should be given legal status. The apprehension stems from the belief that they are a burden to our education and health systems, boost crime rates, increase our unskilled workforce, and take away jobs from U.S.-born citizens. As Marsella and Ring (2003) cogently pointed out, beliefs such as these cause fear, anger, and resentment, resulting in exclusionary practices and unfair treatment. Historically this has been the case not only in the United States, but throughout the world. For example, the Chinese were victims of overt discriminatory policies as evidenced in the Chinese Exclusion Act of 1882, the first immigration law targeting a specific ethnic group.

Throughout history, people have migrated to other geographic regions for a wide variety of reasons. Scholars point to poor economic conditions, escape from political persecution, natural disasters, and terrorism as forcing or "pushing" them out of their countries of origin (e.g., Adler & Gielen, 2003). Others note that the motives to migrate are related to what is known as "pull" factors such as better opportunities for educational advancement or employment in the host country. Many immigrant groups leave their countries of origin searching for a better way of life for themselves and their families. In essence, it can be voluntary, like many of the experiences of immigrants who came from a variety of European countries during the early part of the 19th century, or involuntary, such as the enslavement of Africans who were taken from their homeland. Similarly, the Jews were pushed out of Europe to escape persecution during the early part of the 20th century (Pedraza, 2006).

As a consequence of the unprecedented number of recent arrivals, migration has become a central topic in many public and academic circles. In particular, considerable attention has been given to expanding our knowledge about the migratory patterns of different cultural and ethnic groups (e.g., Hoerder & Knauf, 1992), including sociocultural historical contexts (Gabaccia, 2002), and how such groups have been treated (Aarim-Heriot, 2003). Disciplines such as anthropology, sociology, political science, and history are forerunners of the discourse on immigration and have been studying this phenomenon for decades. In contrast, the field of psychology appears to lag behind even though there is a steady increase in the study of psychological aspects of migration and its impact on mental health and well-being. Based on an analysis of nearly 2,000 publications between 1990 and 1998, Schmitz (2003) identified a number of central themes, of which acculturation, identity, stress, and adjustment were among the most addressed in the literature.

The purpose of this chapter is to provide an overview of psychosocial issues associated with migration including the impact it has on the individual and family. First, we begin with a brief overview of the current immigrant population and define basic terms and concepts that help provide a framework. Second, we discuss acculturation as one of the central themes, and, within this context, we describe changes that may occur in a variety of domains such as social class, gender roles, identity, and familial relationships. We also outline how difficulties with the adjustment process may lead to stress and psychological problems. In addition, access to mental health services continues to be a pervasive problem for the recent immigrant. Therefore, we present a variety of factors that limit access to mental health care. Finally, examples of current psychotherapeutic treatment approaches are described, including recommendations for practice.

Terms

We begin with definitions of basic terms associated with the migration phenomena. The term *migration* refers to the "act or process by which people, especially as a group, move from one location (city, country, region) to another" (Marsella & Ring, 2003, p. 11). *Immigration* is often defined as the process of entering a new country of which one is not a native. An *immigrant* is an individual who comes to this country with the intent of staying here. Sometimes the terms *alien* and immigrant are used interchangeably; however, from a legal standpoint they are not the same. Specifically, an individual entering the United States with intentions to stay is first considered an alien who then becomes an immigrant. Also, there are various labels ascribed to the "alien" term. For instance, an individual who is in the United States on a student or temporary work visa is called a *nonimmigrant alien* or a *legal alien*. Furthermore, a person who comes to this country illegally is referred to as an *undocumented alien* (USCIS, 2007). The challenge is deciding what term to use. Some are vehemently opposed to using the term "alien" because of its pejorative connotation. Therefore, our preference is to use the term legal and undocumented immigrant. A *refugee* refers to a person who has left, and unable or is unwilling to return to his/her country because of the fear or threat of persecution which is motivated by racial, political, and religious conflicts (USCIS, 2007). In presenting the various issues, topics, and themes in this chapter, we refer to the immigrant population as encompassing all recent arrivals to this country regardless of their undocumented, refugee, or legal status.

Who Are the Immigrants Today?

As stated earlier, the immigrant population continues to rise. In fact, the United States witnessed an unprecedented growth between 2000 and 2005, now considered the largest in its history (Camarota, 2005). By far the largest group is of Hispanic/Latino heritage. For example, of the approximately 8 million arrivals between 2000 and 2005, more than half came from Spanish-speaking countries. Immigrants from Mexico are the largest group, with 2.8 million arriving within this 5-year time period alone. Also, Caramota (2005) noted that the Latin American and Caribbean countries literally "dominate the list of immigrant-sending countries, accounting for almost half of the top 25 countries" (p. 9). These countries are: Mexico, El Salvador, Cuba, Dominican Republic, Guatemala, Colombia, Honduras, Ecuador, and Peru.

The second largest group of immigrants comes from East and South Asia, accounting for approximately 18% of the total population. Specifically, the countries are China, Hong Kong, Taiwan, India, and the Philippines. Smaller but significant numbers come from Vietnam, Korea, and Japan. Based on 2000 census data, significant numbers of West Indian and African immigrants came to the United States from Jamaica, Guyana, Trinidad, Nigeria, and Egypt (Tormala & Deaux, 2006). In 2005 the top 10 countries of origin for refugee arrivals in the United States through the resettlement program were Somalia, Laos, Cuba, Russia, Liberia, Ukraine, Sudan, Vietnam, Iran, and Ethiopia, totaling approximately 53,800 (Batalova, 2006). The point to be made here is that immigrants from these countries of origin are diverse in terms of their ethnic/cultural composition, geographic location, and sociopolitical history.

Caramota (2005)[1] outlined a number of socioeconomic characteristics that help to further our understanding of the immigrant population, as a whole, as well as the diversity within the group.

1. Of those individuals who are in the workforce, nearly 31% of all immigrants had less than a high school education compared to nearly 9% of U.S.-born citizens. Of the immigrants who arrived between 2000 and 2005, 34% had less than a high school education. Approximately 25% of all immigrants, including those who arrived within the last 5 years, had a high school diploma compared to 32% of U.S. citizens. Interestingly, the gap is much smaller at the higher levels of education. Specifically, the percentage of both immigrants, including the more recent arrivals, and U.S.-born citizens with bachelor's, graduate, and professional degrees is strikingly similar (approximately 27% and 29%, respectively).
2. The overall income level is lower than the U.S.-born citizen. In 2005 the average household income for immigrants was $56,289 for a family of roughly 3.1 compared to $61,098 for U.S.-born citizens, whose family size is on average 2.5.
3. Immigrants have very little impact on the age structure of U.S. society. In fact, the average age of an immigrant in 2005 was approximately 39 years compared to 35 years for a U.S.-born citizen. However, the average age of those who arrived within the last 5 years is 28.
4. In terms of occupational distribution the report clearly shows that significant numbers of U.S.-born citizens have jobs that are

also held by large numbers of immigrants. Of those occupations shared with U.S.-born citizens that have the highest concentration of immigrants, 43% are in farming, fishing, and forestry; 26% in construction and extraction; 34% in building, cleaning, and maintenance; 24% in food preparation; and 22% in production. It is not the case that immigrants take the jobs that U.S.-born citizens do not want, because the data show that these occupations and all others are predominantly held by U.S.-born citizens. If immigrants were in fact taking over the jobs that no one else wants, they would be overrepresented in one or more of these occupations.

5. Among the various immigrant groups, Russians, Koreans, and Iranians have the highest percentages of self-employment income (28%, 22%, and 20%, respectively), significantly higher than U.S.-born citizens (13%) and most of the groups from Latin American countries (ranging from 4% to 17%).
6. Poverty remains relatively high among the immigrant population. Of the 37 million people living in poverty, about 23% are immigrants and their U.S.-born children. More striking is that 42% of all immigrants compared to 29% of U.S.-born citizens live in and are near poverty, of which the highest percentages (more than 50%) come from Spanish-speaking countries—primarily Mexico, Dominican Republic, Guatemala, and Honduras. These percentages range from 62% to 55%.
7. Nearly 47% of immigrants and their U.S.-born children are either uninsured or receive Medicaid, compared to 25% of U.S.-born citizens and their children.
8. Welfare use is higher among immigrants, as a whole (28%), compared to the U.S.-born population (18%); however, these rates vary across countries of origin. For example, those who come from Mexico and the Dominican Republic have higher welfare use rates (57% and 43%, respectively) than any other immigrant group.

In addition to these data described here, Hernandez, Denton, and Macartney (2007) report that children of recent immigrants account for 20% of all children in the United States. Not surprising, about 40% of these children are from Mexico.

Immigration Laws

The United States has a long history of immigration laws and policies that dates back to the 18th century, involving prohibitions to citizenship based on race such as the Naturalization Act of 1790, which was limited to Western European Whites. Likewise, the national origin quota system established in the late 19th century restricted entry of certain immigrant groups, such as the Chinese Exclusion Act of 1882. It is not our intent to review this history; however, basic knowledge about past and current laws and the public's response to immigration reform is offered.

The Immigration and Nationality Act of 1924 was established to restrict entry to the United States by creating a quota system. Preference was given to individuals from northern and western Europe, while immigration was restricted for southern and eastern European countries. Moreover, immigration was still banned from Asia. This law was in place for nearly three decades before changes were made. As with the Act of 1924, the Immigration and Nationality Act of 1952 was established to control the number as well as the type of immigrant. However, different from the previous act, relatives of U.S.-born citizens and refugees were allowed entry, and a quota was set per year for all other immigrants. Because of the selective nature of the act, the government was allowed to deport individuals who either engaged in unlawful behavior or had political ideologies or practices that were unacceptable to the United States (Phelan & Gillespie, 2007).

Heavily influenced by the Civil Rights Movement of the 1960s, the act was amended. The Immigration and Nationality Act of 1965 eradicated the national quota system that had been in place since 1924, allowing preference to those seeking jobs that had a shortage of workers, and those wanting to reunite with family (Pedraza, 2006). This act was again modified in 1990 to allow more immigrants to enter, with preference given to immigrants seeking jobs and family reunification. In addition, the Immigration Reform and Control Act of 1986 granted amnesty to undocumented persons who had been in this country before 1982. However, this act also imposed severe penalties to employers who knowingly hire illegal immigrants.

Undeniably, the events of September 11, 2001, served as the catalyst for the current debate on immigration. The passing of the bill the Border Protection, Antiterrorism and Illegal Immigration Control Act of 2005 (H.R. 4437), is a clear example of efforts to control immigration. Among the many provisions outlined in the bill, the most controversial aspects center on increasing U.S./Mexico border patrol, raising the penalties for illegal immigration, and its harsh treatment of asylum seekers or refugees. The bill is considered by many as one of the most unjustly harsh anti-immigration bills in nearly a century, targeting undocumented individuals, including the violation of basic human rights and due process for those seeking asylum. By contrast, others believe that it is necessary to establish laws and policies such as this bill in order to regulate their entry and ensure that immigrants are successful in the host country (Esses, Dovidio, Jackson, & Armstrong,

2001). Nonetheless, it has fueled the debate on immigration, culminating in nationwide protests where millions of people have staged demonstrations against the bill (e.g., the May 1, 2006, Great American Boycott).

Dynamics of Migration

The forces that contribute to migration vary, are complex, and may be negative, positive, or both. As stated earlier, driving forces such as severe economic and/or discordant political conditions in the countries of origin, as well as escape from persecution and physical harm, are considered among the main reasons for migration. Others choose to migrate not because they are being forced out, but because they simply want a better life for themselves and their families, which is motivated by economic incentives. They may want to further their education, seek business opportunities, or obtain higher-paying jobs. Knowing the motives provides an important context for understanding the adaptation process. For example, de las Fuentes and Vasquez (1999) acknowledged that individuals who are forced to leave because of threats to physical well-being may be more distressed on the outset than those who come for economic or educational gains. More important, individuals who arrive as political refugees, such as the Vietnamese in the 1970s, and Africans from Ethiopia between 1981 and 1995, may be especially vulnerable to distress and psychological problems because many of them escaped horrifying conditions.

Along this line of reasoning, Castex (1997) articulated a variety of ways immigrants arrive in this country. For example, a person may come to the United States first, to look for employment and housing, then the immediate family comes later. Depending on the situation in the country of origin and regulations established by the government, others arrive as a family unit (including grandparents). Their journey may be very difficult, as is the case for many refugees who are detained in camps for months. Castex argued that they may be living in a "state of almost suspended animation awaiting approval to immigrate" (1997, p. 53). Quite often, family members are separated and many of their personal belongings are left behind in their home country. Many of these processes also apply to undocumented immigrants; however, unlike those who come legally, they often live in a state of fear of being deported.

In addition, the migration experience can be thought of as a stage process involving a variety of factors and conditions that influences the way individuals and families respond and adapt to the new environment in the host country. For example, Zuñiga (1992) described the process as consisting of five dynamic stages: (1) the *preparatory stage* involves the initial decision to leave the country of origin, and the individual and/or the family's preparation for departure. Was it planned or sudden? Did the individual have time to say good-bye to family and loved ones?; (2) the actual *act of migration* involves the quality of the experience. Was it difficult? Did the individual and/or family experience negative or positive events during the process?; (3) during the post-arrival period there might be a *period of overcompensation,* which involves a dramatic shift toward holding on to traditions as practiced in the home country as a way to maintain a sense of stability; (4) there is a *period of decompensation* in which conflicts arise within the family. The root of these conflicts may be related to challenges to traditional gender roles, as well as the stress associated with the demands of securing employment and learning to navigate the new environment; and (5) a *transgenerational impact* on the family occurs as the children begin to adapt to the new country. It is often the case that the younger generation adopts new ways of thinking and behaving that are representative of the dominant culture. In particular, new views on dating, friendships, dressing, and curfew may be vastly different from the parents' values. These changes in values are also tied to the rapid acquisition of the English language among the youth. Consequently, these differences impact family dynamics such as the communication patterns and relationships between and among family members.

PSYCHOSOCIAL ISSUES

It is well recognized that the field of psychology has given considerable attention to the role of culture in how people behave, think, feel, and interpret their environments; however, very little research exists on the psychological study of immigrants. In particular, scholars are beginning to conceptualize new theoretical frameworks that help us to better understand the migration experience, such as the adaptation processes involved in adjusting to a new environment, as well as its impact on psychological well-being (e.g., Akhtar, 1999; Berry, 2001; Mahalingam, 2006). Undoubtedly, immigrants can experience a great deal of stress and strain as they adapt and settle into a new country, which can result in psychological problems.

Acculturation and Stress

The psychological literature on immigrants, albeit scant, tends to focus on the consequences of the acculturation or adaptation process. This process has significant psychosocial impact on the individual who may undergo dramatic changes in gender role expectations, ethnic/racial identity, and familial relationships, for example. To add to the complexity the individual and family's status, whether legal, undocumented, or refugee; age; socioeconomic background; as well as the availability of economic resources and support networks will also affect the type and quality of the adjustment process (Halperin, 2004). Furthermore, these changes become even more challenging when coupled with barriers such as English language proficiency, underemployment, and anti-immigration attitudes (e.g., Chandler & Tsai, 2001; Esses et al., 2001; Pettigrew, 2006).

Acculturation is a concept widely studied in psychology to explain how individuals undergo change. Gerardo Marín (1992) defined it as a:

> process of attitudinal and behavioral change undergone . . . by individuals who reside in multicultural societies (e.g., the United States, Israel, Canada, and Spain), or come into contact with a new culture due to colonization, invasion, or other political changes. (p. 236)

John W. Berry, a pioneer in the study of acculturation, describes it is a process in which two or more cultural groups come into contact, resulting in "mutual" change (Berry, 2001, p. 616). In other words, both groups are affected by the contact. However, as Berry noted, one group will dominate. In addition, acculturation is thought to occur at both the group level, in which the cultural group undergoes change as a whole, and at the individual level. We focus on the individual psychological level as it relates to the immigrant's experience.

Berry (1997, 2001) provided a conceptual framework that helps us to understand how individuals respond to the acculturation experience. This framework consists of four attitudinal strategies that involve interaction and contact with other people: (1) *assimilation* in which individuals give up their cultural heritage and completely immerse themselves in the new culture; (2) *separation* in which individuals hold on to their cultural traditions and practices, and do not wish to engage with people from the larger society; (3) *integration* whereby individuals keep cultural traditions and practices while participating in the larger society; and (4) *marginalizaton* in which individuals either by their own volition or lack of opportunity do not have interest in interacting with others from the larger society. In this case individuals can experience isolation due to discrimination. More importantly, Berry (2001) emphasized that the degree to which individuals fully integrate will depend on the host society's perceptions of and willingness to accept them. For example, in a study examining attitudes toward Black and Asian immigrants, Esses et al. (2001) found that individuals who believed they were competing with an immigrant group for resources harbor negative attitudes toward them. More important, they found that the more visible the immigrant group the greater the threat of competition.

Immigrants will undergo the acculturation process in different ways depending on a complex set of circumstances, such as how the host country perceives them (e.g., attitudes toward immigrant groups), and motivational forces, such as the desire to reunite with family already in this country or escape from political and economic oppression. Their ability to adjust will also depend on the availability of personal (e.g., coping strategies, economic) and social (e.g., community support) resources once they arrive. Moreover, in a review of the literature on leisure activities among different ethnic and cultural immigrant groups, Stodolska and Yi (2003) reported that acculturation is strongly linked to type of recreational activities desired. For instance, they found that the least acculturated Mexican Americans were more likely to spend their leisure time with immediate and extended family, whereas the more acculturated Mexican Americans tended to participate in leisure activity patterns similar to Anglo-Americans.

The move to a new country is considered a significant stressor because it essentially involves uprooting individuals and families. Stress is defined by Berry, Kim, Minde, and Mok (1987) as a "generalized physiological and psychological state . . . brought about by the experience of stressors in the environment, and which requires some reduction . . . through a process of coping until satisfactory adaptation to the new situation is achieved" (p. 492). Moreover, the stress can range from mild with minimal effects to so severe that it leads to serious psychological trauma (e.g., Roysircar, 2003; Steel et al., 2006). In addition, *acculturative stress* can occur when there is a lack of culture-specific activities and social events that were routinely attended in the country of origin, loss of support network, and longing to be back in the homeland with family and friends (Shiraev & Levy, 2004).

Gender, Family, and Postmigration

Espín (1999, 2006) argues that men and women differentially experience the postmigration process of change and adaptation. For example, girls and women are expected to maintain cultural traditions and practices while the men are allowed to develop new ways of thinking and behaving. Moreover, women who come from a patriarchal family structure may challenge traditional gender roles as they acculturate, which may cause greater stress compared to men.

Even second-generation women, that is, women born and raised in the United States whose parents migrated to this country, undergo culture-specific gender role socialization experiences. For example, Mahalingam and Haritatos (2006) extensively interviewed seven second-generation Indian college-age women on how they were raised by their parents. Specifically, these young women reported that their parents instilled the traditional gender role expectation of maintaining family honor and respect by being the "good daughter/woman" (p. 265). According to the authors, this expectation comes from the idealized Hindu cultural gender role of *pativirda*—dedicated wife who is virtuous and self-sacrificing. Although these Indian immigrant parents endorsed high achievement for their daughters, which is considered to be more of an American value (e.g., attending college), they still wanted their daughters to maintain this cultural ideal.

Studies by Dion and Dion (1993, 1996, 2001) have confirmed the existence of gender differences in the socialization processes in that daughters of immigrants are pressured into maintaining cultural traditions and ideals and are closely supervised when it comes to dating and selecting partners for marriage. For instance, Inman, Howard, Beaumont, and Walker (2007) found that Asian Indian mothers continued to place limits on dating for their daughters and not sons. Furthermore, the traditional values and practices of how young girls should be raised and behave may be at odds with the dominant cultural values of the new country, thus creating conflict between parents and daughters (e.g., de las Fuentes & Vasquez, 1999).

Marital problems can also arise because of such struggles. For example, Nah (1993) reported greater marital problems among Korean immigrants because the patriarchal family structure was threatened as women's roles changed. Similarly, Yakushko and Chronister (2005) noted that women may experience increased domestic violence after their arrival, which could be related to the conflicts that surface within the household. By contrast, immigrant women may find a sense of freedom and empowerment as they challenge traditional roles associated with their sexuality and gender including heterosexual identity (Espín 1999).

Citing a major study by Noh, Wu, Speechly, and Kasper (1992) on Koreans who migrated to Canada, Dion and Dion (2001) pointed out that women who were employed had higher rates of depression than the men, attributing it to the stress associated with higher demands placed on them. In particular, these women not only worked long hours, but were responsible for child rearing and all household functions. Also, they speculated that the stress experienced by these women may be in part a result of " . . . the process of renegotiating family, specifically, spousal roles, as a result of changed circumstances associated with immigration" (p. 514).

Scholars such as Hérnandez and McGoldrick (1999) and Hong and Ham (1992) argue that migration has such a profound impact on people's lives that it needs to be considered in existing family life-cycle models, and ideally as a new life-cycle stage for all immigrant families. Migration can disrupt the family's natural developmental process and structure. This is often the case when families are separated for an extended period of time. It is not uncommon for fathers to migrate first, leaving their wives to provide for and take care of children under very difficult economic conditions in their homeland. Month or years can go by before the family is reunited, and by then the children have undergone developmental changes of their own. Consequently, the reunification of the family after a long separation can be stressful since the dynamics within the family are bound to change as new and familiar roles are being renegotiated, children and spouse/partner are undergoing adaptation to the new country, and family responsibilities increase (e.g., Hong & Ham, 1992).

Social Class, Gender, and Postmigration

Social class plays a major role in the acculturation process. More precisely, the immigrant's level of education and qualifications, occupation and skills, as well as the degree of wealth and economic resources will significantly affect the degree to which he or she is successful in negotiating new roles and navigating the new social system. Drawing from clinical work with immigrant couples, Inclán (2003) highlighted that those in the highest class structure with awareness of their social standing may frame and interpret their experiences in unique ways:

> Bourgeois immigrants with a class consciousness . . . accept the dual-earner family structure, understand the need for gender roles change, place less distance between themselves and their poor and working-class countrymen, and come with an interest in remaining different from the American mainstream. They affirm their ethnic identity and uphold the critique of a class-stratified system. (p. 335)

In general, a more egalitarian relationship exists between men and women, and when conflicts arise they tend to resolve them as a couple. By contrast, Inclán's discussion of immigrant couples who are considered upper to middle class (i.e., small- or medium-level businesspeople) respond in ways that are different from the bourgeois class. Specifically, traditional gender roles are emphasized, men remain the sole providers of the family, women are expected to maintain cultural traditions, and women's attempts to renegotiate their roles are met with resistance. With respect to the poor immigrant, Inclán argued that their primary objective is to work, earn money, and provide for their families. The poor immigrant is not concerned with preserving a social class status as might the middle class and bourgeois, but rather aspires to gain social status by working hard to improve his/her economic conditions. Consistent with the perspectives outlined in the previous section, the couple might struggle with many demands and they may not be prepared to deal with the changes in gender roles. Inclán (2003) pointed this out when he stated that "Contradictions between economic and personal adaptation needs, between the values of their culture of origin and those of the new culture, and between old and new gender ideologies are always present and mature at different points along the adaptation time line" (p. 338).

Ethnic/Racial Identity and Postmigration

The postmigration experience is likely to have a profound impact on identity. In the context of the acculturation process scholars have examined how individuals undergo changes in their identity. For instance, ethnic identity among Asian, Black, and Hispanics/Latino adolescents (e.g., Phinney, 1989; Phinney & Chavira, 1992), and gender differences among young adults primarily of Asian backgrounds (e.g., Chinese, Indian, Sri Lankan, Filipino, Korean, Laotian, Vietnamese) (Dion & Dion, 2004) have been explored.

Much of the research on ethnic identity development has focused on adolescents and young adults because this is a time when individuals experience major transitions in their lives related to physical and emotional development. These transitions are compounded by the acculturation process, which involves negotiating traditional values and beliefs instilled by their parents, and the values and beliefs endorsed by the dominant culture. Dion (2006) argued that for immigrant adolescents, in particular, the family plays a vital role in their identity formation, and that its development involves culture-specific beliefs and values. For instance, in many Asian and Hispanic/Latino cultures parents value close family relationships that promote interdependence among its members. The adolescent is expected to develop in an environment that fosters this interconnectedness. In contrast, the U.S. culture values the development of autonomy and independence in youth. However, as Dion noted, the developmental stage of the so-called emerging adulthood, described as a time in which young adults become autonomous and independent in life's tasks such as pursuing career goals and building a relationship with someone, simply does not always fit with many cultural group expectations. Many cultures that endorse a collectivistic orientation expect their adult children to not only remain connected with their parents and siblings, but also decisions about major life transitions are made involving immediate and sometimes extended family members. This is evidenced in the cultural value of *familismo* in Latino culture in which there is a strong sense of obligation to family (e.g., Santiago-Rivera, Arredondo, & Gallardo-Cooper, 2002), and filial piety in Asian culture where the son is expected to take care of the parents once they reach old age (e.g., Hong & Ham, 2001).

With respect to adolescent ethnic identity development, Jean Phinney's pioneering work has provided invaluable insight into its relationship to factors such as self-esteem, psychological well-being, and acculturation (e.g., Phinney, 1990; Phinney, Cantu, & Kurtz, 1997; Phinney, Horenczyk, Liebkind, & Vedder, 2001). Specifically, Phinney and colleagues have consistently shown that the stronger the ethnic identity, the greater the psychological well-being. This is particularly the case as adolescents acculturate. Moreover, adolescents who have what Phinney calls an *integrated identity,* that is, believing that one belongs to an ethnic group and also belongs to the larger society, have a higher sense of well-being (e.g., Phinney et al., 2001).

A similar concept known as *transnationalism,* defined as the process by which immigrants "forge and sustain multi-stranded social relations that link together their societies of origin and settlement" (Pedraza, 2006, p. 45), promotes the notion that immigrants do not completely assimilate into the new society, but rather become *bicultural,* adopting new ways of being while retaining aspects of their culture of origin. A transnationalistic orientation evokes a sense of connection with the homeland and manifests itself in a variety of ways such as sending money home, and frequently calling, and traveling to visit family and friends. Of course, this depends on the affordability and ability to travel. Murphy (2006) also noted that establishing social networks is an important feature of transnationalism, clearly evident in the creation of many ethnic enclaves in the United States. In essence, these ethnic communities serve to buffer the negative consequences of stress associated with the acculturation process.

The discourse on immigration also involves race. How immigrants are perceived and subsequently treated will affect their ability to adapt and achieve their desired goals. Tormala and Deaux (2006) made this point in describing the experiences of Blacks from the West Indies/Caribbean and Africa in the United States. Based on empirically supported research findings, they concluded that Black immigrants are perceived more favorably than U.S.-born Africans (i.e., African Americans), and fare better in educational attainment, labor force participation, and employment compared to African Americans. Equally important, they are more likely to have contact and interact with others outside of their own cultural group during the early stages of the adaptation process; however, similar to African Americans they are just as likely to experience racial prejudice as they acculturate. Because of skin color, Black immigrants are often subjected to the same insidious negative stereotypes ascribed to African Americans. Subsequently, they are forced to renegotiate their identities, which can cause confusion, anxiety, and disillusionment (Tormala & Deaux, 2006).

Children, Parenting, and Postmigration

Children of immigrant parents can experience stress during the postmigration process. They, too, experience loss such as missing friends left behind, familiar surroundings, and personal belongings. Immigrant children also face challenges that are sometimes overlooked by parents because they are overwhelmed with their own adjustment processes. Children need to adjust to a new school environment, which often involves learning English, making new friends, and negotiating new roles. Castex (1997) argued that children of recent immigrants almost instantly become responsible for serving as the translator and interpreter for the parents, who may have more difficulty learning the English language. She also noted that the age at which children migrate will make a difference in their ability to learn English, such that younger child are more likely to learn the language without an accent. Consequently, children are able to mainstream and navigate the system a lot faster than their parents. Unfortunately, however, children are often placed in a precarious situation, as exemplified in this statement:

> . . . a young child may accompany a parent to the hospital and serve as the interpreter, even though the child may be unfamiliar with medical terms in English and may be worried about the condition of the parent. The child may also be placed in a particularly difficult position if he or she is the subject of the conversation that is taking place. (Castex, 1997, p. 56)

Children also may experience developmental delays during the adaptation process. This is especially the case for children dealing with trauma associated with exposure to violence, malnutrition, and abuse encountered in their home country or during their journey to the new country; de las Fuentes and Vasquez (1999) described numerous studies on trauma, pointing out that significant numbers of Southeast Asian (e.g., Cambodian and Vietnamese) and Central American (e.g., Salvadoran) refugee children who were separated from immediate family while escaping persecution from their war-torn countries exhibited symptoms of posttraumatic stress and had difficulty adapting. One of the studies cited by de las Fuentes and Vasquez is a comparative study by McCloskey, Southwick, Fernández-Esquer, and Locke (1995) on immigrant Latino children who experienced either political or domestic violence. The results of their study showed that these children, especially those who had lost their fathers due to political violence, had higher posttraumatic stress disorder (PTSD) symptoms compared to children who were not exposed to violence. Interestingly, they also found that mothers played a major role in buffering the negative effects of exposure to violence by maintaining a strong bond with their children.

The literature suggests that many cultural groups with a patriarchal family structure have common features such as authoritarian parenting styles, strong familial bonds, interdependence among immediate and extended family members, and, as stated earlier, traditional role expectations for sons and daughters (e.g., Dion, 2006; Hong & Ham,1992; Santiago-Rivera et al., 2002). The patriarchal family structure is often threatened during postmigration as individuals within a family try to adapt to a new cultural environment that has different child-rearing practices. This is clearly evident in the parents' struggle to maintain traditions through their parenting styles and, yet, acclimate to new ways of raising children. Inman et al. (2007) found this to be the case among first-generation Asian Indian immigrant parents who needed to incorporate a more "democratic style of parenting," which included mother and father sharing in the responsibility for the care of the children, while instilling traditions such as marrying within the culture and maintaining close family ties.

Personality and Migration

A new area of research on migration focuses on identifying specific characteristics of the immigrant population that differentiates those who want to migrate from those who choose to remain in their homeland. Specifically, Boneva and Frieze (2001) studied this phenomenon in what they call the "migrant personality," arguing that individuals who choose to migrate may possess a specific constellation of characteristics (e.g., predispositions of achievement, power, and affiliation motivation; values of family and work centrality). Interestingly, they found that individuals with high achievement and power motivation, high orientation toward work, and low affiliation motive and low value placed on family have a higher desire to migrate. The implications are far reaching because these predispositions can help counselors not only predict the likelihood of a successful transition, but also develop interventions to aid those who have difficulty adjusting. Understandably, they acknowledge that their model may not apply to refugees because the motives for leaving their homelands are different (e.g., forced out due to threats of harm); however, these same characteristics could be studied when examining the refugee's decision to stay or return to his or her country of origin.

Unfortunately, there is little known about the rates of psychological disorders such as major depression and posttraumatic stress among recent immigrants, especially refugees. However, Martens (2007) has begun to address this need by reporting on a number of studies that detail prevalence rates of depression among different immigrant and refugee groups in the United States, Canada, Netherlands, England, Spain, Israel, and Australia, and examines a diverse sample who come from many countries, such as China, Korea, Cambodia, Mexico, Turkey, Somalia, and Bosnia.[2] He found that not all of these groups have the same rates of depression, nor do they all have higher rates compared to other groups. More important, different factors associated with depression have been investigated, making it difficult to develop interventions that are generalizable across immigrant groups. For example, among the Chinese elderly, poor general physical health, low income, and barriers to health care access have been associated with higher rates of depression. Likewise, poor health, lower levels of acculturation, and separation from children have been related to depression among Mexican immigrants.

ACCESS TO MENTAL HEALTH SERVICES

As previously discussed, immigrants have a number of stressful processes and adjustments to manage. In addition, there are a number of barriers that stand in the way of accessing the services they need.

Differing Conceptualizations of Mental Health Services

From the outset, the immigrant's understandings of mental illness as well as the lack of familiarity with mental health services as they exist in the United States are considered barriers. For instance, Southeast Asian refugees, among others, may equate mental health services only with severe pathology requiring hospitalization (Gong-Guy, Cravens, & Patterson, 1991). The stigma associated with mental health treatment is related to a number of factors. Among them is the belief that mental illness is hereditary and therefore may interfere with future attractiveness of family members to marriage suitors. An immigrant may believe that there is a correlation between mental illness and past wrongdoings, which is perceived as damaging the reputation of the family. Moreover, there may be a fear that identifying mental health issues will lead to deportation or other difficulties in the migration process (Gong-Guy et al., 1991).

Transportation to Mental Health Facilities

Access to mental health facilities is often related to geographic location. Yu (1997) cogently articulated how geographic barriers to mental health facilities develop for this population. Specifically, economic constraints limit the residential choices of newcomers, therefore, they are more likely to live in racially and ethnically similar communities where they feel comfortable, accepted, and find stable employment. These communities are typically low income and are unlikely to be the locations of choice for service providers. Thus, transportation becomes an issue because the mental health treatment centers are located in areas where "mainstream Americans work or live" (Yu, 1997, p. 173).

Learning to drive and obtaining a driver's license in a new country is difficult in and of itself, but affording a car and auto insurance may be an unobtainable goal. Obtaining a driver's license may be a more difficult goal for an immigrant who is undocumented. Consequently, many immigrants will rely on public transportation or friends and family for rides. This presents a significant challenge when making counseling appointments because the individual not only needs to take time off from work but must also coordinate transportation needs.

Many recent immigrants may not be familiar with the public transportation system. A counselor at a community clinic specializing in serving immigrants once shared that she dedicated an entire session to helping her client learn to ride the bus from her apartment to the clinic and back. The counselor met the client at her home and accompanied her on the bus ride (G. Chen, personal communication, September 2004). This clearly demonstrates a good understanding of the practical barriers that must be addressed early in order to increase the likelihood of seeking and staying in treatment.

Lack of Insurance

As mentioned earlier in this chapter, many immigrants are uninsured or underinsured (Yu, 1997). Specifically, between 42% and 51% of noncitizens lack health insurance compared to 15% of native citizens of the United States (Alker & Urrutia, 2004). Another important difference is that about two-thirds of U.S citizens obtain their health insurance coverage through their employers. This is only true for about a third of noncitizens; keeping in mind that many immigrants work in low-paying jobs, labor and trade occupations, or in small companies that may not offer insurance (Alker & Urrutia, 2004). Medicaid and the State Children's Health Insurance Program (SCHIP) fill in the gap in employer-sponsored insurance for some low-income immigrants. However, this coverage has been severely limited by the 1996 Personal Responsibility and Work Opportunity Reconciliation Act (PRWORA).[3]

Foreign-born children under the age of 18 are uninsured at the rate of about 37%, which is three times higher than the rates for U.S. citizen children (American Psychological Association, 2007). SCHIP and Medicaid continue to be important sources of coverage for U.S.-born children of immigrants and immigrants who have been in the United States for longer than 5 years. Some states have also stepped in to provide coverage to fill the gap created by the expiration of PRWORA. However, at times immigrants are reluctant to step forward and take advantage of either federal or state programs, fearing that they will be considered a "public charge," which can lead to citizenship eligibility problems and possibly deportation (Alker & Urrutia, 2004; Ku & Matani, 2001).

Even if an immigrant client has health insurance, he or she may be underinsured or inadequately insured. It is well recognized that comprehensive health plans thin out when it comes to behavioral health care. Having federal- or state-sponsored insurance, versus private insurance that is employer-sponsored, may mean having less choice in where one may receive counseling, although some therapists in private practice do accept Medicaid. If an immigrant has no insurance coverage, community clinics or practitioners who do sliding scale or pro bono work may be options. Unfortunately, community clinics often have waiting lists and therapists in private practice usually take a very limited number of low-paying clients.

Lack of Linguistically Competent Service Providers[4]

We have discussed some of the barriers that may interfere with immigrant clients' access to therapy, such as lack of insurance and transportation issues. However, for those who actually make contact with a service provider there are a number of potential obstacles to overcome. Perhaps one of the most common barriers to obtaining counseling services is language.

As mentioned earlier, individuals of Hispanic/Latino descent make up the largest group of immigrants (Camarota, 2005). A significant number of these immigrants are primarily Spanish monolingual or have very limited English language proficiency. Unfortunately, although the number of predominantly Spanish-speaking immigrants continues to increase, the number of service providers who are able to speak Spanish remains fairly low (U.S. Department of Health and Human Services, 1999).

When Spanish-speaking Latino clients have the opportunity to receive treatment from a Spanish-speaking therapist, the language itself can be utilized in therapeutic ways. For example, an immigrant client may wish to use the second language when describing a recent trauma, as a way to give herself/himself some distance from the event, so she/he is able to give the therapist the basic facts about what occurred. However, later, if the client wants to deal with and integrate the trauma, the native language may be used so that the client can better access the emotions that accompanied the event (Santiago-Rivera & Altarriba, 2002). Utilizing language in this way is not possible without a bilingual service provider.

The complexity of the language issue is even more pronounced for Asian Americans and Pacific Islanders because the majority were born outside of the United States, speak over 100 languages and dialects, and approximately 35% live in households where those over the age of 13 have limited English proficiency. However, there are only about 70 Asian American/Pacific Islander mental health providers for every 100,000 individuals from this group, compared with 173 per 100,000 White individuals (U.S. Department of Health and Human Services, 1999). In situations where the provider does not speak the client's native language, an interpreter will be necessary.

Problems With Interpreters

Working with clients through interpreters presents many challenges. For instance, when trained interpreters are not available, children, other relatives, and people without a background in counseling are often utilized. Although these individuals may be able to translate effectively for basic information exchange, it is unlikely that this arrangement will be sufficient for the purposes of counseling. When using children as interpreters, they are not cognitively at the same level as an adult; therefore, the information being filtered back and forth between the provider and the client may lack sufficient detail and/or may be inaccurate.

For many cultures, the hierarchy between parent and child is much stricter than in mainstream U.S. culture. A parent may feel greatly disempowered or shamed by having to send personal information through his or her child. The use of other relatives, such as brothers and sisters or aunts and uncles, can also be problematic in that they may have strong opinions about the care and treatment of their loved one and may have certain biases about what should be the outcome. As such, the information exchange between counselor and interpreter may be distorted. Although utilizing an interpreter who *is not related* to the client may yield better results, being untrained still presents other difficulties.

Untrained interpreters may not convey questions from the counselor in the manner intended. For example, the counselor may ask, "How have you been sleeping?" but the interpreter asks, "Have you been sleeping?" The client responds "yes" instead of describing the quality of his or her sleep. As a result, misdiagnosis may occur, either in the direction of over- or underdiagnosis (Ruiz, 2002). In this case, the doctor may miss persistent insomnia or, alternatively, hypersomnia if she or he does not persist with follow-up questions, or if the interpreter continues to miss the details of the inquiry. Misdiagnosis is not the only negative result that may occur. A loss of trust and rapport can be experienced by the client, resulting in a likelihood that the client will not return for further services. The mental health provider may also become frustrated as a result of getting less than adequate information, which may lead to less empathy for and patience with the client.

Using a trained interpreter also has its challenges. One of the most common issues centers on the three-way dynamic in the session. For example, *transference,* the feelings projected on the counselor from the client, and *countertransference,* any emotional reactions the counselor has to the client, may occur in the counseling process (Corey, 2004). Not only are these dynamics operating between the client and counselor, but they may also operate between the client and the interpreter, and the counselor and the interpreter. A further complication is that there may be interpreters who are linguistically capable and are trained in translation for therapy, but who do not have the social skills or the temperament for it (E. Sylvester, personal communication, March 23, 2007).

All this being said, sometimes an interpreter is simply necessary. With the wide variety of countries from which immigrants come, it is doubtful that a linguistic match between counselor and client will always be found. Therefore, it is recommended to use interpreters, taking into account the issues addressed. Moreover, it may be helpful to discuss expectations with both the interpreter and the client about the counseling process. Also, in situations where an interpreter is not available, it is appropriate to proceed with some type of helping relationship, especially if there is no better alternative. In situations like this, it is recommended that counselors take a more directive role and work with clients in a concrete fashion and utilize community resources.

Misdiagnosis and Lack of Expertise in Cross-Cultural Conceptualization of Illness

When immigrants access the mental health care system, cultural differences and language barriers may lead to misdiagnosis. This occurs most frequently between non-English-speaking immigrants and English-speaking clinicians. With respect to language differences, misunderstandings may occur concerning the presence of symptoms and the frequency, duration, and severity of those symptoms. This may lead to misdiagnosis (conceptualizing the illness incorrectly), underdiagnosis (not recognizing the true severity of the illness), or, as has been reported in the literature concerning Latinos, "an exaggerated perception of psychopathology" (Ruiz, 2002, p. 86).

The tendency for some immigrant clients to explain psychiatric conditions as being caused by supernatural phenomena (Ruiz, 2002) and the hallucinations and dissociations experienced by many refugees suffering from PTSD (Gong-Guy et al., 1991) may be misinterpreted as evidence of schizophrenia or some other psychotic state. This may occur, in the latter example, even when the mental health provider has documentation of the refugee client's traumatic history. As mentioned in the previous section regarding difficulties in using interpreters, family members who assist with translation may have their own investment in the outcome of a client's treatment. In these cases, the client's pathology and symptoms may be downplayed or exaggerated, depending on the interpreter's motive, thereby influencing the outcome of the diagnosis.

For immigrant clients whose traditional backgrounds discourage the direct expression of feelings or who subscribe to a more holistic view of body and mind, there may be a tendency to focus on physical complaints (Sue & Sue, 2003; Yu, 1997). However, Gong-Guy et al. (1991) argued that somatic complaints rarely suggest somatization disorder in refugees, for example, as this diagnosis and hypochondriasis are not common in this population. They suggest that practitioners should instead be alerted to the possibility of depression since this is much more commonly seen in refugees.

The work of Kleinman (as cited in Fukuyama & Sevig, 2002), who "advocates discovering the narrative behind the illness and promoting dialogue" between the provider and the client (p. 282), is very relevant here. In trying to explain a client's illness, he recommends asking questions such as, "What do you call the problem? What do you think has caused the problem? What do you think the sickness does? What do you fear most about the sickness?" (p. 282). Such an approach is useful because it asks questions that help us understand *how the client makes sense* of his or her illness. These inquiries are quite different from the standard intake questions that many counselors ask, which tend to be oriented toward diagnosis derived from the *Diagnostic and Statistical Manual of Mental Disorders IV (DSM-IV)* (American Psychiatric Association, 1994).

TREATMENT ISSUES AND CURRENT APPROACHES

In this section, we will explore several current approaches that are being used to treat immigrant adults and youth. It is not our intent to cover all the approaches being utilized at this time, but rather present innovative examples. Before exploring this topic, we discuss a number of "critical issues" that should be considered when working with immigrants and refugees.

Critical Issues in Treating Immigrants and Refugees

To begin with, it is important to develop an understanding of the reasons and circumstances under which the client came to this country. For example, it is important to find out if she or he came here voluntarily, for economic or educational purposes, or unwillingly to escape harm and persecution. If the immigrant client is a child, find out if she or he had a choice about coming and was separated from the family at any given time. In addition, it is important to know, historically, what type of relationship the United States has had with the country of origin. (K. Brabeck, personal communication, March 21, 2007). Yakushko and Chronister (2005) recommend that counselors keep a globe or atlas in their offices and ask clients to describe their country of origin and share their migration story, including pre- and post-migration experiences (see also Azima & Grizenko, 2002).

Be prepared and willing to spend a good amount of time building rapport. Immigrants and refugees are often still in shock from their cultural transition to the United States when they arrive to therapy. Dr. Sylvester shared this perspective: "It's pretty easy for them to identify me as a White, middle-aged lady, with an education, who is really different from them . . . to not really be able to relax in my presence." She explains that she spends a lot of time putting people at ease. Furthermore, immigrant clients often do not know what a psychologist, counselor, or therapist is, or they have had bad experiences with mental health professionals. If they did not voluntarily seek treatment, Dr. Sylvester asks them, "Why do you think you are here?" If someone seems really intimidated, she asks, "Who do you think I am? What do you think I'm about?" (personal communication, March 2007).

Clinicians should be prepared to explain their approach to treatment, as many immigrant and refugee clients are only familiar with medical treatment and may immediately expect medication (Gong-Guy et al., 1991). It is also important to spend time with recent immigrants educating them on the different cultural norms and practices of the new culture (Pumariega, Rothe, & Pumariega, 2005).

A key issue in working with immigrant clients is being aware of how isolated they are and of the loss they have experienced. Immigrants may have had a strong sense of community where they lived. In many places in the United States, especially in urban areas, that sense of neighborhood community does not exist. As such, counselors should determine if any extended family lives in this country and can provide support.

Working with refugees posses some challenges as well because they may have abruptly left their country of origin escaping potential harm and death. They may arrive in a state of crisis, which requires immediate mobilization of services. Pumariega et al. (2005) recommend a stage process. The first stage parallels the approach used with individuals who are victims of other disasters—triage, debriefing, and putting into place emergency services. Refugees with symptoms of severe trauma, for example, are given support and structure, as well as help to regain control of their lives. The second phase involves assisting with housing and employment needs, as well as helping to place refugee children in school. The last phase centers on connecting them with appropriate mental health and social services in a community-based system that is familiar with their culture.

It is important to meet clients *where they are,* and tune in to their hierarchy of needs. Although many of us who train as psychologists and counselors may be eager to engage the client in therapy, there often are a variety of practical issues that need to be addressed. For example, meeting basic needs (e.g., finding a place to live, a job, learning to get around on a bus) may take priority. The counselor needs to know what services and resources he or she can seek for meeting these basic needs. Informing clients about national organizations that work for immigrant rights, such as the National Network for Immigrant and Refugee Rights, and educating them about how to cope with the barriers that they may face will assist them in their transition (Yakushko & Chronister, 2005).

Finally, it is helpful to expand the use of service providers such as social workers, case managers, psychiatric nurses, and psychiatrists, especially in cases of severe pathology. The goal is to work "collaboratively and interdisciplinarily" with other health care professionals because many clients may have coexisting medical conditions and may be on psychotropic medication, requiring coordination with psychiatrists and other physicians. Social workers and other professionals with different training and perspectives may raise issues that would not have been otherwise considered (K. Brabeck, personal communication, March 21, 2007).

Assessment Challenges

Treatment and diagnosis are often informed by psychological evaluations. However, in the case of immigrant clients, these assessments also may affect asylum status, other resident/immigration issues, or government benefits. Unfortunately, there is a lack of well-translated, standardized, and normed psychological instruments for individuals who do not speak English and/or are foreign-born. Furthermore, few counselors and psychologists are experienced in cross-cultural assessments. Often, an interpreter is utilized to translate test items for instruments that have been standardized in English, "a process that can effectively invalidate results" (Gong-Guy et al., 1991, p. 646). With proper training and knowledge of cross-cultural assessment issues, a counselor can give impressions and draw tentative conclusions from evaluations in which an interpreter and/or nonverbal assessment tools have been utilized. However, cautions and caveats should be included throughout the report. Beyond the issue of language and assessment tools, the interests of the client and the purpose of the testing must be taken into consideration. It is recommended that a good deal of time be spent in the beginning clarifying what the purpose of the assessment is and what will be done with the results. It is important to tell the client who will and who will not have access to it, and what control the client does and does not have over the information (E. Sylvester, personal communication, March 23, 2007).

Theoretical Orientations

Although there may be some theoretical orientations that are a better fit for particular problems, we cannot conclude that there is one particular theoretical orientation that is most helpful in working with recent immigrants. Dr. Brabeck reports that "a lot of things have been helpful at different times" in her work with clients. For her, "A feminist, multicultural orientation is the water that everything else swims in." She says that there are instances when cognitive-behavioral therapy (CBT) is most helpful, but other times when she has been able to do more psychodynamic, insight-oriented work with the client than she thought would be possible (personal communication, March 21, 2007). Dr. Sylvester thinks that there is a "[c]onfounding between education and immigration," meaning that it is not simply the newness to this country and the cultural differences that may make deeper, insight-oriented work less suitable for immigrant clients. Education may be the key factor in determining at what level and with what approach the work with the client will take place. However, when working with clients with less education, a solution-focused, practical approach may be the best strategy at the beginning, then moving on to exploring deeper issues might make sense (personal communication, March 23, 2007). Finally, as mentioned before, it may be the issue that dictates the approach. Because so many refugees suffer from PTSD, this may be more important than cross-cultural factors. Some of these individuals have very fresh trauma, and the approach utilized should be chosen with this in mind (E. Sylvester, personal communication, March 23, 2007).

The Empowerment Program: Psycho-Education and Prevention

The Empowerment Program, located in the Kansas metropolitan area, was specifically designed to meet the social and emotional needs of immigrant and refugee women by combining prevention and psycho-educational outreach (Khamphakdy-Brown, Jones, Nilsson, Russel, & Klevens, 2006). The entities that collaborated to offer the program included a university counseling psychology department and its clinic, a local domestic violence shelter, and a not-for-profit organization whose mission already included serving immigrant women. The program employed services such as, but not limited to, counseling, psycho-educational home visits and workshops, advocacy, and case management. Bilingual and bicultural paraprofessionals, who receive ongoing training, were also an important part of the program, acting as translators, interpreters, and resource specialists. These advocates are refugee and immigrant women who were active in their own communities.

The Empowerment Program served 128 women during the first year, and 172 women participated in the second year. Although a study of the effectiveness of the program was not reported, the authors gave their impressions of what factors appeared to be most critical (Khamphakdy-Brown et al., 2006). Interestingly, a relatively small number of women accessed counseling as part of their services, but a substantial number of women utilized other outreach services. This phenomenon is consistent with the argument that shame and lack of knowledge about what counseling is may be common in many cultures. Reporting on lessons learned, the authors noted that they had to become more "mobile and creative" in reaching out to the women (p. 45). Along those lines, home visits and workshops appeared to be successful ways to reach clients. Psycho-educational approaches and case management appeared more effective than traditional counseling approaches that focused on emotional issues or developing insight. The authors cautioned that boundary issues and dual relationships were ongoing challenges considering that advocates, counselors, and clients interacted in a number of settings. Finally, the authors recommended the utilization of bicultural-bilingual advocates when serving refugee and immigrant communities, as they felt this was "[a]n essential component of gaining credibility, visibility, and access to the women in need" (p. 45).

The Empowerment Program (Khamphakdy-Brown et al., 2006) offers a good example of not only the blend of services, but the willingness of psychologists, counselors, social workers, health care workers, and paraprofessionals to join together to provide a cohesive program of services. However, an evaluation of the program's success would be important in the future, as empirical support would provide a basis for the creation of similar programs.

Drama Therapy

Meeting the needs of adolescents and children immigrants can be especially challenging as they are struggling with developmental challenges along with their transition to the United States. They may also be less receptive to one-on-one, primarily verbal therapy. A unique approach designed to facilitate the adjustment of newly arrived adolescent immigrants is a drama therapy program developed by an interdisciplinary team in Montreal (Rousseau et al., 2004). The program, serving teens ages 12 to 18 from all over the world, was designed to give them an opportunity to share their stories and struggles.

The drama workshop, which consisted of 10 weekly 75-minute sessions, was part of the students' regular school day. The workshop was not about artistic performance, but instead aimed to give teens a safe space where they could address difficult issues and emotions. During each session, a topic was introduced, and the students were then invited to express their experiences and concerns. Sound, movement, and simple props were favored over dialogue to represent the teller's perspective. Stories developed by members to express specific themes, such as loss, were also acted out using improvisation and music. In these cases, the goal was to alter the situation in such a way that empowered the storyteller and other members, either by changing the ending to the story, or creating a dialogue with others that was missing from the original story (Rousseau et al., 2004).

An informal, qualitative assessment of the program took place over a 3-year time period. Students, teachers, and team members from a local children's hospital participated in the evaluation. Teachers reported that the program helped them to get to know their students better and "noted positive changes in the student's behavior and self-esteem" (Rousseau et al., 2004, p. 19). By sharing their stories, students felt less isolated, and a stronger sense of community was built. Moreover, students were motivated to support each other as they developed a better understanding of what their peers were experiencing. The workshops represented a safe place for the teens to participate in respectful discussions about the cultural, social, and political diversity that surrounded them. Finally, the workshop provided a mechanism to explore identity development issues related to the migration experience.

A School-Based Mental Health Program

Because children spend most of their time at school and because of the transportation issues many immigrants face, it is best if treatment is available in the educational setting, much as it was in the drama therapy program just described. Having mental health services at school increases the possibility for compliance and follow-through on the part of both parents and children.

Newly arrived immigrant children in the Los Angeles Unified School District (LAUSD) receive a variety of services through the Emergency

Immigrant Education Program (EIEP), such as medical and dental screening, tutoring, and language classes (Stein et al., 2002). However, it was found that mental health services were lacking. Local academic institutions and the LAUSD paired together to form the Mental Health for Immigrants Program (MHIP). MHIP employed a CBT group intervention, which was modified to better fit the needs of immigrant children, such as developing examples that were culturally relevant, addressing language issues, and dealing with supernatural experiences (seeing spirits or ghosts) that were shared by several children (Stein et al., 2002).

The first study to be released from the MHIP focused on 198 Latino children, in third through eighth grades. They were treated for trauma-related depression and/or PTSD symptoms in an eight-session, CBT group delivered in Spanish. A waitlist control group was employed (Kataoka et al., 2003). A significant decrease in depressive and PTSD symptoms was observed in the treatment group, while depressive symptoms remained the same and PTSD symptoms had a slight, nonsignificant decrease in the waitlist group. Interestingly, with regard to both depressive and PTSD symptoms, when controlling for other factors, boys, as well as children from other Latin American countries compared with Mexican children, were doing better at follow-up (Kataoka et al., 2003).

Kataoka et al. (2003) do note some limitations to their study, including the modest symptom changes obtained, which, on average, remained in the clinical range at short-term follow-up. Also, there were compromises made in the research design in order to treat all children who wanted to participate in the intervention in a timely manner. For this reason, only a portion of the participants were randomized. The authors recommend that these issues, among others, be addressed in subsequent evaluations of the program.

CONCLUSION

In conclusion, it is important to focus on both practical and emotional needs, as well as to consider the immigrant's support systems, environment, and culture in planning interventions. Children and adolescent immigrants need programs that address not only their migration experiences, but the developmental challenges they are facing. Creative approaches, whether it be drama groups (Rousseau et al., 2004) or an adapted CBT intervention (Kataoka et al., 2003; Stein et al., 2002) may benefit children and teens more than traditional play therapy or verbal approaches. Most important, it appears that offering these services in a school context, where children already spend a great deal of their time, is of utmost importance. If working for a clinic that treats children and teens, explore collaborations with schools where treatment can be offered at their campuses.

Interventions with immigrants must be culture relevant. Compliance with treatment requires that services be conceptualized with the worldview of the client in mind. For instance, a mental health clinic that serves Cambodian immigrant clients might provide culturally appropriate services, such as acupuncture, or employ a Buddhist monk and provide him with formal social work training (Gong-Guy et al., 1991). Even if cultural expertise such as indigenous healers cannot be accessed, the manner in which one works with clients can still be culturally relevant. For example, asking a client how he/she would like to be helped may bring about useful brainstorming. Perhaps a client would like to pray, recite a chant, or drink a special tea at a session. Accommodations for the incorporation of healing rituals such as these can easily be made.

Empirical studies on the efficacy of mental health interventions with newly arrived immigrants or just immigrants in general are virtually nonexistent. One, concerning the treatment of Latino immigrant children (Kataoka et al., 2003), was included in this chapter. This dearth of quantitative studies needs to be addressed. Likewise, well-designed, qualitative studies would strengthen the literature in this area. The systematic evaluation of programs similar to those described in this chapter is also needed.

In this chapter, we have attempted to offer basic information pertaining to the experiences of recent immigrants and refugees. A description of the current immigrant population in the United States was given, along with terminology and a history of laws pertaining to immigration in this country. The importance of the process of acculturation as it pertains to the experiences and well-being of immigrants was discussed, as were several intersecting identity issues, such as social class and gender roles. As you have learned in this chapter, the migration process can be quite stressful, and many pre- and postmigration events contribute to mental health issues for immigrants. Unfortunately, there are many barriers to mental health services, as discussed here, such as language, transportation, insurance, and lack of cultural competence on the part of service providers. Critical issues in conducting assessment and counseling with immigrants were identified, and a few examples of current psychotherapeutic approaches were presented.

Endnotes

1. These figures are excerpted from the report titled "Immigrants at mid-decade: A snapshot of America's foreign-born," by Steven Camarota, Director of Research at the Center for Immigration Studies. This report is based primar-

ily on the March 2005 Current Population Survey. The report defines the foreign-born as persons living in the United States who are not U.S. citizens.

2. Martens (2007) examined the following immigrants and refugee groups: Chinese, Koreans, Cambodians, Mexicans, Hispanics from Central and South America, Africans and Caribbean Blacks, Ethiopians, Somalis, Bengalis, Hindus, Pakistani, Russian-Jewish, including immigrants from the Maghreb and former Soviet Union. Martens found that the rates vary across these groups. Intervention programs must be specifically tailored to meet the needs of each group because of the diversity of cultures, languages, life circumstances, and migration histories in the immigrant population.
3. PRWORA has restricted immigrants, including pregnant women and children, who arrived after August 22, 1996, from federally funded health coverage and other public benefits for their first 5 years in the United States (American Psychological Association, 2007). Although PRWORA has expired, the program continues to be funded until a new bill is enacted (Wikipedia, 2007). Passage of the proposed Immigrant Children's Health Improvement Act (ICHIA) (National Immigration Law Center, 2007) would improve the health insurance coverage for children and pregnant women by lifting the 5-year ban imposed by PRWORA. ICHIA is scheduled to be introduced in 2007 as part of the SCHIP reauthorization and would give states more flexibility to provide health coverage to eligible, documented, pregnant women and children (National Immigration Law Center, 2007).
4. Two psychologists with many years of experience with immigrants were interviewed for this chapter. Their input and comments were incorporated throughout sections of the chapter. Dr. Kalina Brabeck is currently completing a postdoctoral internship in neuropsychological assessment in Providence, Rhode Island. She has extensive experience working with recent immigrants, refugees, and survivors of torture. Her experiences include working at a battered women's center, where the majority of her clients were Spanish-speaking women from Mexico and Central America, and conducting both therapy and assessment at a community-based counseling center that specialized in serving immigrants and refugees, where her clients were from countries such as Honduras, Mexico, Columbia, Bosnia, Brazil, and Cuba. Her postdoctoral internship was at Bellevue Hospital in New York City on the Cross-Cultural Psychology Track, where she worked at the Bilingual Treatment Program Clinic with immigrants from all over the world, including China, Poland, and Russia. When asked about what she identifies as "critical issues" in working with immigrants and refugees, Dr. Brabeck identified language barriers, isolation, understanding a client's migration experience, and managing the balance between providing therapy and addressing practical issues. Dr. Elizabeth Sylvester is a psychologist, now in private practice, who has experience working with recent immigrants, refugees, and clients seeking political asylum. Dr. Sylvester says that she is doing less therapy with immigrants these days but is currently conducting a number of asylum assessments. Most of her experience with recent immigrants came from working at a community mental health center that specialized in serving immigrants and refugees. In that setting, she worked with immigrants from all over the world. Dr. Sylvester received most of her early training in bilingual therapy in Spanish at a local child guidance center, where she worked almost exclusively with Latin American immigrants, mostly from Mexico, and also U.S.-born children with

immigrant parents. She is constantly getting calls for services for immigrants from all over the world. Unfortunately, she knows of few people in her area who are trained to work with an interpreter or who are competent to work with immigrant children. Dr. Sylvester shared her knowledge of building rapport with immigrant clients and court assessment issues for refugees, among other information.

BIBLIOGRAPHY

Aarim-Heriot, N. (2003). *Chinese immigrants, African Americans, and racial anxiety in the United States,* 1848–82. Urbana, IL: University of Illinois Press.

Adler, L. L., & Gielen, U. P. (Eds.). (2003). *Migration: Immigration and emigration in international perspective.* Westport, CT: Praeger.

Akhtar, S. (1995). A third individuation: Immigration, identity, and the psychoanalytic process. *Journal of the American Psychoanalytic Association, 43,* 1051–1084.

Akhtar, S. (1999). *Immigration and identity. Turmoil, treatment, and transformation.* London: Jason Aronson.

Alker, J. C., & Urrutia, M. (2004). *Immigrants and health coverage: A primer.* The Kaiser Commission on Medicaid and the Uninsured. Retrieved April 16, 2007, from http://www.kff.org/uninsured/upload/Immigrants-and-Health-Coverage-A-Primer.pdf

American Psychiatric Association. (1994). *Diagnostic and statistical manual of mental disorders IV.* Washington, DC: Author.

American Psychological Association. (2007). *The mental health needs of immigrants.* APA Online, Public Policy Office. Retrieved April 16, 2007, from http://www.apa.org/ppo/ethnic/immigranthealth.html

Azima, F. J. C., & Grizenko, N. (2002). *Immigrant and refugee children and their families: clinical, research and training issues.* Madison, CT: International Universities Press.

Batalova, J. (2006). *Spotlight on refugees and asylees in the United States.* Washington, DC: Migration Policy Institute. http://www.igrationinformation.org/SFocus/print.cfm?ID=415

Berry, J. W. (1997). Immigration, acculturation, and adaptation. *Applied Psychology: An International Review, 46,* 5–68.

Berry, J. W. (2001). A psychology of immigration. *Journal of Social Issues, 57,* 615–631.

Berry, J. W., Kim, U., Minde, T., & Mok, D. (1987). Comparative studies of acculturative stress. *International Migration Review, 21,* 491–511.

Boneva, B. S., & Frieze, I. H. (2001). Towards a concept of a migrant personality. *Journal of Social Issues, 57,* 477–491.

Camarota, S. (2005, December). *Immigrants at mid-decade: A snapshot of America's foreign-born population in 2005.* Washington, DC: Center for Immigration Studies. Retrieved April 16, 2007 from http://www.cis.org/articles/2005/back1405.html

Castex, G. M. (1997). Immigrant children in the United States. In N. K. Phillips & S. L. A. Straussner (Eds.), *Children in the urban environment: Linking social policy and clinical practice* (pp. 43–60). Springfield, MA: Charles Thomas Publishers.

Chandler, C. R., & Tsai, Y. (2001). Social factors influencing immigration attitudes: An analysis of data from the General Social Survey. *The Social Science Journal, 38,* 177–188.

Corey, G. (2004). *Theory and practice of counseling and psychotherapy* (7th ed.). Belmont, CA: Wadsworth.

de las Fuentes, C., & Vasquez, M. J. T. (1999). Immigrant adolescent girls of color: Facing American challenges. In N. G. Johnson, M. C. Roberts, & J. Worell (Eds.), *Beyond appearances: A look at adolescent girls* (pp. 131–150). Washington, DC: American Psychological Association.

Dion, K. (2006). On the development of identity: Perspectives from immigrant families. In R. Mahalingam (Ed.), *Cultural psychology of immigrants.* Mahwah, NJ: Lawrence Erlbaum Assoc.

Dion, K., & Dion, K. L. (1993). Individualistic and collectivistic perspectives on gender and the cultural context of love and intimacy. *Journal of Social Issues, 49,* 53–69.

Dion, K., & Dion, K. L. (1996). Cultural perspectives on romantic love. *Personal Relationships, 3,* 5–17.

Dion, K., & Dion, K. L. (2001). Gender and cultural adaptation in immigrant families. *Journal of Social Issues, 57,* 511–521.

Dion, K., & Dion, K. L. (2004). Gender, immigrant generation, and ethnocultural identity. *Sex Roles, 50,* 347–355.

Espín, O. M. (1999). *Women crossing boundaries: A psychology of immigration and transformation of sexuality.* New York: Routledge.

Espín, O. M. (2006). Gender, sexuality, language and migration. In R. Mahalingam (Ed.), *Cultural psychology of immigrants.* Mahwah, NJ: Lawrence Erlbaum Assoc.

Esses, V. M., Dovidio, J. F., Jackson, L. M., & Armstrong, T. L. (2001). The immigration dilemma: The role of perceived group competition, ethnic prejudice, and national identity. *Journal of Social Issues, 57,* 389–412.

Fukuyama, M. A., & Sevig, T. D. (2002). Spirituality in counseling across cultures. In P. B. Pedersen, J. E. Draguns, W. J. Lonner, & J. E. Trimble (Eds.), *Counseling cross cultures* (5th ed., pp. 273–295). Thousand Oaks, CA: Sage.

Gabaccia, D. R. (2002). *Immigration and American diversity: A social and cultural history.* Malden, MA: Blackwell.

Gong-Guy, E., Cravens, R. B., & Patterson, T. E. (1991). Clinical issues in mental health service delivery to refugees. *American Psychologist, 46,* 642–648.

Halperin, S. (2004). The relevance of immigration in psychodynamic formulation of psychotherapy with immigrant. *International Journal of Applied Psychoanalytic Studies, 1,* 99–120.

Hernandez, D. J., Denton, N. A., & Macartney, S. E. (2007). *Children in America's newcomer families.* (Research Brief Series, # 2007–11.) University at Albany, SUNY, Center for Social and Demographic Analysis.

Hérnandez, M., & McGoldrick, M. (1999). Migration and the life-cycle. In B. Carter & M. McGoldrick (Eds.), *The expanded family life-cycle: Individual, family, and social perspectives* (pp. 169–184). Boston: Allyn & Bacon.

Hoerder, D., & Knauf, D. (1992). *Fame, fortune, and sweet liberty: The great European migration.* Bremen, Germany: Temmen.

Hong, G. K., & Ham, M. D. (1992). Impact of immigration on the family life-cycle: Clinical implications for Chinese Americans. *Journal of Family Psychotherapy,* 3, 27–40.

Hong, G. K., & Ham, M. D. (2001). *Psychotherapy and counseling Asian American clients: A practical guide.* Thousand Oaks, CA: Sage.

Inclán, J. (2003). Class, culture, and gender in immigrant families. In L. B. Silverstein & T. J. Goodrich (Eds.), *Feminist family therapy: Empowerment in social context* (pp. 333–347). Washington, DC: American Psychological Association.

Inman, A. G., Howard, E. E., Beaumont, R. L., & Walker, J. A. (2007). Cultural transmission: Influence of contextual factors in Asian Indian immigrant parents' experiences. *Journal of Counseling Psychology, 54,* 93–100.

Kataoka, S. H., Stein, B. D., Jaycox, L. H., Wong, M., Escudero, P., Tu, W., et al. (2003). A school-based mental health program for traumatized Latino immigrant children. *Journal of the American Academy of Child and Adolescent Psychiatry, 42,* 311–318.

Khamphakdy-Brown, S., Jones, L. N., Nilsson, J. E., Russel, E. B., & Klevens, C. L. (2006). The Empowerment Program: An application of an outreach program for refugee and immigrant women. *Journal of Mental Health Counseling, 28,* 38–47.

Ku, L., & Matani, S. (2001). Left out: Immigrants' access to health care and insurance. *Health Affairs, 20,* 247–256.

Mahalingam, R. (ED.) (2006). *Cultural psychology of immigrants.* Mahway, NJ: Lawrence Erlbaum Assoc.

Mahalingam, R., & Haritatos, J. (2006). Cultural psychology of gender and immigration. In R. Mahalingam (Ed.). *Cultural psychology of immigrants* (pp. 259–275). Mahwah, NJ: Lawrence Erlbaum Associates.

Marín, G. (1992). Issues in the measurement of acculturation among Hispanics. In K. F. Geisinger (Ed.), *Psychological testing of Hispanics* (pp. 235–251). Washington, DC: American Psychological Association.

Marsella, A. J., & Ring, E. (2003). Human migration and immigration: An overview. In L. L. Adler & U. P. Gielen (Eds.), *Migration: Immigration and emigration in international perspective* (pp. 3–22). Westport, CT: Praeger.

Martens, W. H. J. (2007). Prevalence of depression in various ethnic groups of immigrants and refugees: Suggestions for prevention and intervention. *International Journal of Mental Health Promotion, 9,* 25–33.

McCloskey, L. A., Southwick, K., Fernández-Esquer, M. E., & Locke, C. (1995). The psychological effects of political and domestic violence on Central American and Mexican immigrant mothers and children. *Journal of Community Psychology, 23,* 95–116.

Murphy, E. J. (2006). Translational ties and mental health. In R. Mahalingam (Ed.), *Cultural psychology of immigrants* (pp. 79–92). Mahwah, NJ: Lawrence Erlbaum Associates.

Nah, K. -H. (1993). Perceived problems and service delivery for Korean immigrants. *Social Work, 38,* 289–296.

National Immigration Law Center. (2007, January). Facts about the Immigrant Children's Health Improvement Act (ICHIA). Retrieved April 18, 2007, from http:www.nilc.org/immspbs/cdev/ICHIA/ichia_facts_2007–01–25.pdf

Noh, S. H., Wu, Z., Speechley, M., & Kaspar, V. (1992). Depression in Korean immigrants in Canada: Correlates of gender, work, and marriage. *Journal of Nervous and Mental Disease, 180,* 578–582.

Pedraza, S. (2006). Assimilation or transnationalism: Conceptual models of the Immigrant experience in America. In R. Mahalingam (Ed.), *Cultural psychology of immigrants* (pp. 33–54). Mahwah, NJ: Lawrence Erlbaum Associates.

Pettigrew, T. F. (2006). A two-level approach to anti-immigrant prejudice and discrimination. In R. Mahalingam (Ed.), *Cultural psychology of immigrants* (pp. 95–112). Mahwah, NJ: Lawrence Erlbaum Associates.

Pew Hispanic Center (2006, March). *No consensus on immigration problem or proposed fixes: America's immigration quandary.* Washington, DC: Pew Pedraza Research Center.

Phelan, M., & Gillespie, J. (2007). *Immigration law handbook.* New York: Oxford University Press.

Phinney, J. S. (1989). Stages of ethnic identity development in minority group adolescents. *Journal of Early Adolescents, 9,* 34–49.

Phinney, J. (1990). Ethnic identity in adolescents and adults: A review of research. *Psychological Bulletin, 108,* 499–514.

Phinney, J., Cantu, C., & Kurtz, D. (1997). Ethnic and American identity as predictors of self-esteem among African American, Latino, and White adolescents. *Journal of Youth and Adolescence, 26,* 165–185.

Phinney, J. S., & Chavira, V. (1992). Ethnic identity and self-esteem: An exploratory longitudinal study. *Journal of Adolescence, 15,* 271–281.

Phinney, J., Horenczyk, G., Liebkind, K., & Vedder, P. (2001). Ethnic identity, immigration, and well-being: An interactional perspective. *Journal of Social Issues, 57,* 493–510.

Prewitt-Diaz, J. O., Trotter, R. T., & Rivera, V. A. (1990). *The effects of migration on children: An ethnographic study.* State College, PA: Centro de Estudios Sobre la Migración.

Pumariega, A. J., Rothe, E., & Pumariega, J. B. (2005). Mental health of immigrants and refugees. *Community Mental Health Journal, 41,* 581–597.

Rodriguez, R. R., & Walls, N. E. (2000). Culturally educated questioning: Toward a skills-based approach in multicultural counselor training. *Applied & Preventive Psychology, 9,* 89–99.

Rousseau, C., Gauthier, M. F., Lacroix, L., Alain, N., Benoit, M., Moran, A., et al. (2004). Playing with identities and transforming shared realities: Drama therapy workshops for adolescent immigrants and refugees. *The Arts in Psychotherapy, 32,* 13–27.

Roysircar, G. (2003). Understanding immigrants: Acculturation theory and research. In F. D. Harper & J. McFadden (Eds.), *Culture and counseling: New approaches* (pp. 164–185). Boston, MA: Allyn & Bacon.

Ruiz, P. (2002). Hispanic access to health/mental health services. *Psychiatric Quarterly, 73,* 85–91.

Santiago-Rivera, A. L., & Altarriba, J. (2002). The role of language in therapy with the Spanish-English bilingual client. *Professional Psychology: Research and Practice, 33,* 30–38.

Santiago-Rivera, A. L., Arredondo, P., & Gallardo-Cooper, M. (2002). *Counseling Latinos and la familia: A practical guide.* Thousand Oaks, CA: Sage.

Schmitz, P. G. (2003). Psychosocial factors of immigration and emigration: An introduction. In L. L. Adler & U. P. Gielen (Eds.), *Migration: Immigration and Emigration in international perspective* (pp. 23–50). Westport, CT: Praeger.

Shiraev, E., & Levy, D. (2004). *Cross-cultural psychology: Critical thinking and contemporary applications.* Boston: Pearson Education.

Steel, Z., Silove, D., Brooks, R., Momartin, S., Alzuhairi, B., & Susljik, I. (2006). Impact of immigration detention and temporary protection on the mental health of refugees. *British Journal of Psychiatry, 188,* 58–64.

Stein, B. D., Kataoka, S., Jaycox, L. H., Wong, M., Fink, A., Escudero, P., et al. (2002). Theoretical basis and program design of a school-based mental health intervention for traumatized immigrant children: A collaborative research partnership. *The Journal of Behavioral Health Services & Research, 29,* 318–326.

Stodolska, M., & Yi, J. (2003). Impact of immigration on ethnic identity and leisure behavior of adolescent immigrants from Korea, Mexico and Poland. *Journal of Leisure Research, 35,* 49–79.

Sue, D. W., & Sue, S. (2003). Culturally appropriate intervention strategies. In *Counseling the culturally diverse, theory and practice* (4th ed., pp. 123–150). New York: John Wiley & Sons.

Tormala, T. T., & Deaux, K. (2006). Black immigrants to the United Status: Confronting and constructing ethnicity and race. In R. Mahalingam (Ed.), *Cultural psychology of immigrants* (pp. 131–150). Mahwah, NJ: Lawrence Erlbaum Associates.

U.S. Citizenship and Immigration Services (USCIS).(2007). Definition of refugee from the Immigration and Nationality Act. Retrieved March 11, 2007 from http://www.uscis/portal/site/uscis

U.S. Department of Health and Human Services, Office of the Surgeon General, SAMHA (1999). Fact Sheets. Asian Americans/Pacific Islanders. Mental Health: Culture, Race, Ethnicity—Supplement. Retrieved April 16, 2007, from http://mentalhealth.samhsa.gov/cre/fact2.asp

U.S. Department of Health and Human Services, Office of the Surgeon General, SAMHA (1999). Fact Sheets. Latinos/Hispanic Americans. Mental Health: Culture, Race, Ethnicity—Supplement. Retrieved April 18, 2007, from http://mentalhealth.samhsa.gov/cre/fact3.asp

Wikipedia Foundation, Inc. (2007). *Personal Responsibility and Work Opportunity Act.* Wikipedia. Retrieved April 18, 2007, from http://en.wikipedia.org/wiki/Personal_ Responsibility_ and_Work_Opportunity_Act

Yakushko, O., & Chronister, K. (2005). Immigrant women and counseling: The invisible others. *Journal of Counseling and Development, 83,* 292–298.

Yu, M. (1997). Mental health services to immigrants and refugees. In T. R. Watkins & J. W. Callicutt (Eds.), *Mental health: Policy and practice today.* Thousand Oaks, CA: Sage.

Zuñiga, M. E. (1992). Families with Latino roots. In E. W. Lynch & M. J. Hanson (Eds.), *Developing cross-cultural competence: A guide for working with young children and their families* (pp. 151–179). Baltimore, MD: Brooks.

Chapter Twelve

Social Problem Solving and Health

Timothy R. Elliott
Morgan Hurst

Counseling psychology is committed to helping people meet the challenges and solve the problems they encounter in daily routines and in stressful circumstances. To a great extent, this holds true for other professional psychology specialties (including clinical, educational, and health psychology) as clients usually seek professional assistance in solving the problems they face. Thus, the study of problem-solving abilities—their measurement and correlates—and efficient ways to improve these abilities is of keen interest to clinicians and researchers.

Counseling psychology has played an influential role in this area of inquiry. Historically guided by early cognitive-behavioral theorists (D'Zurilla & Goldfried, 1971), counseling psychology contributed essential theoretical refinements (Heppner & Krauskopf, 1987) and measurement tools (Heppner, 1988) that remain landmark events. However, related and subsequent theoretical and empirical contributions—appearing primarily in outlets associated with clinical and health psychology, and in the larger, multidisciplinary literature—have yet to be sufficiently integrated with contributions from counseling psychology. This lack of scholarly integration has not necessarily impeded advancements and applications, but it has thwarted a deeper theoretical understanding of the mechanisms at work in the learning and application of social problem-solving abilities.

Historical Backdrop

The historical backdrop of theory and research must be considered for us to appreciate the subsequent developments in the current literature. The D'Zurilla and Goldfried (1971) paper is the intellectual wellspring for this area: In this paper, the authors described the elements that would eventually characterize the problem-solving process. Specifically, it was argued that successful problem solving consists of identifying a problem, defining the characteristics and important aspects of the problem, generating possible solutions and alternatives for the problem, choosing a viable solution and implementing it, and then monitoring and evaluating the progress of the solution.

Two important features of this paper should be emphasized. First, as Nezu (2004) observes, the proposed model of this work was *prescriptive* rather than *descriptive;* that is, D'Zurilla and Goldfried construed effective problem-solving principles as they should be and as they should operate, in theoretical terms. Second, the authors did not recommend a specific measure for assessing problem-solving skills; their essay was primarily concerned with the ramifications of their straightforward model for cognitive-behavioral interventions.

The implications of this model for counseling psychology were spelled out in an important conceptual review by Heppner (1978) and demonstrated in an impressive intervention study by Richards and Perri (1978). These papers—both published in the same volume of the *Journal of Counseling Psychology*—exemplified the two different approaches to the study of problem-solving abilities that persist to this day. In the former, Heppner considered the larger cognitive-behavioral framework in which problem solving was a part, drawing out implications for counseling practice and research. Eventually, Heppner's work produced the Problem Solving Inventory (PSI; Heppner, 1988), accompanied by an impressive program of empirical research that demonstrated the correlates and properties of the PSI (for reviews of this work see Heppner & Baker, 1997; Heppner, Witty, & Dixon, 2004). In contrast, Richards and Perri took initiative from the prescription of problem-solving abilities stipulated by D'Zurilla and Goldfried, developed an intervention based on these principles, and provided evidence of their utility in significantly improving self-management skills of undergraduates (Richards & Perri, 1978).

In surveying the current landscape, we find relevant research that extends from the Heppner research program. This influence is rather easy to identify, as most of this work relies on the PSI (perhaps the most frequently used problem-solving measure). This work appears predominately in the counseling psychology literature. The most comprehensive theoretical commentary on this scholarship appears in Heppner and Krauskopf (1987), in which an information-processing model is used to help us understand how individuals learn, regulate, and execute problem-solving abilities.

Running parallel to this stream of work (with a few intriguing moments of empirical overlap) are studies that integrate the problem-solving principles into interventions with considerable success. Although D'Zurilla and colleagues were apparently uninterested in developing a measure of problem-solving abilities at first—indeed, some of the initial intervention studies used Heppner's PSI (Nezu & Perri, 1989)—this camp provided theoretical refinements of the cognitive-behavioral mechanisms of the problem-solving process (D'Zurilla & Nezu, 2007). A measure of social problem-solving abilities was eventually developed (featuring 70 items; D'Zurilla & Nezu, 1990) and empirically refined (52 items; D'Zurilla, Nezu, & Maydeu-Olivares, 2002). However, this research stream is best characterized by the number of intervention studies that appeared in journals associated with clinical and counseling psychology, and the far-reaching implications of this work are now being realized by multidisciplinary research teams across the health professions.

Theoretical Distinctions

Although these two streams of work often complement the other, a few compelling theoretical distinctions should be noted. In the Heppner and Krauskopf (1987) model, for example, problem solving is construed as a metacognitive variable that has organizational properties. In a manner akin to Bandura's self-efficacy model (Bandura, 1986), problem solving is a self-appraisal process, as behavior is influenced by subjective beliefs and perceptions of abilities, competencies, and potential. These cognitions regulate emotional experiences and expression, overt behavior, personal goals, and goal-directed activity. The PSI features three empirically derived factors (Personal Control, Problem-Solving Confidence, and Approach-Avoidance), but it is not construed as a measure of actual problem-solving abilities, per se. The favored terminology emphasizes the phenomenological processes stipulated in this model (e.g., "problem-solving appraisal" and "self-appraised problem-solving abilities").

The Social Problem-Solving Inventory-Revised (SPSI-R; D'Zurilla & Nezu, 1990) was developed as the authors recognized two broad functions of social problem-solving abilities they termed *problem orientation* and *problem-solving skills* (see Nezu & D'Zurilla, 1989). The problem orientation component, based on converging evidence from research at that time, served to regulate emotions, maintain a positive attitude necessary for solving problems, and motivate a person toward solving problems in routine and stressful circumstances. The problem-solving skills component encompassed the actual skills individuals use in solving problems, including rational skills, avoidance, and impulsive and careless styles. This model guided much of the contemporary research that has used this scale. The theoretical and clinical focus of this group centers on the prescriptive nature of the original model (D'Zurilla & Nezu, 1999; Nezu, 2004) and consistently uses the term "social problem-solving abilities." Recently, D'Zurilla and colleagues recognized the strong associations that have occurred between the positive orientation scale on the SPSI-R measure and the rational problem solving scale, and between the negative problem orientation scale and the impulsive/careless and avoidance scales (D'Zurilla, Nezu, & Maydeu-Olivares, 2004). They use the terms "constructive problem-solving style" and "dysfunctional problem-solving style" in their recent conceptualization.

PERSONAL ADJUSTMENT AND HEALTH

We acknowledge that personal adjustment is an important aspect of "health," generally, and it is a dubious enterprise to separate adjustment into dualistic notions of "mental" and "physical" health. The study of social problem solving and emotional adjustment has largely dominated the relevant counseling literature, and only recently have we begun to appreciate the theoretical and clinical implications of social problem-solving abilities and physical health. From our perspective, we are fairly confident in the established associations between ineffective problem-solving abilities and depression, anxiety, and distress among people in general (Heppner et al., 2004; Nezu, 2004). However, ineffective problem-solving abilities are inconsistently associated with indicators of health-compromising behaviors (e.g., sedentary behavior, substance abuse; Elliott, Grant, & Miller, 2004). Social problem-solving abilities can be significantly predictive of important self-reported outcomes (e.g., disability, well-being; Elliott et al., 2004) and with objectively rated indicators of therapeutic adherence (although the directions of these relationships are not always clear; see Herrick & Elliott, 2001).

In the remainder of this chapter, we address recent advancements in our understanding of social problem-solving abilities from recent research in emotional, interpersonal, and social adjustment associated with health, with health outcomes and secondary complications, and from problem-solving interventions among persons with various health conditions. We then turn our attention to major issues and findings raised in published reviews of the research to date, and conclude with a discussion of the problems we see in this work and offer our recommendations for future research. We use the term "social problem-solving abilities" in deference to the original model and in light of the currency of this concept in the larger multidisciplinary literature (in which much of the research relevant to our discussion has appeared).

Emotional, Interpersonal, and Social Adjustment

In a previous survey of problem-solving abilities and health, the connections between dysfunctional social problem-solving styles and depression and distress were theoretically consistent across the relevant literature; data linking effective problem-solving abilities with optimal adjustment were decidedly mixed (Elliott et al., 2004). Empirical research over the ensuing years has yielded similar results. A negative problem orientation has been associated with higher depression scores among older persons with vision loss (Dreer, Elliott, Fletcher, & Swanson, 2005) and among family caregivers of persons with severe disabilities (Grant, Elliott, Weaver, Glandon, & Giger, 2006; Rivera et al., 2006). A dysfunctional problem-solving style—as measured by the SPSI-R—may be particularly characteristic of individuals who meet diagnostic criteria for a suspected major depressive disorder (Dreer, Elliott, Shewchuk, Berry, & Rivera, 2007; Grant, Weaver, Elliott, Bartolucci, & Giger, 2004; Rivera, Elliott, Berry, Oswald, & Grant, 2007).

Indicators of function and quality of life among persons with debilitating conditions rely heavily on self-report measures of these constructs. These measures may be influenced by respondent problem-solving styles, independent of objectively defined indicators of disability severity (Elliott, Godshall, Herrick, Witty, & Spruell, 1991; Shaw, Feuerstein, Haufler, Berkowitz, & Lopez, 2001). Consistent with these data, Rath and colleagues found ineffective problem-solving abilities were significantly associated with self-reported psychosocial impairment among persons with traumatic brain injuries (TBI; Rath et al., 2004). Similar results have been found among persons in a chronic pain rehabilitation program (Witty, Heppner, Bernard, & Thoreson, 2001). A negative problem orientation is a stronger predictor of psychosocial impairment than health locus of control variables (Shanmugham, Elliott & Palmatier, 2004).

In fact, among persons with TBI, there is evidence that social problem-solving abilities may be a better predictor of community integration following medical rehabilitation than several neuropsychological measures often used to predict adjustment in this population (Rath, Hennessy, & Diller, 2003). These results—consistent with prior evidence of the social adaptability associated with effective problem-solving (see Heppner et al., 1982; Neal & Heppner, 1986)—may prove particularly enlightening in our appreciation of interpersonal and social dynamics of adjustment following disease and disability.

Although the results from these studies have been largely consistent with previous research, the evidence linking social problem-solving abilities and optimal adjustment remains thin. For example, prospective research has found a positive orientation predictive of well-being among family caregivers of stroke survivors over 13 weeks after discharge from an inpatient rehabilitation program (Grant et al., 2006). Cross-sectional research has found a negative orientation to be inversely associated with caregiver mental health and life satisfaction (Rivera et al., 2006), and Dreer et al. (2005) found elements of constructive and dysfunctional problem-solving styles were associated with the life satisfaction reported by individuals in an outpatient low-vision rehabilitation program.

A more detailed analysis of subgroups within a large sample of individuals with disabilities suggests that the relationship of problem-solving abilities to measures of distress and well-being may be theoretically consistent at the extremes: Effective problem-solving abilities are associated with a more optimal profile, and ineffective abilities are associated with the opposite clinical picture (Elliott, Shewchuk, Miller, & Richards, 2001). However, two other clusters revealed that some individuals who harbor a negative orientation and who report rational problem-solving skills also experience considerable distress. Our lack of insight into the actual mechanisms by which problem solving influences adjustment in routine, daily experiences hinders our interpretation of these data and their implications.

A similarly complicated pattern emerges in our understanding of self-reported health and social problem-solving abilities. Prospective research has found a negative orientation to be productive of family caregiver health complaints over the course of a year (Elliott, Shewchuk, & Richards, 2001). Yet cross-sectional study with family caregivers of persons with various disabilities did not replicate this finding (Rivera et al., 2006), and Grant et al. (2006) found a significant—albeit tenuous and diminishing—relationship between a positive orientation and general health over 13 weeks. Despite early evidence that a negative orientation is predictive of self-reported health complaints in cross-sectional and prospective designs (Elliott & Marmarosh, 1994), it appears that several unmeasured factors may account for these inconsistent findings.

There is reason to believe that social problem-solving abilities operate within interpersonal and social contexts to exert an influence on adjustment. An effective problem-solving style has been associated with greater relationship satisfaction among family caregivers of stroke survivors (Shanmugham, Cano, Elliott, & Davis, under review). Related research suggests that children of families that rely on problem-solving coping fare better over time than families who rely less on these strategies (Kinsella,

Ong, Murtagh, Prior, & Sawyer, 1999; Rivara et al., 1996). Furthermore, persons living with severe disability and with family caregivers who have impulsive and careless ways of solving problems were more likely to have a pressure sore within the first year of acquired disability than other individuals (Elliott, Shewchuk, & Richards, 1999). Caregiver dysfunctional styles have also been implicated in the distress and decreased life satisfaction reported by patients with congestive heart failure (Kurylo, Elliott, DeVivo, & Dreer, 2004).

A comprehensive study by Johnson and colleagues (2006) suggests that the effects of problem solving on distress may be defined by several adaptive correlates of social problem-solving abilities. In this study, distress—as a latent construct—was composed of decreased social support, elevations in depression and negative mood, and high stress among 545 HIV+ adults, and distress was predicted by constructive and dysfunctional problem-solving styles (accounting for over 60% of the variance). Although prior research has indicated that social problem-solving abilities are usually related to these separate variables in a theoretically consistent fashion, this was the first study to demonstrate these relationships in a comprehensive model, and the associations were best understood within the context of this model.

Health Outcomes and Secondary Complications

In many respects, social problem-solving abilities have demonstrated considerable utility as a predictor of important health outcomes in several studies of depression among persons living with chronic health conditions. Depression is often conceptualized as an important health outcome because it is associated with increased heath care costs and it compromises the overall health of persons with conditions as varied as diabetes, paralysis, and congestive heart failure.

It has been difficult to ascertain the ways in which problem-solving abilities might influence other, more objectively defined health outcomes. Data concerning the relations of problem solving to substance use, exercise, and other health behaviors have been mixed (see Elliott et al., 2004), although among individuals who live with a disability there is some indication that a dysfunctional style may be associated with health-compromising behaviors (Dreer, Elliott, & Tucker, 2004).

The Johnson et al. (2006) study again informs us of the ways in which problem-solving abilities may influence health outcomes. In this attempt to predict adherence to antiretroviral therapy (assessed by a survey of the number of pills skipped during a 3-day period), the final model revealed no significant, direct paths from the two social problem-solving latent variables (constructive, dysfunctional) to adherence. Rather, social problem solving exerted significant indirect effects to adherence through its substantive effects on distress. Thus, social problem-solving abilities were significantly associated with therapeutic adherence through its palliative, beneficial (and perhaps, regulatory) effects on personal stress, distress, and social support.

Studies that demonstrate connections between social problem-solving abilities and objectively diagnosed biomedical variables are particularly impressive, but the lack of clarity (or, in some cases, theory) raises intrigue and speculation about the nature of these relationships. Social problem-solving abilities were significantly predictive of pressure sores diagnosed over the first 3 years of traumatically acquired spinal cord injury (SCI), and these associations were more influential than clinically important variables like severity of disability and demographic characteristics (e.g., race, gender, age; Elliott, Bush, & Chen, 2006). These data are among the first to document the potential of social problem-solving abilities to prospectively predict individuals who may be at risk for expensive and often preventable health complications, above and beyond the predictive value of variables deemed medically important. Nevertheless, the exact mechanisms by which problem solving exerted this observed effect cannot be determined from this study.

We can speculate from other relevant studies that problem-solving abilities may have prevented pressure sores (and promoted healthier skin) among participants in the Elliott et al. (2006) study in a couple of ways. Effective problem solvers may have had fewer health-compromising behaviors than persons who had dysfunctional styles (e.g., less sedentary, inactive behaviors, less alcohol intake; Godshall & Elliott, 1997); perhaps they were more successful in regulating their emotions and stress levels so they were more likely to attend to recommended regimens for skin care and maintenance (i.e., therapeutic adherence; Johnson, et al., 2006). However, a compelling study of glycemic control among African American men raises other possibilities.

In a study of 65 African American men with diabetes, Hill-Briggs and colleagues (2006) found avoidant and impulsive/careless styles (as measured by a short form of the SPSI-R) were significantly predictive of elevated hemoglobin A1C levels, indicative of poor glycemic control. The relationship between avoidant scores and A1C levels was not mediated by participant depression. These data are further supported by focus group research, in which a group of persons with poor glycemic control reported more avoidant and impulsive/careless responses to a problem-solving task than a group of individuals with good glycemic control (Hill-Briggs, Cooper, Loman, Brancati, & Cooper, 2003). It is possible that a dysfunctional problem-solving style—in the context of chronic disease and stress—may have definite correlates with impaired immune system functioning (these correlations do not permit causal explanations; glycemic control may have been influenced by unmeasured variables such as diet, exercise, and distress that may, too, be influenced by problem-solving abilities).

Lessons Learned From Intervention Research

Problem-solving therapy (or training; PST) has promulgated as an attractive therapeutic option in many multidisciplinary health care settings. Indeed, the broader concept of "problem solving" is considered an essential element in chronic disease education and self-management programs (Hill-Briggs, 2003). PST grounded explicitly in the principles espoused by D'Zurilla and Goldfried has been applied with notable success in alleviating distress among persons with cancer (Nezu, Felgoise, McClure, & Houts, 2003; Nezu, Nezu, Friedman, & Faddis, 1998) and in improving coping and self-regulation skills among persons with TBI (Rath, Simon, Langenbahn, Sherr, & Diller, 2003). Problem-solving interventions have documented success in individual sessions provided in primary care settings (Mynors-Wallis, Garth, Lloyd-Thomas, & Tomlinson, 1995), in structured group therapy (Rath et al., 2003), in telephone sessions with community-residing adults (Grant, Elliott, Weaver, Bartolucci, & Giger, 2002), and in online Web sessions for parents of children with TBI (Wade, Carey, & Wolfe, 2006a; and with observed benefits on child functioning, Wade, Carey, & Wolfe, 2006b). When null effects have appeared in the peer-review literature, these may be attributable in part to a perceived lack of relevance or lack of "tailoring" of the intervention to problems—as they are perceived and experienced—of immediate concern to participants (Shanmugham et al., 2004; Study 2).

The positive effects of PST are usually ascribed to the treatment, particularly when significant increases are observed on self-appraised (Grant et al., 2002) and observed problem-solving abilities (Rath et al., 2003). There is some evidence that decreases in dysfunctional styles may be particularly essential in realizing significant decreases in depression (Rivera, Elliott, Berry, & Grant, in press). Participants may display increased skills in finding more solutions to their problems following PST than persons assigned to a control group (Lesley, 2007). In one impressive multisite clinical trial, Sahler et al. (2005) found the beneficial effects of PST on lowering negative affect among mothers of children with cancer were pronounced among young, single mothers; Spanish-speaking mothers demonstrated continued improvements over a 3-month period. Nevertheless, there is perplexing evidence that PST can be associated with lower depression scores over time with no corresponding changes in social problem-solving abilities (Elliott, Brossart, & Fine, 2007).

Critical reviews point out that this work has recurring problems with the theoretical integrity of interventions, a lack of methodological details, and a lack of clarity regarding the "dosage" sufficient for therapeutic change. Nezu (2004) has been especially critical of the lack of theoretical integrity, as the general flexibility of the original D'Zurilla and Goldfried model may be melded into or added on to any loosely defined cognitive-behavioral intervention. In some cases, it may appear that a published report used a "problem-solving intervention" but there is no elaboration of principles of the model or how these were implemented in any replicable fashion (e.g., Smeets et al., 2008). There are some high-profile trials in which training in "problem solving" was presented as a marquee feature of the multisite intervention, and this evidently meant training in rational, instrumental ways to cope with certain problems, but there is no mention or recognition of the problem orientation component and its theoretical function in self-regulation and motivation (e.g., Project REACH, Wisniewski et al., 2003). Nezu (2004) adamantly argues that PST must address issues germane to the problem orientation component, and strategies that strictly address the problem-solving skills component will not be successful.

The broad range in the number of sessions across studies frustrates our ability to determine the dosage sufficient for therapeutic change. Some studies report clinical success with after a few sessions (Mynors-Wallis et al., 1995), but other work shows no effects after two sessions administered 6 months apart (Elliott & Berry, submitted). Weekly sessions seem to have considerable benefits over several weeks (Grant et al., 2002; Rath et al., 2003; Sahler et al., 2005). In some clinical scenarios, however, therapeutic change may occur with monthly sessions over the course of a year (Rivera et al., in press). Currently, we cannot conclude from the extant literature the minimal dosage of PST sufficient to effect beneficial, therapeutic changes. This is an issue that should be addressed in future work.

A critical review of problem-solving interventions for family caregivers of stroke survivors concluded that the inconsistent use of a theoretical framework and concepts, and a recurring neglect in measuring participant problem-solving abilities, limits our understanding of PST in this area (Lui, Ross, & Thompson, 2005). Very few of the studies reviewed used standardized measures of problem-solving abilities despite their availability; many studies use the term without regard to the prevailing theoretical models and corresponding directives for training and assessment. Multidisciplinary research teams are often unfriendly to psychological theories. The Lui et al. critique reveals a high regard for cognitive-behavioral theories and a considerable respect for conducting theory-driven research and service. In particular, this critique conveys a premium on theory for organizing and interpreting multidisciplinary research, and for guiding service programs and their evaluation.

The most critical and informative review of this literature appeared in a recent meta-analysis of 31 studies of PST (Malouff, Thorsteinsson, & Schutte, 2007). This paper stayed true to the basic, organizing principles of the social problem-solving model and recognized the theoretical fidelity of authors across studies. PST demonstrated a significant effect size across studies, indicating a superiority over no treatment and treatment-as-usual. Although no moderating effects were found by mode of delivery (group, individual) or in the number of hours of PST (further confounding our ability to determine adequate "dosage"), these colleagues found significant effects for the presence of problem orientation training (consistent with the Nezu position) and homework assignments. Unfortunately, they also found an "investigator" effect: Studies conducted by one of the developers of PST had a significant contribution to the overall effects of PST. This contribution was stronger than the contributions of homework assignment and problem orientation training. Finally, PST was not significantly different from bona fide treatment alternatives.

Identifying and Solving Problems in the Research Base

As these recent reviews and preceding comments attest, there are several problems that have lingered in this literature that impede our appreciation of social problem-solving abilities and the mechanisms by which they have beneficial effects on health. Yet the available research is generally supportive, as we continue to see positive and theoretically consistent findings in multidisciplinary outlets (e.g., *Stroke, Journal of Behavioral Medicine, Pain, British Medical Journal, Patient Education and Counseling*) that signify an acceptance of social problem solving far beyond the usual confines of counseling psychology research (which also may signify the far-reaching impact of counseling psychology research). With these optimistic thoughts in mind, we assert the following issues should receive greater theoretical and empirical scrutiny in future work.

Utilize and Promote Theory-Driven Research and Instrumentation

Exploratory studies are unquestionably compelling and intriguing, and they arguably broaden our vision and stoke our intellectual curiosity (e.g., Hill-Briggs et al., 2006). But the ordinary, rank-and-file, "stopgap" studies do not advance our understanding of social problem-solving abilities if they fail to make explicit ties to the prevailing theoretical models, ignore instruments tied to these models (PSI, SPSI-R), or make vague, obscure references to "problem solving" with no appreciation for the implications of prior work, subsequently squandering the opportunity for informed, relevant research that advances existing knowledge. It is frustrating to read studies that ignore prior work, and wonder how the results could have differed if proper attention had been given to the implications of previous theory-driven research (e.g., De Vlieger et al., 2006).

These are not trivial matters: The most egregious and harmful incidents occur in large, multisite clinical trials that purport to use "problem-solving interventions" with no ties to relevant theory-driven research, and then report null effects for their intervention (as in the case of Project REACH). For those invested in policy-relevant research, small-scale studies that yield positive results are held in suspicion because smaller samples often overestimate actual treatment effects (and thereby dismiss the convergence of data across methodologically diverse studies); large-scale, multisite randomized controlled trials (like Project REACH) are assumed to be more robust, generalizeable, and necessary for determining the true efficacy of an intervention (Califf, 2002). Consequently, a perceived lack of evidence from a multisite clinical trial can irreparably smear the reputation of theory-driven PST, and cultivate unjustified disinterest among funding sources and policymakers for further study of PST.

There is some concern that the primary measures of problem-solving abilities—the PSI and the SPSI-R—may be too time-consuming and cumbersome for use in many clinical settings. Interestingly, a shorter, 25-item form of the SPSI-R has been used successfully in several studies (e.g., Grant et al., 2002) and some researchers have read the SPSI-R aloud to participants to ensure administration (with theoretically consistent results among persons with visual impairments, Dreer et al., 2005, and with disabling mobility impairments, Elliott, 1999). This may be asking too much for everyday clinical applications, and shorter versions should be developed for telehealth applications and in primary care clinics. Preliminary item analysis of the SPSI-R suggests that a briefer version for greater use may be possible, with results generally consistent with contemporary reformulations of the social problem-solving model (Dreer et al., 2007).

Broaden the Scope of PST Across Research Teams and Clinical Settings

The effects of PST on depression and distress permeate the literature (Malouff et al., 2007). Recent applications have unsuccessfully tried to use PST to elevate life satisfaction (Rivera et al., 2007). More promising areas include the use of PST principles to promote healthier diets and lifestyles

(Lesley, 2007; Perri et al., 2001) and to facilitate the use of problem-solving strategies in social interactions (essential for community reintegration; Rath et al., 2003). Although much of this work is hampered by the lack of specificity about the actual implementation of PST and relevant theory (rendering the results suspect and thwarting generalizability and replicability; e.g., Van den Hout, Vlaeven, Heuts, Zijlema, & Wijnen, 2003), these studies collectively illustrate the potential of PST in various applications. Other colleagues, for example, incorporate PST in promoting healthier lifestyles (including matters of impulse control, adherence, mood regulation) among persons who are HIV+ (the Health Living project, Gore-Felton et al., 2005) and who have substance abuse histories (Latimer, Winters, D'Zurilla, & Nichols, 2003). PST may prove to be quite adaptable in long-distance, community-based telehealth programs, in which ongoing services may be provided to underserved people and to those in remote areas (e.g., Grant et al., 2002; Wade et al., 2006a).

Identify the Mechanisms of Therapeutic Change

It appears that there is no clear evidence of the "dosage" of PST necessary to effect change. Moreover, when change occurs, it is unclear if the changes are uniquely attributable to PST. One persistent issue concerns the intricate relationship between a negative orientation and self-report measures of distress. Even when we find evidence linking effective problem-solving abilities with objectively defined outcomes (e.g., skin ulcers), we do not know if effective problem-solving abilities influenced greater behavioral adherence to therapeutic regimens, or if the problem orientation component was instrumental in regulating emotional adjustment and prevented distress that could have compromised health. We do know that PST is more successful when the issues germane to the problem orientation component are addressed, and there is evidence that decreases in negative orientation and dysfunctional problem-solving styles can be associated with decreases in depression in response to PST (Rivera et al., in press).

There is legitimate concern that—with respect to social problem-solving abilities—the "absence of the negative" may be more powerful than the "presence of the positive." It is important for us to understand how and why a negative, dysfunctional style is associated with negative outcomes (and a greater likelihood of a positive outcome), and why and under what conditions a constructive problem-solving style proves uniquely beneficial. This could entail studies of social problem-solving abilities and biomedical indicators of stress and adjustment. We believe this is a pressing issue given current interest in social problem solving as an important variable in positive psychology (Heppner & Wang, 2003).

Attend to Matters of Diversity

Few cognitive-behavioral variables appear to be as culturally resilient as social problem-solving abilities (Heppner et al., 2004). Large-scale studies that have controlled for possible effects of ethnicity have shown the relationships of social problem-solving abilities to distress and adherence (Johnson et al., 2006) and to health outcomes (Elliott et al., 2006) are not mediated by race. Studies of race-specific issues have yielded some of the most intriguing data to date among problem-solving and biomedical markers of health (among African-American men; Hill-Briggs et al., 2006); other work has shown some effects for PST tailored to address health promotion issues among African Americans with hypertension (Lesley, 2007). There is also some indication that Spanish-speaking participants may experience greater benefits from PST than others (Sahler et al., 2005).

There are many health problems that are disproportionately experienced by ethnic minorities in the United States (e.g., diabetes, stroke, disability incurred in acts of violence). Collectively, available evidence suggests that PST may be used in prevention and remedial programs to assist persons from minority backgrounds who live with these conditions. Although this work is promising, we have yet to see robust effects of PST across health conditions, and research has yet to be conducted in any substantive fashion with certain ethnic groups (e.g., Chinese, although initial work has been consistent with extant theoretical models; see Siu & Shek, 2005). Ideally, the next wave of intervention research will document effects of PST among people across ethnic groups and cultures.

Problem Solving for the People

Research to date suggests that PST can be effectively provided by psychologists, physicians, nurses, and counselors. As the needs of our society demand greater attention to and support for the increasing number of people who live with a chronic health condition that necessitates routine adherence to prescribed regimens (and currently this number constitutes almost 50% of the population of the United States; Partnerships for Solutions, 2004), health promotion programs will increasingly rely on paraprofessionals and community health workers to reach a larger number of individuals. These public health efforts already work with community groups (schools, churches) and with respected paraprofessionals within certain communities (e.g., *promotoras* in Latino communities) to educate people about health and health promotion skills. We believe problem-solving principles can be taught in public health interventions to reach a greater percentage of people who are affected by chronic health conditions (including family members of an individual with a diagnosable condition). We also know that PST can be effectively provided in the community via telehealth, so a greater use of existing technologies is expected in community-based programs. PST can be a useful modality for prevention programs for teaching health promotion skills (e.g., nutrition, sexual health and behaviors, exercise and activity) to individuals, generally.

A real concern lurking in this sea of possibility is the difficulty in determining when and how to best apply PST: People experience a wide range of problems in our communities, and paraprofessionals may be overwhelmed by the depth and severity of certain problems they will inevitably encounter in their clientele. Furthermore, we know that some individuals live with considerable distress and face many problems that have a restricted range of options and solutions. In these clinical scenarios, a strict reliance on the rather linear application of PST principles may be frustrating to paraprofessionals and clients. Research is needed to determine the best and optimal use of PST by paraprofessionals in public health interventions, and when doctoral-level providers are best suited for using PST in more complex cases that demand greater clinical expertise.

SUMMARY

The study and application of social problem-solving abilities has matured beyond its early years in the counseling psychology literature to be embraced by a larger, multidisciplinary audience. Many theoretical issues remain for counseling psychologists to examine and refine, and an influx of new researchers would do much to assuage concerns of "investigator" effects in PST research. Perhaps the next wave of PST research will be conducted in public health programs. It behooves counseling psychology to be involved in this activity so that the theoretical tenets of social problem solving are accurately integrated and realized in this work, and in the process, ensure a more accurate realization of the effects and applicability of social problem-solving theory and research for the public good.

AUTHORS' NOTE

This chapter was supported by grants to the first author awarded by the National Institute on Child Health and Human Development (#ROI HD37661), the National Institute on Disability and Rehabilitation Research (H133A020509), and from the National Center for Injury Prevention and

Control (#R49/CE000191) to the Injury Control Research Center at the University of Alabama at Birmingham.

The contents of this study are solely the responsibility of the authors and do not necessarily represent the official views of the funding agencies.

BIBLIOGRAPHY

Bandura, A. (1986). *Social foundations of thought and action: A social cognitive theory.* Englewood Cliffs, NJ: Prentice Hall.

Califf, R. M. (2002). Large clinical trials: Clinical research institutes. In J. I. Gallin (Ed.), *Principles and practice of clinical research* (pp. 225–250). San Diego, CA: Academic.

De Vlieger, P., Crombez, G., & Eccleston, C. (2006). Worrying about chronic pain. An examination of worry and problem solving in adults who identify as chronic pain sufferers. *Pain, 120*(1–2), 138–144.

Dreer, L., Berry, J., Rivera, P., Elliott, T., Swanson, M., McNeal, C., et al. (2007). *Efficient assessment of social problem-solving abilities: A Rasch analysis of the social problem-solving inventory-revised.* Manuscript submitted for publication.

Dreer, L., Elliott, T., Fletcher, D., & Swanson, M. (2005). Social problem-solving abilities and psychological adjustment of persons in low vision rehabilitation. *Rehabilitation Psychology, 50*, 232–238.

Dreer, L., Elliott, T., Shewchuk, R., Berry, J., & Rivera, P. (2007). Family caregivers of persons with spinal cord injury: Predicting caregivers at risk for depression. *Rehabilitation Psychology, 52*, 351–357.

Dreer, L., Elliott, T., & Tucker, E. (2004). Social problem solving abilities and health behaviors of persons with recent-onset spinal cord injuries. *Journal of Clinical Psychology in Medical Settings, 11*, 7–13.

D'Zurilla, T. J., & Goldfried, M. R. (1971). Problem solving and behavior modification. *Journal of Abnormal Psychology, 78*, 107–126.

D'Zurilla, T. J., & Nezu, A. M. (1990). Development and preliminary evaluation of the Social Problem-Solving Inventory. *Psychological Assessment, 2*, 156–163.

D'Zurilla, T. J., & Nezu, A. (1999). *Problem-solving therapy* (2nd ed.). New York: Springer.

D'Zurilla, T. J., & Nezu, A. M. (2007). Measures of social problem solving ability. In T. J. D'Zurilla & A. M. Nezu, *Problem solving therapy: A positive approach to clinical intervention* (pp. 33–47). New York: Springer.

D'Zurilla, T. J., Nezu, A. M., & Maydeu-Olivares, A. (2002). *Social problem-solving inventory-revised (SPSI-R): Technical manual.* North Tonawanda, NY: Multi-health Systems.

D'Zurilla, T. J., Nezu, A. M., & Maydeu-Olivares, A. (2004). Social problem solving: Theory and assessment. In E. Chang, T. J. D'Zurilla, & L. J. Sanna (Eds.), *Social problem solving: Theory, research, and training* (pp. 11–27). Washington, DC: American Psychological Association.

Elliott, T. (1999). Social problem solving abilities and adjustment to recent-onset physical disability. *Rehabilitation Psychology, 44*, 315–332.

Elliott, T., & Berry, J. W. (2007). *Brief problem-solving training for family caregivers of persons with recent-onset spinal cord injuries: A randomized control trial.* Manuscript submitted for publication.

Elliott, T., Brossart, D., & Fine, P. R. (submitted). *Problem-solving training via videoconferencing for family caregivers and effects on family members with spinal cord injury: A randomized clinical trial.* Manuscript submitted for publication.

Elliott, T., Bush, B., & Chen, Y. (2006). Social problem solving abilities predict pressure sore occurrence in the first three years of spinal cord injury. *Rehabilitation Psychology, 51,* 69–77.

Elliott, T., Godshall, F., Herrick, S., Witty, T., & Spruell, M. (1991). Problem-solving appraisal and psychological adjustment following spinal cord injury. *Cognitive Therapy and Research, 15,* 387–398.

Elliott, T., Grant, J., & Miller, D. (2004). Social problem solving abilities and behavioral health. In E. Chang, T. J. D'Zurilla, & L. J. Sanna (Eds.), *Social problem solving: Theory, research, and training* (pp. 117–133). Washington, DC: American Psychological Association.

Elliott, T., & Marmarosh, C. (1994). Problem solving appraisal, health complaints, and health-related expectancies. *Journal of Counseling and Development, 72,* 531–537.

Elliott, T., Shewchuk, R., Miller, D., & Richards, J. S. (2001). Profiles in problem solving: Psychological well-being and distress among persons with diabetes mellitus. *Journal of Clinical Psychology in Medical Settings, 8,* 283–291.

Elliott, T., Shewchuk, R., & Richards, J. S. (1999). Caregiver social problem solving abilities and family member adjustment to recent-onset physical disability. *Rehabilitation Psychology, 44,* 104–123.

Elliott, T., Shewchuk, R., & Richards, J. S. (2001). Family caregiver social problem-solving abilities and adjustment during the initial year of the caregiving role. *Journal of Counseling Psychology, 48,* 223–232.

Godshall, F., & Elliott, T. (1997). Behavioral correlates of self-appraised problem solving ability: Problem solving skills and health compromising behaviors. *Journal of Applied Social Psychology, 27,* 929–944.

Gore-Felton, C., Rotheram-Borus, M. J., Weinhardt, L. S., Kelly, J., Lightfoot, M., Kirshenbaum, S., et al. (2005). The Healthy Living Project: An individually tailored, multidimensional intervention for HIV-infected persons. *AIDS Education and Prevention, 17,* 21–39.

Grant, J., Elliott, T., Weaver, M., Bartolucci, A., & Giger, J. (2002). A telephone intervention with family caregivers of stroke survivors after hospital discharge. *Stroke, 33,* 2060–2065.

Grant, J., Elliott, T., Weaver, M., Glandon, G., & Giger, J. (2006). Social problem-solving abilities, social support, and adjustment of family caregivers of stroke survivors. *Archives of Physical Medicine and Rehabilitation, 87,* 343–350.

Grant, J., Weaver, M., Elliott, T., Bartolucci, A., & Giger, J. (2004). Family caregivers of stroke survivors: Characteristics of caregivers at-risk for depression. *Rehabilitation Psychology, 49,* 172–179.

Heppner, P. P. (1978). A review of the problem-solving literature and its relationship to the counseling process. *Journal of Counseling Psychology, 25,* 366–375.

Heppner, P. P. (1988). *The problem-solving inventory.* Palo Alto, CA: Consulting Psychologist Press.

Heppner, P. P., & Baker, C. E. (1997). Applications of the problem-solving inventory. *Measurement and Evaluation in Counseling and Development, 29,* 229–241.

Heppner, P. P., & Krauskopf, C. J. (1987). An information processing approach to personal problem solving. *The Counseling Psychologist, 15,* 371–447.

Heppner, P. P., & Wang, Y.-W. (2003). Problem-solving appraisal. In S. J. Lopez & C. R. Snyder (Eds.), *Positive psychological assessment* (pp. 127–138). Washington, DC: American Psychological Association.

Heppner, P. P., Hibel, J., Neal, G. W., Weinstein, C. L., & Rabinowitz, F. E. (1982). Personal problem solving: A descriptive study of individual differences. *Journal of Counseling Psychology, 29,* 580–590.

Heppner, P. P., Witty, T. E., & Dixon, W. A. (2004). Problem-solving appraisal and human adjustment: A review of 20 years of research utilizing the problem-solving inventory. *The Counseling Psychologist, 32,* 344–428.

Herrick, S., & Elliott, T. (2001). Social problem solving abilities and personality disorder characteristics among dual-diagnosed persons in substance abuse treatment. *Journal of Clinical Psychology, 57,* 75–92.

Hill-Briggs, F. (2003). Problem solving in diabetes self-management: A model of chronic illness self-management behaviors. *Annals of Behavioral Medicine, 25,* 182–193.

Hill-Briggs, F., Cooper, D. C., Loman, K., Brancati, F., & Cooper, L. (2003). A qualitative study of problem solving and diabetes control in type 2 diabetes self-management. *Diabetes Educator, 29,* 1018–1028.

Hill-Briggs, F., Gary, T., Yeh, H.-C., Batts-Turner, M., Powe, N., Saudek, C., et al. (2006). Association of social problem solving with glycemic control in a sample of urban African Americans with type 2 diabetes. *Journal of Behavioral Medicine, 29,* 69–78.

Johnson, M., Elliott, T., Neilands, T., Morin, S. F., & Chesney, M. A. (2006). A social problem-solving model of adherence to HIV medications. *Health Psychology, 25,* 355–363.

Kinsella, G., Ong, B., Murtagh, D., Prior, M., & Sawyer, M. (1999). The role of the family for behavioral outcomes in children and adolescents following traumatic brain injury. *Journal of Consulting and Clinical Psychology, 67,* 116–123.

Kurylo, M., Elliott, T., DeVivo, L., & Dreer, L. (2004). Caregiver social problem-solving abilities and family member adjustment following congestive heart failure. *Journal of Clinical Psychology in Medical Settings, 11,* 151–157.

Latimer, W. W., Winters, K., D'Zurilla, T., & Nichols, M. (2003). Integrated family and cognitive-behavioral therapy for adolescent substance abusers: A stage I efficacy study. *Drug and Alcohol Dependence, 71,* 303–317.

Lesley, M. L. (2007). Social problem solving training for African Americans: Effects on dietary problem solving skill and DASH diet-related behavior change. *Patient Education and Counseling, 65,* 137–146.

Lui, M. H. L., Ross, F., & Thompson, D. (2005). Supporting family caregivers in stroke care: A review of the evidence for problem solving. *Stroke, 36,* 2514–2522.

Malouff, J. M., Thorsteinsson, E., & Schutte, N. (2007). The efficacy of problem solving therapy in reducing mental and physical health problems: A meta-analysis. *Clinical Psychology Review, 27,* 46–57.

Mynors-Wallis, L. M., Garth, D. H., Lloyd-Thomas, A. R., & Tomlinson, D. (1995). Randomised controlled trial comparing problem solving treatment with amitriptyline and placebo for major depression in primary care. *British Medical Journal, 310,* 441–445.

Neal, G. W., & Heppner, P. P. (1986). Problem solving self-appraisal, awareness and utilization of campus helping resources. *Journal of Counseling Psychology, 33,* 39–44.

Nezu, A. (2004). Problem solving and behavior therapy revisited. *Behavior Therapy, 35,* 1–33.

Nezu, A. M., & D'Zurilla, T. J. (1989). Social problem solving and negative affect. In P. Kendall & D. Watson (Eds.), *Anxiety and depression: Distinctive and overlapping features* (pp. 285–315). San Diego, CA: Academic Press.

Nezu, A. M., Felgoise, S. H., McClure, K. S., & Houts, P. (2003). Project Genesis: Assessing the efficacy of problem-solving therapy for distressed adult cancer patients. *Journal of Consulting and Clinical Psychology, 71,* 1036–1048.

Nezu, A., Nezu, C., Friedman, S., & Faddis, S. (1998). *Helping cancer patients cope: A problem-solving approach.* Washington, DC: American Psychological Association.

Nezu, A. M., & Perri, M. G. (1989). Social problem solving therapy for unipolar depression: An initial dismantling investigation. *Journal of Consulting and Clinical Psychology, 57,* 408-413.

Partnerships for Solutions (2004). *Chronic conditions: Making the case for ongoing care.* Baltimore, MD: Johns Hopkins University Press.

Perri, M., Nezu, A., McKelvey, W., Shermer, R., Renjilian, D., & Viegener, B. (2001). Relapse prevention training and problem-solving therapy in the long-term management of obesity. *Journal of Consulting and Clinical Psychology, 69,* 722–726.

Rath, J. F., Hennessy, J. J., & Diller, L. (2003). Social problem solving and community integration in postacute rehabilitation outpatients with traumatic brain injury. *Rehabilitation Psychology, 48,* 137–144.

Rath, J. F., Langenbahn, D., Simon, D., Sherr, R. L., Fletcher, J., & Diller, L. (2004). The construct of problem solving in higher level neuropsychological assessment and rehabilitation. *Archives of Clinical Neuropsychology, 19,* 613–635.

Rath, J. F., Simon, D., Langenbahn, D., Sherr, R. L., & Diller, L. (2003). Group treatment of problem-solving deficits in outpatients with traumatic brain injury: A randomised outcome study. *Neuropsychological Rehabilitation, 13,* 461–488.

Richards, C. S., & Perri, M. G. (1978). Do self-control treatments last? An evaluation of behavioral problem solving and faded counselor contact as treatment maintenance strategies. *Journal of Counseling Psychology, 25,* 376–383.

Rivara, J., Jaffe, K., Polissar, N., Fay, G., Liao, S., & Martin, K. (1996). Predictors of family functioning and change 3 years after traumatic brain injury in children. *Archives of Physical Medicine and Rehabilitation, 77,* 754–764.

Rivera, P., Elliott, T., Berry, J., & Grant, J. (in press). Problem-solving training for family caregivers of persons with traumatic brain injuries: A randomized controlled trial. *Archives of Physical Medicine and Rehabilitation.*

Rivera, P., Elliott, T., Berry, J., Oswald, K., & Grant, J. (2007). Predictors of caregiver depression among community-residing families living with traumatic brain injury. *NeuroRehabilitation, 22,* 3–8.

Rivera, P., Elliott, T., Berry, J., Shewchuk, R., Oswald, K., & Grant, J. (2006). Family caregivers of women with physical disabilities. *Journal of Clinical Psychology in Medical Settings, 13,* 431–440.

Rob, J. E. M., Smeets, J. W. S. Vlaeyen, A. H., Arnold, D. M., Kester, G. van der Heijden, J. M. G. and Knottnerus, J. A. (2008). Chronic low back pain: Physical training, graded activity with problem solving training, or both: The one-year post-treatment results of a randomized controlled trial. *Pain, 134*(3), 263–276.

Sahler, O., Fairclough, D., Phipps, S., Mulhern, R., Dolgin, M., Noll, R., et al. (2005). Using problem-solving skills training to reduce negative affectivity in mothers of children with newly diagnosed cancer: Report of a multisite randomized trial. *Journal of Consulting and Clinical Psychology, 73,* 272–283.

Shanmugham, K., Cano, M., Elliott, T., & Davis, M. (under review). *Social problem solving abilities, relationship satisfaction and adjustment of family caregivers of stroke survivors.* Manuscript under review.

Shanmugham, K., Elliott, T., & Palmatier, A. (2004). Social problem solving abilities and psychosocial impairment among individuals recuperating from surgical repair for severe pressure sores. *NeuroRehabilitation, 19,* 259–269.

Shaw, W. S., Feuerstein, M., Haufler, A., Berkowitz, S., & Lopez, M. (2001). Working with low back pain: problem-solving orientation and function. *Pain, 93,* 129–137.

Siu, A. M. H., & Shek, D. T. L. (2005). Relations between social problem-solving and family well-being among Chinese adolescents in Hong Kong. *Social Indicators Research, 71,* 517–539.

Smeets, R. J. E. M., Vlaeyen, J., Hidding, A., Kester, A., van der Heijden, G., & Knottnerus, J. (2008). Chronic low back pain: Physical training, graded activity with problem solving training, or both? The one-year post-treatment results of a randomized controlled trial. *Pain, 134,* 263–276.

Van den Hout, J. H., Vlaeven, J. W., Heuts, P., Zijlema, J., & Wijnen, J. A. (2003). Secondary prevention of work-related disability in nonspecific low back pain: Does problem-solving therapy help? A randomized clinical trial. *The Clinical Journal of Pain, 19,* 87–96.

Wade, S. L., Carey, J., & Wolfe, C. R. (2006a). An online family intervention to reduce parental distress following pediatric brain injury. *Journal of Consulting and Clinical Psychology, 74,* 445–454.

Wade, S. L., Carey, J., & Wolfe, C. R. (2006b). The efficacy of an online cognitive-behavioral family intervention in improving child behavior and social competence in pediatric brain injury. *Rehabilitation Psychology, 51,* 179–189.

Wisniewski, S. R., Belle, S., Coon, D. W., Marcus, S., Ory, M., Burgio, L., et al. (2003). The resources for enhancing Alzheimer's caregiver health (REACH): Project design and baseline characteristics. *Psychology and Aging, 18,* 375–384.

Witty, T. E., Heppner, P. P., Bernard, C., & Thoreson, R. (2001). Problem solving appraisal and psychological adjustment of persons with chronic low back pain. *Journal of Clinical Psychology in Medical Settings, 8,* 149–160.

Author Index

A

B

C

D

E

F

G

H

I

J

K

L

M

N

O

P

Q

R

S

T

U

V

W

Y

Z

Subject Index

A

B

C

D

E

F

G

H

I

Q

R

S

T

U

V

W

Y

Z